The Pleasure Garden, from Vauxhall to Coney Island

The Pleasure Garden, from Vauxhall to Coney Island

Edited by
JONATHAN CONLIN

PENN

UNIVERSITY OF PENNSYLVANIA PRESS

PHILADELPHIA

PENN STUDIES IN LANDSCAPE ARCHITECTURE

John Dixon Hunt, Series Editor

This series is dedicated to the study and promotion of a wide variety of approaches to landscape architecture, with special emphasis on connections between theory and practice. It includes monographs on key topics in history and theory, descriptions of projects by both established and rising designers, translations of major foreign-language texts, anthologies of theoretical and historical writings on classic issues, and critical writing by members of the profession of landscape architecture. The series was the recipient of the Award of Honor in Communications from the American Society of Landscape Architects, 2006.

Copyright © 2013 University of Pennsylvania Press

All rights reserved.
Except for brief quotations used for purposes of review or scholarly citation, none of this book may be reproduced in any form by any means without written permission from the publisher.

Published by
University of Pennsylvania Press
Philadelphia, Pennsylvania 19104-4112
www.upenn.edu/pennpress

Printed in the United States of America
on acid-free paper
10 9 8 7 6 5 4 3 2 1

Library of Congress Cataloging-in-Publication Data
The pleasure garden : from Vauxhall to Coney Island / edited by Jonathan Conlin.
  p. cm. (Penn studies in landscape architecture)
  Includes bibliographical references and index.
  ISBN 978-0-8122-4438-0 (hardcover : alk. paper)
  1. Amusement parks—England—History. 2. Amusement parks—United States—History. 3. Resorts—England—History. 4. Resorts—United States—History. 5. Amusements—England—History. 6. Amusements—United States—History. I. Series: Penn studies in landscape architecture
  GV1853.4.G7 P54 2013
  635.90942
  2012014198

Frontispiece: *Vauxhall Gardens* (c. 1859). Lambeth Borough Archives. Landmark 1259.

Contents

Introduction
JONATHAN CONLIN   1

Chapter 1. Theaters of Hospitality: The Forms and Uses of Private Landscapes and Public Gardens
JOHN DIXON HUNT   29

Chapter 2. Pleasure Gardens and Urban Culture in the Long Eighteenth Century
PETER BORSAY   49

Chapter 3. Guns in the Gardens: Peter Monamy's Paintings for Vauxhall
ELEANOR HUGHES   78

Chapter 4. Performance Alfresco: Music-Making in London's Pleasure Gardens
RACHEL COWGILL   100

Chapter 5. Pleasure Gardens of America: Anxieties of National Identity
NAOMI STUBBS   127

Chapter 6. Pleasure Gardens in Nineteenth-Century New Orleans: "Useful for All Classes of Society"
LAKE DOUGLAS   150

Chapter 7. Night and Day: Illusion and Carnivalesque at Vauxhall
DEBORAH EPSTEIN NORD   177

Chapter 8. "Strange Beauty in the Night": Whistler's Nocturnes of Cremorne Gardens
    ANNE KOVAL   195

Chapter 9. Edwardian Amusement Parks: The Pleasure Garden Reborn?
    JOSEPHINE KANE   217

Notes   247

Select Bibliography   299

List of Contributors   303

Index   307

Acknowledgments   315

The Pleasure Garden, from Vauxhall to Coney Island

Introduction

JONATHAN CONLIN

When London's Vauxhall Gardens closed in July 1859 many felt that it represented the end of an era. Whether under the moniker "New Spring Gardens," "Vauxhall Gardens," or "Royal Vauxhall Gardens," at its close the Lambeth resort could claim a history stretching back to the Restoration, almost two centuries. Together with its many rivals, such as Ranelagh and Marylebone, Vauxhall Gardens provided jaded urbanites with a pleasant suburban retreat, a place in which to amuse themselves and entertain family and friends. Here they ate and drank, listened to music, admired paintings and sculpture, and enjoyed a variety of other spectacles, the most important of which was the crowd itself.

Though the first pleasure garden, London's Spring Gardens (Figure I.1), had offered little more than bowls in the 1630s, eighteenth- and nineteenth-century pleasure gardens such as Vauxhall incorporated elements of masquerade, *chinoiserie*, and other exotic fantasies that transported visitors to new realms of fancy. Promenading along their shaded walks of a summer evening, visitors could escape the pains of the city while still enjoying its pleasures. Sudden contrasts of light and dark, familiar and strange, pleasure and danger that would have seemed deeply unsettling anywhere else became a source of excitement and wonder.

For tourists to eighteenth-century London, a visit to Vauxhall was almost obligatory. For composers and performers, it offered the quickest way of attracting a public following. For novelists such as Fielding, Smollett, Burney, Dickens, and Thackeray, it was the perfect place to send heroes and villains alike. The significant and illustrious contingent of foreign visitors was struck by the resort's success in bringing different ranks together without any obvious police. They admired this order, concluded it to be an inimitable product of a free British nation, then rushed home to establish their own gardens, adding yet more "Vauxhalls" to the many already found

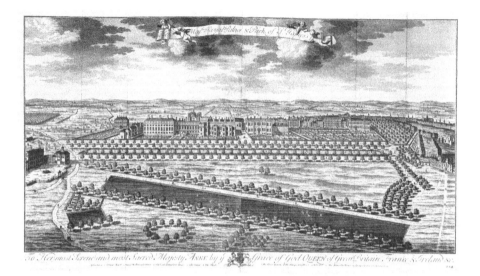

Figure I.1. *Her Majesties Royal Palace and Park of St. James's*, colored engraving. From *Nouvelle Théâtre de la Grande Bretagne,* 5 vols. (London: David Mortier, 1715). © Dumbarton Oaks Research Library and Collection, Rare Book Collection, Washington, D.C.

elsewhere in Britain—in Norwich, Shrewsbury, Tunbridge Wells, and other places. Though several opened near established hostelries or were operated by former publicans, it was clear that these resorts were not the same thing as beer gardens or taverns. They were something else, something new: Vauxhalls.

Over the course of the eighteenth and nineteenth centuries the word *Vauxhall* duly entered the French, Dutch, Swedish, German, Russian, and Danish languages.[1] Pleasure garden fashions and frissons could even be enjoyed by those who did not visit in person. For every visitor who made the journey to a Vauxhall on foot or by boat or carriage many more journeyed there in their imaginations, by viewing a print, reading a newspaper, or singing the latest pleasure garden songs in their own homes. Pleasure gardens were London's gift to the world.

Pleasure gardens have been seen as typifying a nascent public sphere, one identified with the "commodification of culture," the rise of the "middling rank," and other symptoms of modernity. Our knowledge of these gardens, however, is largely restricted to London resorts, and much of what we know about even those renowned sites derives from works by Warwick Wroth, now more than a century old.[2] Despite the importance of the individual artists (such as Hogarth and Whistler) and musicians (Handel, Haydn, and many others) active within them, pleasure gardens have been neglected by historians of painting, sculpture, and music. Those art historians and literary scholars who have addressed London pleasure gardens have focused almost exclusively on the 1760s and 1770s, ignoring their Caroline origins and Victorian development. Gardens outside London and abroad have been almost entirely ignored. Other pleasure gardens have been seen as little more than pale imitations of London's Vauxhall.

This volume is the first to consider the pleasure garden as an international phenomenon, as well as the first to survey these resorts from their origins in the seventeenth century to the early twentieth century. Building on an interdisciplinary dialogue started by the 2008 Tate Britain/Garden Museum conference "Vauxhall Revisited: Pleasure Gardens and Their Publics," the chapters in this book address a number of areas that have yet to receive any scholarly attention, such as musical programming and American pleasure gardens. One of the most dynamic social spaces of modern Britain and the United States, as the range of disciplines represented here (art history, literary studies, musicology, the history of designed landscapes, and others) indicate, pleasure gardens can be approached in a number of different ways.

Although geographic and chronological parameters vary from chapter to chapter, the contributors share a number of concerns that must be central to understanding the pleasure garden as a designed landscape: the relative accessibility of the gardens to different social classes, the melding of different media and genres, and the relationship between town and country as well as that between reality and willed complicity in illusion. This introduction will return to these themes, as well as indicate avenues for future research; as with all the other contributions, it is as much an invitation as an investigation.

But first, a working definition is in order. Eighteenth- and nineteenth-century nomenclature is unhelpful here, as "pleasure garden" was used interchangeably with "pleasure ground" to refer to privately owned gardens open only to friends and to the odd visitor, and they were usually located at some distance from town. In such parks visitors might never spy their host, though they might on occasion see fellow guests.[3] It was nonetheless clear that the gardens were an expression of that host's authority and taste. Visitors were expected to praise and show deference.[4]

Figure I.2. Detail of Figure I.1. Spring Garden is the triangular enclosure at center. Note the gate allowing entrance from St. James's Park.

Pleasure gardens lacked a clearly identifiable "host."[5] When Lord Digby was arrested in Spring Garden "for striking in the King's Garden, he answered, that he took it for a common Bowling Place where all paid Money for their coming in."[6] On the other side of the wall, in St James's Park, Lord Digby was a courtier, or at least subject to the raft of ordinances controlling behavior within the verge of the court. By stepping through the entrance into Spring Garden (Figure I.2), Digby had entered a different space, where he could meet, converse with, and beat up fellow customers without regard to a host. Even at that early date (1634) we have the sense of the pleasure garden as a resort where access is controlled by a fee at the door. Once gained, access brings with it a certain license, a right to "make oneself at home" in the space. Unlike at court, however, money, rather than place or rank, is the main criterion for admission. Closed down in May 1654, Spring Garden nevertheless reopened the next month. Cromwell's London was willing to go without its theaters and fairs, which were successfully suppressed, but they weren't going to let the Puritans rob them of Spring Garden.

Thomas Myers Garrett's 1978 dissertation on the pleasure gardens of New York offers a useful definition of "pleasure garden": "a privately owned (as opposed to a governmentally owned) enclosed ornamental ground or piece of land, open to the public as a resort or amusement area, and operated as a business."[7] This seems a helpful place to begin, more helpful than the definitions found in more recent dictionaries of landscape architecture, which either conflate pleasure gardens and public parks or acknowledge the distinction only to posit a prurient opposition between the "uplifting, educative environment" fostered by parks and the "louche" or commercial (as in tawdry) attractions afforded by the former.[8] Most pleasure gardens were seasonal (that is, open only in the summer), suburban, and designed to be visited in the late afternoon or evening. Though some resorts may be challenging to categorize, pleasure gardens had a number of characteristics that distinguished them from tea gardens and spa gardens. Tea gardens were a Sunday-afternoon retreat aimed at a predominantly middling clientele (Figure I.3), and offered much less by way of musical or staged performances. Spa gardens were organized around the taking of medicinal waters, although this activity paled before the other attractions on display at the largest spas, such as Sadler's Wells or Beulah Spa in London, which were effectively pleasure gardens.[9]

That pleasure gardens were performative spaces is beyond doubt. John Dixon Hunt's chapter places pleasure gardens alongside Chiswick and Stowe as places where hospitality was performed. Rather than viewing Vauxhall from the gardens of Brown and Repton, Hunt notes how French and Italian designs and models of behavior were naturalized in the English pleasure garden. This chapter as well as Hunt's earlier work challenges historians of designed landscapes to abandon old approaches to garden history (in particular the "formal"/"informal" dyad) in favor of a new garden history focused on (among other things), the history of the reception and consumption of gardens.[10] Scholars outside garden history might choose to interpret this as a case of garden historians "catching up" with developments outside their own field. On the contrary, in reaching out to other historical disciplines garden historians bring with them much that is of

Figure I.3. Carington Bowles, *Mr. Deputy Dumpling and Family Enjoying a Summer Afternoon* (c. 1780), mezzotint. Guildhall Library, City of London.

value to those in other disciplines, particularly to the study of pleasure gardens.

Peter Borsay's chapter describes the patterns of circulation and interaction that made these resorts so exciting for visitors. Though these rituals were common to resorts situated in London, Norwich, Tunbridge Wells, and other towns in this period, they carried significant hidden costs in terms of dress and time, costs that, he argues, would have led many would-be visitors to exclude themselves. Borsay also locates "an evolving green agenda" within these resorts, a movement "towards introducing green spaces and leisure services into the town." John Evelyn's account of pleasure gardens in his 1661 treatise *Fumifugium: or the Inconveniencie of the Aer and Smoak of London Dissipated* as at once a "place of Recreation" and a means of sweetening polluted city air suggests that such language is not anachronistic but was present from the beginning.[11]

Pleasure gardens were multimedia environments that played sensory games with visitors. Focusing for the most part on Vauxhall and other London resorts, the chapters by Eleanor Hughes, Rachel Cowgill, Anne Koval, and Deborah Nord consider how the gardens and their visitors were represented in painting, music, and fiction. As these chapters show, the paintings, novels, and concertos, important works of art in their own right, also functioned as cues: entertaining visitors but also instructing them on how to behave, when and where to move, and even how to think. In addition to providing a much-needed survey of the composers, musical forces, and forms popular at the London gardens from the eighteenth through the nineteenth century, Cowgill's chapter sheds light on the shape of a typical evening's entertainment, in which the movements of performer and audience alike were carefully choreographed. The chapter also indicates just how much pleasure garden performances have to teach us about canon formation, listening habits, and the Georgian and Victorian soundscape.

The commissioning by Jonathan Tyers of paintings to decorate the supper boxes at Vauxhall in the 1730s and 1740s has been identified as a key moment in the emergence of a self-aware art public in Britain.[12] Compared to the pastoral revels depicted by Francis Hayman in his supper-box paintings, however, the naval history paintings by Monamy of around 1740 addressed by Eleanor Hughes have received little attention.[13] Considered alongside songs celebrating hearty English tars, they provide fascinating examples of a form of patriotic discourse familiar from work on empire and identity in the early to mid-eighteenth century.[14] Although reenactments of

Waterloo and other battles, which brought casts of uniformed actors, horses, and special effects to Vauxhall in the following century, marked a change in scale, those Regency spectacles were clearly part of a long tradition of celebrating military heroes and staging patriotic rituals of remembrance within pleasure gardens.

Charmed by twinkling lamps, excited by fireworks, or undone by the gloaming of the ill-famed "dark walks," visitors to pleasure gardens enjoyed a range of light entertainment. Semidarkness was dangerous but also exciting. Though it covered a manifold of sins, it also revealed a "fairy-land." Deborah Nord and Anne Koval share an interest in pleasure gardens as places for the willed suspension of disbelief, for a complicity in illusion that caused moral and class distinctions between "audience" and "performer" to melt away. As Nord indicates, complicity was often associated, oddly perhaps, with the innocence of childhood and youth. Maturity could come at too high a price for those who, like Charles Dickens, preferred the comforting illusion to the tawdry truth of a "Vauxhall Gardens by day," when there were no shadows in which to hide.

Though the Whistler "nocturnes" that Koval considers date from a later period and depict a different London resort, she shares this interest in nostalgia with Nord. Her discussion of Whistler's *Nocturne in Black and Gold: The Falling Rocket* (1875) in the context of the closure of Cremorne Gardens gives an added layer of significance to the painting as well as to the Ruskin/Whistler trial in which it featured so prominently. In John Keats's ode "To a Lady Seen for a Few Moments at Vauxhall" (1818) as well as in Whistler's nocturnes, Nord and Koval find parallels to Baudelaire's project of "distilling the eternal from the transitory" within the city of modernity. The thrill experienced by these visitors was bittersweet precisely because they recognized that the relationships realized (if only for a moment) within a pleasure garden were of a kind that could not be conceived anywhere else. Such hypothetical encounters could be recollected, without having actually been experienced, long after the lady vanished, the music stopped, or the brilliant rocket fell to earth.

Pleasure gardens and Vauxhalls thrived in cities across the United States in the nineteenth century, from Butte (Montana) to Charleston (South Carolina). With the exception of Garrett's dissertation mentioned earlier, these resorts have been entirely neglected. Confronted with a vast new field to explore, Naomi Stubbs and Lake Douglas adopt different approaches. Stubbs provides a geographically and chronologically broad survey of resorts located in major cities on the East Coast. Her chapter explores how resorts struck a balance between imitation of renowned London pleasure gardens and attempts to create a home for "American" pleasures. Douglas focuses on New Orleans, a city famed, then as now, for its leisure facilities, and which had more pleasure gardens (fourteen) than any other city in the nineteenth-century United States.

As Douglas shows, the Vauxhall, Eliza, and New Vauxhall pleasure gardens of that city provide compelling examples of how the pleasure garden responded to the challenges posed by a remarkably diverse community; diverse not only in racial terms but also in terms of the different European communities (French, German, English) that jostled in the city. These resorts were exceptional in being patronized by free blacks as well as whites, if on slightly different terms. They offer a case study of how New Orleans society operated before the introduction of physical segregation. Viewed more broadly, the resorts described by Douglas and Stubbs represent an unexplored world of urban green space absent from traditional histories of designed landscapes in the United States, with their focus on municipal projects of "reform" or "improvement" centered on the public parks of the second half of the century.

Did pleasure gardens die or did they evolve into new forms of entertainment in the years around 1900? Josephine Kane's chapter suggests that a better knowledge of the Victorian pleasure garden will help us to situate amusement parks in their historical context, resisting the tendency to view them as American novelties or simply as spin-offs of world's fairs. Historians of amusement parks, such as Gary Cross and John Walton, have proposed the pleasure garden as part of their ancestry. Kane's chapter is nonetheless the first attempt to evaluate the nature and extent of the pleasure garden legacy.[15] Though they did not have rides of the sort that provided visitors to New York's Coney Island with physically jarring thrills and license to squeal, pleasure gardens did provide the thrill of encountering what one might call the expected unexpected.

This book focuses exclusively on the pleasure gardens of England and the United States. Irish pleasure gardens such as Dublin's Vauxhall (1793–?) have yet to be studied. Although Parisian "Wauxhalls" have received some attention, that attention has focused on the pre-Revolutionary period.[16] During the French Revolution these resorts were suspected of harboring royalist plotters and so were subject to heavy surveillance. Despite this, they enjoyed a resurgence under the Directory and Empire, adding new roller-coaster–style rides and helping to reestablish Paris as Europe's capital of pleasure.[17]

Tantalizing shreds of information attest to pleasure gardens elsewhere in Europe. A remonstrance survives from the musicians of Brussels complaining to Emperor Joseph II that his military bands who were playing in the city's Vauxhall robbed them of business. They pleaded for the Emperor to prohibit such bands from playing "chez des Bourgeois."[18] Although Joseph II's decision in this case is unknown, it is clear that he encouraged public access to similar spaces in his capital, Vienna.[19] In 1745 Frederick II gave permission for two Huguenot entrepreneurs to open a pleasure garden, "In den Zelten," in the Berlin Tiergarten.[20] As in ancien régime France, encouragement of these resorts may have represented a public relations exercise on the part of self-consciously "enlightened" regimes.

From Court to Town

Though pleasure gardens have been far less studied over the past fifty years than theaters, parks, and other spaces for recreation, they have not failed to arouse antiquarian interest. Such interest has focused almost entirely on Vauxhall and Ranelagh Gardens. Alfred Bunn clearly took an interest in the Georgian history of Vauxhall Gardens in the 1840s, when he was manager of the resort, and used extracts from what may have been the gardens' own institutional archive to promote a wigs-and-powder vision of "Old Vauxhall."[21] Victorian scrapbooks indicate that there was a body of amateurs interested in collecting pleasure garden ephemera, especially the admission tokens.[22] The numismatist and British Museum curator Warwick Wroth was the first to research the history of pleasure gardens, however. Aided by his brother Arthur, Wroth collated accounts of pleasure gardens from earlier parish histories with topographical prints, published diaries, and literary accounts to produce a garden-by-garden survey of *The London Pleasure Gardens of the Eighteenth Century* (1896) with details of admission charges and opening times, layout, ownership, and musical performances.[23] Until the publication in 2011 of David Coke and Alan Borg's *Vauxhall Gardens: A History*, most historical studies of London gardens drew heavily on Wroth.[24] Perhaps because of a certain po-faced aversion to pleasure, these gardens were ignored by Marxist social historians of the 1970s.

In the 1990s an important historiographical shift led by Roy Porter and John Brewer renewed interest in pleasure gardens. It became clear that pleasure gardens had more interesting stories to tell than ones revolving around quaint old fashions or what "dear old Pepys" had noted in his diary.[25] Chief among these was the shift from a court-centered to a public-centered culture. Porter and Brewer championed a new approach to eighteenth-century studies, one that focused on audiences, reception, and in particular the intermediaries such as dealers, print sellers, and impresarios whose business was the retailing of "the pleasures of the imagination" to the middling audiences that constituted that "public." Thanks to Peter Borsay's 1989 book on the "urban renaissance" in the English provincial town it was now possible to show how far these networks spread outside London.[26] Brewer and Porter's approach also chimed in well with publications on London's concert life by scholars whose interest in reception and performance practice had been piqued by Cyril Ehrlich in the late 1970s and 1980s.[27]

Brewer described the pleasure garden as a natural successor to the satirical bricolage he found in John Gay's *The Beggar's Opera* (1728). "It offered a mixed audience a variety of entertainments from opera arias to ballads in a place where high and low life, respectability and intrigue could combine."[28] This bricolage represented "the commodification of culture" within an emergent "public sphere," but the process appeared ludic rather than dismally economic. Upon its translation into English in 1989, Jürgen Habermas's *The Structural Transformation of the Public Sphere* (1962) afforded an intellectual framework. For Habermas, resorts such as opera houses and theaters were sounding boards for a "public opinion" carefully crafted and monopolized by an emerging middle class. Though they drew heavily on Habermas, Brewer, Porter, and others working in the 1990s overlooked his pessimism, particularly regarding the "commodification of culture": "To the degree that culture became a commodity not only in form but also in content, it was emptied of elements whose appreciation required a certain amount of training—whereby the 'accomplished' appropriation [i.e., the training] once again heightened the appreciative ability itself.... Of course, such enjoyment is also entirely inconsequential."[29] In the 1990s "commodification of culture" was celebrated, rather than bemoaned, and inspired a number of articles, essays, and books on the visual arts, literature, and society of eighteenth-century America and Europe. "Commodification" was linked to the "commercialization of culture." Both were about upward social mobility and the trickle-down of elite fashions, in the spirit of that "consumer revolution" of Wedgwood plates and print sellers.[30] Although one suspects that Habermas would not have viewed consumption as an equivalent to participation on his public sphere, a focus on consumption was welcomed as a way of valorizing the private sphere and enfranchising women, something seen as a correction of Habermas's account.[31]

The "rehearsal" of Handel's *Music for the Royal Fireworks* organized by Jonathan Tyers at Vauxhall in April 1749 was highlighted as the ideal illustration of this shift from a court- to a public-centered culture.[32] The piece was commissioned by George II to celebrate the Peace of Aix-la-Chapelle, and performed in Green Park on 27 April, to the accompaniment of a pyrotechnic display launched from a "firework pavilion" designed by Jean-Nicholas Servandoni. Tyers secured the right to stage a "rehearsal" at Vauxhall on 21 April as a quid pro quo for supplying the court with equipment and technical expertise needed for the official performance. Although Tyers's performance was a great success and supposedly drew a crowd of 12,000, the Green Park performance was a failure.[33] Dampened by recent rain, the fireworks initially refused to light. Servandoni and the King's Master of Ordnance got into a fight. After some time, inattentive staff accidentally set fire to the pavilion, which burned to the ground. For Brewer the episode "perfectly expresses the longstanding inability of the monarch and his court to represent themselves effectively on a public stage," which he contrasted with the commercial success and professionalism of Tyers, "a man who viewed culture as a commodity to be sold rather than as a means to praise monarchs."[34]

An Inclusive Space?

Pleasure gardens are hailed, therefore, for their undiscriminating accessibility, for offering a space in which members of a rising middling rank could mingle with their superiors, hone their social skills, and learn how to consume and comment intelligently on "the polite arts" of painting, sculpture, and music. Although the eighteenth-century private pleasure ground has been described as a "landscape of exclusion," diverting public roads, depopulating villages, and blocking views of other habitations in order to isolate the house, the public pleasure garden has appeared as a landscape of inclusion.[35] A middle class is needed, we feel, to explain Wilkite agitation in the 1760s, the "Consumer Revolution," the failure of radical reformers in the 1790s—and their success in the 1830s. Demographic historians have struggled to dampen this excitement, pointing out how small the "middling rank" was (10 to 12 percent of the total population) and that it did not grow as a percentage of the overall population.[36] Meticulous research into the audience for the April 1749 "rehearsal" of Handel's *Music for the Royal Fireworks* has demonstrated that it would have been physically impossible for the often-quoted 12,000 people to have attended at Vauxhall. Close analysis of tides, turnpike tolls, and advertisements (which only gave two days' notice of the event) suggest that an estimate of 3,500 is more realistic.[37] Far from successfully courting a wide following through such events, Handel tried to cancel it, and Tyers probably ended up losing money.

The one shilling or (in America) dime/"one bit" admission fee paled before the considerable costs in time, transport (including bridge and turnpike tolls), and, above all, dress—all before one reached the pleasure garden entrance. Once inside, it was hard to resist the social pressure (or pressure from one's own family) to buy notoriously overpriced food and drink. Given the license that seems to have been afforded visitors within the gardens to stare at or comment loudly on the dress or deportment of other visitors, many less wealthy visitors would have found their first visit less pleasant than they had imagined it would be. American pleasure gardens seem to have been more willing than English ones to post additional entry requirements based on dress, decorum, and race.

If it is so easy to describe pleasure gardens as inclusive spaces then that is partly because that is how pleasure gardens liked to describe themselves. Lockman's 1739 song *The Charms of Dishabille* refers to "Red ribbons" (a reference to the red sash of the Order of the Bath) "grouped with aprons blew": "This is the famous Age of Gold / Mankind are merely Jack and Gill [*sic*]."[38] In fact those in working clothes and liveried servants were prohibited from entering most pleasure gardens. Many similar accounts referring to different ranks, trades, and professions mingling in pleasure gardens could be cited.[39]

This is not to deny that domestic servants such as footmen and ladies' maids, middling shopkeepers, and a smattering of what we might call "white-collar" (rather than Lockman's blue-aproned) workers such as lawyers' clerks did patronize eighteenth-century pleasure gardens. At tea gardens they predominated; however, at pleasure gardens they would have been in the minority. There is evidence that employers in the 1740s paid for their servants to attend as an annual treat.[40] For the shopkeepers and professionals, for the hangers-on they brought as their guests, and for visitors from out of town, a visit would also have been a rare treat. Perhaps timed to celebrate a birthday, an engagement, or another rite of passage, a visit would have been much anticipated, intensely enjoyed, and endlessly analyzed once one returned home.

For the elite beau monde who were steady patrons of pleasure gardens, being in a space alongside servants and middling people did not mean one treated them as equals. On the contrary, pleasure gardens "performed exclusivity."[41] As an example one might cite the case of a certain Mrs. Cary in summer 1765, who presumed she had developed a friendship with Lady Sarah Bunbury, daughter of the Second Duke of Richmond, after Bunbury spoke to her at Ranelagh. There seems to have been some misunderstanding as to the significance of this meeting, as Lady Bunbury's letter to a friend the following January indicates: "I was vastly diverted with my *friendship* with Mrs. Cary: you know she dined one day at the Pay Office. I saw her at Ranelagh one night this year, & went up to make her a civil speech: & that is our friendship. As to her fashions, I am sorry to say they are but too true among the common run of people here, for such figures as one sees at publick places is [sic] not to be described; I am sorry for our English taste, but so it is."[42] Mrs. Cary may have been the wife of a senior Pay Office functionary, one of those who worked under Bunbury's much older brother-in-law Henry Fox, who was Paymaster General until May 1765. Cary clearly took a speech Bunbury saw merely as "civil" as the sign that a friendship had begun, misunderstanding the unwritten rule that conversations solicited within a pleasure garden did not "count" outside the garden. Borsay notes a similar rule in force at the Pantiles in Tunbridge Wells.

Lady Bunbury is clear in her mind that such a friendship is impossible. The gap in status is wide enough, indeed, for the suggestion to be amusing to her. Both parties have derived a kind of pleasure (a slightly unpleasant kind, in Bunbury's case) from this exchange among "equals," but for both sides it derives from knowing in the back of their minds that they are *not*, in fact, on the same level. Though it is hard to speak of "middling values" in this period, one suspects that there would have been many "Mrs. Carys" who did not wish to emulate Lady Bunbury (who by then had broken off one engagement, married, and was engaging in adulterous affairs) but who derived pleasure from being able to watch Bunbury and her friends walk the same walks and listen to the same music.

The importance ascribed to such voyeurism may explain why we sometimes conclude that pleasure gardens are caught in a downward spiral once the beau monde ceased to patronize them. The elite stopped attending London's pleasure gardens in the 1820s, but we can no longer see that as tantamount to the beginning of the end.[43] Complaints that a pleasure garden was less splendid than one recalled, the company less select, and the effect less intense should be recognized for what they so often were: a way of indicating that one was "at home" in the garden. Mock disappointment was one form of vicarious proprietorship, a role performed before one's own guests and the company as a whole. In a resort where variety and novelty were important, such declarations were bound to be insistent.

There were pleasure gardens where the company of what we might consider the elite (defined by wealth) was neither sought nor desired. Though very little documentation survives, black pleasure gardens such as New York's African Grove (1821–?) and the Haytian Retreat (1829–?) would surely have had their own elites and may well have excluded whites.[44] Lake Douglas's chapter on New Orleans pleasure gardens shows that mixed-race resorts can and did thrive in a community divided into free whites, slaves, and "free people of colour." Although slaves were entirely excluded, otherwise pleasure gardens appear to have coped very well with *plaçage*, the convention for white men to have mixed-race concubines and families. They did not divide their grounds into segregated "white" and "black" areas.

We are relatively adept at considering how gardens changed "over time": season to season or even century to century. But we are only beginning to appreciate how gardens changed "in time." The makeup of the crowd, the entertainment, and the behavior was different on a weekday from what it was on a Saturday and different at five o'clock from what it was at ten. One strategy that made the New Orleans system work was having separate nights of the week for "people of color" and for whites. In 1825 Simon Laignel of the Faubourg La Course had three nights for subscribers (whites of both genders), one for white men and free "women of color," and one for "free people of color of both sexes." Though race was not a factor there, even quite small English pleasure gardens had unwritten rules that shaped what sort of people and what behaviors were acceptable at a certain hour. For the prostitutes and others intent on "Keeping it up" at 1870s Cremorne, the ten o'clock fireworks display marked not the end but the "real" beginning of a night at the pleasure garden.

The lamps used at Vauxhall Gardens in the 1760s only had enough oil to last an hour, from nine until ten o'clock, when the concert ended. As the technology of lighting advanced from lamps to gas to electricity, so pleasure gardens colonized more of the evening, from late afternoon to past midnight, affording several different kinds of reveler the opportunity to make the resort their own, for an hour or two at least. Pleasure gardens thus form an important chapter in what Craig Koslofsky has recently dubbed "the colonisation of the night" in the early modern period.[45] Light could also be used to divide a pleasure garden into brightly lit "core" areas and darker, fringe areas.

Though the fireworks were an unavoidable cue, often the time or spatial dividing line separating the "safe" zones from the more experimental or disreputable zones was not clear. As several chapters demonstrate, to understand pleasure gardens we need to be careful not to base too much on a series of uniformly lit, bird's-eye snapshots.[46] We need to be careful how we use newspaper items, which were often puff pieces, and—in the case of Vauxhall—fictional accounts. Etherege, Addison, Fielding, Smollett, Burney, Egan, Ainsworth, Dickens, Thackeray, and, much later, Georgette Heyer and Jean Plaidy: a raft of English authors sent characters to Vauxhall. Often enough something extraordinary happened—or, as Nord notes in her discussion of the scene in *Vanity Fair*, almost happened. On the one hand, we may ask whether Vauxhall ever witnessed the suicides (Burney) or elopements (Ainsworth, Heyer) described in such accounts.[47] On the other hand, we should remember that these authors were describing an actual place in Lambeth. Readers were also visitors, something that presumably held authors back from making their Vauxhall scenes so dramatic as to be unbelievable.

Many visitors liked "their" pleasure gardens to have light and dark areas. Concern about the dark walks occasionally led managers to block off dark walks or to illuminate them better, to ensure that all areas could be easily surveyed. When the macaronis tore up the fences blocking off the dark walks or smashed lamps in 1770s Vauxhall they were not simply a bunch of overdressed inebriates engaging in random acts of vandalism; rather, they were asserting their concept of the pleasure garden as a collection of spaces for different types of person and forms of behavior, spaces whose borders were blurred and so easily (or unwittingly) transgressed.

The "spatial turn" is helping us understand behaviors as a haggling over space and its uses rather than as a dispute between politeness and its opposites. Recent scholarship on the history of popular pastimes affords a useful model. Nineteenth-century antiquarians such as Joseph Strutt and latter-day Marxists alike have structured their histories of such pastimes teleologically: as a progress from "barbarism" to "civilization" on the one hand,

and as erosion or commercialization of an "authentic," single plebeian culture on the other.[48] It is more helpful to understand this story as a process by which town squares changed from being mixed-use spaces (commercial and recreational) to being exclusively commercial ones. Though the recreations had not changed, the space had, as urban space became more neatly classified into distinct settings for different activities. So those who continued to use squares and streets for recreations such as cock-throwing were criminalized—not for causing cruelty to animals but for causing a disorder or public nuisance. "Different spaces had the power to invest popular recreations with new meanings."[49] Such changes were part of a new economy of time, as increased use of machinery and wage rather than piece labor created a "right" and a "wrong" time for recreation, as well as a right and a wrong place.[50]

Though the world of wakes, fairs, and bull-baitings seems somewhat removed from that of pleasure gardens, such work provides useful tools. Among other things, it suggests we should be careful before attributing the closure of pleasure gardens to campaigns for "rational recreation," temperance, or improved national morals.[51] Economic opportunities played a far more important role. In many cases, the lure of making a fortune by selling a site for residential development proved too great, leaving devotees distraught, snapping off twigs from the trees as mementos at Vauxhall's last night in 1859. As Koval shows, in Cremorne's case Whistler's evanescent "nocturnes" served as unlikely, if more effective, mementos of that temple of transience after its closure in 1877.

Recovering "Gardenhood"

Throughout their two-hundred-year history, these resorts were celebrated by visitors and promoters alike as new Edens and as an escape from the cramped, crowded, and care-worn city. Though the birdsong might be manufactured and the pleasant country views nothing but canvas, it is clear that these resorts retailed a certain idea of "countryside." Patrons' fine clothes, their modes of transport, and the resorts' location on the city's edge all conspired to lend the journey the feel of a holiday jaunt or excursion. Traveling "by water to Vauxhall" or even simply crossing the gangplank to Castle Garden at the southern tip of Manhattan in the 1840s created a sense of passing out of the city and out of the everyday.[52]

But these places did not aim to create an accurate representation of the countryside. It is sometimes suggested that this or that pleasure garden's doom was sealed by the unstoppable growth of the city, which supposedly made it harder to pretend that the resort lay in the country. Yet, as John Dixon Hunt points out in Chapter 1, many visitors knew the countryside all too well, found it boring, and wanted something different. They agreed with the character Olivia from Sedley's *The Mulberry-Garden* (1675), who remarked to her sister Victoria that the walks in the garden were "much better than the long Walk at home: for in my opinion Half a score young men, and fine Ladies Well drest, are a greater Ornament to a Garden, than a Wilderness of Sycamores, Orange, and Lemmon Trees; and the rustling of rich Vests and Silk Pettycoats, better Musick than the purling of Streams, Chirping of Birds, or any of our Country Entertainments."[53] It is clear that pleasure gardens are a distinct type of entertainment resort, with much to teach us about class, gender, the self, and the relationship between town and country. But the "gardenhood" (to use a word coined by Horace Walpole) of these resorts has often been ignored. Such resorts were not mentioned in nineteenth-century garden encyclopedias or histories of gardening by John Claudius Loudon or Alicia Amherst.[54] Practitioners of "the new garden history" who profess to see gardens as a function of "changing patterns of social organization" are happy to leave out pleasure gardens.[55]

Pleasure garden design between 1660 and 1860 seems to have moved through three phases. The first, a market garden *ornée*, lasted from 1660 to around 1730. Its layout consisted of one or more squares with grass walks edged by shrubbery, containing beds for flowers and fruit, the produce of which might be consumed in the garden itself or sold in the city's markets. Evelyn's *Fumifugium* describes a garden of this kind, which he saw as affording recreation for city-dwellers as well as being a means of perfuming the air before it flowed into the city. "All low-ground circumjacent to the City," he wrote, should

> be cast and contriv'd into square plots, or Fields of twenty, thirty, and forty *Akers*, or more, separated from each others by Fences of double *Palisades,* or *Contr'spaliers,* which should enclose a Plantation of an hundred and fifty, or more, feet deep, about each Field; not much unlike to what His *Majesty* has already begun by the wall from Old *Spring-garden* to *St. James's* in that *Park*; and is somewhat

resembled in the new *Spring-garden* at *Lambeth*. That these *Palisad's* be elegantly planted, diligently kept and supply'd, with such *Shrubs*, as yield the most fragrant and oderiferous *Flowers* . . . *Sweet-brier*, all the *Periclymena's* and *Woodbinds*; the Common *white* and *yellow Jessamine*, both the *Syringa's* or *Pipe trees*. . . . That the *Spaces*, or *Area* between these *Palisads*, and Fences, be employ'd in Beds and Bordures of *Pinks, Carnations, Clove, Stock-gilly-flower, Primroses, Auriculas, Violets.*

Evelyn goes on to note that beans, peas, and other vegetables "*marketable* at *London*" could also be grown within "these Closures."[56] His account tallies closely with French physician Balthasar Monconys's account of Vauxhall in 1663.[57] Though the largest pleasure gardens had wide sand walks, most had narrower grass walks. Without lighting and without much musical or theatrical programming, parties probably did not stay more than a couple of hours. Scattered arbors (often made of old carriages) provided limited, somewhat ramshackle seating. Sadly, no images survive of this first phase, apart from the odd map.[58]

The second phase is that most commonly associated with the pleasure garden and was closely modeled on Jonathan Tyers's Vauxhall improvements of the 1730s and 1740s. Walks were now categorized into main *allées*—wide, graveled, processional routes—and subsidiary walks (Figure I.4). Walks and spaces for performance were framed with isolated lime or elm trees at regular intervals. At Vauxhall the original plots seem to have been filled in with such trees, except for one corner, the so-called "Rural Downs." Bushes and low trellises beneath these trees kept visitors from straying off the walks, although some of these bosky blocks were "wildernesses," riddled with curving, irregular paths of the sort found in 1720s designs by Charles Bridgeman. In the 1740s Tyers introduced three new ranges of supper boxes, arranged in curving lines so as to facilitate the mutual admiration of supper parties and those promenading. These boxes, the orchestral pavilion, and other follies mingled Gothic, Turkish, *chinoiserie*, and other styles, while massive false perspectives were placed at the end of walks to create an impression of distance or to translate the viewer to locales associated with Antiquity or the Grand Tour.

There is evidence to suggest that these features were part of a carefully worked-out scheme. Tyers's private family garden at his Surrey estate of Denbies had an unusually sophisticated design, which took death as its

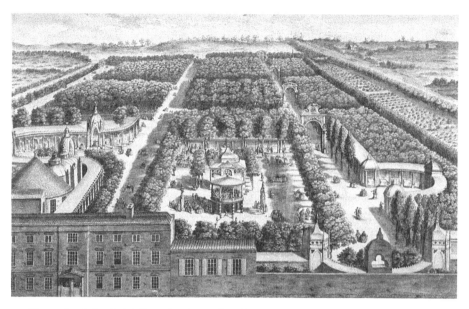

Figure I.4. John S. Muller after Samuel Wale, *Vauxhall Gardens* (1751), colored engraving. Guildhall Library, City of London.

theme. It included a monument to Robert James Petre, Eighth Baron Petre, a noted garden designer and patron of the American John Bartram.[59] The thousands of trees and shrubs Bartram supplied made Petre's Essex estate (Thorndon Hall) a bridgehead for the exotic American plants. Although the new "shrubberies" (the word itself was novel), which appeared in noble pleasure grounds around mid-century tended to have serpentine rather than straight walks, it is surely reasonable to propose that Tyers may have consulted Petre about his commercial garden.[60] The apsidal shape of the supper boxes at Vauxhall has been linked with the exedras or theater-like spaces Evelyn and other seventeenth-century English Grand Tourists would have admired at Marlia, Mondragone, Florence's Boboli, and other Italian gardens. These same gardens also had mechanical special effects similar to the famous tin cascade Tyers introduced at Vauxhall in 1752.[61]

Vauxhall's design also indicates French influences, particularly in its walks. The phrase "pleasure garden" derived originally from the *jardin de plaisir*, in translations of French gardening books such as John James's of Dézallier d'Argenville (1728). In James's translation "pleasure gardens" were

Figure I.5. John S. Muller after Samuel Wale, *The Triumphal Arches, Mr. Handel's Statue &c. in the South Walk of Vauxhall Gardens* (after 1751), etching and engraving, hand colored. Yale Center for British Art, Paul Mellon Collection B1977.14.18703.

described as "those that we take care to keep with the greatest Delicacy and Neatness, and where we expect to find Regularity, good Order, and whatever may most please the Eye, as Parterres, Groves, and Grass-Plots, set off with Portico's, and Cabinets of Arbor-work, Figures, Fountains, Cascades, &c."[62] D'Argenville devoted considerable attention to walks and to discussing what types of trees had the right attributes for planting on them: tall, smooth trunks; high, spreading crowns; roots that won't trip promenaders. Smooth trunks and high crowns had the benefit (for Tyers) of making it easy to attach lanterns, effectively using the trees as lampposts.

The final phase of pleasure garden design began around 1820 and continued until the gardens disappeared. Yet as Vauxhall remained stuck in the second phase, we must look to Surrey Zoological Gardens (Figure I.5), to Cremorne, and to American pleasure gardens for examples. Insofar as these resorts are far less documented, evidence is in short supply. It is clear nonetheless that this phase placed a great emphasis on displays of bedding plants, which were probably "plunged" into beds. An unusually early example of such design, Brighton's Promenade Grove (1793–1802) had rows of elms planted on either side of a path but also had colorful bedding plants and shrubs.[63] Along with exotic trees in pots, the emphasis seems to have been on creating bright patches of color that could be changed relatively easily. Were the technology available then, Victorian impresarios might well have availed themselves of plastic plants, much as a smaller shopping mall might do today, to embellish a concourse or glazed piazza. As shrubberies and trees were cleared to make room for "monster" wooden dancing platforms, covered performance spaces, or wooden floors on which movable tables and chairs could be set, much "gardenhood" was lost.

In the "history of gard'ning" which formed the opening chapter of Stephen Switzer's *Ichnographia Rustica* (1718), John Evelyn was hailed as the font of English garden theory. "If he was not the greatest Master in Practice, 'tis to him is due the Theorical [sic] part of Gardning."[64] Considering that Switzer saw the Restoration as the period in which "those preliminary Foundations of Gard'ning were laid," it is both striking and unhappily proleptic that less than sixty years later he should have already been able to distinguish "practice" from "Theorical" gardening.[65] The latter has not been kind to pleasure gardens, nor has Horace Walpole. Walpole's *History of the Modern Taste in Gardening* (1780) contrasted the French style, which he associated with formality, monotony, and symmetry, with the "modern" English style discovered by the designer William Kent, who (in Walpole's memorable phrase) "leaped the fence, and saw that all nature was a garden."[66] Or rather *rediscovered*, as Walpole held that the English style had always been there, slumbering unnoticed since the days of Henry II.[67]

Roping in willing or unwilling accomplices such as John Milton and Alexander Pope, Walpole established a teleological historiography of gardens that progressed from a "bad" absolutist restraint and formality to a "good" and "natural" informality that has since come to be associated with "Capability" Brown and Humphry Repton. Although Alicia Amherst noted in 1895 how often "so called reforms, undertaken with the aim of increased simplicity, resulted in greater stiffness and formality," the majority of British as well as foreign scholars accepted the teleology of "formal" and "informal."[68] What with their seemingly "old-fashioned" or "French" emphasis on straight graveled walks, pleasure gardens had no place in a narrative of English informality.

The English landscape style heavily influenced the parks "movement" of the next century, particularly in the United States. As Heath Schenker has shown, the ostensibly "natural" Greensward plan adopted in New York's Central Park (1858) embodied a Republican elite's claim to represent "a true American aristocracy."[69] The decision to lay out these great American public parks in the English landscape style may seem a natural or an obvious choice. By revealing the hidden history of the pleasure garden in antebellum America, Naomi Stubbs and Lake Douglas's chapters show that there was an alternative model—the pleasure garden—that had been developed in the years between 1800 and 1840. Many associated it with an easygoing sociability they found preferable to the staid, elitist, and supposedly "improving" landscape style. In the case of Central Park this pleasure garden model was considered, only to be rejected as so much "claptrap and gewgaw."[70] In 1832 the United States Congress rejected a proposal to turn the Washington Mall into a pleasure garden, for which the would-be lessee wished to charge admission.[71]

In a sense the formal/informal opposition resulted from a partial misreading of Walpole, who noted in his *History* that the history of gardening was marked more by the odd flash of genius than by "progressive improvement," and who could express regret at seeing the drive for "nature" leaving a house "gazing by itself in the middle of a park."[72] His letters reveal a Walpole who took great delight in visiting pleasure gardens and who permitted his own taste to be influenced by what he saw in them. He could find himself preferring his tree trunks with lamps attached (as at Vauxhall), rather than au naturel. As Hunt's essay indicates, such views make it difficult to situate Vauxhall and its imitators within familiar narratives of garden history as progress from French formality to English landscape "naturalism." Though foreign visitors ceaselessly commented on the "English" mingling and freedom they saw in such resorts, pleasure garden layouts can seem "foreign." A garden history more attentive to expectations, experience, and reception is, Hunt's chapter suggests, one in which pleasure gardens have much to teach us, one less likely to fall victim to the neat theory-driven distinctions to which "Vegetative Philosophy" (to use Switzer's phrase) has been prone.[73]

To view gardens as stages on which hospitality was performed reminds us that, English national stereotypes notwithstanding, gardens were not exclusively devoted to solitary indulgence of melancholy in a rural retreat from the cares of the city. For visitors from the country a pleasure garden was one of the main, if not the main, "sight" in "town." Though song after song told of how the pleasure gardens' trees "Waft us, in fancy, far from town," it was only "in fancy." Pleasure gardens packaged the most exciting aspects of city living—encounters with the elite and other people one did not know, the latest music and fashions—as a countrified fantasy. Nobody, least of all "Rude Colin," the stereotypical pleasure garden visitor up from the sticks, took it for real countryside.

As with the boulevards in seventeenth- and eighteenth-century Paris, the graveled walks of the suburban pleasure garden created a new kind of movement, which could not be indulged in either in city or in countryside. "Walks in Gardens, like Streets in a Town, serve to communicate between Place and Place," d'Argenville wrote, "they make one of the principal Beauties of Gardens."[74] Modeled on the temporary structures such as those designed by Inigo Jones to line the route by which James I performed his royal entry to London in 1604, the arches installed at Vauxhall in 1732 (Figure I.6) made a royal act of procession into "an amusement for the crowd."[75] Unwritten rules seem to have choreographed how visitors proceeded around several of the larger pleasure gardens. Smaller pleasure gardens and the smaller walks of Birmingham's Vauxhall and Liverpool's Ranelagh were more suited to strolling or rambling than to the processing that went on in London's Vauxhall and Ranelagh.[76] Between 1670 and 1676 the ramparts of Paris had been transformed into *les beaux boulevards*—avenues for promenading that were closed to carts and other commercial traffic. The boulevards consisted of a wide, graveled central *allée* for coaches with a narrower, shaded *contre-allée* on either side, for pedestrians. When minimum street widths were laid down in Paris in 1787, the boulevards' planting was explicitly cited.[77]

Though the grid-like layout of Vauxhall might remind us of the city block, in an important sense Enlightenment city planning involved accommodating a pursuit until then restricted to royal and elite gardens: walking for pleasure. The French seventeenth-century visitor Misson observed how the circular area for coaches in seventeenth-century Hyde Park ("the Tour") was used by the elite in much the same way as the Cours la Reine in Paris was. "When they have turn'd for some time round one way," he noted, "they face about and turn t'other. So rowls [*sic*] the world."[78] This type of circulation was only possible for those wealthy enough to keep a

Figure I.6. *Summer Fashions for 1844 by B. Read and Co.* [Surrey Zoological Gardens] (1844), colored engraving. Guildhall Library, City of London.

carriage, and a fine one at that. At Ranelagh similar circulation (also with a signal to indicate when to change direction) was possible on foot, allowing one to inspect the company and be inspected much more closely.

Pleasure gardens took promenaders out of their coaches and gave them opportunities to learn new types of walking, new ways to "go nowhere," as Peter Borsay puts it. Songs describing Vauxhall show an almost Impressionist eye for how fixed objects can seem to rearrange themselves as the lovers walk, creating an endless variety:

> In the gay square, how oft have we
> Observ'd the diff'rent objects play?
> A statue, tent, alcove or tree,
> Now seem to join, now break away.

But step, and we the picture change,
For other objects groop'd we view:
Wond'ring, from shade to shade we range,
Ever delightful, ever new.[79]

Walking in town was, by contrast, a dangerous chore best left to those of a menial condition who never had time to walk for pleasure.[80] Of course, city streets would eventually become places for such walking, even for the solitary walk of the *flâneur* but only after they had been redesigned to function more like gardens.[81]

Finding "Something Else"

The pleasure garden first appeared on the fringes of a royal park (St. James') and its layout borrowed heavily from French-style *cours*, which had formed a "land of promenade" ("païs des promenades") in seventeenth-century Paris.[82] But it also took elements from market gardens and from private pleasure grounds, and the absence of royal guards and the petty rules of decorum and precedence fostered a more easygoing mood. The admission fee was not the only criterion for admission to the "charms of dishabille," however, and "dishabille" had its own formalities. It is surely possible to recognize the importance of the classless trope as a source of pleasure gardens' thrill and of patriotic pride at their success without ourselves falling victim to this myth's seductive charms. If this book leads scholars to adopt a more considered approach to "classless" pleasure gardens, it will have achieved one of its aims.

Pleasure gardens offered a wide range of visual and musical sensations. Rather than being distractions, the subjects, lyrics, and other cues constantly referred the viewer and listener back to the crowd. The crowd afforded the thrill of the expected unexpected. If you wanted to slip the bounds of sexual decorum, you knew when and where to find willing accomplices inside the pleasure garden. For most visitors, however, it was enough just to know they were there. Pleasure gardens thus remind us that urban green space does not have to be about retreat or escape from the city. On the contrary, pleasure gardens satisfied a distinctly urban hunger for novelty, fashion, and sensory stimulation. Though the layout and vision of "nature" found in public parks fit the stories we like to tell about garden

Figure I.7. After J. Louth, *Miss Mary Taylor & Mr. F. S. Chanfrau in the New Piece, called* A Glance at New York (c. 1835). Harvard Theatre Collection, Houghton Library, Harvard University.

history better than pleasure gardens do, those parks were a later development, one many erstwhile patrons of the pleasure garden found dull.

This essay earlier quoted two fictional visitors' impressions on entering a London pleasure garden: Victoria and Olivia, from Sedley's play *The Mulberry-Garden* (1675). The "Bowery boy" hero and heroine of Benjamin Baker's play *A Glance at New York* (1848), Mose and Lize, are comparatively déclassé. Though separated by two centuries and several thousand miles, their arrival in New York's Vauxhall inspires the same sense of wonder and delight:

Mose: Say, Lizey, ain't this high?
Lize: Well, it ain't nothing else.[83]

Chapter 1

Theaters of Hospitality: The Forms and Uses of Private Landscapes and Public Gardens

JOHN DIXON HUNT

One of the central issues of eighteenth-century English garden history is how we might situate within our habitual narratives the phenomenon of Vauxhall Gardens (and indeed other so-called public pleasure grounds in London and the provinces). A cluster of more specific issues emerges in the process of answering the general questions: how did the idea of what Horace Walpole called "gardenhood" undergo changes when private designs were transferred into the public sphere? Did its sceneries and other representations—of "countryside," for example—require modifications as a result not only of changing taste but also of the different contexts in which they were exhibited? Did some of the assumptions and expectations of private-garden experience and reception transfer readily to public places like Vauxhall, and how did its distinctive theatrical character affect them? And, perhaps most interesting, how may we best register Vauxhall's particular identity as a British site, not least when late eighteenth-century landscape fashions were being touted as essentially new, modern, and above all "English"?

Gardens as Theater and Sites of Hospitality

Sir Henry Wotton, in his 1624 book, *The Elements of Architecture*, wrote that a gentleman's house and garden constituted a "Theater of his Hospitality, the Seate of Self-fruition, the Comfortablest part of his own life . . . an epitome of the whole World."[1] We may construe the phrase "theater of . . .

hospitality" as indicating how a country estate both offered a collection or compendium (a "theater") of hospitable features and itself conspicuously performed hospitality, providing a stage where giving and receiving of hospitality were visible and, if well done, applauded.[2] Wotton expresses largely traditional assumptions about the responsibilities and opportunities of the landed classes but ones that assumed special significance in the English sociopolitical context; he assumed that such obligations, well performed, guaranteed not only personal satisfaction and fulfillment but also civic and patriotic virtue.

When certain elements of country estates were borrowed for consumption in public pleasure grounds, the theatrical possibilities still existed—visitors at Vauxhall and Ranelagh both acting in and spectating a range of entertainments.[3] But the performance of hospitality would be different, not least because it was played out against somewhat exotic and self-conscious scenery but also because the roles of both host and guest are radically challenged, along with the modes of their "self-fruition." The host was now variously the garden proprietors or their agents (who nonetheless collected entrance fees and money for refreshments provided), sometimes owners of the land (Vauxhall was royal property, so the attendance of the Prince of Wales may well have provided some visitors with the wholly gratifying sense of enjoying royal hospitality), or the very crowds themselves, many of whom had no estates of their own in which to play host. As early as the 1710s, Joseph Addison had glanced at these new possibilities in landscape experience when he mused upon the "greater satisfaction" that somebody might take in "the prospect of fields and meadows" than he or she might in the actual possession of such land itself.[4]

There were 1,500 people at Vauxhall in June 1736 when Horace Walpole visited; on another occasion he estimated "above five-and-twenty hundred people," and he assumed (wrongly, of course) that its "vogue" would not last long.[5] That these crowds saw themselves as both hosts and guests interchangeably (as well as actors and spectators) is clear from Walpole's own enthusiastic reports of frequenting in the 1740s the "immense amphitheatre with balconies full of little ale-houses" at Ranelagh or, as his enthusiasm for Ranelagh waned, in joining a "party of pleasure" bound for Vauxhall, hosted by Lady Caroline Petersham in June 1750.[6] He described this excursion as some military exercise—after "drumming up the whole town" and assembling a company, they paraded "for some time" up the river and disembarked at the gardens. The vivacity of their party was much increased by a quarrel or fracas that erupted after their arrival—not the first or last to disturb the peace there. The metaphor changes once the group has settled into their booth, preparing their own minced chicken and cherries and strawberries; now the group's performance is admired by other visitors: "The whole air of our party was sufficient . . . to take up the whole attention of the garden."

The "Country" as Setting for Hospitality

But that was in 1750. Much earlier the New Spring Gardens, before Jonathan Tyers took over the lease in 1728, was valued for its country atmosphere, an effect that over the years had to be more and more vigorously contrived, with the result that the place would come to please less those who really knew and had opportunities to visit the countryside and enthral those who did not or who wanted something rather different than rural bromides.[7] We might apply here what I call the "nightingale" test: Jonathan Swift went to the gardens because of the nightingales' song; Addison's Sir Roger de Coverly wished there had been more nightingales and fewer strumpets, but otherwise it "put him in mind of a little coppice by his house in the country, which his Chaplain used to call an Aviary of Nightingales"; by mid-century the management positioned men in the dense shrubberies to imitate nightingales, presumably because that's what clients wanted to hear and the birds themselves had fled the "motley crowds";[8] by 1769 Horace Walpole advised his foreign guests that this fabled birdsong could be heard only at his Strawberry Hill and not when they arrived at Vauxhall.[9] On yet another occasion he told Mme. du Deffand that if she wished to hear nightingales she'd have to travel far from town and not hear remarks about either Wilkes or Vauxhall.[10]

We have, unfortunately, no visual documents of the New Spring Gardens. But John Evelyn, no mean commentator on gardens, described it as a "pretty contriv'd plantation," which implies a pleasantly organized ground of shrubs and trees, perhaps subdivided into different planting areas, a layout that is confirmed by the Frenchman Balthazar Monconys in 1663, who found there "a large number of squares, 20 or 30 paces across, enclosed with gooseberry bushes; and all these square plots are planted with raspberries, rose bushes . . . and with vegetables like peas, beans, asparagus, strawberries etc."; on 23 April 1688 Samuel Pepys watched "citizens" eating the cherries off the trees.

That all suggests how these Spring Gardens in Lambeth initially enjoyed the appearance of a prosperous and productive rural property, already no doubt somewhat factitious but thriving on the complicit acceptance by city visitors of its being the genuine, or real, thing. Restoration comedies confirm this sense of a constructed but highly appreciated country-ness in resorts like Vauxhall; if people wanted to play at being in the country, this was a plausible stage on which to do so.[11] Especially after Tyers finally purchased the property in the 1750s, its "rurality" and "gardenness" depended increasingly on a careful match of its much developed physical conditions with the expectations its visitors brought to it. Some, indeed, did not find it country-like at all: "'Tis not the country, you must own; / 'Tis only London out of town."[12] But others sang of "groves," "glades," "greenwood," an Eden without snakes lurking in the grass, an Arcadia, and an example of "rural art."[13] Yet it was not so much that Vauxhall would lose its rural appeal as that it responded to more and more sophisticated ideas of what city folks would expect of a country retreat: its music adopted a distinctly pastoral message; its paintings, too, increasingly promoted an imagery of imagined but somewhat rosy country pleasures like Hayman's *Blind Man's Buff*, artlessly imagining rural pursuits and pastimes. Other public resorts in and around London maintained their distinctive rural air longer than Vauxhall (Figure 1.1), partly because they were smaller; partly because they were less capable of expensive refurbishments; and (one suspects) partly because, in the face of Vauxhall's relentless show-business, to maintain a rural ambience was strategic and shrewd. Especially the tea gardens in and around London, to which Vauxhall was compared before Tyers took it over, were created around gardens, orchards, and other open-air amenities, like the Pancras Wells, Bagnigge Wells adjacent to Hyde Park, or the London Spa.[14] Yet even some of these, without any extensive exterior facilities, sought to project a country air even as late as the 1790s—the Apollo music room, even called a "Petit Vauxhall," boasted a painted country scene (Figure 1.2) behind which the orchestra of seventy musicians was concealed.

Scenery in the London Pleasure Grounds

By the time we have visual records of Vauxhall in the late 1730s and early 1740s, Evelyn's and Monconys's descriptions of a rural and somewhat utilitarian country garden no longer seem so apt. The "large number of

Figure 1.1. Entrance to Cuper's Gardens, Lambeth (c. 1820), pen and ink with watercolor over pencil. Guildhall Library, City of London.

squares" is still there, at least in the further reaches and sides of the site, but the emphasis—in both graphic and verbal reports—is now upon the walks, both straight and meandering, some of which are graveled, others grassed. (As I shall suggest later, these could be construed as either perfectly familiar features of English gardens or the accustomed layout of urban promenades, an already well-established European phenomenon.) There were also groves of trees, lawns, a scattering of sculptures and pavilions or *fabriques*, other insertions like triumphal arches, a Gothic obelisk, a cascade, and "vistas" into the surrounding countryside. The surroundings of Vauxhall were indeed still rural and indicated as such in the post-1751 engraving by J. S. Muller after Samuel Wale (see Figure 1.4). The northernmost edge of the site was a representation of "Rural Downs," with turf interspersed with fir trees, cypresses and cedars, and a statue by Roubiliac of John Milton on a hillock. But other admired views were contrived by paintings on large canvases, and later *fabriques* like the Hermitage and Smuggler's cave were no more than stage scenery constructed of lathe and painted canvas. Some

Figure 1.2. Orchestra Room of the Apollo Gardens (c. 1820), brush and ink with watercolor. Guildhall Museum, City of London.

of these insertions were changed over the years, perhaps in an effort to meet either the expectations of "nature" in a garden or a fashion for the exotic: by 1762, for example, a new one showed a "view in a Chinese garden," which perhaps addressed both. But one thing remained stable: The theatricality of these public grounds, as of private ones, resided in more than the fact of their scenery; as in actual theaters, so here, there needed to be a complicity between the creators/performers and the audience/visitors to use their imaginations to make surroundings that are palpably inadequate into something with the power of the real.[15] Not everybody had such imagination; some who disliked the whole business of theater wouldn't suspend their disbelief, but many Vauxhall-goers did.

Now all of that design repertoire would have been perfectly familiar to those with some experience of gardens elsewhere in the years before 1750. It may not match our habitual history of English landscapes becoming more and more natural, but in fact it almost certainly approximated the expectations of a "garden" for the majority of visitors. The much commented on walks at Vauxhall, for instance, have their parallels elsewhere: the larger ones, well illuminated, were contrasted with the dark walks in which couples could lose themselves (in more ways than one); as early as 1700 we hear that the "windings and turnings" at New Spring Gardens are "so intricate" that they provided fruitful scope for escapades, a use also confirmed by Restoration comedies.[16] By 1718 the incorporation in landscape designs of what Stephen Switzer called "private and natural turns" within more regular garden spaces was commonplace; in Wray Wood at Castle Howard Switzer admired the "intricate Mazes" of Nature's "much more Natural and Promiscuous Disposition."[17] By the 1730s Lord Burlington's Chiswick gardens were laid out with wide goosefoot alleys interspersed by narrow and winding paths through the shrubberies that were established between the main walks. A painting by Rysbrack of circa 1730, nearly contemporary with Tyers's reopening of Vauxhall, shows a lady emerging from the thickets (Figure 1.3), which maybe throws fresh light on what is natural and promiscuous about such spaces.[18]

Nor were the various *fabriques* anything unusual in contemporary English landscaping, if perhaps sometimes more tacky in the manner of stage scenery: triumphal arches, temples dedicated to Comus, Neptune, fountains or simulations of such. They were also stylistically eclectic—Chinese, Turkish, Gothic, Grecian. Even those illusionistically painted and illuminated backdrops were an old device for enlarging urban garden

Figure 1.3. Detail of Pieter Andreas Rysbrack, *Chiswick Villa: View of the Bagnio and Domed Building Alleys, and the Alley with the Statue of Cain and Abel* (c. 1729–30), oil on canvas. © Devonshire Collection, Chatsworth. Reproduced by permission of Chatsworth Settlement Trustees.

space—Evelyn had admired some in Paris in the 1640s, and they were still being promoted by Batty Langley in 1728 in his *New Principles of Gardening*.[19] Vauxhall made considerable use of them (Figure 1.4), both to extend visitors' sense of space and to amuse and edify them. One in particular at Vauxhall, a landscape with a cascade, was animated briefly, after a bell had been rung to gather people to the site, with strips of tin to represent flowing water. By 1771 it failed to stimulate some visitors' imaginations—Tobias Smollett's Matthew Bramble saw it as "a puppet-shown representation of a tin cascade"; but its success in others' eyes ensured that as late as 1810, for instance, Sydney Gardens in Bath (Figure 1.5) exhibited "a very large & ornamental piece of Scenery & Machinery" in the form of a very popular cascade.[20]

Vauxhall was, therefore, under Tyers's management, a deliberate creation to please his clientele with an acceptable, even wonderful, theater of gardenhood for those who were happy and willing to see it as such. There may have been some who had different notions of a country retreat—as

Figure 1.4. Edward Rooker after Canaletto (Giovanni Antonio Canal), *A View of the Center Cross Walk &c.in Vauxhall Gardens* (1751), hand-colored engraving. Yale Center for British Art, Paul Mellon Collection B1977.14.18719.

Brian Allen showed us many years ago, Tyers's own country estate presented an entirely different form and experience of a garden.[21] In many ways, though, Vauxhall's layout and décor can be paralleled in private gardens throughout England that seem wholly compatible with the public taste of Vauxhall. After all, William Kent produced some exuberantly Chinese pavilions for Henry Pelham at Esher Place during the 1730s.[22] Other places like Percy Lodge (the former property, Riskins, of Lord Bathurst, in Buckinghamshire) were reworked by the Earl and Countess of Hertford in the late 1740s in a bucolic, faux rural mode with a host of fantastic insertions: a temple, statues, grotto, gothic, classical and Chinese *fabriques*, rustic huts, and views into adjacent agricultural land.[23] It was said to be both "enchanted Ground" and responsive to "ev'ry change of Pleasure." Similar insertions and effects could be found in many private gardens throughout England and were not exceptional one way or another, even if some critics decried them. Furthermore, the description of such private landscaping was usually "pleasure grounds" (to distinguish them from walled gardens for

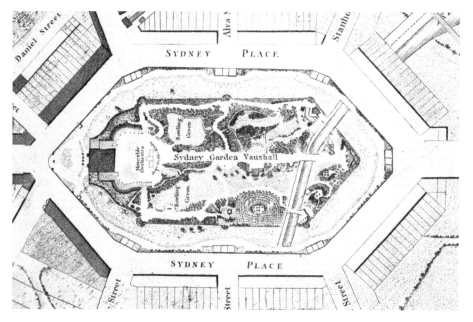

Figure 1.5. S. I. Neele after C. Harcourt Masters, Map of Sydney Garden Vauxhall, Bath (1808), engraving. Bath in Time—Bath Central Library.

vegetables and cutting flowers and from other necessarily practical elements of a country estate), and this same word, *pleasure*, would be on the lips of so many Vauxhall visitors: *The Ambulator*, for instance, constantly asserts how much "pleasure" the "beauties of the place" afforded, and there was even an insertion after 1750 termed a "Temple of Pleasure."[24] Even if the phrase "pleasure garden" was not generally used in English, the assumption that the "walks" and "groves" were "for pleasure" was universal.[25]

Questions of Ethnicity and National Profile

However, the pleasures that were taken at Vauxhall obviously differed widely—and one person's pleasure could be another's discomfort or misery—and these varieties of response also fluctuated over time. A hugely experienced visitor to both French and English gardens, Horace Walpole, first seems to have preferred Ranelagh, but then switched his affections to Vauxhall; later still, he admitted to finding the "disposition of the gardens" at Vauxhall only "a little better" than at Ranelagh, and otherwise thought its "gardenhood" was negligible.[26] What he did like in fact was the artificiality of Vauxhall: he allowed it was beautiful only at night, when it was "lighted up";[27] this suggests that he viewed it very much as a species of theatre, a "representation" of a certain kind of "gardenhood."[28] He was told by his expatriate friend Mann that a garden in Florence was "lighted up very prettily with such lamps as you have in Vaux Hall, which are suspended on green poles surrounded with vine branches."[29] Yet by 1770 Walpole has again changed his mind: he tells another correspondent that he "used formerly to think no trees beautiful without lamps to them, like those at Vauxhall" but now finds "trees beautiful without" them.[30] In the same year, 1770, as he tells Mann, he is extremely skeptical about attempts to transfer some of the fashionable "theater" of Vauxhall to private estates. That summer he had attended the reception and entertainment of Princess Amelie at Stowe, where "a small Vauxhall was acted for us at the grotto in the Elysian fields." He disliked the cold and thought "there were not half lamps enough," but the illuminations in the thickets and in boats on the lake were passably pleasing. Supper in the grotto was "as proper to this climate, as a sea-coal fire would be in the dog-days at Tivoli." He found the gathering of notables and "a crowd of people from Buckingham" risible for "such an Arcadian entertainment."[31] Clearly, Walpole felt that the Vauxhall apparatus and its theatrical mode of hospitality did not translate well to the Elysian Fields of Stowe.[32]

Much of Walpole's later references to Vauxhall and Ranelagh are couched in terms of their difference from the landscaping he inhabited and sought to celebrate. Partly it pitted the excitement and throngs of crowds that frequented public gardens against a vogue for the solitudes of private gardens and landscapes. Walpole drew sharp distinctions between London's public gardens and what neologistically he called the "greenth" and "gloomth" of his own Strawberry Hill.[33] In 1764 he entertains a party of French at Strawberry Hill where he stresses its rural and English qualities (offering them a very English "syllabub" from his own cows) before they "all went away to Vauxhall," though not before he had in a true spirit of hospitality shown them a "fashionable" French song printed on the Strawberry Hill Press; but then (as he writes) "at eight [in the evening they all] went away to Vauxhall."[34] The implication here and elsewhere in his correspondence is that the French would be perfectly at home in Vauxhall. In a similar vein five years later, Walpole entertains another group of French at

Strawberry Hill, which he recounts in a letter to Lady Mary Wortley Montagu: he greets the French guests facetiously wearing a carved wooden cravat by Grinling Gibbons and a pair of embroidered gloves once belonging to James I, which he is amused to think the French considered the habitual "dress of English country gentlemen."[35] He takes them to see "Pope's grotto and garden" nearby, at least for him one of the major icons of English landscape gardening. The French guests are also "saluted" by his nightingales, the "tenants of the manor." Having described this French visit to Montagu, in the very next paragraph of his letter he reports on a "ridotto al fresco at Vauxhall," where a covered passageway all around the site "took off from the gardenhood." It is clear that Walpole distinguished easily between the seclusions, rurality and Englishness of places like his own Strawberry Hill and the exotic contrivances of the public gardens.

Walpole's changing responses to these public pleasure grounds doubtless kept pace with his own careful charting and promotion of landscape design, in particular its appeal to nature and to an endemic Englishness, which become the dominant note of his garden work; thus his comment about preferring trees without lights comes at precisely the time he was finalizing his essay on the modern taste in English gardening. Quite how much Vauxhall fits then or now into a narrative of English garden design is intriguing, especially the Walpolian narrative to which we still cleave. The site which began (in the New Spring Gardens) as an epitome of rurality and natural countryside, to which ideal later landscaping would aspire, gradually acquired exotic forms and scenic effects that brought it more into line with that strand of garden art that went in for *fabriques* and follies of all sorts. Those extravagances were not, however, wholly inimical to the landscaping tendency, either because many canonical landscaped sites indulged in them (Stowe, for example) or because landscaped sites were neither ubiquitous nor uniform across the land. In short, Walpole's view of the Englishness of English landscaping did not command universal assent: a distinctly natural aspect was utterly boring for many people; endless opportunities for reverie and introspection in solitary excursions did not please everybody. The "naturalism" of "Capability" Brown annoyed designers like Chambers (a political rival anyway); Joshua Reynolds (who frequented Ranelagh with Goldsmith) doubted that gardens purged of all artifice counted as gardens at all;[36] and in 1737 Lord Hervey and Lady Montagu each found the idea of nature "boring": "As for the Beautyfull Scenes and the pleasing verdure of Country Prospects," she wrote to him, "when people talk of the Pleasures these things exhibit to them I always either think they lye egregiously or have almost execrable taste."[37] For those so disenchanted with the "pleasing verdure" of the countryside, the illuminations and songs and company of the public gardens were an ideal and truly pleasurable alternative to a bare, Brownian mode.

The claims that English garden design was separating itself from continental patterns had come early—with Addison at the very least—and therefore its indigenous qualities were deemed a virtue (versus, say, French forms in the Le Nôtrean mode); as Linda Colley argues, notions of Britishness at this time were often determined vis-à-vis an "Other," and this no more than in gardening.[38] There was therefore an implicit assumption and even assertion that the "new" gardening was definitely English and "spoke" of Englishness—English hospitality, self-fruition, comfort, and political stability. It was left to Horace Walpole in the 1760s to give this full articulation, to pursue and promote unambiguously (for him at least) an indigenous, English landscaping: "The reason why [English] taste in [natural] Gardening was never discovered before the beginning of the present Century, is that It was the result of all the happy combinations of an Empire of Freemen, an Empire formed by Trade, not by a military & conquering Spirit, maintained by the valour of independent Property, enjoying long tranquillity after virtuous struggles, & employing its opulence & good sense on the refinements of rational Pleasure."[39]

Thus for Walpole and for those who followed his lead, the "English" landscape garden played a distinctive role in that forging of a British nation, the idea of which, as Colley has written, is of a generous umbrella under which many different but indigenous entities and ideas would be able to shelter, something like Walpole's "happy Combinations" of trade, politics, landed prosperity, and social customs.[40] The emphasis was on what *we* were doing over here on this island as opposed to what *they* had been doing over there for too long—and "here" could include territories in Scotland (Mavisbank) or Wales (Hafod), taken as part of a larger entity, what Colley terms "a language of Britishness." So the ever-increasing number of tourists who visited private estates in the pursuit of landscape experience would have understood the role of new landscaping in the promotion of a post-1707 nation.

But that the English landscape garden, as promoted by Walpole and celebrated tendentiously by him in the work of William Kent and "Capability" Brown, was not the only access to a "language of Britishness" is clear from the case of Vauxhall, where "th'astonish'd foreigner [was invited to] applaud" many and various illustrations of Britishness.[41] It was never, especially after the 1730s, exactly cutting-edge garden design, though its décor had some fashionable moments (ruins, cascades, *chinoiserie*, meandering walks). But as theater its scenography was both more versatile and better suited to the diverse clientele; indeed, Walpole even thought Vauxhall was eclipsing London's operas and playhouses.[42] Its often tawdry and seemingly miscellaneous scenery was an invitation to the garden visitors to exercise their imaginations, as they would in the theater, and respond to a rich repertoire of Britishness: paintings like Hayman's *Triumph of Britannia*, statues of Milton and Handel (good to appeal to Hanoverian sympathies, after all), illustrations of "our divine Shakespeare," "busts of distinguished Britons" in the circular music room, walks dedicated to the Druids, and patriotic songs (even the verses of the song "Bacchus and Mars" allowed as how "Britons deserve to have plenty of wine").[43] A Gothic obelisk (an odd notion in itself) was substituted for the statue of the classical Aurora around 1762.[44] All in all it was an indigenous ensemble of items and emblems that was hailed as being "far beyond the imaginations" of the East and equal to those of Greece.[45]

Furthermore, into this "language of Britishness" were absorbed from a very early stage a host of exotic elements. The exotic contrivances of Vauxhall became for many its trademark. In 1712 Addison's *Spectator* "could not but look upon the place as a kind of *Mahometan* paradise," even if a later painting in the gardens showed "Two Mahometans gazing in wonder at the beauties of the place" (presumably it took such exotic visitors to recognize the true significance of Vauxhall).[46] Indeed, a writer (possibly Henry Fielding) in the *Champion* thought the pavilions went "far beyond the imaginations of the East."[47] Walpole, too, clearly appreciated this oriental ambience, even when seen from a distance: when the fireworks at Ranelagh or Marylebone "illuminate[d] the scene [at his Strawberry Hill], he told a correspondent that it imparted an air of Araby or Haroun Alraschid's paradise."[48] When Tyers had opened Vauxhall on 7 June 1732, it was with a "ridotto al fresco," and such *ridotti* continued to be a feature of the entertainments there: the term derived from private entertainments in the city of Venice,[49] by the eighteenth century renowned for its exotic and endless commitment to pleasure.[50] Ranelagh, too, would invoke Venice as part of its ambience. Indeed, in 1771 the Venetian architect Giannantonio Selva found himself entirely at home in the "casino" at Ranelagh, for garden casinos were where many such Venetian *ridotti* were held. Selva (who would become the designer of Napoleon's public gardens in Venice early the next century) went to Ranelagh to promenade or walk up and down ("passeggiare"); he found the site consisted of a high terrace that gave views over a great deal of territory ("terrazzo superiore da cui si domina molto paese"), and he termed the rotunda itself a "casino," noting that from it one went down to the river. At Vauxhall he liked both its grand alley of trees ("un gran viale di alberi"), of the sort he would himself establish in the Venetian public gardens after 1812, and he appreciated its various theatrical elements—illuminations, transparencies, calling one a "scena" that represented a cascade of well imitated water ("una caduta di acqua bene imitata"), and other such effects ("simile oggetti di trattenimento").[51] He might (as a Venetian) also have shared Walpole's early preference for Vauxhall because the best way to reach the gardens was by water; however, Ranelagh did have a canal.[52]

It was then an essential part of Vauxhall's appeal as a British institution that it was so hospitable to foreign effects—Chinese pavilions, Venetian *ridotti*, its aptness for French promenade or Italian *passeggiare*, a place Walpole would readily assume his French guests would find congenial. All of those elements could be absorbed, as Britain was itself absorbing foreign trade and customs and making them her own. It was, after all, a theater of hospitality. Had not a writer in *The World* in 1754 (and I take it he was not being ironic) argued that Britain's improvement in architecture had been achieved by a "happy mixture" of Chinese with native Gothic?[53]

It is indeed useful to look out from Vauxhall into the other English gardens and into garden history rather than in the reverse direction. If—as Lady Mary Wortley Montagu wrote to Alexander Pope—"an excessive prodigality of ornaments and decorations" were the mark of French gardens, because of the "levity and inconstancy of the French taste, which always pants after something new, and heaps ornament upon ornament without end or measure," the promenade was yet another largely French fashion that found its best opportunity in public gardens like Marylebone.[54] Public gardens, whatever other opportunities and entertainments were provided, whatever structures were erected to accommodate and amuse, were above all places to promenade and be seen. The Venetian Selva went to Ranelagh, as we've noted, *per passaggiare*, a term for which, interestingly, no exact equivalent exists in English. The French term for describing the place where such activity takes place was *promenade*, or sometimes *promenoir*, which we may obviously render as promenade, though—even when invoked for the seaside promenade—it lacks a certain important nuance; it is a place to walk, but walking is not promenading ("taking a turn," however, or "strolling" may get us a bit nearer). Given Selva's perspective, it helps to consider both the designs and uses of these English public pleasure grounds in continental terms.

A dominant feature introduced into French urban planning in the seventeenth century was the promenade, what Richard Clary has termed "a new type of landscape in Paris."[55] And in the eighteenth century the promenades were hailed, by the amateur architect Louis De Mondran, as key "embellishments" of a city.[56] An early prototype was the Mail near the Arsenal in Paris, where the game of *Jeu de Mail* was played and where spectators walked up and down to watch it; the Mail was shaded with lines of trees. Such installations became very popular throughout France and, of course, London had its own malls, too, all of which survived even when the game lost much of its early popularity, just as it also had places like the New Exchange in the 1630s for indoor promenades. But in 1616 Marie de Medici commissioned the Cours la Reine in Paris, 1,500 meters long and 50 wide, with separate lanes for pedestrians and carriages, divided by lines of trees, and this had no function as a ball field. Such layouts proliferated, sustained by a new fashion for strolling and driving around in carriages. The essential design features of a promenade were that it was a green space and that it was suburban, and those created (as many were) on disused battlements enjoyed views into the countryside. Its linear form encouraged movement, and there was little else to distract the stroller (no sculpture, paintings, garden features).

I have no need to pursue the history of this French feature any further because in a crucial way what was significant about it found an English manifestation about the time that Jonathan Tyers obtained the lease (in 1728) and then (in 1752 and 1758) became the proprietor of the former Spring Gardens. In the early 1730s the French artist Jacques Rigaud arrived in London, according to George Vertue "at the request of Mr. Bridgeman the Kings Gardner," to take the views of Lord Cobham's gardens at Stowe in Buckinghamshire, subsequently engraved and published by Bridgeman's widow in 1738; Rigaud would also be employed by Lord Burlington at Chiswick in 1733–34.[57] He was a fashionable artist and print seller with a shop

Figure 1.6. Jacques Rigaud, *Orangery and Ha-Ha, Lord Burlington's Chiswick Villa* (c. 1734), pen and ink with grey wash. © Devonshire Collection, Chatsworth. Reproduced by permission of Chatsworth Settlement Trustees.

in the rue Saint Jacques, in Paris, and once arrived in this country he brought to bear the skills that he had honed before leaving France in a series of engravings, among which was a set titled significantly *Les Promenades de Paris*, images that displayed the new and fashionable spaces and their activity of promenading, though some also showed these same social functions taking place within French aristocratic gardens that were often opened to the larger public.

So when Rigaud comes to England, he chooses, perhaps with a rather French esprit, to view Burlington's and Lord Cobham's gardens through these very French, urban spectacles (Figure 1.6). John Harris calls Rigaud "mischevious" and even doubts that we can rely on the accuracy of some of his visualizations.[58] I don't believe we can either, not because he was being an irresponsible Frenchman or because he couldn't depict what was there but because he saw in these English gardens, with their straight lines, gathering points, and elegant visitation, something familiar that he could exploit and augment in his drawings. His views of both Chiswick and Stowe, for example, show implausibly large crowds of people (Figure 1.7), the kind of attendance that would thrill the National Trust. The company

Figure 1.7. After Jacques Rigaud, *View from the Foot of the Pyramid* [Stowe] (1739), engraving. © Dumbarton Oaks Research Library and Collection, Rare Book Collection, Washington, D.C.

shown in the gardens at Stowe has been scrutinized by Richard Quaintance who argues that we may identify a whole Burke's Peerage there.[59] I cannot doubt his eagle eye, but I seriously wonder whether on most occasions such a gathering took place rather than being Rigaud's vision of the promenade potential of Stowe. Big crowds needed generously wide spaces, which Stowe maybe could offer, but Chiswick could not: Rigaud's drawings made Lord Burlington's place seem much larger than it was.[60] But we are dealing with an artist whose job was not to please architectural historians who want imagery to declare exactly what was there and who are accordingly dismayed at his "fictionalized" views. From an alternative point of view that considers how gardens were perceived and used, Rigaud's imagery is very suggestive: he sees the gardens peopled by promenaders, by folk responding to the different opportunities of the sites yet also seeing and being seen as they saunter. If Rigaud draws "theatrical" spaces that Harris says were never installed at Chiswick, these "entirely fictitious" projections of "an ambience that never existed" are better seen as responses to the social opportunities of these private gardens that as a Frenchman he would readily perceive.[61] He is indeed capturing an ambience rather than a specific and precise architectural space. What Lord Burlington himself thought about these views of his gardens is unclear; after all, he much frequented Paris and might have

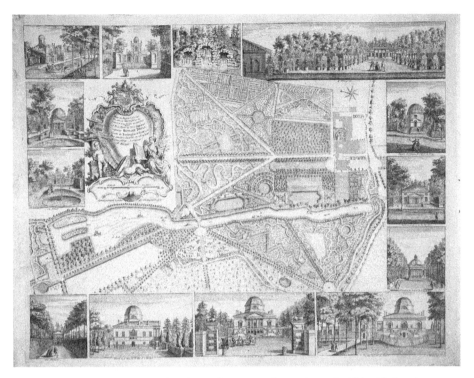

Figure 1.8. John Rocque, *Plan du Jardin & Vuë des Maisons de Chiswick* (1736), etching. © Devonshire Collection, Chatsworth. Reproduced by permission of Chatsworth Settlement Trustees.

found something to tolerate if not admire, his Palladianism notwithstanding, in how Rigaud taught him to see his gardens.[62] However, we have some evidence that Burlington and Rigaud disagreed at least about the fees and the Frenchman was sent away "like a lying ras[cal]."[63] It is interesting to note, however, in Rigaud's plan of Chiswick (Figure 1.8), with its characteristic little boxes of views around the edge (a graphic device he popularized), these scenes are virtually devoid of the elegant crowds and cast of dozens that the drawings show (and this is not simply a question of their limitations of scale).

Rigaud never got (as far as we know) to draw in Vauxhall Gardens, but his imagery of Stowe and Chiswick makes very clear the potential of gardens for this very continental activity of the promenade. And as most owners of gardens, however much they opened their estates to visitations, would not generally tolerate such public promenades, it was precisely places like Vauxhall that welcomed and could indulge them. Indeed, I would argue that Vauxhall offered a way of thinking about garden use and reception at the polar extreme from the more usual English bias toward solitude in gardens, which conversation paintings in particular celebrated during this period. Walpole frequently expressed his relief at being able to relax "once more in the gay solitude of my own little Tempe" at Strawberry Hill.[64]

Yet Vauxhall did not lose its own determined sense of national or patriotic status, even when its "gardenhood" seemed foreign to fashionable taste in English landscaping. It was certainly in the "grand taste," as *England's Gazetteer* said of "Fox-Hall" in 1751, a phrase often applied to larger continental sites. Its wonderful as well as tawdry versatility allows us, then, to register the sheer diversity and range of garden experiences in the later eighteenth century. We are used to understanding a decisive revulsion against gardens overburdened with "stuff"; already by mid-century the mockery of overdesigned sites was mounting, especially when it involved absurd exoticisms or misjudged scale: Francis Coventry had been satirizing the fictitious but not implausible Squire Mushroom with his Chinese bridge, Temple of Venus, and ridiculously brief serpentine stream.[65] More seriously, Joseph Warton's *The Enthusiast* (1744) voiced a revulsion from "gardens deck'd with art's vain pomps." In that climate Vauxhall, though it clearly made some adjustments to cater to changing tastes, was not in a position, even if it wanted to, to make radical changes in design; it espoused and declared alternative ideas of Britishness, pleasure, and hospitality.

Chapter 2
───────

Pleasure Gardens and Urban Culture in the Long Eighteenth Century

PETER BORSAY

For well-off visitors to London in the eighteenth century, a trip to one or preferably both of the great pleasure gardens of Vauxhall and Ranelagh was de rigueur. Dazzling and vibrant, particularly once illuminated at night, they were among the top tourist attractions of the capital; in 1772 M. Grosley thought them "finer in appearance than the Houses of Parliament, Courts of Justice or the King's Palace."[1] However, their very brilliance, reported in coruscating prose by contemporary observers, has emphasized their individuality, encouraging commentators to investigate them as one-off phenomena. This has obscured the extent to which the great gardens were part of a movement—which was not confined to London but swept across Britain as a whole in the long eighteenth century—toward introducing green spaces and leisure services into the town. This chapter seeks to place the pleasure gardens in the context of this wider cultural transformation. It does so initially by exploring separately the "pleasure" and "gardens" elements in eighteenth-century urban culture; it then investigates the way space and time were deployed in pleasure gardens and walks to construct, challenge, and ultimately reinforce the social norms that underpinned the dynamic growth of polite urban leisure.

Pleasure

Contemporaries may not have used the term "pleasure gardens," but pleasure was undoubtedly what the spaces were about. On crossing the boundaries of the gardens, visitors (though, of course, not those for whom it was a site of employment, such as waiters, musicians, thieves, and prostitutes) entered a special zone of unmitigated leisure, in which all notions of work and toil were banished, as the emphasis was on play, symbolism, and otherness.[2] Lewis Mumford, whose *The City in History* (1961) is cited by the *OED* for the use of the term "pleasure garden," states of the best-known establishments in Europe, "these gardens consisted of a large central building, often gaudily decorated, where dances and routs could be held, and where great feasts could be given; surrounded by gardens with recessed arbours and woods where people might roam on a fine evening, eating, drinking, flirting, copulating, watching fireworks or lantern displays: the gaiety and licence of the carnival offered daily." Mumford argued that "the pleasure garden grew on one stem of the palatial baroque life" disseminated from the palace and court to the city in the seventeenth and eighteenth centuries.[3] However, in Britain this simple line of transmission was less than clear. Lawrence Klein has argued that "in the course of the seventeenth century the tripartite model [court, country, and city] broke down and was replaced by a new and more integrated model and practice of élite culture, centred on the Town," so that by the early eighteenth century "the Town had taken over the central space occupied previously in elite culture by the Court."[4] John Brewer has contended that in the late seventeenth century the court and church were declining as sites and sources of cultural leadership, leaving a vacuum whose spaces were rapidly colonized by a new type of intensely urban, public, accessible, profit-driven, and pleasure-seeking culture; and that this "mix of commerce and hedonism promoted by cultural middlemen was embodied in the chief cultural sites of eighteenth-century London."[5] The pleasure garden thus has to be seen alongside the assembly room, theater, concert room, circulating library, exhibition hall, and coffeehouse, as part of a broader movement delivering commercialized urban public culture on an unprecedented scale. Moreover, it is clear that this movement and culture was not confined to London, or even to the metropolitan centers of Dublin and Edinburgh, but permeated at varying rates and intensities much of the urban system of Britain.[6]

If the pleasure garden was part of a bigger picture, where exactly did it fit into the composition as a whole? Did it simply replicate the services being offered in other types of entertainment facilities? In the case of the larger gardens it could be argued that their special qualities lay not so much in that they provided any pastime different from that which could be found elsewhere but that they brought together in one place a uniquely varied *combination* of entertainments. Thus Vauxhall, when fully developed, possessed an ornate saloon or rotunda, a picture gallery, a theater, an orchestra or a concert pavilion, supper boxes (decorated with paintings), a supper room and bar, together with illuminations and a fireworks tower, catering for shows, spectacles, dancing, music, and food. Multidimensional and multisensual, the sheer variety and intensity of the pleasure experience at Vauxhall accounted for its kudos and popularity. However, few gardens could rival the level of investment in and multifaceted character of Vauxhall. Warwick Wroth, in his study of the London gardens, identifies more than sixty establishments, but he places only four of these—Cuper's, Marylebone, Vauxhall, and Ranelagh—in the top division, with the great majority consigned to a "second division" associated with mineral springs, and a "third division," mainly tea gardens.[7] The great gardens thus present a skewed picture of the role of the pleasure garden as a leisure type. If there is a common factor that defines its special position in the pleasure system, it is probably the *garden* element in its makeup. This has tended to be neglected, as the focus in horticultural history has been on the rural and particularly country-house garden, and urban historians have concentrated on the nongreen built environment.[8] But town dwellers were as if not more interested than country dwellers in the *cultural* phenomenon of green space, as their access to such space became more and more attenuated with urbanization. The pleasure garden offered one means to remain in contact with nature.

Greenscapes

It is at this point, where we engage not so much with garden as with a broader environmental history, that we need to place the pleasure garden within another series of widening contexts. The first is that of green space within London itself. A map of the period—such as John Rocque's of the 1740s (Figure 2.1) shows that pleasure gardens are simply one fragment in the capital's greenscape. The built area of the metropolis is pitted with small pockets of vegetation—such as private gardens, allotments, churchyards, and squares—and the sprawling edges of the city merge seamlessly into closes, fields and meadows of varying types. In Rocque's map Vauxhall, Ranelagh, and Marylebone Gardens are embedded within this marginal

Figure 2.1. Detail of John Rocque, *Plan of the Cities of London and Westminster and Borough of Southwark* (1747), etching. Guildhall Library, Museum of London.

zone, pleasure gardens surrounded by a working agricultural and horticultural landscape.[9] During the seventeenth century, Laura Williams argues, "the key trend, in the character of London's green spaces . . . is the shift of focus away from peripheral open fields, meadows, and pasture for walking and recreational use, and towards more ordered and formal sites."[10] In such sites the planting of tree-lined and gravel-laid walks was one of the most characteristic features. Well-to-do inhabitants and visitors to the capital had access to a range of such spaces, of which commercial pleasure gardens were but one element. When the German tourist Zacharias Conrad von Uffenbach came to London in 1710, he visited Cuper's (or Cupid's as he called it, not without good reason); the Spring Gardens (the forerunner of Vauxhall); and the spas, with their attached facilities, at Hampstead, Lambeth, and Richmond. But he also made several excursions to St James's Park and Hyde Park; took in Greenwich Park, Moorfields, Lincoln's Inn Fields, the London apothecaries' herb garden, and the gardens at Somerset House and Hampton Court; and visited the gardens at the homes of the Duke of Somerset at Isleworth and the Earl of Radnor at Chelsea.[11] At the end of the eighteenth century one guide to London listed, in addition to the commercial gardens, "the private-gardens where genteel company are admitted"—Kensington Gardens, Gray's Inn Gardens, Lincoln's Inn Gardens, Middle Temple Gardens, and the Charter House Gardens.[12] There therefore existed alongside the pleasure gardens a spectrum of other formally arranged green spaces—parks, institutional and private gardens, and planted squares—to which there was a measure of public access.

What went for the metropolis also pertained in the provinces. From the later seventeenth century and in some cases before, towns across Britain were modifying green spaces, in a formalized or semiformalized way, for purposes of public recreation.[13] Full-blown pleasure gardens were one feature of this, many adopting the nomenclature of their metropolitan counterparts. Eighteenth-century Birmingham, for example, had an Apollo Gardens and Vauxhall Gardens, Bristol a Vauxhall Gardens, Coventry "Spire's Spring Garden," Newcastle a New Ranelagh Gardens, and at one point in the 1770s Norwich—which possessed commercial gardens as early as 1663—had four pleasure gardens competing with each other, two of which acquired the names "New Spring Gardens" (and later Vauxhall Gardens) and Ranelagh Gardens.[14] From the late 1730s Bath had the Spring Gardens (like Norwich, later renamed Vauxhall) in Bathwick; from 1770 the Bagatelle at Lyncombe Spa; from 1777 the rival King James's Palace higher up Lyncombe Vale, Bathwick Villa Gardens, which were revamped in 1783; and from the 1790s the large-scale Sydney Gardens and Grosvenor Gardens, located on the northern and eastern edges of the expanded city, and representing the death-knell for the original Spring Gardens.[15]

Pleasure gardens were only the tip of the iceberg, particularly in smaller towns unable to support a commercial establishment. Beyond the pleasure garden, as was the case of London, stretched a spectrum of public or semi-public planted green spaces. These ranged from the many simple tree-lined corridors to arbors and groves (such as the Queen's Grove at Tunbridge Wells, laid out at the accession of Anne),[16] planted squares (as in Queen Squares, Bristol and Bath),[17] churchyards laid out with walks (as at Painswick and St Philip's Birmingham),[18] institution-based gardens (such as those attached to the Barber Surgeons Hall at Newcastle and the Infirmary, built in 1755, at Manchester),[19] private gardens open to the public (like those of Sir Charles Musgrave at Durham and Lord Viscount Hereford at Ipswich),[20] and larger-scale gardens or parks such as those at Shrewsbury. In 1698 Celia Fiennes described the town's Abbey Gardens as, "gravel walks set full of all sorts of greens, orange and lemmon trees; . . . there were alsoe firrs, myrtles and hollys of all sorts and a greenhouse full of all sorts of Curiosityes of flowers and greens, there was the aloes plant; out of this went another Garden, much larger with severall fine walks kept exactly cut and roled for the Company to walke in; every Wednesday most of the town, the Ladyes and Gentlemen walk there as in St. James's Parke." Twenty years later the mayor laid out the extensive Quarry walks on the sloping ground to the south of the town that filled the loop in the Severn. Across the river in Kingsland in 1728 an area was set aside, access to which could only be obtained by key, "for ladies and gentlemen to air their coaches and horseback."[21] Such spaces might be furnished with seats, summer houses, refreshment booths, a musicians gallery and even shops; the Pantiles at Tunbridge Wells (Figure 2.2) and Gravel Walks (later Orange Grove) at Bath (Figure 2.3), were both lined on one side with luxury retail outlets, and in the case of the Pantiles also a tavern, coffee house, assembly rooms, and gaming rooms.[22] This emphasized their role as places of general entertainment and blurred the distinction between them and pleasure gardens. It is difficult, for example, to know how to classify the spaces in Leeds described by Thoresby in 1724 as the "very pleasant meadows by the Spring-Garden, where an house of entertainment was, of late years, erected," and the "Pasture-Spring, a house of entertainment, upon the Little Rill,

Figure 2.2. After Thomas Loggan, *The Upper Walks, Tunbridge Wells* (1804, original gouache after 1748), colored engraving. Museum and Art Gallery Tunbridge Wells.

commonly called Holbeck-beck."[23] Were these pleasure gardens or simply walks with a refreshment facility attached?

Whatever the answer, these places, in London and the provinces, shared the common characteristic of being green spaces engineered in some way for public leisure. And it is their common *green* characteristics that should be emphasized. Their proliferation suggests the negotiation of a new sort of relationship between town and country, where spaces were being constructed in which the growing numbers of citizens and visitors to towns were able to draw the natural world and the countryside into their lives, albeit at an essentially aesthetic and vicarious level. This function was reinforced by the location of the majority of public gardens and walks on the urban periphery, allowing them to mediate between town and country. The capital's pleasure gardens were situated predominantly on its edge.[24] Provincial walks and gardens were placed in similar marginal locations. Many followed the line of the city walls (as at Dorchester, Exeter, Chichester, and Hereford)[25] or deployed them as elevated promenades (as at York, Chester, and Tenby);[26] many also meandered along the banks of a river as

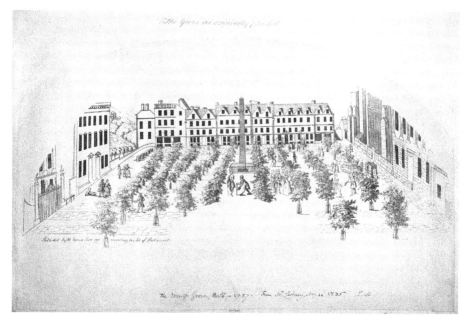

Figure 2.3. G. Speren, Fan Mount Showing the Orange Grove, from *Four Prints for Mounts of Fans, Designed and Curiously Engraved of Places in and about Bath* (1737), engraving. Bath in Time—Bath Central Library.

it wove its course through or around a town (as at Bath, Shrewsbury, York, Bristol, Maidstone, Leeds, and Exeter).[27] The walk and gardens, "for people of rank and fortune," attached to Thomas Harrison's assembly room at Bath (opened in 1708) (Figure 2.4) followed the bank of the Avon and according to Mary Chandler, writing in the 1730s, immersed those who perambulated them in nature:

> Round the green walk the river glides away
> Where 'midst espaliers balmy zephyrs play,
> And fan the leaves, and cool the scorching ray:
> View the brown shadows of yon pathless wood;
> And craggy hills irregular and rude!
> Where nature sports romantick.[28]

At Liverpool Richard Pococke reported in 1750 that "at the corner of the town next the sea is a very fine situation, commanding a view of the sea; it

Figure 2.4. Thomas Robins, View of Bath showing Harrison's walks and gardens, and the Orange Grove (at right) (c. 1750), watercolor. © The Trustees of the British Museum.

is called the Ladies Walk, and is divided into three parts by two narrow strips of grass and two rows of trees."[29] This inclusion of the marine edge into the notion of the margin was indicative of the major redefinition of nature, underway in the eighteenth century, to incorporate the sea. It led to the emergence of the seaside resort as a new type of urban center and with it beach, promenade, and cliff walks as zones of recreation.[30] Pococke's account of the Ladies' Walk in Liverpool emphasizes the idea of the "view." This suggests that the use of such walks involved not only a passive presence *in* but also an active engagement *with* nature. Many of the walks laid out in provincial inland towns and seaside resorts were conceived of and constructed as viewing platforms. In 1760 Lybbe Powys found in the ruins of Rougemont Castle at Exeter that "the inhabitants have for some years been filling up the ditch and on it planting trees, which on one side of a fine terrace form a grove, and on the other being what one may style a natural hanging shrubbery, beyond which the rising country forms a charming prospect, which together make the walk (called Northern Hay) very delightful"—a raised tree-lined walk clearly identified on the Bucks's west prospect of the city of 1736—while at Shaftesbury, perched on a hilltop, "The prospects surrounding it are indeed charming, more so, I suppose, from the novelty of the place. They have two sweet walks, one call'd Park Hill, and Castle Hill."[31]

In the walks at Exeter and Shaftesbury, positioned on naturally elevated sites and with the countryside in close proximity, obtaining a spectacular view of and engaging with nature was easy enough. The geography of London offered less potential, particularly in the case of the pleasure gardens. The larger gardens were enclosed establishments, operating in some cases at night, and increasingly finding their peripheral rural locations compromised by the city's relentless growth. Moreover, the question might be asked, were they, particularly in the case of the major gardens, actually conceived of as green spaces; or was this simply a secondary consideration to their role as venues for music, dancing, eating, and such? Caution should be exercised in dismissing outright the green credentials of the gardens. They were planted spaces. The presence of trees and other greenery seems universal. Vauxhall was described in 1775 as possessing "several noble vistas of very tall trees, where the spaces between are filled up with very neat hedges; and within are planted a variety of flowers and sweet smelling shrubs."[32] Most appear to have been laid out in a formal fashion, perhaps because of the need to provide space within which those promenading were highly visible. For this reason design may have been resistant to the more "naturalizing" tendencies in country-house landscape gardening, gathering pace particularly from the mid-eighteenth century.[33] Mark Girouard claims that Sydney Gardens in Bath (Figure 2.5), opened as late as 1795, "were perhaps the first [pleasure gardens] to be laid out, at least in part, in the naturalistic landscape manner."[34] It would appear that the redesigning of Marylebone in 1752–53 made little change to the formal character of the gardens; if anything, more straight walks and vistas were introduced.[35] However, after its makeover and reopening in 1732, one visitor to Vauxhall in the 1740s described how "right before me extended a long and regular vista; on my Right Hand, I stepp'd into a delightful Grove, wild, as if planted by the Hand of Nature."[36] This would seem to refer to Vauxhall's so-called "wildernesses," not a novel element in garden design, but in the "late geometric garden" of the early eighteenth century one occupying a more prominent role, and one whose name implied something that was the antithesis of urban.[37] Other features at Vauxhall had an overtly bucolic character. There was an area called the Rural Downs, "where lambs are seen sporting . . . covered with turf, and pleasingly interspersed with young cypress, fir, yew, cedar and tulip-trees"; a display that was activated at nine

Figure 2.5. J. C. Nattes, "Sydney Gardens and Rear of Sydney House," from William Miller, *Bath: A Series of Illustrated Views* (1805), hand-colored etching and aquatint. Bath in Time—Bath Central Library.

o'clock each evening and showed "a very fine landscape, illuminated by concealed lights, in which the principal objects that strike the eyes are a cascade, or a water-fall, and a miller's house"; and some of the paintings in the supper boxes were of country scenes, such as "a shepherd playing on his pipe" and "country dancers round the maypole."[38] The "noble gravel-walk" that led from the main entrance gate was said in 1767 to be "planted on each side with very lofty trees" and "terminated by a landscape of the country, a beautiful lawn of meadow-ground." The rear of the gardens was protected only by a ha-ha, intended to open up "a View into the adjacent Meads; where Haycocks, and Haymakers sporting, during the mowing season, adds a Beauty to the Landskip."[39] What reinforced this Arcadian ambience was the heavily rustic content of the songs delivered during the concerts in the gardens. Not untypical of the genre was one, sung at Vauxhall in the mid-eighteenth century, which opened with the lines:

More bright this sun begins to dawn,
The merry birds to sing,
And flow'rets dappled o'er the lawn,
In all the pride of spring.[40]

By the early nineteenth century, if not before, the rural character of the view from Vauxhall had been disturbed by the construction of terraced housing along Kennington Lane and Vauxhall Street, but this should not deflect from the original green agenda of the gardens.[41]

Space: Journeying and Walking

The London gardens owed much to *where* they were located, and this is indicative of the importance of space in understanding their operation and meaning. Getting to and from the establishments was the first essential step in the pleasure garden experience. A position on the periphery of the capital necessarily implied a significant journey for many customers living in the fashionable residential areas nearer the center. For the more well to do, the coach and carriage was the preferred method of conveyance (by the 1760s there were about 800 licensed hackney coaches in London alongside private conveyances),[42] offering comfort, a measure of safety, and protection from the elements. But the volume of traffic generated at the major gardens could create its own problems.[43] So "full" was London on 15 May 1776 that it took the Harris family of Salisbury an hour in their relatively short journey from Piccadilly to Ranelagh "and an hour and five and twenty minutes from the time we left the room, getting back." When Edward Pigott had visited Ranelagh two weeks earlier on May Day he found it "very crowded . . . there is tolerable good regulation for the coaches, but has [*sic*] there was too many, generally some accident happens."[44] Traffic mishaps were a common occurrence when using coaches in the restricted spaces of the town, but the vehicles' importance as symbols of power and status, and the opportunities they provided for social networking, guaranteed their appeal to the elite.[45] During his stay in London for the season 1762–63, James Boswell, traveled—along with other members of a party assembled for the occasion—to Vauxhall and Ranelagh in the coach of the tenth Earl of Eglinton (one of Boswell's circle of acquaintances in the city).[46] The interface between vehicles and gardens was a sensitive point, partly because of the volume of traffic and partly because this was where visitors became exposed to the potential threat posed by the open streets. There appears to have been spaces where coaches could wait for the company at Vauxhall, and—at least by 1795—"near the coach-entrance, is a large convenient room for the reception of the company, who are waiting for their carriages," but at Ranelagh in the 1770s it was "a common thing" reported a Chelsea innkeeper "for gentlemen when they go to Ranelagh to send their chariots, and put them up at my house till they want them again."[47] During von Uffenbach's visit to London he drove to Lambeth Springs and the Spring Gardens but returned from the latter by river and also took a boat from Westminster to Cuper's Gardens. He reasoned that because London is built along the Thames "one can go almost everywhere by water; this is exceedingly pleasant, not only because one is rowed past the town, but because one travels swiftly. . . . It is more comfortable to travel in these boats than in the Heckney-Coaches, which jolt most terribly."[48] It is likely that travel by boat to Vauxhall and Ranelagh, a common option,[49] appealed not only for practical but also for aesthetic reasons, reinforcing the proximity to nature (the Spring Gardens in Bath were also accessed by ferry across the Avon until the Pulteney Bridge was built)[50] in the same way as promenading along riverbanks. Walking to the gardens was also an option, even for the well off. A footpath existed from the fashionable Cavendish Square to Marylebone, and it was possible to access Ranelagh "on foot through St James's Park, from the west-end of which the distance does not exceed a mile."[51] In 1767 Sylas Neville, though arriving by coach, walked back from Ranelagh at half past twelve, presumably not through the park at this time of night, "a Westminster watchman was so civil as to leave his box to show me the way into Great George Street," just below Hanover Square.[52] For those unfamiliar with London, however, there was always the possibility of getting lost, as Carl Philip Moritz did in 1782 on the way to Ranelagh. He had the sense to take a coach home.[53] Given the level of demand a vehicle was not always available for hire. Two ladies who exited Vauxhall in 1769 and were unable to find a coach, rejected the opportunity to travel by boat and instead walked, for protection, with a waiter from the gardens (whom they paid a shilling) until they spied a conveyance for hire, "got in, and ordered the coachman to drive to the New Buildings near the Middlesex Hospital."[54]

For most fashionable visitors, walking was an activity generally to be undertaken *inside* rather than *outside* the gardens. However, this was a very particular sort of perambulation, fundamentally different from that of the ordinary world, where progressing from point A to point B is the principal objective. In the special space that constituted the pleasure gardens, progressive was replaced by circular motion. Accounts of Vauxhall in 1739 note how on arrival the company "take a hasty circuit around the walks," before the music strikes up, and "after the first piece of musick is finish'd, a silence ensues, of a length sufficient to allow the company time to take a circuit of the gardens before another begins."[55] In the visitors' movement to and from the gardens, there was a sense of purpose and direction; movement was linear. Once in the gardens the world of normal motion was suspended; when the company moved they were effectively going nowhere. This concept of circular motion reached its apogee in the rotundas constructed at Ranelagh, Vauxhall, and—in a downmarket version—on Spa Fields.[56] Ranelagh was by far the largest of the rotundas, constituting, according to Maximilien de Lazowski, "an immense round room. I no longer remember its diameter but at least 130 or 140 feet." Edward Pigott upped the odds, claiming a diameter of "very nearly 200 feet," but most guides repeat the standard dimensions of an exterior diameter of 185 feet, and an interior one of 150 feet.[57] Moritz observed that "everything here was circular." In the center of the huge covered space was "the chimney" or "four high black pillars containing ornate fireplaces where coffee, tea and punch were being prepared," and on the circumference were two tiers of sixty boxes, into which was recessed an orchestra. Around the chimney, according to Moritz, "all fashionable London revolved like a gaily coloured distaff, sauntering in a compact throng." James Boswell praised the "noble Rotunda all surrounded with boxes to sit in and such a profusion of well-dressed people walking round is very fine." Tobias Smollett's Matthew Bramble observed that there were two positions that the visitors could take, in or out of the human snake; "One half of the company are following at the other's tails, in an eternal circle; like so many blind asses in an olive-mill . . . while the other half are drinking hot water, under the denomination of tea, till nine or ten o'clock at night, to keep them awake for the rest of the evening." Moritz relates how when "tired of the crowd and of strolling around in a circle I sat down in one of the alcoves in order to take some refreshment," before ascending to a box in the gallery, "from which, like a solemn watcher of the world, I looked down on the concourse still turning round and round in circles."[58]

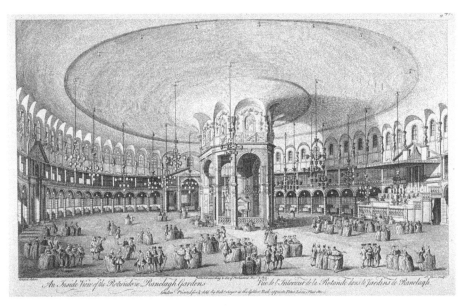

Figure 2.6. Nathaniel Parr after Canaletto (Giovanni Antonio Canal), *The Interior of the Rotunda at Ranelagh* (1751), engraving. Guildhall Library, City of London.

The rotunda at Ranelagh represented an extreme version of circular walking. But many formal walks encouraged promenaders to saunter backward and forward in a vaguely circular fashion. A similar mode of movement was to be found in the Ring in Hyde Park, where "the usage was to drive round and round, but when they had turned for some time round one way, then, as if tired with the sameness, they were to face about and turn round the other during some time also, for variety-sake."[59] It was a pattern of motion that had its parallel, as Mark Girouard has noted, in the changing design of fashionable houses and buildings of public entertainment. The enfilade alignment of rooms associated with the "formal house" (1630–1720) was giving way to the circular arrangement of the "social house" (1720–70), a form of design also reflected in the larger assembly rooms, like those at York and Bath, where guests could move easily between the main ballroom and the linked refreshment and card rooms.[60] What was the point of this form of circular space and motion? First, it possessed a repetitive hypnotic quality associated with ritual forms of behavior that suggested to participants that they had entered a different sphere of experience. Norms of behavior were changed and expectations modified and heightened. Second, circular motion provided the ideal performative context in which people could engage in intensive types of display and voyeurism. As Moritz noted in the rotunda at Ranelagh, "Some who wished to see and to be seen were going round in an everlasting circle."[61] Miles Ogborn has emphasized that "Vauxhall Gardens was made of spectacles. . . . The audience itself was very much part of this spectacle," and Peter de Bolla argued that "what the spectator is going to see, and be seen seeing, in Vauxhall Gardens is visuality itself." For those seeking social or sexual status, or for those combining the two in the pursuit of a marriage partner, walks and gardens were among the key auditoriums from which to observe, and stages on which to perform.[62]

Third, Laura Williams has stressed the relationship in the period between circulation, walking, gardens, and health in what was a nascent form of environmentalism. She argues that "good health was vested in movement as opposed to stagnation, applicable not just to circulation within the body of the individual, but the body of the town itself."[63] Building on scientific ideas such as William Harvey's discovery of the body's circulatory system, and contemporary views on the importance of allowing the free flow of air, public walks, and gardens—anticipating later ideas of the park as "the lungs of the city"—came to be seen as an antidote to the increasing congestion, pollution, and ill health associated with the city. This was reinforced by their frequent waterside location, as rivers would be seen as an integral part of nature's own circulatory system. Fourth, as Jonathan Conlin has pointed out, the pleasure gardens and the movement of people within them had a sociopolitical dimension. The "circulation-friendly planning" encouraged a pattern and created a representation of social relationships that made it appear to contemporaries that "equality, independence and police went together."[64] Here encapsulated was the "British system"—praised by many foreigners and reflected in their admiration of the British pleasure gardens—that allowed citizens of different ranks to consort informally together and circulate as one undifferentiated body, without creating disorder and threatening the structure of authority. The contact generated by circulation encouraged sociability and politeness rather than prompting social fissures, therefore walks and gardens were considered a powerful force for promoting social harmony and sustaining the social order.

Space: Politeness and the Public Sphere

With their emphasis on mass circular motion and their informal and open ethos, pleasure gardens can be seen as an archetypal example of the public sphere, to be ranked alongside the coffeehouse and assembly room. Contemporaries, particularly foreign tourists, were struck by the wide social mix found at the gardens. Moritz understood that "the poorest families make an effort to go to Ranelagh at least once a year, my landlady assures me" and reported that in the rotunda "old and young, nobility and commoners, I saw them all crossing and recrossing in a motley swarm."[65] Historians have followed this contemporary lead and emphasized the accessibility of the gardens. A. H. Saxon has suggested that "all classes spent their leisure hours at these establishments," Penelope Corfield that "an important part of Vauxhall's appeal was its relative openness. It was not a location reserved for any one social group," John Brewer that the pleasure garden was "available to almost anyone who could pay," and David Solkin that "eighteenth-century London offered very few other places where the different classes could mix more freely at such close quarters."[66] There is no doubt much truth in this picture of *relative* accessibility and social heterogeneity, but we should remain cautious about exaggerating how "public" the public sphere was. Much more is needed to be known about who actually visited the gardens and walks. In Wroth's hierarchy of gardens, the top four attracted "people of rank and fashion" (though, with the possible exception of Ranelagh, the gardens were "by no means exclusive or select"), whereas the tea and generally the spa gardens—the bulk of establishments—"had an aristocracy of aldermen and merchants, young ensigns and templars, and were the chosen resort of the prentice, the sempstress, and the small shopkeeper."[67] The fact that the smaller gardens clustered to the north of the City of London, whereas the four major gardens lay in close proximity to the fashionable West End, reinforces this picture of a garden hierarchy serving different social clienteles.

Admission to Vauxhall, after John Tyers's revamp of the gardens in the 1730s, was one shilling for an ordinary event, less than a day's wage for an artisan (Marylebone was only six pence initially, rising to one shilling by 1767; Ranelagh was two shillings and sixpence, though this included refreshments) and not beyond the pockets of the lower middle class.[68] However, subscription tickets for the season—which carried the kudos of patronage and often took the form of attractively decorated metal tokens (Figure 2.7)

Figure 2.7. Perpetual Pass to Vauxhall Gardens Presented to William Hogarth (1733), gold. © The Trustees of the British Museum.

that owners could treat as a fashion accessory and show off—cost considerably more; at Marylebone the price for a ticket for two rose from 12 shillings in 1738, to £1.11s. 6d. in 1766 and two guineas in 1774.[69] Admission to prestigious events could also be pricey. A ticket (which admitted two) to the two balls held at Marylebone in August 1746 was 10s. 6d. for each occasion, attendance at the Vauxhall rehearsal of the Royal Fireworks Music in 1749 was 2s. 6d., and admission to the Festivale di Campagna held at Marylebone in 1776 was one guinea per person, and one and a half guineas for two.[70] Moreover, focus on ticket prices ignores the substantial additional expenses of food and drink,[71] and, even more important, the major hidden costs of clothing, personal accoutrements, and education. To perform effectively at one of the top gardens, to play a significant part in the drama that was underway, and thus to enjoy any meaningful social return from the occasion, visitors had, prior to entry, to have invested sums of money that were beyond the incomes of the vast majority of the population. This in itself would have guaranteed a measure of exclusivity. Such was also the case for provincial public walks, where financial barriers to entry were rare, and where most ordinary people appear simply to have excluded themselves. Where there was a risk of contamination of polite space it was not because the common people desired to share in polite promenading, but because they wanted to continue their customary uses of spaces that had been appropriated to meet the needs of fashionable society. Thus at York formal action had to be taken in the 1740s to exclude washerwomen and naked bathers from the fine new walk laid out, using corporation finance and with the aim of attracting gentry society to the city, along the north bank of the Ouse.[72] Jonathan Conlin has argued that Vauxhall Gardens saw a change in the social makeup of its clientele between 1770 and 1859, with a shift toward middle- and then lower middle-class use, and this may reflect a wider trend in the status of those visiting public gardens, parks, and walks.[73] But when in guides of 1767 and 1782 Ranelagh, admittedly always more exclusive than Vauxhall,[74] was described as "a public place of pleasure, where the first quality, and best families in the kingdom resort" and being "frequented by the nobility, gentry and citizens of the higher ranks," it is unlikely that this was entirely tourist hyperbole.[75]

Not that the common people were entirely absent from these polite green spaces. Cooks, waiters, musicians, operatives, gardeners, and the like had to be present, particularly in the larger pleasure gardens, to service the needs of the company, who would also bring their own servants (though at

Vauxhall domestic servants in livery were banned from the walks and were segregated in a "coop" outside the gardens).[76] Moreover, in the case of some of the walks and gardens there was a significant presence of prostitutes[77] and thieves.[78] In 1775 a General Plestow described how "I was at Vaux hall upon the 3rd day of August, I missed my pocket-book, with some notes; it was in my waistcoat pocket; I am convinced it must have been picked out of my pocket, either in Vauxhall gardens, or going from the garden to the coach next morning"; another victim in 1771 described how a pair of criminals worked in tandem while he was attending Marylebone Gardens, "While I was there I was jostled about a good deal by the crowd, and my hat fell off; I immediately suspected the jostle might be done by some body, with an intention to steal my watch. I felt for my watch, and it was gone; the prisoner was close to me; I observed him stoop and extend his hand forward, as if delivering something to another person."[79] In *The Spectator* of 1712 Joseph Addison has Sir Roger de Coverley complain to the "Mistress of the House" at Spring Gardens "that he should be a better customer to her gardens, if there were more nightingales, and fewer strumpets," and a witness at a criminal case in 1745 told how he "knew Mrs. Moore twenty years ago, she used to go under the name of Chamberlain. She walked in Spring Gardens at Vaux Hall, and picked up men there."[80] For the pickpockets and prostitutes who attended the gardens the entrance fees and expense of purchasing the fine clothes necessary to cut a plausible figure, and to get past any check on admission, was part of the professional costs of doing their job. They were there not to socialize with their superiors but to fleece them. As such their presence—in numbers relatively small in relation to the overall visitor population—did not represent a serious challenge to the social exclusivity of the gardens.

Far more significant was the threat that they posed to the safe and polite image of the pleasure garden experience. In this respect the danger was not confined to the geographical limits of the establishments but also embraced the space traversed by visitors—seen as prime targets because of their wealth and possession of high value status accessories like watches—on their journeys to and from the gardens. Criminals operated in the vicinity of the leading pleasure gardens and along the main arteries of communication to them. The victim in a case in 1738 described what must have been a not uncommon ploy that combined prostitution and theft: "I was at Vauxhall, and got a little in liquor, but I remember I had a guinea in my pocket, beside-silver, when I came on this side of the water. The prisoner (I suppose) pick'd me up, and we went to a house in Vinegar-Yard, by Russel Court. I was so much fuelled, that I do not know where I was, 'till the landlord waked me in my chair the next morning." The victim discovered that he had been fleeced of his valuables.[81] Anthony Bell, a gentleman, was similarly relieved of money and a watch in 1773 while he slept with a prostitute: "As I was coming from Vauxhall, between two and three in the morning, I met with the prisoners. . . . Davis ran after me and asked me to go home with her; I offered her a shilling to see her bubbies: then we had a long conversation. I agreed to go home with her, and did. I and Davis went to bed."[82] Most at threat, at least potentially, were those who walked. The organist at Vauxhall, James Worgan, was attacked and injured in August 1740 on the Kennington Lane by a "foot-pad" as he was returning from the gardens.[83] Two years earlier a servant John Udall was returning home alone from Ranelagh at 11:30 P.M. when "in Chelsea Fields a man took me by the collar . . . he said, let me have what you have got: he threw me down, and took out my watch; it was a silver one with two cases: then he took my buckles, which were plated: my watch had a steel chain to it, with a silver setting of a seal . . . he took four shillings and sixpence in money from me. There was another man in company with him."[84] Thieves often seem to have worked in teams. A notorious gang of four robbers "being out another evening waiting for their prey, they met two gentlemen coming from Ranelagh-Gardens, they directly accosted them with the usual terms of G-dd-n you, stand and deliver! and the gentlemen drew their swords . . . but the rogues soon overpowered them, and took from one of them a watch, some silver, and his sword, and from the other, a watch with a triangle crystal seal, set in gold, a guinea, and his sword."[85] It was not only those on foot who were at risk. There are several cases of people returning from the gardens by coach or chaise being held up (including one, coming from Ranelagh, in Duke Street, Lincoln's Inn Fields, and another, coming from Marylebone, between Tottenham Court Road and Fig Lane) by armed thieves.[86] Pleasure garden proprietors faced a constant battle to keep such criminal elements at bay and ease the anxieties of their customers, employing doorkeepers and watchmen inside the gardens, and deploying armed patrols to escort clients back to their homes in the West End and elsewhere.[87] Moreover, as David Solkin has shown in the case of Tyers's remodeling of Vauxhall, proprietors were acutely conscious of the need to maintain the respectability of their establishments. This was not just to avoid adverse action of the part of the authorities—the Disorderly Houses Act of 1752 required that a "house, room, garden or other place kept for public dancing, music or entertainment" in London, Westminster, and twenty miles around had to be licensed—but also to deliver the polite image customers desired.[88]

But if the company aspired to politeness it is also clear that their lesser faculties craved something else. When under pressure Tyers cordoned off the notorious Lovers' Walk at Vauxhall and erected lighting, 150 young men among his customers duly tore down the fencing and smashed the lamps.[89] The pleasure gardens were seen as spaces in which polite norms could be both celebrated *and* challenged. A good part of the appeal of the gardens was that they were perceived as dangerous spaces in which customers could indulge their impolite passions and play at crossing the boundaries of class and gender.[90] This was particularly so in the case of the masquerade, described by Terry Castle as projecting "an anti-nature, a world turned upside down, an intoxicating reversal of ordinary sexual, social, and metaphysical hierarchies," for which the gardens were a primary venue.[91] In 1732 a witness in a case at the Old Bailey described how a person known as Princess Seraphina, a "gentleman's servant" who frequented Vauxhall, "commonly us'd to wear a white gown, and a scarlet cloak, with her hair frizzled and curl'd all round her forehead; and then she would so flutter her fan, and make such fine curtsies, that you would have not known her from a woman: she takes great delight in balls and masquerades, and always chooses to appear at them in a female dress, that she may have the satisfaction of dancing with fine gentlemen."[92] However, in the final analysis it was play. As in the case of carnival (to use Mumford's term), the gardens constituted spaces and moments in which the social and sexual norms could be inverted temporarily but which ultimately served to reaffirm these norms. Impoliteness helped to define rather than undermine politeness. It has also to be said that whatever the challenge posed on occasions to sexual norms it is likely that the general expectations of behavior tended to reinforce rather than undermine conventional sexual roles. A 1796 guide noted that Vauxhall was "justly celebrated for a display of living beauty and fashion in the persons of English ladies" and the sentiments expressed in the myriad songs performed at the gardens, if occasionally erotic, nonetheless put the sexes firmly in their orthodox places. One sung by Mr. Sedgwick at

Vauxhall in the later eighteenth century, and directed at the female audience, was not untypical:

> First, you that woul'd join in the conjugal band,
> And wish to get married as soon as you can,
> Let love and good temper e'er go hand in hand,
> And then never doubt but you'll conquer your man.[93]

Much of the run-of-the-mill business of Vauxhall and Ranelagh, such as the staging of concerts, offered little scope for carnivalesque antics, and by the end of the eighteenth century unconventional and transgressive modes of sexual behavior were facing growing disapproval. This was particularly so in the case of the masquerade.[94] It had long been the focus of criticism. During the moral panic that followed the earthquake that shook London in 1750, an anonymous pamphleteer railed against a masquerade ball advertised for Ranelagh, "assured, that all people, who have any sense of religion, or common decency, are fully determined to show their abhorrence and detestation, in the most public manner, against all that are audacious enough to presume to go," and warning darkly "though I am . . . an enemy to riots and commotions of any kind, yet I will not be answerable for the resentment of the lower kind of people, which no guards ought to protect them from . . . sure the Invalids of Chelsea Hospital may be better employed than in guarding the roads on that occasion."[95] Over time the masquerade appears to have been adapted to reduce the element of concealment that lay at its heart; in Paul Langford's words, "It was left to the English to take the masque out of masquerade."[96] It must also be remembered—and this is where focus on the major gardens may seriously mislead us—that many, probably most of the proliferating public walks and gardens appearing in London and provincial towns did not have the risqué reputation of Vauxhall and Ranelagh and did not aim to push the boundaries of appropriate behavior too far. Social exclusivity would have been maintained and in all likelihood the presence of thieves and prostitutes relatively limited. There would have been excitement and some risk taking as perambulators showed off their finery and suitors and their chaperones eyed potential catches. The pursuit of status and marriage partners, and the two were intimately linked, was a deadly serious business. Yet all this would have been contained within a prevailing discourse of politeness.

Time

If space did much to define the public sphere and discourse of politeness in pleasure gardens, so also did time. The London gardens were predominantly a summer phenomenon, open between April/May and August/September. In 1795 it was reported that entertainment at Ranelagh began about mid-April and that "Vauxhall is generally open from May to August."[97] This pattern of operation was to be expected, given the open-air character of the gardens and their dependence on shrubbery and trees, but it also nicely plugged the gap left between the closing and opening of the metropolitan winter season, the period in the year into which the majority of London's fashionable events were crammed. By the later eighteenth century the middle of the year was also a phase of relative inactivity in Bath, where the Sydney Gardens, it was said, "amply supplies the absence of other amusements during the summer months."[98] For most of the smaller spas summer would have been the *peak* period, but in the county towns it was the winter season, as in the city, which was dominant. This was probably reflected in the fact that the New Walk at York was open throughout the year between 7 A.M. and 6 P.M. However, the essentially summer character of the promenade can be seen in the way that between 1 May and 1 September the gates were unlocked an extra two hours earlier and later.[99] As well as being a convenient way of giving shape to the recreational calendar, the notion of a winter and summer season resonated with the "natural" temporal order, celebrated in literary works like James Thomson's widely admired *The Seasons* (1726–30). In this sense the summer character of gardens and walks reinforced their spatial role in reconnecting their urban clientele to nature. The season opened on 9 May 1763 at Marylebone Gardens with a song:

> Now the Summer advances and Pleasure removes
> From the Smoak of the Town to the Fields and the Groves
> Permit me to hope that your Favours again
> May smile as before on this once happy Plain.[100]

Most walks and gardens would have operated to a daily and weekly rhythm. John Wood recorded in the 1740s how at Bath public breakfasts followed a visit to the baths and Pump Room earlier in the morning.[101] Commercial pleasure gardens were a common location for such meals; in the 1760s and

Pleasure Gardens and Urban Culture

Figure 2.8. Charles Grignion after Nathan Drake, *Prospect of Noble Terras Walk* (1756), etching and engraving. York Museum Trust (York Art Gallery).

1770s the Spring Gardens at Bath accommodated sumptuous breakfasts on Monday and Thursday mornings, attended by music and dancing, for which there was an entry fee of 1s. 6d.[102] About 12 p.m., Wood continues, "some of the Company appear on the *Grand Parade*, and other Publick Walks, where a Rotation of Walking is continued for about two Hours"; the company reassembled again on the walks after dinner and evening prayers.[103] Most London gardens operated for several days every week in season; Islington for two to three days, opening its doors at 7 a.m. and already full by 10 to 11 a.m., with dancing all day.[104]

The sort of daily and weekly routines associated with walks and pleasure gardens were essential to guarantee that all participants turned up at the right places at the right times. They were effectively a herding mechanism to ensure that the company moved in unison and maximized the corporate experience of the occasions. In the rotunda at Ranelagh a bell rang at midday to reverse the direction in which the crowd circulated, clockwise in the morning and counterclockwise in the afternoon.[105] But time—as with space—not only enforced social integration, it also engineered social separation. The regimens found at Bath or the major London gardens depended on the availability of free time during weekdays, something that would have been impossible for the mass of the working population. The only spare time regularly open to working people was Sunday. Significantly, Vauxhall closed on this day, and von Uffenbach observed of St. James's Park that "during the week gentlemen of the highest fashion are to be met here," but on a Sunday "no genteel persons come there, but only those who cannot get there in the week or who live too far from Westminster." However, the Pantheon in Spa Fields (the haunt of small tradesmen) was open on a Sunday, as were the small tea gardens for which this was the key day of the week.[106]

Most gardens and walks were places of daylight pleasure. But the major commercial gardens also mounted concerts, which could run from any time between 6 P.M. and 11 P.M.,[107] and lavish evening events like masquerades and ridottos. The pleasure-making could extend deep into the night. In June 1765 Gertrude Harris attended a benefit concert and "very fine fire works" at Ranelagh, and "came away about eleven oclock."[108] In the same month two years later Sylas Neville set out for Ranelagh at 6:30 P.M. and did not exit the gardens until half past midnight.[109] In May 1776 Edward Pigott arrived at Vauxhall at 9 P.M. and departed at 12 A.M., but leaving about half of the company still remaining.[110] Lazowski reported in 1785 "that one doesn't reckon to go promenading at Ranelagh before midnight or one o'clock."[111] Six years later the Oakes family (of Bury St. Edmunds), having suppered at their London lodgings on a Friday evening in May, "all went to Ranelagh [at] 11 o'clock & return'd home at 3."[112] In 1785 one witness in an Old Bailey case reported how he and a companion "had been at Ranelagh, and about two in the morning we were in Duke-Street, Lincoln's-Inn-Fields," and another in a case two years later testified "I drive a hackney coach, I came from Ranelagh, between three and four in the morning."[113] The Festivale di Campagna staged at Marylebone in June 1776 began at 8:30 with an instrumental concert, followed by catches and glees after 10:00, a cold collation at 11:00, and dancing after midnight. It was advertised of the same gardens that at the two balls in August 1746 "the whole band will perform until three o'clock."[114] Events of this kind were not only beyond the pockets of working people, but keeping these hours was only feasible for those able to rest during the following day.

The daily rhythms of the leisure class were, therefore, in vital respects an inversion of those of the working class. For the latter the evening was a period of recuperation and sleep, for the former it was effectively the working part of the day. In the fashionable towns, but especially in London, night took on a new dimension for the polite classes. At a practical level this was only possible because of the extensive use of illuminations both inside leisure facilities and on the streets.[115] Most accounts of the great London gardens emphasize the extensive and brilliant nature of the lighting. The rotunda at Ranelagh was reported in 1776 to be illuminated by 2,080 lights, a quarter of these located in the eighteen chandeliers.[116] In 1767 it was said of Vauxhall that "when it grows dark, the garden near the orchestra is illuminated, almost in an instant, with about 1,500 glass lamps; which, by their glittering among the tress, renders it exceedingly light and brilliant"; during the Ridotto Al Fresco held at Vauxhall in June 1769 the whole gardens were illuminated by about 5,000 lamps; and in 1796 it was claimed of Vauxhall that "up to 14,000 lamps have been used, at one time, in the lighting of these gardens, which, every night this season, are illuminated with uncommon splendour."[117] What made the spectacle so exciting and the illuminations so brilliant was the contrast with the darkness of the night. Philip Moritz in 1782 recorded how during a visit to Ranelagh "every now and then I would compare for my own satisfaction the glitter of this scene [in the rotunda] with the darkness in the garden outside, in order to recapture some of the thrill I had enjoyed when I first entered the building. Well into the night I amused myself thus."[118] The play on light and dark was at its most thrilling in the fireworks displays that became a feature of the major gardens in the later eighteenth century, orchestrated by pyrotechnists like Jean-Baptiste Torré.[119] The Sydney Gardens in Bath hosted "four or five gala nights in the course of the summer, which for brilliancy, taste, and elegance, cannot be excelled: about 5,000 variegated lamps are then lighted, and a splendid display of fireworks then set off. On these occasions a company of three or four thousand persons frequently assemble to witness this enchanting scene, and present a spectacle the most sprightly and animating that the imagination can conceive."[120]

The contrast between night and day was a feature of literary and visual representations of London like those of John Gay's *Trivia* (1716) and William Hogarth's *Four Times of the Day* (1738); "Evening" from the Hogarth sequence formed one of the supper-box paintings at Vauxhall.[121] Gay refers specifically to the "dang'rous Night" and goes on to catalog the risks facing the inadvertent walker who might be accosted by thieves, drunks, violent rakes, pickpockets, and prostitutes. All of these could be found in and on the outskirts of the major gardens during an evening event. Though undoubtedly posing a threat to the polite credentials of the occasions, dubious characters of this sort were also an integral part of the gardens' appeal. The sense of risk and insecurity created a frisson of excitement for participants. At night the natural order was inverted and it was possible to cross the boundaries of normality and flirt with danger. The heroine of Fanny Burney's *Evelina* (1778) exclaims, "We came home from the ridotto so late, or rather so early, that it was not possible for me to write. Indeed, we do not *go*, you will be frightened to hear it,—till past eleven o'clock: but nobody does. A terrible reverse of the order of nature! We sleep by the sun, and wake with the moon."[122] However, there were always the illuminations to banish the darkness and restore order. The ridottos and masquerades that featured in the evening entertainment at the gardens were thus to some extent a play on the contrasts between day and night, black and white, politeness and impoliteness. The contrast between light and dark was emphasized in the inversion ritual that accompanied the final night of the season at Vauxhall when "there are commonly from three to four thousand spectators, and a kind of riot generally ensues before morning, during which the lamps are broken, and other irregularities are committed." Young Branghton in *Evelina* advised that "Miss ought to stay in town till the last night . . . there's always a riot,—and there the folks run about,—and then there's such squealing and squalling!—and there all the lamps are broke,—and the women run skimper scamper;—I declare I would not take five guineas to miss the last night!"[123] This further emphasized the carnivalesque character of the gardens and their role in both challenging and establishing the norms of the polite world.

The polite public sphere was not confined to pleasure gardens and walks. Many of the new fashionable urban pastimes, such as attending assemblies and concerts, served similar purposes. What marked out gardens and walks was their commitment to an evolving green agenda, as rapid urbanization drove many people—inside and outside towns—to renegotiate their relationship with nature. Not that that agenda was a purely environmental one. The capacity to relate to nature at an aesthetic as opposed to a working level, the ability to stand *outside* rather than *inside* nature, was a sign of refinement, and therefore very much part of that socially defined world of politeness that circumscribed the meaning of the urban pleasure garden. The norms of that world did not go unchallenged, but the relative exclusivity of many of the green spaces involved, the care taken by proprietors to protect their image, and the ritualistic nature of the entertainment limited the potential for social subversion. Fashionable walks and gardens were an important part of the new system of urban pleasure that characterized the long eighteenth century, and that facilitated a limited but significant expansion and redefinition of the elite while simultaneously reinforcing the underlying social order.

Chapter 3

Guns in the Gardens: Peter Monamy's Paintings for Vauxhall

ELEANOR HUGHES

The reopening of the Vauxhall pleasure gardens in 1732 under the proprietorship of Jonathan Tyers has been identified as a key moment in the development of the relationship between British visual culture and the public sphere. In an effort to deliver the gardens from their former reputation—the fictional Sir Roger de Coverley commented that his visit to the gardens would have been more pleasurable had there been "more Nightingales, and fewer Strumpets"—Tyers made a number of improvements, including the installation of gravel walks, an open-air bandstand (the Orchestra), and a series of supper boxes.[1] By the early 1740s the boxes had been decorated with paintings, the majority of which were executed by Francis Hayman and his studio, from designs by Hayman, Hubert Gravelot, and William Hogarth (Figure 3.1).[2]

Hayman's supper-box pictures have made the gardens of some interest to art historians as the place where, for the first time, paintings by native British artists were made available to the public, more than a decade before the first public art exhibitions in London and more than two decades before the founding of the Royal Academy. In keeping with Tyers's aims for propriety, the supper-box paintings depicted rustic pursuits and children's games in compositions that constitute largely de-eroticized versions of the fêtes galantes by Watteau and his followers that were then popular in England.[3] Based on these works, the artistic program at Vauxhall has been characterized as helping to demarcate a place of leisure and pleasure that was meant to both attract and define polite society. The paintings aided

Guns in the Gardens

Figure 3.1. Francis Hayman, *Jonathan Tyers, with His Daughter Elizabeth, and Her Husband John Wood* (between 1750 and 1752), oil on canvas. Yale Center for British Art, Paul Mellon Collection B1981.25.328.

in the putative transformation of the gardens from a place of "libidinous assembly" to "an arena of purity and chaste delight, for the delectation of the human mind" and where "commerce had tamed passion into refinement."[4] Other work on Vauxhall has examined the "distinct political/cultural dimension" of the gardens, focusing on the patronage of Frederick,

Prince of Wales, the symbolic head of the "Patriot" Opposition and landlord of the gardens. It has been noted that the authors of several of the theatrical and literary productions on which some of Hayman's paintings were based—Henry Fielding, Robert Dodsley, George Lyttleton—as well as other cultural figures linked with Vauxhall (John Gay, Thomas Arne), moved in Opposition circles.[5]

Almost completely overlooked in these studies are four supper-box paintings by Peter Monamy, now lost and known only through engravings by Pierre Foudrinier and Remi Parr, which were published by Bowles and Carver in 1743. Monamy's paintings were integrated into the overall decorative schema, providing counterpoints to the other supper-box pictures.[6] They have received only cursory mention in scholarship on the artistic program at Vauxhall, while published works focusing on the paintings themselves do not consider their immediate context.[7] At the same time, historical scholarship on the cultural reception of the events depicted by Monamy stops short of consideration of pictorial responses, as does work on evidence of the political/cultural dimension of Vauxhall.[8] Coke and Borg contend that Monamy's pictures were "a reflection of, and focus for, popular feeling, and presaged no move towards a politicalisation of the gardens."[9] This chapter seeks to draw together these strands of inquiry through a more thorough and nuanced reading of Monamy's paintings in the context of the political pressures of the 1730s and early 1740s. By so doing, it aims to reposition the gardens as a key location for the promotion of national and patriotic ideologies, most explicitly through Monamy's paintings and through the related songs and ballads in circulation both at Vauxhall and throughout the wider metropolis and beyond. Not only do Monamy's paintings bring into the gardens interrelated themes of imperial acquisition and conquest, violence, national duty, slavery, liberty, and naval supremacy, they also articulate patriotic themes more explicitly than any form of cultural production at the gardens, visual or musical.

The Taking of Porto Bello

Two of Monamy's pictures, *The Taking of Porto Bello by Vice Admiral Vernon on the 2nd of Nov 1739 with Six Men of War Only* and *The Taking of the St. Josef a Spanish Carracca Ship Sept 23rd 1739*, portray events concerned with hostilities between England and Spain that had been mounting during the 1730s, breaking out into the War of Jenkins Ear (which would merge into the War of Austrian Succession). Britain and its colonies had been essentially at peace with other European powers since 1714 and the end of the War of Spanish Succession; the signing of the Treaty of Utrecht brought crucial Mediterranean and North American bases and an *asiento*, which gave Britain a monopoly over the slave trade in the Spanish West Indies and a license allowing one British ship each year to trade with Spanish-American colonies. British trade with the Americas, however, was increasingly seen to be threatened by the unwillingness of Spanish authorities to tolerate British violations of the *asiento*, characterized in England as the piracy of the Spanish *guardacostas*, vessels that were charged with seizing contraband goods from British vessels. The situation became a focus for parliamentary discontent with the ministry of Robert Walpole, reaching its climax in 1738 when a Spanish Customs officer sliced off the ear of an English merchant captain, Robert Jenkins, and suggested that it be sent to George II. Encouraged by the accession of vital commercial markets through warfare in 1714, the opposition waged a propaganda campaign, including petitions from merchants in major cities, for a naval corrective to assuage the blow to national pride.[10]

Admiral Edward Vernon, a vociferous opposition Whig, had claimed in 1729 that he could take Porto Bello with only six ships and 300 men.[11] After a naval career during which he had gained much experience in the West Indies, Vernon had become involved in politics during the peace after the Treaty of Utrecht. He had openly and fiercely criticized Walpole for his neglect of the Navy and would advocate, through speeches and pamphlets, for a maritime economy and "the humane encouragement of seamen to man the fleet."[12] The major trading port between Spain and her colonies on the coast of present-day Panama, Porto Bello, "the only mart for all the Wealth of Peru to come to Europe," was the point of export of sugar, cocoa, aromatic gums, indigo, cochineal, pearls, emeralds, gold, and silver from Chile and Peru to Spain; the supplier of European goods to Lima and Panama; and the fitting-out place of the *guardacostas*.[13] The port was not only a strategic but also a highly symbolic target; in 1729 Admiral Francis Hosier had attempted and failed to take the seemingly impregnable fortress, subsequently succumbing to yellow fever along with some 4,000 men from his squadron. The blame for this disaster, spun as an instance of naval martyrdom at the hands of a ministry reluctant to act, was placed squarely—and unfairly—on Walpole.[14]

Vernon set sail from Plymouth in August 1739 with instructions from the Admiralty to "commit all sorts of hostilities against the Spaniards in such manner as you shall think proper."[15] His plan was to enter the harbor of Porto Bello in line of battle, each ship firing on the Iron Castle (Castillo de Todofierro) as it passed. The first ships would proceed up the harbor and then separate to attack its smaller forts, while the last ships would concentrate their attack on the Iron Castle, which should by then have been weakened by the close range broadsides of the leading ships. However, as the first ship, the seventy-gun *Hampton Court*, entered the harbor on the morning of 21 November, the wind turned, making it impossible to sail toward the town. Vernon had issued unusual and innovative additional fighting instructions to his captains, delegating authority to them over minor tactics if circumstances so demanded: "And as it is impossible to fix any general rule to occurrences that must be regulated from the weather and the enemy's disposition, this is left to the respective captains' judgment that shall be ordered out of the line to govern himself by[,] as becomes an officer of prudence and resolution."[16] The narrative of the action that appeared in the *London Magazine* for 13 March 1740 demonstrates the complexity of the subsequent attack:

> The Admiral luffing up as near to the Fort as he could, the Fire of his small Arms commanded the Enemies lower Batteries, and had a good Effect in driving them from those Batteries, from which they could do most Harm; and by this Means the Men were also secured at Landing. . . . As the Boats came near the Admiral's ship, he call'd down to them to go directly on Shore under the Walls of the Fort, tho' there was no breach made; but this answered as was expected, by throwing the Enemy into a general Consternation, the Officers and Men who had stood to the lower Battery, flying to the upper Part of the Fort, where they held up a White Flag. . . . In the mean time the Seamen had climb'd up the Walls of the lower Battery and struck the Colours, and then drew the Soldiers up after them, to whom the Spaniards, who had retired to the upper Part of the Fort, soon after surrendered at Discretion.[17]

With the fall of the Iron Castle, the rest of the town surrendered. Vernon's dispatches to the Admiralty reached England in March 1740, and the news of his victory was greeted by enthusiastic (albeit not entirely spontaneous) popular and civic celebrations. Responses included official and civic honors and promotions for Vernon, now a national hero, and his captains. Vernon was nominated for six parliamentary constituencies, and birthday celebrations in his honor outstripped those for the royal family. Popular expressions of praise and gratitude included bonfires and illuminations in at least fifty-four towns throughout the country and the production of souvenir objects such as jugs, medals, and ladies' fans. The pottery industry in particular underwent a "minor revolution" in its production of Vernon memorabilia: bowls, mugs, and plates decorated with Vernon's likeness and celebratory slogans.[18]

Much of the cultural response centered on the figure of Vernon and his six ships; this was equally the case in the poems and songs written to celebrate the victory. Many of the songs were collected in chapbooks and disseminated by ballad singers and sellers; they celebrate the event in a generalized language of victory with nautical overtones:

> Come, my lads, with souls befitting,
> Let us never be dismay'd;
> Let's avenge the Wrongs of BRITAIN,
> And support her *injur'd Trade*.
> . . .
> Spain no longer shall assume, Boys,
> The *free ocean* as her own;
> For the Time, *at last*, is come, Boys,
> We'll their Topsails lower down.
> Tho' in Politics contesting,
> *Round and round* they *were about*;
> All their ships and *manifesting*
> With our *Broadsides* we will rout.[19]

Using Vernon's biographical details to flesh out classical allusions, these poems frame the capture of Porto Bello as a patriotic victory for those opposing what was perceived as a corrupt ministry and cast Vernon in the age-old role of single-combatant, the solitary warrior-hero, whose "Genius" saves the nation. Others take a less elevated tone: The "Satyrical and Panegyrical Instructions to Mr. William Hogarth, Painter, on Admiral Vernon's taking Porto Bello with Six Ships of War Only," invites the reader to envisage the scene in typically Hogarthian terms:

Spread, noble Artist, spread thy Canvas wide,
And take thy Pencil with exulting Pride,
Full of the Glory of thy *Britain* fraught,
Truth in thy Hand, and *Freedom* in thy Thought;
Thy animated Colours shall relate
How VERNON rais'd his Country's drooping State.[20]

As the final line suggests, both the campaign that led to the declaration of war and the cultural response to Vernon's victory partake of the politically libertarian, patriotic ideologies of empire that "worked to establish and naturalize exclusive, gendered definitions of citizenship and political subjectivity that valorized an aggressive masculinity as a touchstone of Englishness, while devaluing and marginalizing 'effeminate' others both within and without the polity."[21] The poem continues:

Here let a powder'd *Fopling* seem to prate
In gentle Tone about the *Nation's State*,
Say *Wars* and *Battles* are most horrid Things
But sweet the Charms a blest *Convention* brings,
That *Trade* and *public Virtue's* all meer *Stuff*—
If we have *Peace* and—*Taxes*,—that's enough.

These responses—whether in the form of spectacle, souvenir, poem, or song—effectively efface the role of the ships that conveyed Vernon and his crews across the Atlantic, the captains who commanded them, and the sailors and soldiers who actually fired the broadsides. They reduce the complexity of the action as reported in the newspapers to the superhuman actions of a single figure.

Marine paintings, however, operate not at the scale of the human figure but at the scale of the ship—or rather, of squadrons and fleets of ships. Monamy's representation of the action (Figure 3.2) offers the pictorial framework for rehearsing a narrative with which his viewers could be assumed to have a high degree of familiarity. At the time of Vernon's victory, Monamy was in his mid-fifties and had been England's foremost marine painter for twenty years, but the capture of Porto Bello was his first opportunity to depict a contemporary British sea battle.[22] Monamy's *The Taking of Porto Bello by Vice Admiral Vernon* was installed at Vauxhall by 19 May 1740, a matter of weeks after news of the victory reached London.[23] To

Figure 3.2. Remi Parr after Peter Monamy, *The Taking of Porto Bello by Vice Admiral Vernon on the 22nd of Novr. 1739 with Six Men of War Only* (1743), hand-colored engraving. Yale Center for British Art, Paul Mellon Collection B1995.13.138.

compose the painting, Monamy must have availed himself of the same sources that were available to those who saw the painting at Vauxhall, including a diagram that had been sent with Vernon's dispatches to the Admiralty and was immediately published in *London Magazine*'s "Monthly Chronologer" for 1740 as a "plan of the town and harbour of Porto Bello (Taken by Edward Vernon Esq. Vice Admiral of the Blue on the 22 November with six Men of War only)"[24] as well as accounts such as the following, which appeared in the *London Evening Post*:

> The Action lasted some Hours, and one of the Castles was better defended than the other; but as soon as our Men were ordered to land, the Affair was soon-ended, for (as we are assured the Admiral

writes) never did Bravery excel theirs, the Sailors jumping on Shore, Cutlass in Hand, and with the most intrepid Resolution climb'd the Ascent, those who were first up helping the others to ascend, and in the midst of a dreadful Discharge of great and small Arms, seal'd the Walls, drove the Spaniards before them, and made themselves Masters of the Place."[25]

The Taking of Porto Bello by Vice Admiral Vernon compresses the temporal scope of the action. Boats are still bringing soldiers and marines to shore, ships are still firing, and fighting continues on the battlements even as the white flag of surrender is being lowered to be replaced by the Union Jack. These activities are placed along a trajectory that moves from right to left across and up the picture plane to the site of victory; figures in the boats lean, pointing, toward the forts, while those already landed climb up the walls to the top of the Iron Castle. The depth of field has been compressed to bring the town of Porto Bello closer to the picture plane, the shore filled with structures that lead the eye back to the Iron Castle. These elements result in a highly legible picture from which the narrative of the action can be easily reconstructed. Unlike the poems and songs, Monamy's picture displaces (or re-places) the heroics of the action onto the six ships, the sailors and marines, representing the capture of Porto Bello as a collective victory rather than a singular one.

The Taking of the St. Joseph

It has been observed that "determining the audience for a particular cultural production . . . goes beyond the necessary empirical inquiry into its social composition, to embrace the broader question of how an audience comes to identify itself as a social entity (a class, a gender, a race, etc.) by consuming certain images, texts, and objects."[26] *The Taking of Porto Bello* is predicated on an audience knowledgeable about national events and almost certainly influenced by the nation's naval fortunes; as Geoff Quilley has noted, "Whether in naval ceramics, sea-songs, nautical melodrama, catchpenny prints or the prominence in popular discourse of issues to do with trade and navigation, the idea or image of the sea permeated all aspects and all levels of society."[27] Another of Monamy's Vauxhall pictures speaks clearly to that interest: *The Taking of the St. Joseph a Spanish Carracca Ship*

Figure 3.3. Remi Parr after Peter Monamy, *The Taking of the St. Joseph a Spanish Carracca Ship, Sept. 23 1739, by the Chester and Canterbury Men of War, This Prize Was Valued at Upwards of 150,000 Pounds* (1743), hand-colored engraving. Yale Center for British Art, Paul Mellon Collection B1995.13.134.

Sept 23rd 1739 by the Chester and Canterbury Men of War, This Prize Was Valued at Upwards of 150,000 Pounds (Figure 3.3). The picture depicts the end of a chase; the English ship on the right is firing, while at the stern of the *St. Joseph* a white flag is being raised. Significantly, the capture appears to have been relatively nonviolent; none of the ships appears to have suffered any damage. The portrayal of such a capture in its most generic sense would have signified to viewers of every class the bloodless acquisition of capital.

The chance to win prize money was one of the major incentives for able-bodied young men to join the navy following the Cruisers and Convoys Act of 1708, which confirmed the jurisdiction of the Admiralty and its legal processes in governing the capture and condemnation of prizes.[28] In men of war, the value of a prize was shared among the crew of every rank, from the commander-in-chief and officers down to seamen and marines, the proportion for each rank dictated by the Act.[29] The professional division between commissioned officers and the lower ranks roughly corresponded to social-class differences, insofar as despite varying social backgrounds, lieutenants and above were considered to be gentlemen: "Whatever their personal origins, commissioned officers as a class historically represented the military and governing classes came to sea to take their natural place in command of those who merely earned their living afloat."[30] Prize money was an incentive for all. In discussing the profession of the naval officer, N. A. M. Rodger says, "The young man contemplating a career at sea . . . had more attractive prospects than promotion for its own sake, and first among them all was prize money. It was considered entirely proper in the eighteenth century that patriotism should have its own reward, and no class of persons were so highly rewarded for serving the Crown as sea officers."[31] From the Admiralty's point of view, the consequences of taking prizes in the mercantilist wars of the mid-eighteenth century extended beyond pecuniary rewards. Prizes were "not just an adjunct of war, but one of the prime instruments of strategy . . . enemy commerce could be crippled, colonies cut off, outposts harried or occupied and war supplies curtailed."[32] The incentive of prize money equally helped to shape the popular image of the sailor. Later in the century the capture of another Spanish register ship, the *Hermione*, would bring each seaman of the *Favourite* and *Active* £300 in prize money, famously enabling them to fry gold watches on Portsmouth Hard—as Rodger comments, "It was the sort of thing that stuck in the memory."[33] The capture of the *St. Joseph* would have similarly seized the imagination:

> Letters from Admiral Haddock to the Duke of Newcastle, give an account, that on the 23rd of September a rich Spanish ship, called the St. Joseph, bound from the Caraccas . . . was taken off of Cadiz. She is since arrived in Portsmouth, under the convoy of the Chester, and 1900lb wt. of silver, taken out of her, lodged in the bank of England, also 1,467,648lb of cocoa, in the Excise warehouse. Her invoice consists of 10,000 faregas of cocoa, each 110lb weight, above 100,000 lb wt of varinas tobacco, and 30,000 pieces of eight, registered; which is valued at 100,000 l. besides silver and other effects not mention'd in the bill of lading.[34]

The *Gentleman's Magazine* reported that the "several Tons of silver" taken out of the ship were brought from Portsmouth "guarded by a Troop of Horse, with the King's Trumpets and Drums playing before them, and lodged in the Bank of England."[35]

It would not be going too far to say that these paintings functioned as recruitment posters for the war effort, marshaling the desire for prize money in the service of patriotic interest among an audience affected at all ranks by the opportunities—and threat—of the sea. Later in the century, the need for sailors to join the navy was sufficiently acute that "a Press-gang, having information that one of the Lamplighters at Vauxhall had been at sea, went to that place and pressed him; the Waiters assembled to rescue their fellow-servant, and being joined by those from several adjoining houses, a battle ensued, in which, after a very severe conflict, the gang were forced to quit the field."[36]

Black-Eyed Susan

If the taking of the *St. Joseph* can be seen to lure young men to sea, *Sweet William's Farewell to Black-Eyed Susan* (Figure 3.4) both romanticizes their departure and similarly mobilizes the domestic front toward its duty. Based on John Gay's poem of 1713, the first two stanzas of which are included on the print, it centers on the theme of parting lovers, as William takes leave of Susan to go to sea with the Navy:

> O Susan, Susan Lovely Dear,
> My vows shall ever true remain;
> Let me Kiss off that falling Tear,
> We only part to meet again;
> Change as ye list ye Winds, my Heart shall be
> The faithful Compass that still points to thee.
>
> The Boatswain gave the dreadful Word,
> The Sails their Swelling Bosom spread.
> No longer must she stay aboard:
> They kissed, She Sigh'd, he hung his head:
> Her less'ning Boat unwilling rows to Land,
> Adieu. She cries, and wav'd her Lilly Hand.

Figure 3.4. Pierre Fourdrinier after Peter Monamy, *Sweet William's Farewell to Black Eyed Susan*, hand-colored engraving. Yale Center for British Art, Paul Mellon Collection B1995.13.141.

The picture shows a ship moored in the Downs, with the figures of William and Susan just discernible, dwarfed by the scale of the ship and of the departing fleet beyond. Susan stands in the boat that is pulling away from the three-decker and waves to William who leans on the rail of the ship. In the absence of contemporary comment on the original painting—and indeed on any of Monamy's paintings for Vauxhall—it becomes necessary to recover meanings that would have been self-evident to eighteenth-century viewers. For example, even in print form, the picture derives poignancy from its inscription of the theme of separation into the depiction of movement and distance. The ship's sails are still being hoisted and are beginning to catch the breeze, while the rowers in the boat are poised at full reach, about to pull on their oars. Monamy's picture prompts the viewer to

Figure 3.5. B. Cole after Francis Hayman, *The Humorous Diversion of Sliding on the Ice* (1753), engraving. Guildhall Library, City of London.

imagine the continuation of these movements, the translation of potential into kinetic energy as the ship's sails belly out to catch the wind and the ship heels round to join the rest of the fleet, while at the same time the rowers pull and the distance between the lovers increases. So much would have been instantly, even unconsciously recognizable to an audience that had arrived at Vauxhall Stairs by ferry.

Moreover, this picture partakes of a pictorial idiom that repeats in a number of Francis Hayman's supper-box pictures, the suspended moment of chance and balance, followed by inevitable and potentially hazardous motion, as seen in, for example, *The Humorous Diversion of Sliding on the Ice* (Figure 3.5) and *The Play of Blindman's-Buff*. It has been suggested that many of these had a moral component, representing the vanity of earthly pursuits.[37] Whereas Hayman's *The Play at See-Saw* tantalizes the viewer with the "erotic allure and consequent dangers of an illegitimate coupling of high and low," *Sweet William's Farewell* uses its suspension of movement to allow the viewer to experience vicariously the pain of separation.[38] Here we are balanced in the moment when the distance between the two lovers can be measured in the span of a glance. The shadow of the ship very nearly reaches the stem of the boat to connect the two, creating an axis of tension that impels the viewer to gauge the distance of the ship to the fleet and the boat to the shore.

Rather than presenting a popular ritual to be both repudiated and embraced, as did many of Hayman's pictures, Monamy's picture expresses themes to be emulated by its viewers and seems to have inspired other versions: Dominic Serres's *A Fleet Sailing Out of the Downs, with the Story of Black Ey'd Susan* was exhibited at the Royal Academy in 1771, and John Nixon's *Black Eyed Susan, Drawing, Last Verse* in 1786. George Cruikshank later parodied the scene in his series "Incident on a Party to Vauxhall" (1794), in a print titled *Black-Eyed Sue, and Sweet Poll of Plymouth, Taking Leave of Their Lovers, Who Are Going to Botany Bay*.[39] The character of Black-Eyed Susan became a popular figure for female loyalty during the eighteenth century, embodying feminine patriotism and acting as the means by which women were interpolated into the support of war. An ex-naval officer recalled that while moored at Hamoaze in 1782 "our midshipmen carried on a roaring trade when rowing guard in the middle watch. They would sometimes set off to Catwater to visit a house where a very handsome girl lived, who would get up at any hour to make flip for them and felt highly flattered at their calling her Black-eyed Susan."[40] The slightly bawdy nature of this anecdote mediates the tragi-sentimental tone of the Gay poem and Monamy prints, and the outright deviance and comedy of Cruikshank's print, with its literal black eye and the association of the women with criminals, as well as the suggestion that their fidelity may be less than a defining characteristic. At the earlier date of Monamy's pictures, the figure of Black-Eyed Susan seems to have served as a strategy for enlisting popular support for war akin to that of the Jack Tar. Although patriotic duty might compel men to go to sea, the age-old role of women included maintaining the social fabric by remaining faithful to their men: Gay's poem focuses on William's reassurances to Susan that he will be faithful to Susan, while her fidelity is taken for granted:

> Believe not what the Landmen say,
> Who tempt with Doubts thy constant Mind;
> They'll tell thee, Sailors, when away,
> In ev'ry Port a Mistress find.

Women's roles in times of war were understood to be predicated on social class: A revealing "Address to the Females of Great Britain," published during the threat of French invasion in 1803, exhorted women of all ranks to participate in the war effort. "Labouring women" were considered able to "get in the Harvest, and feed the Horses tho' they cannot clean them"; along with middle-class women, they were encouraged to tend wounded soldiers and to employ their sewing needles; nothing was asked of "Ladies," however, than to abstain from "Screamings, Faintings, &c. when our Enemies appear" and to refrain from placing emotional pressure during times of separation: "and as you value Happiness or Honour, cling not around you Parents, Husbands, Lovers: holding their Hands and weakening their Exertions when every Exertion is necessary."[41] Susan provided a model for behavior at any level of society, both in her farewell and in her fidelity, in a situation that would confront plenty of Vauxhall's female visitors.[42] By departing to do duty for his country, of course, William did the same for men.

English and Algerines

Monamy's fourth Vauxhall painting, *A Sea Engagement Between the English and Algerines* (Figure 3.6), presents a very different kind of naval warfare than that depicted in *The Taking of Porto Bello* and *The Taking of the St. Joseph*. The picture shows three English ships, heavily damaged in the sails and rigging, and a fourth English ship sinking in the right background, in what appears to be a vicious and losing struggle against Barbary corsairs, identifiable from their lateen-rigged (triangular) mainsails. In the left foreground one of the galleys is sinking, and on the right a boat tips dangerously under the struggle of its occupants, bearded figures in turbans who use spears and a curved sword to stave off sailors in the water who are attempting to climb in. The composition appears to be based on similar subjects by the marine painters Willem van de Velde, Elder and Younger, who had come to England in 1672 at the invitation of Charles II (Figure 3.7). In the absence of a native tradition of maritime art, their drawings and paintings for the court and Admiralty served as models for Monamy and successive generations of British marine painters.[43] According to George

Figure 3.6. Pierre Fourdrinier after Peter Monamy, *A Sea Engagement Between the English and Algerines* (1743), hand-colored engraving. Yale Center for British Art, Paul Mellon Collection B1995.13.133.

Vertue, for example, Monamy had been "put to ordinary painting but haveing an Early affection to drawing of ships and vessels of all kinds and the Imitations of the famous masters of that manner Vandevelds &c by constant practice he disti[nguished] himself and came into reputation."[44]

The subject reflects a concern still current in the eighteenth century. As Linda Colley has demonstrated, the Mediterranean was still as much a focus for British maritime trade activity as the Atlantic and Indian oceans combined, and the predations of corsairs operating from the Barbary coast—Morocco, Algiers, Tripoli, Tunisia—were of very real and visceral concern. These were light, fast vessels that could snap up merchant shipping and take passengers and crew captive, selling them into slavery within the Ottoman Empire and, it was feared, forcibly converting them to Islam. Colley notes

Figure 3.7. Willem van de Velde the Younger, *An Action off the Barbary Coast with Galleys and English Ships* (c. 1695), oil on canvas. Yale Center for British Art, Paul Mellon Collection B1981.25.641.

that "Barbary corsairing alarmed and angered out of all proportion to its actual extent because it seemed the negation of what England and ultimately Britain and its empire were traditionally about"—liberty, Protestantism, naval and commercial supremacy.[45] The decision to install such a picture at Vauxhall in c. 1741–42 may have been influenced by the publication in 1739 (followed by a second edition in 1740) of one of the most remarkable captivity narratives of the eighteenth century, *The History of the Long Captivity and Adventures of Thomas Pellow in South Barbary*, which describes the author's twenty-three-year captivity, beginning at the age of eleven, when his uncle's ship was taken by corsairs operating from Sale, on the Moroccan coast. At the same time, viewers may have registered the contrast between the enemy's treatment of sailors in the picture—both British and Algerian seamen struggle in the water—and Vernon's much-vaunted clemency toward his Spanish captives after the capture of Porto Bello. Among his Articles of Capitulation, which were reported in the press, he had allowed the inhabitants of the garrison to stay or leave, with a guarantee of security, and granted the crews of the Spanish ships three days to retire "with all their personal effects." The return of Spanish prisoners already taken was guaranteed if Vernon's conditions for the evacuation of the forts and ships were met. The *London Magazine* reported that "the Governor and Inhabitants of Porto Bello expressed the greatest Sense of the Humanity and Generosity, with which they were treated by the Admiral, and his Majesty's Squadron under his Command."[46] *A Sea Engagement Between the English and Algerines* complicates the view presented in *The Taking of Porto Bello* and *The Taking of the St. Joseph* of Britain as an equal combatant in the contest for commercial dominance. It suggests—as Colley points out—that Britons *can* be slaves and reminds us that, in the early 1740s, the imagined empire was by no means assured.

Guns in the Gardens

Monamy's pictures must also be considered within the context of other cultural productions taking place in the gardens. The music performed in the gardens by professional singers and musicians was also available for consumption in the form of ballad sheets and songbooks (Figure 3.8). Published under a variety of fanciful titles ("The Court of Apollo," "The New Festino Songbook"), the songbooks claimed to collect "new songs . . . Sung this season at Ranelagh, Vauxhall, Sadler's Well, the Theatres, and in the most polite Companies" or "all the songs, Sung This Season at Vauxhall, Ranelagh, Marybone [*sic*] Gardens, Sadler's Wells, at both the Theatres, & C."[47] Although many of the songs included have the sorts of pastoral themes that one might expect to correspond with the imagery of Hayman's rustic supper-box paintings—"Lovers and Shepherds," "The Unkind Shepherdess," "The Maid of Primrose Hill"—there are also a number of nautical songs, suggesting thematic parameters within which Monamy's paintings could have been viewed. The majority concern the separation of lovers as a result of war and are generally told from the point of view of either the sailor thinking of home or the woman who waits for him. "The Sailor's Wish" is the lament of a sailor who has been in an action between one English ship and five French men of war and is dying, wounded on deck; he wishes himself at home with his love, "tis for her sake I die." Other songs take naval events as their topics. "Admiral Parker's Late Engagement" celebrates the battle of Dogger Bank between the English and Dutch fleets,

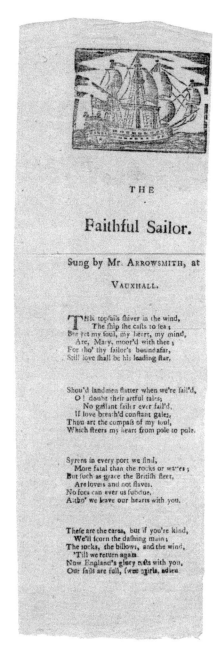

Figure 3.8. *The Faithful Sailor* (c. 1783), songsheet with woodcut. Beinecke Rare Book and Manuscript Library, Yale University.

although its description of the engagement resonates with the imagery of Monamy's *A Sea Engagement Between the English and Algerines*:

> Stout the vessels, great the slaughter,
> Many from the boody fray,
> Lay like wrecks upon the water,
> Masts and rigging tore away.
> Close and fierce began the firing,
> Briskly answering gun for gun:
> Ev'ry moment lives expiring,
> Not a ship attempts to run:
> Forty minutes and three hours,
> Did this dreadful combat hold;
> And of two contending powers,
> Which prevail'd could scarce be told.

In the space of the gardens, then, the themes of Monamy's paintings were reinforced by other media.

Taken as a group, Monamy's paintings for Vauxhall suggest the incorporation of issues of political, national, and imperial concern into the itinerary of refined pleasure. If "bourgeois public opinion and class identity were formed in the cultural and social spaces of theatres, art exhibitions, and concerts," then the gardens would be a prime locus of formation of national and imperial identities.[48] A representation of the taking of a large prize like the *St. Joseph*, for example, inscribed a libertarian, mercantilist view of empire into the spaces of Vauxhall. At the same time, through its depiction of such an acquisition as straightforward, even uncontested, *The Taking of the St. Joseph*—and, it could be argued, *The Taking of Porto Bello*—not only seems to suggest that supremacy is destiny but also mediates between the "aggressive masculinity" of imperial acquisition and the politeness of the culture of the gardens. Just as rustic pastimes were cleaned up, sanitized, and submitted to "the ordering imperatives of a high-cultural aesthetic" so that they could at once be condemned and used to construct respectability, marine paintings could present the desirable separated from its dangerous origins; they make available the acquisition of wealth and the pleasure of dominance, national glory and even a certain visceral excitement, without detailing the violence, bloodshed, foul play, and avarice of the event. David Solkin has commented that "Jonathan Tyers knew his customers; and as time went on he seems to have become increasingly aware of their desire for a dignified art that addressed them as equals, without imposing any cultural demands beyond the reach of a 'common' understanding. One might say that it became Tyers's particular business to make his patrons feel that they collectively embodied an art public, simply by virtue of their participation in the sphere of polite discourse."[49] Monamy's marine paintings, however, may have also made Tyers's patrons feel that they embodied a nation.

Chapter 4

Performance Alfresco: Music-Making in London's Pleasure Gardens

RACHEL COWGILL

Pausing in Paris on a tour through France and Italy in 1770, the English music-historian Charles Burney noted his impressions on visiting a French version of a familiar haunt:

> I went to one of the Vaux Halls (they have 3 or 4 here) paid half a crown for my admission and had my eyes put out by the quantity of lights and my ears stunned by the number of fiddles etc for the dancing. When I have described this Vaux Hall it will be easy—no it will not be easy—to find the resemblance. It is on the Boulevard. At the first entrance is a rotund—not very large—with galleries round it well light up [*sic*] and decorated. Then you pass through a quadrangle in the open air well illuminated and the galleries continued on each side to another square room still larger with a row of Corinthian pillars on each side with festoons and illuminations. This is a very elegant room. In this and in the Ist room minuets, allemands, cotillons and contre danses, when the weather is cold, which was now the case, in the extream. There was a great number of people all at present in mourning for a Queen of Denmark and this was all the change that was given for my half crown. Not a morsel of garden.[1]

The venue in question can be identified as Jean-Baptiste Torré's "Wauxhall," which opened in 1764 on the boulevard Saint-Martin, its name making capital from the growing reputation of one of the largest and most

Figure 4.1. A. C. Pugin and J. Bluck after Thomas Rowlandson, *Vauxhall Garden* from Ackermann's *Microcosm of London* (1809), etching with aquatint. Lambeth Borough Archives, Landmark 5057.

spectacular of the 631 commercial pleasure gardens known to have operated in eighteenth- and nineteenth-century London.[2] In his travel journals, Burney was generally willing to admire where admiration was due; to put his reservations about this Parisian imitation simply down to national prejudice, therefore, would be to miss the point. Although he highlights the venue's deficiencies and particularly the price of admission—at two and a half times what it cost to enter Vauxhall—his description is broadly appreciative.[3] There is music here as well as illuminations, ornaments, and interesting architecture; and unlike its English namesake this venue also appears to have been licensed for public dancing. But somehow for Burney the Torré is just not Vauxhall, the absence of garden restricting the *rus in urbis* experience so crucial to the ambience of London's pleasure gardens. Compare, for example, Tobias Smollett's description of the charms of Vauxhall in his novel *The Expedition of Humphry Clinker* (1771), where his character Lydia Melford emphasizes the delights of socializing alfresco:

> Image to yourself my dear Letty, a spacious garden, part laid out in delightful walks, bounded with high hedges and trees, and paved with gravel; part exhibiting a wonderful assemblage of the most picturesque and striking objects, pavilions, lodges, groves, grottos, lawns, temples, and cascades; porticos, colonnades, and rotundas; adorned with pillars, statues and painting: the whole illuminated with an infinite number of lamps, disposed in different figures of suns, stars and constellations; the place crowded with the gayest company, ranging through those blissful shades, or supping in different lodges on cold collations, enlivened with mirth, freedom and good humour, and animated by an excellent band of musick.[4]

The multifarious features so cherished in accounts such as this have attracted the attention of scholars from many disciplines in recent years, but the contribution of music, which was central to the London pleasure garden experience, has tended to be overlooked and underplayed. Musicologists have tended to find the naked commercialism of garden proprietors in pursuit of novelty, spectacular entertainment, and multimediality off-putting; but for those who have been willing to forage through the extensive surviving sources of garden repertoire, the rediscovery and recuperation of music by the likes of Charles Dibdin, J. C. Bach, and Henry Bishop, much of it either written for or made famous through performances at Vauxhall, has proved ample reward.[5] Indeed, some of the most celebrated composers of the day were contracted to the gardens, not least because they offered employment over the summer months, from late May to September, when theaters and concert halls across the capital were mostly dark: Samuel Arnold (1740–1802), for example, directed the music at Marylebone in the early 1770s, and his organist, James Hook (1746–1827), went on to serve as composer and organist for Vauxhall from 1774 to 1820, taking over from Thomas Arne (1710–78) who had held the post of composer since 1745, and who also arranged many of the concerts at Ranelagh.[6] While acknowledging such fruitful reevaluation of repertoire, this chapter sets off in a different direction, to explore the extraordinarily creative uses to which music was put by London's garden proprietors seeking to shape a luxurious, pleasurable, and sensational aural dimension to this unique form of evening entertainment. This chapter will focus principally on the pleasure gardens at Vauxhall, which, as far as musicological scholarship is concerned, seem to have been the most neglected of the three main London pleasure garden venues—Marylebone, Ranelagh, and Vauxhall.[7] As we shall see, proprietors used music as a sonic equivalent to the sensual delights they achieved with sculpture, decorations, and illuminations, and to influence mood and affective response to these visual attractions; but they also used it to define and differentiate physical spaces, to enhance illusion, to choreograph the movements and behavior of the crowd, and to structure the passing of time from twilight through midnight. Alfresco musical performance—whether in street, park, or garden—was experienced by all classes in eighteenth- and nineteenth-century England. Indeed, for some it may well have been their only access to music outside the home, church, or tavern. Yet it is easy not to take this music-making seriously, assuming that it is limited by disregard both for acoustic and aesthetic subtleties and makes free with what might be construed as the "composer's intentions." As this chapter will show, exploring the aural landscape of the pleasure garden—its "soundscape"— helps to round out our understanding of this aspect of metropolitan sociability and to identify the key elements of music's place within it.[8]

Entertainment at Vauxhall began as an informal affair, with the impromptu music-making of wandering minstrels mingling with the natural sounds of birdsong, as Samuel Pepys observed in his diary entry of 28 May 1667: "To hear the nightingale and other birds, and here fiddles and there a harp, and here a jews trump, and here laughing, and there fine people walking, is mighty divertising."[9] When the Bermondsey entrepreneur Jonathan Tyers (1702–67) took over the lease of the gardens in 1728, he remodeled what was essentially an easygoing country tavern with wooded grounds and walks, located just a short boat or coach ride away from the city, into a formal garden laid out on a grid, with groves of trees divided by long gravel paths, or *allées*, meandering grassy paths, and far-reaching vistas across neighboring hayfields. The French influence perceptible in fashionable aristocratic gardens in England at this time is readily apparent. Vauxhall reopened as "Spring Gardens" on 7 June 1732, with illuminations and a ridotto al'fresco, or open-air masquerade, then all the rage at the playhouses among the ton.[10] Under Tyers's control the gardens at Vauxhall would develop into what Miles Ogborn has described as a "key site in the geography of eighteenth-century cultural production" and "a landscape of commodified consumption."[11] Through capital investment in luxurious facilities; diverting, mesmerizing spectacles; and careful marketing and charging for entry at the gates, he was able to create a unique sociable experience pitched to a polite and an elegant clientele, based on the pleasures of the senses, of exoticism, and of the imagination. Knowing what Vauxhall would have become by the 1770s and 1780s, however, can obscure our understanding of Tyers's original vision for the gardens, which was more in the order of a princely court shaped by the political agenda of his patron, the Prince of Wales, than a public pleasure resort.

John Rocque's representation of Vauxhall Gardens on his 1747 map of London (see Figure 2.1) shows the first of two structures built by Tyers to provide the gardens with music.[12] In the first quadrant, we see two pavilions—one circular or possibly octagonal, to which an oblong extension has been added, and one square. The circular pavilion was an open-air orchestra or wooden performance platform, where musicians could be seated under a domed roof, providing them with shelter and natural amplification in the manner of a bandstand (Figure 4.3).[13] The square pavilion, by contrast, was built with stone and named for Frederick, Prince of Wales (1707–51).[14] Scholars have long known that the prince was the ground landlord for the gardens, but architecture historian Nebahat Avcıoğlu has argued that Frederick assumed an active interest in their redevelopment, confirmed by the central position his pavilion occupied and his marking the opening of the gardens in 1732 with a ceremonial entry via the Thames from a state barge specially designed for the occasion by William Kent.[15] She points out that Tyers took on the lease in the same year Frederick was recalled by his father, King George II, from the Hanover family seat at Herrenhausen in order to calm national concern over the succession, and she argues further that the prince's pavilion represented Frederick's aspirations to power through its emulation of the architecture of the Topkapı Palace (the primary residence of the Ottoman sultans on the Bosphorus River). These initial essays in *turquerie* at Vauxhall would soon be extended to new structures: In 1742 a Turkish Tent was erected in the grove just behind the orchestra and used, often by the prince himself, for dining, and a fourth structure, the rotunda (music room) with a picture-gallery extension, was finished just before Frederick's untimely death in 1751 (Figure 4.7).[16] The rotunda was tucked away on the east side behind the supper boxes and was Vauxhall's response to the celebrated circular hall for music-making and promenading at Ranelagh (Figure 2.6). Avcıoğlu points out that these buildings "emulated Ottoman palatial forms" as they were perceived and described by British travel-writers such as Lady Mary Wortley Montagu and Aaron Hill, rather than by direct experience (although the Topkapı Palace was situated close to the headquarters of the Levant Company).[17] Vauxhall gave Frederick a canvas on which to fashion himself both as cultivated patron of the arts and as principal heir to the British throne, but rhetorical elaboration of this self-image by the anti-Walpole Opposition seeking to promote Frederick as the "ideal patriot king," caused the prince's already tense relations with the king and queen to deteriorate drastically and threatened to undermine his hopes for the succession.

The attraction of this Turkish style to the prince was probably not only its distinctiveness and novelty but also, as Avcıoğlu suggests, its connection with one of the three great political leaders he made reference to in order to shore up his cultural authority: Edward, the Black Prince, who had once owned the manor of Vauxhall on which the gardens now stood; Alexander the Great; and Ibrahim Pasha, the enlightened Ottoman statesman, reformist, patron of arts, and intellectual. In 1722 Ibrahim Pasha had initiated the building of the imperial complex of Sa'dabad (meaning "abode of happiness") for Ahmed III, which, although it was destroyed in 1730, had stood for a new sense of sociability—the palace was open to the public, representing an interconnectedness between "ordinary" people and their ruler. This model appealed to the Opposition notion of Frederick as "patriot king" and encouraged Tyers to make of Vauxhall, in Avcıoğlu's words, "a socially inclusive morally refined and commercially viable public space."[18] If Avcıoğlu is right, here, then some of the published responses to the redeveloped

Vauxhall can be seen to have been politically motivated. The Vauxhall site in its earliest years had acquired a reputation as a place for illicit dalliances and sexual liaisons, which Tyers worked hard to eradicate from his repackaged and refined version; several commentators, however, took the opportunity of the opening masquerade to play on these sensitivities. The anonymous author of a poem titled "The Ladies Delight, Containing . . . IV. Ridotto al'Fresco," for example, quipped that the aristocracy no longer needed to visit distant health spas to cure infertility:

No more shall *Duchesses* to *Bath* repair,
Or fly to *Tunbridge* to procure an Heir;
Spring-Gardens can supply their every Want,
For here whate'er they ask the Swain will grant
And future Lo-ds (if they'll confess the right)
Shall owe their Being to this blessed Night;[19]

In a similar vein, the *Universal Spectator* likened Vauxhall to Plato's academy, but credited "the Midnight Academy" at the gardens with instructing "both Sexes in *good Letters, good Manners* . . . and a nameless *Et cetera*."[20]

The proximity of and alignment between the musicians' platform and the Prince's Pavilion (and later the Turkish Tent), together with its high sides and elevation, which ensured that the music would carry while preventing audiences from seeing the musicians themselves, and the fact that the first concerts were purely instrumental, strongly suggests that the orchestra was conceived as a court band. The Turkish or Moorish modeling of the musicians' platform doubtless added another level of meaning, connecting with the fascination for janissary bands that was typical of European monarchs from the late seventeenth century onward. This had arisen from their military encounters with the Ottoman Empire,[21] however, whereas the purpose of the Vauxhall band was to harmonize and refine garden clientele rather than to stir warlike passions. *The Turkish Paradise or Vaux-Hall Gardens; Wrote at Vaux-Hall Last Summer; The Prince and Princess of Wales, With Many Persons of Quality and Distinction Being in the Gardens* (London: T. Cooper, 1741) acknowledges the depravity seen at Vauxhall in the past—"In Times, not yet forgot, this Ground was trod / By *Lust*, and *Folly*, this was their Abode"—but identifies Frederick as the bringer of great prosperity, national unity, and well-being:

Hail Prince of glorious Race! hail Royal Heir!
Hail darling Object of the Peoples Care!
Thou common Good, propitious Heaven has sent
To silence Faction, and beget Content.

The role of the Vauxhall band was made clear—to focus the attention of listeners on this promising future:

No longer ye soft soothing Lyres be mute,
O now or never touch the breathing Flute;
Raise my sunk Mind—where has my Fancy stray'd?
How wander'd in the Maze itself had made!
But hark! the Organ penetrates the Air,
As if *Cecilia*'s Soul were Vocal there;
The Trumpet lives again, my Spirits wake,
And gloomy Thoughts my raptur'd Soul forsake.

It is a commonplace in the pleasure garden literature that Vauxhall played a role in establishing a sense of patriotism among Londoners, but here it is a radical patriotism focusing on the heir to the throne rather than on the king, and indeed an heir whom the king himself was known to detest:

O could our neighbouring Nations see this Sight,
But the Appearance of this happy Night,
Such natural Charms, Complexions all in Grain,
Such Modesty, unlike what others feign,
Such Excellence of Shape: how would they bear
Their Olive Beauties daily painted fair?
How would they gaze, and feast their wond'ring Eyes,
And call VAUX-HALL, a TURKISH PARADISE?

"Turkish paradise" here is meant not in a colonial sense, as Avcıoğlu notes, but as a specific reference to the sultan's palace in Istanbul,[22] and the phrase is used interchangeably with "the Elysian Fields" in the Opposition-inspired rhetoric that surrounded the gardens during this period.[23] This explains why, despite the *turquerie* built into the garden's early architecture, it was not considered incongruous for the band to play, for the most part, music by George Frederick Handel; moreover, why it was not thought inappropriate for the proceedings to be watched over by Roubiliac's figure of the composer himself, as Orpheus, playing the lyre in relaxed pose as if to harmonize and civilize the assembly (Figure I.5).[24] Travelers saw the Ottomans as having inherited and preserved the cultural legacy of the ancients, thus classical notions of paradise could be blended with Muslim notions without apparent controversy; in 1751, for example, the orchestra was being referred to as the "Temple of Pleasure."[25] Among the scores under the elbow of the statue of Handel, as Avcıoğlu notes, the only one named after a specific work is *Alexander's Feast*: The proximity of the statue to the Turkish Tent and Prince's Pavilion, Alexander's associations with clemency, and his victory over despotism and political corruption would therefore have created further meaningful connections for Vauxhall's clientele.[26] How much time Handel himself actually spent in the gardens is unclear, but he wrote a hornpipe for performance at Vauxhall and his *Music for the Royal Fireworks* was given a public rehearsal there in 1749.[27] Frederick would revisit this idea of Handel when planning his "Mount Parnassus" project at Kew, when in his pairing of ancient and modern cultural figures Handel was matched with Timotheus, poet and musician to Alexander the Great.[28] Sadly, however, the prince did not live to realize these plans.

Vauxhall mourned the passing of the Prince of Wales with a "Solemn Dirge," penned by Christopher Smart, set to music by John Worgan (who had succeeded his brother James as Vauxhall's organist earlier that year), and performed on the morning of 17 April.[29] The fifth stanza depicts the arts now languishing without the prince's patronage ("Music's dumb, and Painting sighing, / Drops her Pencil from her Hands, / Sculpture with her Sisters dying / See! Herself a Statue stands") while the ninth stanza passes the mantle of the "patriot king" to Frederick's son George ("Such another?—We possess him, / To revive his Father's Fame, / Honour, Glory, Wisdom, bless him, / Not another, but the same").[30] With Frederick's death Vauxhall Gardens played a less explicitly political role, and the previously understated Turkish and Gothic influences became more pronounced[31]— princely court was transformed into public entertainment venue, and exoticism and eclecticism took hold, designed to fuel the imagination, blur boundaries, and achieve an enjoyably disorienting sense of dislocation. The gardens continued to be associated with princes of Wales, and some if not all of the orchestra, rotunda, Turkish Tent, and Prince's Pavilion continued to bear their decorative plumes of feathers in his honor, although when war

Figure 4.2. Thomas Bowles after Samuel Wale, *A View of the Chinese Pavillions and Boxes in Vauxhall Gardens* (after 1751), etching and engraving, hand-colored. Yale Center for British Art, Paul Mellon Collection B1977.14.18706.

came there was a shift toward a more loyal form of patriotism focused on the figure of the king.[32]

The orchestra, situated so close to the entrance, was the gardens' natural hub—"the grand rendezvous of the company who constantly assemble in this part, if the weather be fine[,] to hear the vocal performers and as soon as the song is ended stray about the gardens."[33] The music would easily have been heard by the crowds as they approached the gardens through the dimly lit streets, and the platform's orientation toward the setting sun, its colors of white and bloom and plaster-of-Paris moldings, would have rendered it a striking sight in the last rays of daylight. As we see from this print dating from 1751 (figure 4.3), the quadrangle or grove in which it was situated was illuminated brightly after dark and fringed with supper boxes and pavilions, many of them decorated with paintings. Several of these paintings featured scenes of rustic music-making and dancing, simultaneously idealized and othered for polite company, such as Francis Hayman's *May*

Figure 4.3. John S. Muller after Samuel Wale, *Vauxhall Gardens Shewing the Grand Walk at the Entrance of the Garden and the Orchestra with the Music Playing* (c. 1751), etching and engraving, hand-colored. Yale Center for British Art, Paul Mellon Collection B1977.14.18699.

Day, or the Milkmaid's Garland.[34] The supper boxes enabled the clientele to enjoy their refreshments under cover and to watch others of the ton as they promenaded nearer the orchestra: "The groups of figures varying in age, dress, attitudes, &c. moving about on this occasion cannot fail giving great vivacity to the numberless beauties of the place and a particular pleasure to every contemplative spectator."[35] The band could be heard as far away as the Dark Walks, however—the notoriously low-lit pathway across the eastern end of the gardens where lovers could find some seclusion and prostitutes would ply their trade despite the best efforts of the garden constables.[36] The oblong extension to the orchestra visible on Rocque's map of 1747 had enabled an organ to be installed at the back of the upper story, which provided greater volume and more robust intonation as a solo or continuo instrument than a harpsichord would have been able to offer in the open air.

As previously mentioned, concerts at Vauxhall were purely instrumental affairs until vocalists were engaged to add solo songs to the mix and to provide a focal point for the spectator. A one-off vocal item—appropriately enough, the air Galatea addresses to the birds, "Hush Ye Pretty Warbling Choir," from Handel's serenata *Acis and Galatea*—was listed for evening performance there during 1739,[37] but otherwise Vauxhall was slow to introduce vocalists. Things changed when Ranelagh, Vauxhall's main competitor, opened in 1742. A year later, Jane Pellet, the fashion-conscious daughter of a celebrated physician, observed, "Among the people of Tast le Delicatesse I think Ranelagh is now the darling pleasure for the sake of Mr. Sullivan, who sings the Rising Sun & Stella & Flavia."[38] Sure enough, Marylebone began to offer vocal items the following year, with Vauxhall falling into line the season after. The extra expense of hiring male and female vocal soloists was absorbed by the proprietor, for a night's admittance to Vauxhall remained at a shilling for most of the century, until 1792, when it was increased to two shillings, causing alarm to James Boswell who feared that the "honest commonalty" would be excluded.[39] After refurbishments and the addition of new attractions in 1812 (probably intended to counteract the effects of general economic hardship caused by the French Wars) entrance was hiked to four shillings but dropped back to three in 1822, the year Vauxhall became the Royal Gardens, Vauxhall, with George IV as patron.[40] Ranelagh, by comparison, charged 2s. 6d. for a night's entry for much of the eighteenth century, the same amount as Burney had paid to attend Torré's Wauxhall in Paris in 1770. The new licensing restrictions of the 1750s limited musical activities in London's public venues, and, as Simon McVeigh has shown, Vauxhall, Ranelagh, and Marylebone emerged from the melee with a virtual monopoly on summer music-making in the capital.[41]

As many others have pointed out, once songs had been introduced, Vauxhall became an important venue for the promotion of native vocal music and for expressing notions of imperial Britishness musically. Dibdin's blustery naval songs, for example, would have been doubly effective when rendered from the orchestra in sight of the ships on the Thames, particularly by Charles Incledon, who was himself a former sailor.[42] Vauxhall's singers were generally of British rather than imported Italian talent, and many had already established reputations at Covent Garden and Drury Lane, though there were a few notable exceptions. The soprano Fredericka Weichsel, wife of Carl Friedrich Weichsel, who was principal oboist at the gardens and originally from Saxony, became extremely popular as a Vauxhall singer from 1766. She sang there for twenty-two seasons, but, judging by a receipt that survives from around 1776 in the Harvard Theatre Collection, her wages remained relatively modest. The £52 10s. she received from Tyers represents around a tenth of what a "middling" soprano could expect to get at the King's Theatre at that time, which would of course have included travel expenses from the Continent. She was also active as an oratorio singer.[43] Weichsel was acquainted with the darker side of Vauxhall, when the Italian violinist Joseph Agus attempted to rape her eleven-year-old daughter there in 1777, for which he was tried and sentenced the following year.[44] Weichsel's daughter became the celebrated English soprano Elizabeth Billington.

Fredericka Weichsel is thought to be the singer depicted by Rowlandson in a well-known watercolor of the Vauxhall orchestra from around 1784 (Figure 4.4). By this time, as we can see, there had been major changes: Originally the instrumentalists had been seated in a circle, facing inward, at a round table (serving as a music stand) on the same level (cf. figure 4.3); by 1784, however, the band had turned to face forward, and then, to accommodate new tiered seating and music stands and to create space for a soloist, a dropped platform with a separate sounding-board had been added to the front, in the manner of an illuminated garden balcony. This had the advantage of promoting the soloist as spectacle, positioned just out of the audience's reach, and indeed of promoting the band as spectacle too. But it also elided the roles of performer and spectator, by effectively inverting the relations of box and stage familiar from more conventional (interior) performance spaces, such as the opera house. Garrick may have been playing with this spectacular ambiguity even further when he created a scene in a production at Drury Lane featuring a replica of the Vauxhall orchestra on stage and poached Vauxhall's Miss Burchell to sing from it, both to the audience beyond the proscenium and to an audience of actors on stage; Tyers was sufficiently piqued by this to trump Garrick's stage representation of a cascade, producing what would become a favorite exhibit at the gardens for many years and giving us another demonstration, should we need it, of Vauxhall's closeness to the theatrical world.[45]

The alterations made to the orchestra required the Prince's Pavilion to be moved to the west wall, next to the main entrance, but they also reflected the growth of the band. Rowlandson's depiction seems to be in line with what we can glean of the size and makeup of the Vauxhall band in the 1780s

Figure 4.4. Thomas Rowlandson, *Vaux-Hall* (c. 1784), watercolor with pen in black and gray ink over graphite. Yale Center for British Art, Paul Mellon Collection B1975.4.1844.

and 1790s, which was probably between twenty and twenty-five players strong. The songs written for and performed at Vauxhall give us our best data on this. Initially they had been simple strophic ballads with continuo accompaniment such as those found in *A Collection of Favorite Songs* by James Hook (figure 4.5). This was published in 1794 but continued the earlier style, with the sort of patriotic texts that proved just as popular with garden audiences as sentimental and amatory songs, pseudo-Scottish songs, sea songs, military songs, comic songs, political songs, hunting and drinking songs, and songs celebrating local topographical themes. With the influence of the Italian and Mannheim schools, however, accompaniments became more intricate and vocal lines more challenging, as in Hook's song "The Lass of Richmond Hill" from 1789. Catches, glees, and other forms of unaccompanied part-song were included in the concerts from 1775, and were a highly popular addition.[46]

Figure 4.5. Unknown Artist, Title Page of *A Collection of Favorite Songs Sung . . . at Vauxhall Gardens* (1794), engraving with etching. Lambeth Borough Archives, Landmark 1369.

The idea that this musical repertoire lacked sophistication needs adjusting, as we see from this number, "See the Kind Indulgent Gales," which was among a group of songs with English texts composed by J. C. Bach for Weichsel to sing at Vauxhall. An expanded wind section is needed—two horns, clarinets, and a bassoon—in addition to four-part strings—two violins, a viola, and a bass—which in outdoor performance would have helped the music to carry further, as would the coloratura vocal line, requiring much agility, and bravura passagework energized by syncopations. If this looks operatic, it is partly because it was a reworking of the aria "Se spiego le prime vele" from Bach's second London opera *Zanaida* of 1762. It was not dumbed down for Vauxhall, however. As Christopher Hogwood has observed, the fact that Bach extended the aria, raised the tessitura, and increased the amount of coloratura is testimony to Fredericka Weichsel's exceptional vocal abilities, and suggests that the audience was content to hear settings that were more elaborate.[47]

Though rosters for the band have not survived, we know that some of the capital's most distinguished orchestral players were engaged at Vauxhall from the comments of contemporaries such as the glee composer R. J. S. Stevens.[48] An all-male group, the band meshed well socially, meeting with the gardens' male vocalists each year for a summer dinner at a local tavern,[49] and occasionally welcoming to the platform a visiting musical amateur who wished to join their number for the evening,[50] something that also happened at the Italian Opera House in the Haymarket. They were equally tolerant of the more eccentric of the garden's clientele, as Charles Edward Horn (composer of "Cherry Ripe") testified in relation to the stockbroker Edward Wetenhall, who chose the wettest and coldest evenings to attend and call for endless encores.[51] In terms of the orchestral repertoire offered at Vauxhall, the most important document available to us is the "Vauxhall Lists"—a manuscript held at the Minet Library in Lambeth, and first discussed by Charles Cudworth in 1967.[52] Probably compiled by the band librarian, the lists provide details of evening concerts given at the gardens in 1790 and 1791. In places, the compiler added a comment or two: Frustration is expressed over singers who sometimes provided inadequate parts for favorite vocal solos, or who were unable to overcome difficulties with intonation, something those not used to performing in the open air must have found quite tricky. One entry in the lists observes that a Mrs. Leaver had sung progressively sharp in the course of a song, to which the orchestra responded as best they could, finishing the song a tone higher in pitch

Figure 4.6. Opening of J. C. Bach, *See the Kind Indulgent Gales: A Favorite Song Sung by Mrs. Weichsell, at Vaux Hall Gardens* (London: Longman & Broderip, 1780).

than they had begun.[53] The orchestral repertoire was challenging and up to date—here we have symphonies by Haydn, Stamitz, Toeschi, and Pleyel, as well as solo concertos for organ (played by the composer); wind or string instruments were consistently featured in both halves of the program until the second decade of the nineteenth century.

According to the amateur composer John Marsh, writing in his journal in June 1770, it was the "fashion [at Vauxhall] only to attend to the songs & to walk about during the performance of the instrumental music."[54] Rowlandson's depiction of the crowd seems to confirm a level of attentiveness to the songs; but when we consider the design of the Vauxhall programs, Marsh's comment implies something interesting about the behavior of the crowd. The strict alternation of short solo songs and extended instrumental works—overtures, symphonies, and concertos—would have encouraged periods of promenading, perhaps around a quarter of an hour at a time, interspersed by a few minutes of standing and attending to the singer. This routine would have facilitated a natural and fluid (but controlled) reconfiguring of social groupings over the course of the evening. As general practice, the bill of the evening's music, posted on a tree next to the orchestra, usually consisted of around sixteen items, opening with an orchestral piece (later this became a vocal item) and closing with a finale for singers and orchestra. The first half of the concert concluded with a glee—glees having been introduced to the garden concerts in 1775—and at Vauxhall women would have taken the upper parts.

The orchestra remained a fixture in the gardens until they closed in 1859, though it increased in size and splendor during that time and drew on technological innovations wherever possible—its shape outlined in tiny gas lights, for example—to enhance the sense of spectacle and accommodate larger ensembles (frontispiece). Initially, in 1735, the concerts had begun at 5 P.M. Toward the end of the century this moved to 7:30 P.M., reflecting a fashion for keeping later hours, and by 1822, the first half of the evening concerts began at 8 P.M. and concluded at 10 P.M. A one-hour intermission allowed the audience to move through the gardens to other attractions—the rope dancing, waterworks, or French Theatre, for example—and the second half concluded as close as possible to midnight, when fireworks were let off and the Ascent on the Rope was performed by a ropewalker. By this stage the gardens were opening only three nights a week, on Monday, Wednesday, and Friday, the Bishop of Winchester having outlawed Saturday-night opening in 1806, for fear of encroachment on the Sabbath.[55] In 1829, cut-down versions of Italian operas were performed concert-style in the rotunda—namely Rossini's *Il barbiere di Siviglia* and *La cenerentola*, starring Fanny Ayton—under the directorship of Tom Cooke and Jonathan Blewitt. Two years earlier, the rotunda had been the venue for the premiere of Cook and Blewitt's vaudeville *Actors Al Fresco; or, The Play in the Pleasure Grounds*, to a text by William Thomas Moncrieff, one of the most active theater men in early nineteenth-century London; and in 1828, a "new vaudeville" by Blewitt, Cook, and R. Hughes—*The Statue Lover*—with text by Douglas Jerrold had been offered to the public.[56] The reconnection with opera at least in part probably reflected the interests of the Gye family: Frederick Gye Sr. was co-proprietor of Vauxhall, having bought the gardens in 1821 with Thomas Bish and William Hughes under the name "London Wine Company," and Frederick Gye Jr. would lease the Royal Italian Opera, Covent Garden, from 1848 until 1877.[57] On these nights, the concert ran from 8:30 P.M., making way for ballet in the new Ballet Theatre at 9:30 P.M., a *fantoccini* (or shadow puppet show, which first appeared around 1823) at 10 P.M., and the opera from 10:30 P.M. until the fireworks at midnight. Other Italian opera performances, some instigated by singers from Her Majesty's Theatre themselves, occurred in 1834, and again as part of a grand musical festival in 1852. Formal music-making in the gardens appears to have been scaled back somewhat from 1835, with the concerts beginning at 9:30 P.M., and the second half lasting only thirty minutes before the fireworks at 11:30 P.M.

Interest in opera at Vauxhall continued into the early 1830s, Henry Bishop having been appointed as musical director in 1826–27 and 1830–33. He had produced a *Waterloo Cantata* for Vauxhall in 1826, used for the first of soon-to-be annual enactments of the Battle of Waterloo with 1,000 soldiers on horse and foot. Now he followed that with a series of five light one-act English operas to texts by Edward Fitzball, variously classified as a vaudeville opera, a nautical burletta, and operettas, all of which are in manuscript still at the Royal College of Music. His *The Magic Fan*, produced in 1832, was billed as a "Turkish operetta," and not least because of its dramatis personae—characters such as Kabri, Alzoff, Ali Muffrutzkin, Ilfonoblunderbronx, and his slave Fum-Fum—seems to anticipate the Savoy operas of Gilbert and Sullivan.[58] English opera had a substantial tradition at the London pleasure gardens, mainly because the addition of music or even a few chords and songs could get around the prohibition of theatrical performance there under the Licensing Act.[59] We have ample evidence for this in the twenty-one all-sung dialogues produced by Charles

Figure 4.7. Benjamin Cole, *The Inside of the Elegant Music Room in Vaux-Hall Gardens* (1752), engraving. Guildhall Library, City of London.

Dibdin for Sadler's Wells, and Storace's English burlettas at Marylebone in the 1750s.[60]

Generally when performances of opera were given at Vauxhall they replaced the second half of the concert and were located in the rotunda rather than on the open orchestra. Initially called the "music room," the rotunda had been built around 1750 on a newly acquired segment of land to provide an indoor performance space during inclement weather (Figure 4.7). It was accessed through the grove and was circular, with a diameter of sixty-seven feet and an orchestra, or platform for the band, with an organ at one end, divided from the main room by a balustrade. A spectacular chandelier, a sofa around the walls, mirrors, candelabra, painted columns, busts in alcoves, carvings, and festoons of artificial flowers gave the impression of a luxurious interior. The roof, to one observer, resembled a clamshell, but others referred to it initially as "the umbrella," partly for its function as cover for the performances in wet weather. The acoustics were considered extremely good.[61] The audience, it seems, would have promenaded about the rotunda, but perhaps not so much as in the larger rotunda at Ranelagh (see Figure 2.6), with which the Vauxhall version was intended to vie. The size of the Ranelagh rotunda made it essentially an indoor performance venue, unlike Vauxhall.

By 1822, the decoration of the rotunda had changed to imitate the interior of an Indian garden room, in scarlet, blue, and yellow, with painted views of Hindoostan on the walls near the orchestra. Now floored for country dancing, the adjoining saloon was decorated with views of Hampton Court Palace, Great Walk Windsor Park, and Fulham Church.[62] Such views played with the viewers' sense of space and place—Are we inside or outside? Are we in Lambeth or another part of town or the empire? Or are we simply everywhere at once? The blurring of boundaries between interior and exterior space became more pronounced as more of the garden was placed under cover. The Covered Walk, for example, visible on a map of 1826 (Figure 4.8) was constructed in 1811. The additional shelter, of course, was to mitigate the damage that could be inflicted on the manager's purse by a season of bad weather. John Marsh records how, if it was wet, he sometimes changed his plans and went to the theater rather than to the garden. Even with the concert relocated to the rotunda, however, rain could reduce audiences for the concerts to eight or ten people.[63]

The music, of course, served both to orient the spectators and to encourage the suspension of disbelief. The concert provided a central frame of reference for the passing of time. But other sonic cues were given, such as the ringing of a bell to signal the commencement of the "cascade" exhibit: "About nine o'clock the curtain is drawn up, and at the expiration of ten or fifteen minutes let down again, and the company return to hear the remaining part of the concert: the last song is always a duet or trio, accompanied with a chorus."[64] The fireworks were less easy to miss. The deployment of military, Caledonian, pandean (a type of panpipe), Milanese, Savoyard, German, Turkish, Silver Miners, and eventually brass bands about the gardens—for example to accompany the ropewalking and the dioramas, and eventually to provide music for dancing—created a dynamic soundscape by which the crowd's circulation through the gardens could be coordinated. Those occupying the supper boxes and pavilions could hire garden musicians to play to them at table after the concert: Described as "two bands of wind music," these were French horns and probably clarinets, which played from small orchestras that could be moved around the grove and walks and were strictly forbidden to take money or drink at the table.[65] When fireworks were not scheduled, music was played

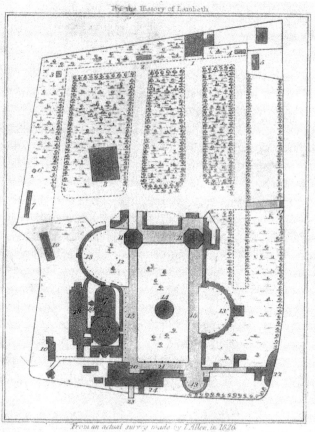

Figure 4.8. Thomas Allen, map of Vauxhall, from Thomas Allen, *The History and Antiquities of the Parish of Lambeth* (1826–27). Lambeth Borough Archives, Landmark 1255.

by a small band in a rolling carriage, drawn along one of the more distant walks, sometimes by a pair of elephants. This seems to have been carried over from the performance of "Hindostan Airs" by members of the band of the Coldstream guards from a "magnificent triumphal car" drawn by elephants during the Oriental Gala celebrating recent successes in India on 24 July 1800: "In the course of the Evening will be displayed, in honour of the late victorious Armies of the East, Conquerors of Tippoo Saib Sultan, a most magnificent Triumphal Car, decorated with superb military trophies, attended by Sepoys, &c. &c. and drawn by Elephants, richly caparisoned in a stile of Oriental grandeur, which will parade majestically along the principal walk. His Royal Highness the Duke of York's Band, placed in the front of the Car, will heighten the effect, by performing several favourite Hindostan Airs."[66] Groups of musicians were also sent out from the gardens in a "magnificent car" and on boats whenever the Vauxhall Sailing Cup regatta was held on the Thames.[67]

Music was also used to evoke the supernatural in several exhibitions. The oldest example of this was staged in 1750 in the section of the garden called the "rural downs," which took in vistas across neighboring fields although these views became less open as the nineteenth century dawned. Groups of musicians were embedded in the landscape itself—playing from pits underground, concealed by shrubbery, and from platforms in the trees, in emulation of what some styled the "Genius of the Wood," or "Fairy Music," perhaps, as Lawrence Gowing has suggested, encouraged by Hogarth's painting *Fairies Dancing on the Green by Moonlight*, which hung in a supper box on the south side of the Grove.[68] This particular musical illusion did not last long, however—a clipping from an unidentified and undated source announced that because of "the natural damp of the earth, being found prejudicial to the instruments[,] this romantic entertainment has ceased";[69] ever after, however, the "rural downs" were also referred to as the "musical bushes," perhaps encouraged by the figure of Milton placed close by, seated on a rock, "in an attitude listening to soft music" in the manner of his *Il penseroso*.[70] These events may have been what was alluded to in the opening of *Sketch of the Spring-Gardens, Vauxhall*:

Verdant Vistoes, melting Sounds
Magic Echoes, Fairy Rounds
Beauties e'vry where surprize:—
Sure this Spot dropt from the Skies![71]

Accounts of Vauxhall often imply that its survival into the nineteenth century was a struggle against the odds—the long slow death of an outdated entertainment—but unlike Ranelagh, which closed in 1803, Vauxhall displayed remarkable adaptability to new economic conditions, particularly in its musical departments, and did not close until 1859.[72] Under Gye, in the 1820s, the number of exhibitions and attractions offered at Vauxhall multiplied dramatically; and in 1837 the gardens, which had been spruced up for the occasion (including the addition of an illuminated coronation crown at the top of the orchestra), came under the patronage of the new Queen Victoria, whose coronation was celebrated in the performance of a *Victoria Ode*, composed by the then musical director G. Stansbury.[73] Ballooning and parachuting exhibitions began at Vauxhall in the early nineteenth century, pioneered by Garnerin, Green, and Cocking, and the arrival of the Nassau balloon in the 1840s triggered another musical experiment, one of the pseudoscientific sort lampooned by Dickens in his account of "Vauxhall by Day" in *Sketches by Boz*. Ten instrumentalists from the military band were sent up in the balloon to see how high they could go and still be heard. Increasingly Vauxhall became a stop on the circuit for touring virtuosi, for Paganini, for example, and the cornet player Jean-Baptiste Arban and his orchestra. The celebrated black dancer William Henry Lane ("Master Juba") performed at Vauxhall with the Ethiopian Serenaders; Master Juba was admired as a source of insights into "the negro life and character" as well as for his demonstrations of 200 different steps.[74] In the 1840s the rotunda became a circus for horsemanship, for example, and for dancing, and the appearance of flamboyant conductors Louis-Antoine Jullien and Philippe Musard, so crucial to the development of the Promenade concert, put Vauxhall directly in touch with the open-air music and dancing on the Champs-Elysées and in the Jardin Turc of fashionable Paris.[75] The result was an increasingly diverse program of entertainment, in which sheer novelty seemed at times to swamp the musical components offered on the colorful bills that would have been plastered across the city. But at other times the centrality of the orchestra was still readily apparent. We can still see the original blend of serious orchestral music and song playing out in new, arguably more "popular" configurations—Mozart's overture to *Idomeneo* or Beethoven's *Prometheus* heard alongside the quadrilles of Jullien, for example—but Vauxhall was no longer, it seems, quite the venue for first performances of new British instrumental music it had been in the 1780s and 1790s.

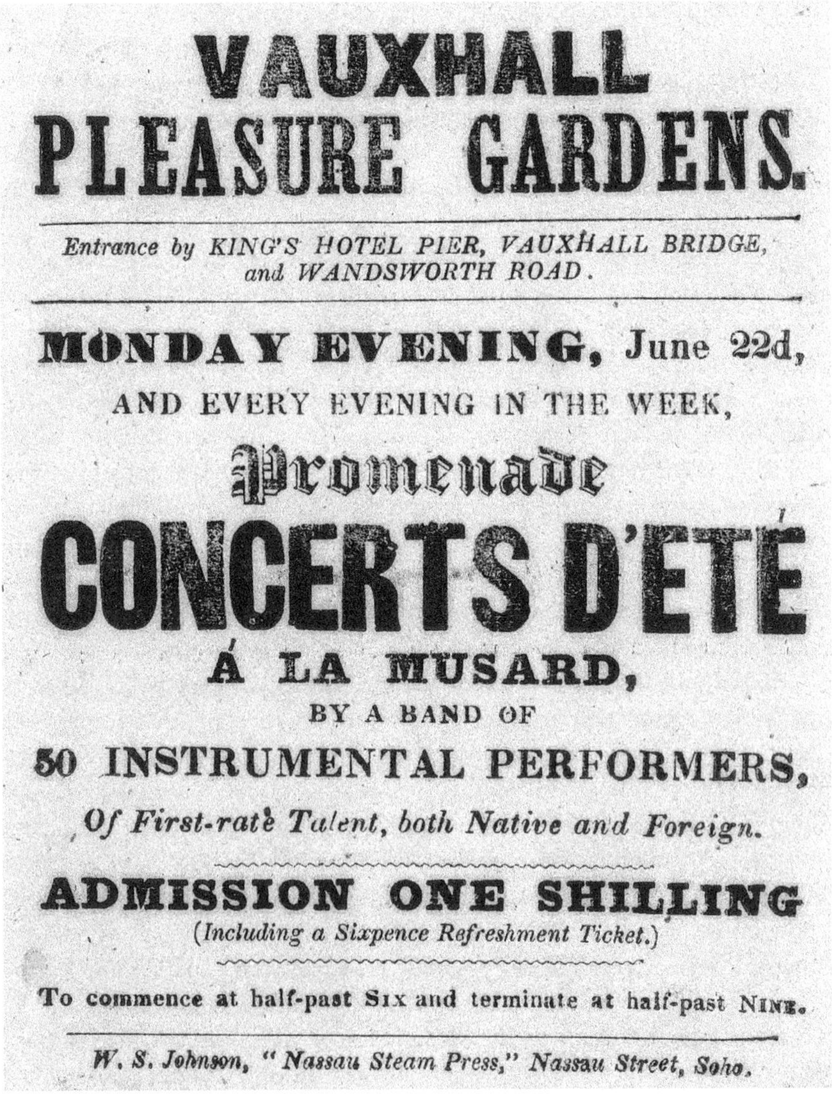

VAUXHALL
PLEASURE GARDENS.

Entrance by KING'S HOTEL PIER, VAUXHALL BRIDGE, and WANDSWORTH ROAD.

MONDAY EVENING, June 22d,
AND EVERY EVENING IN THE WEEK,
Promenade
CONCERTS D'ETÉ
Á LA MUSARD,
BY A BAND OF
50 INSTRUMENTAL PERFORMERS,
Of First-rate Talent, both Native and Foreign.

ADMISSION ONE SHILLING
(Including a Sixpence Refreshment Ticket.)

To commence at half-past SIX and terminate at half-past NINE.

W. S. Johnson, "Nassau Steam Press," Nassau Street, Soho.

Figure 4.9. Bill for Promenade Concert at Vauxhall Gardens (1846). Lambeth Borough Archives, Landmark 1424.

Vauxhall's influence on British musical culture did not end with its closure in 1859. It was influential in the development of the municipal park, for example, as well as of the botanical and zoological gardens of the Victorian period, with their carefully sited bandstands and walks. In terms of the nation's concert life, it contributed in two very distinctive ways. First, in the design of some of the most important and prestigious Victorian venues for music-making, sites with *rus in urbe* appeal that were designed to promote holistic rational recreation for the masses. These include Joseph Paxton's Crystal Palace, rebuilt in Sydenham after the Great Exhibition (1852–54) and set in landscaped gardens with fountains and bandstands.[76] His colleague in that project, the architect Owen Jones, conceived an equivalent building for north London, the Alexandra Palace on Muswell Hill. Built to an "Italian" design and opened in 1873, the first Alexandra Palace (which burned down and had to be rebuilt in 1875) was constructed of materials salvaged from the International Exhibition buildings located south of the Royal Albert Hall.[77] The Royal Albert Hall, a giant (elliptical) rotunda in the Italian Renaissance style, was originally integrated into the Royal Horticultural Society gardens (laid out 1859–61), its south door opening directly into the Society's glasshouse.[78]

Second, the influence of the pleasure gardens can be felt in the development of the promenade concerts. Recent discussion of the Proms as an institution has tended to downplay their continuation of modes of musical engagement characteristic of the eighteenth-century pleasure gardens.[79] Queen's Hall (where the Proms were held until 1941) does seem an uncompromisingly urban, interior space—the fountain, fernery, promenading, and picnicking in the auditorium notwithstanding. But, as a closing thought, we should take a lead from Charles Cudworth's delighted recognition of Proms ancestry in his 1967 discussion of "the Vauxhall Lists" from the 1790s, in terms of the rituals and "hooliganism" of the "last night," for example, but principally in the idea of serious music-making taking place in a sympathetically informal, quasi alfresco setting.[80] Vauxhall's legacy, it seems, is still very much with us.

Chapter 5

Pleasure Gardens of America: Anxieties of National Identity

NAOMI STUBBS

> I am convinced that amusements of this sort are beneficial in many respects. . . . [They] promote domestic circulation . . . [and provide] a channel of industry, which retains a part of that golden current we have so long lavished on foreign toys. . . . [As] an agricultural people, [they] awaken [in us a] taste so natural and noble, and by displaying the native charms of our country, will make us love it the more. . . . Rural entertainments are congenial with republican manners . . . [and in them,] people of all conditions mix in friendly, pleasing society.
> —"A Votary of the Patriotic Muses,"
> *Pennsylvania Packet*, 28 May 1789

Regularly described in very positive tones as "object[s] worthy at once of the notice of the connoisseur and the admiration of the community at large," the pleasure gardens of eighteenth- and nineteenth-century America were a source of pride, touted as a symbol of cultural accomplishment.[1] These sites were seen as distinctly American both in character and in the ideals they represented, as the epigraph here attests. Whether through their promotion of American industry, their association with agriculture and rural ideals, or their supposed lack of class divisions, this Philadelphian commentator was in no doubt that the pleasure gardens lay at the heart of what it meant to be American.

Figure 5.1. Bandbox with Image of Castle Garden, New York (1835–36), cardboard and paper. New York Historical Society. Purchased from Elie Nadelman.

Yet pleasure gardens were certainly not pure American sites. English in origin and in the associations they held, these entertainment venues seem curious sites in which to assert American cultural and national identities, given the importance of independence from England in contemporaneous politics. As the main pleasure gardens operated during the period between the Revolutionary War and the Civil War, they operated at a time when the concept of "America" was especially fluid. Lacking a shared history, unique language, or historic territory, Americans were continuously redefining what it meant to be American from the moment the nation was created. In order to sustain American identities (as opposed to British, French, or colonial—elements formerly central to both individual and group identities), an American national consciousness had to be developed and sustained through a process that was rarely a conscious or an organized endeavor, but rather that was ongoing and unconscious.

As Anthony D. Smith argues, a national identity is created and sustained through "the maintenance and continual reinterpretation of the patterns of values, symbols, memories, myths, and traditions that form the distinctive heritage of the nation."[2] From the late eighteenth century, when pleasure gardens began to emerge as a common entertainment venue in America, certain "values, symbols, memories, myths, and traditions" had begun to be established as being quintessentially American, including values such as honesty and simplicity, and freedom and equality. These values were to be seen in the writings of many important figures, such as Benjamin Franklin, Thomas Jefferson, and Alexander Hamilton, and they were explored by many city-dwelling citizens in their responses to and interactions with the pleasure gardens of America. Despite the apparent contradiction inherent in using an English form to assert American nationalism, the pleasure gardens of America were able to participate in this ongoing process of exploration and (re)negotiation of American identities in part because of the way in which three central ideals of early American national consciousness were addressed: independence, agrarianism, and equality.

With populations ranging from around 20,000 to more than 60,000 people, the East Coast cities of New York, Philadelphia, Boston, Baltimore, and Charleston were among the largest urban centers in the United States when pleasure gardens were at their peak, and many such venues were found in each of these cities.[3] Operating from June or July until September (when the theaters were typically closed), these gardens were open during the day and evening, offering structured entertainment on two or three evenings each week. Tensions between the past and the future, between reliance on England and independence, and between rural simplicity and urban industrialization were especially strong in these sites. This chapter begins by exploring how American identity functioned in opposition to and in alignment with Britain, looking at the relationship between the pleasure gardens of England and those of America. Moving then to the relationship between country and city, the concept of the *rus in urbe* is examined in relation to the gardens' success (and also to their ultimate demise). Finally, this chapter considers the ideal of equality and how it played out in these social spaces. As we shall see, operations of race and class within the gardens of America demonstrated that, as in England, assertions of equality could be highly misleading.

Independence

America and Britain share a past fraught with intimate connections and passionate conflicts, and any attempt to forge American national identities inevitably involved renegotiating links with Britain in order to assert cultural and economic independence. Freedom from British taxation was initially a defining feature of America, but this led to questions of how independent America as a nation really was in other respects. In theater and drama, for example, there were concerns over the English origin of the majority of the plays performed on American stages, with calls for "native themes" and "homespun arts" in the 1780s becoming increasingly frequent into the nineteenth century.[4] While trying to establish a culture that was distinctly American, English forms continued to pervade theater, art, museums, and outdoor amusement areas.[5] Although there were many indications that the gardens were English in form and content, I argue that the gardens displayed a simultaneous rejection of English connections and an assertion of American values and national pride through embracing this English form. In the main, direct ties to the English site were emphasized as a means of asserting a cultural legitimacy (by invoking the acknowledged superior standing of English culture); simultaneously, attempts were made to distance the American sites from all other associations with England. This apparent contradiction speaks to the problematic nature of establishing a new national cultural identity, and the tension between embracing

VAUXHALL GARDEN AND THEATRE, AND COOK'S CIRCUS,
Bowery, New York, 1835.

Figure 5.2. *Vauxhall Garden and Theater, and Cook's Circus* (c. 1835), engraving. New York Public Library.

and resisting the English connections with this form can be seen through many of the sites.

One clear indication that the pleasure gardens of America were directly referencing those of England can be seen in the names of the gardens. Among the numerous gardens found in America, a great many were called Vauxhall, including one in Charleston (which opened in 1795), one in Philadelphia (open from 1813 to 1825), and at least six in New York.[6] Of the New York sites, three were opened by a French confectioner named Joseph Delacroix:[7] the first (1796–97) located at 112 Broadway, the second (1798–1805) on the Bayard estate near Bunker's Hill (which approximates to today's Grand, Broome, Crosby, and Lafayette Streets), and the last (1805–55) located between Broadway and the Bowery, "between Great Jones and Eighth streets," to the north of the earlier sites (Figure 5.2).[8] Other Vauxhalls could be found in Nashville, Tennessee (1834–36), Richmond, Virginia (1802), and New Orleans, Louisiana (1837); indeed, it was this name that was used more than any other, and "Vauxhall" became shorthand for any pleasure garden.[9]

It was not only the name that was borrowed from the London site, however; the explicit highlighting of features shared by London's Vauxhall and its American counterparts was a common tactic in advertising. When the first pleasure garden in Boston was advertised, for example, London's Vauxhall was specifically invoked, with it being announced that the gardens will be planned "on the scale of Raneleigh [sic] and Vauxhall Gardens in the vicinity of London," and that the elegant design will compare with "the celebrated Gardens of that name near London."[10] Indeed, there were physical similarities between the London Vauxhall and several American sites; the layout of London's Vauxhall is well known, and its rectangular divisions and straight paths were echoed in the Charleston garden, with its "several square fathoms of grass plots," and in the last Vauxhall in New York, with its "seven irregularly sized [rectangular] seed beds separated by wide grass-filled avenues, bordered with hedge, and filled with low, bushy plants."[11] Detailed images for each of these sites do not survive, so we cannot fully understand their layout, but generally a trend can be seen in which the gardens were laid out much along the lines of London's Vauxhall.[12] In adopting and reinforcing through advertisements these physical similarities, proprietors were assuring would-be patrons of the sophistication of the venues by invoking the cultural legitimacy of the English Vauxhall.

The ties between the London Vauxhall and the American venues were further reinforced by the types of entertainment offered. For example, under the management of Alexander Placide from 1799, Charleston's Vauxhall presented a combination of fireworks, illuminations, transparencies, ice cream and other refreshments, puppet shows, musical and vocal concerts, and dramatic interludes.[13] Philadelphia's gardens offered grand balls, galas, concerts, refreshments, exhibitions (such as the "velocipede" in 1819), and a variety of performances (such as the *Lecture on Heads*), while New York's provided exhibits, concerts, balls, and fireworks.[14] These varieties of performances were similar to what could be found at London's Vauxhall in the same period.

In addition, specific references were made to performances and songs as being *of* Vauxhall, London. For example, the "Pandean Music Band" of London's Vauxhall was to appear at New York's Vauxhall every Thursday through most of the 1811 season.[15] The fact that song lyrics of London Vauxhall ballads were frequently printed in American newspapers suggests that the English pleasure garden music enjoyed as high a profile in American musical life as the "Vauxhall Song" did in Britain.[16] Though we do not see the number of paintings found in London's Vauxhall, we can find instances of sculptures being presented: Delacroix's third Vauxhall in New York, for example, contained a series of busts.[17] The similarities between the various sites were no mere coincidence, and proprietors often explicitly invoked the London sites (especially Vauxhall) in their descriptions in order to draw ties between the accepted cultural legitimacy of the English venues and the American gardens.

However, the American venues were different from the English ones, and while geographic differences alone would have made it impossible for American sites to actually replicate English ones, there were also overt attempts to assert deliberate deviations from the London model. In several comments printed in newspapers, it was made clear that the London Vauxhall was perceived as being vastly inferior to the American gardens.[18] A 1785 newspaper article stated that "white necks, red cheeks, and lilly hands" could be found at London's Vauxhall, in a piece that suggested the venue was little more than a place to display young girls, while another implied Vauxhall had openly become little more than a marriage market as early as 1765, contrasting with the associations the American venues held with innocence and rural retreat.[19] Writing in 1833, one New York journalist was more direct in his criticism of English gardens: "Noise, plenty of noise, is all they care for in music; and their Vauxhall is so tedious, that one leaves it for home with the gravity of a monk on quitting his chapel for his cell."[20] Although cultural legitimacy was embraced through highlighting similarities between the English and American sites, the moral legitimacy (and superiority) of the American gardens was affirmed through disavowing similarities. In this simultaneous adoption and rejection of the English associations the form held, pleasure gardens allowed patrons and proprietors to claim a cultural identity with both historic roots in and distinction from England.

American pleasure gardens also allowed patrons to address American identities through participation in patriotic activities. Trumpeted as a place suitable for the display of patriotic endeavors, American pleasure gardens were used for exhibits of American industry and for celebrations of the founding of the nation. Patriotic exhibits of American industry were common in the American sites, especially of crafts that supported American goals of reducing economic reliance on Britain. In Washington Gardens (Boston), for example, a display of "Mechanic Arts" (including casks and ship blocks) was advertised as being "intimately connected with the real

Independence of our country."[21] From 1829, Niblo's (New York) hosted numerous American Institute exhibits, which included silk, fruits, flowers, agricultural products, and mechanical items intended to replace English imports.[22] Advertisements in the run up to such exhibits encouraged citizens to become part of the patriotic display by contributing to the show.[23] These exhibits hailed the industrial innovations of the nation and were accompanied by fireworks displays and other events, celebrating the nation's achievements and independence.

By far the most widespread public celebration of the American nation within the gardens was the Fourth of July, and each garden hosted special events. Newspaper accounts record a great number of Independence Day celebrations at the pleasure gardens, with toasts, dinners, special concerts, and transparencies being exhibited specifically in honor of the founding of the country.[24] Joseph Delacroix was particularly notable for the extravagance of his Fourth of July celebrations, and his detailed programs allow us to obtain a more comprehensive view of what a patron could expect to encounter at New York's Vauxhall on that day. For example, on the Fourth of July 1817, Delacroix presented a "Grand Concert" (opening with "Monroe's March"), an address, twenty-nine fireworks exhibits (including the "Star of Freedom, 12 feet in diameter" and "The United States, represented by 19 suns revolving around a center"), and the "Eruption of Mount Etna." These were accompanied by "several thousand lights" and "transparent paintings" commemorating the peace treaties of 1783 and 1813."[25]

Fireworks were the most important and widespread type of entertainment offered at such events, and by 1820 Joseph Delacroix could observe that "the productions of the Pyrotechnic Art are now considered the most elegant and appropriate" for the Fourth of July celebrations.[26] Indeed, fireworks are still considered indispensable to Fourth of July celebrations throughout America and their display has become emblematic of American Independence. The use of fireworks in promoting republican nationalism did not originate in the United States; Michael Lynn has noted that the court's monopoly of such displays was gradually loosened in Europe over the course of the eighteenth century. By the close of the century, he argues, their value as a "republican tool for promoting nationalism" had been recognized in both France and America.[27] Although the first use of fireworks to mark the Fourth of July did not occur within a pleasure garden, pleasure gardens soon emerged as the primary site for such displays. Indeed, newspaper accounts of Fourth of July celebrations in the early nineteenth century indicate that pleasure gardens had a monopoly on such patriotic displays.[28] In establishing sites for patriotic displays that citizens could attend and thus be part of, the gardens encouraged the practice of the "traditions" that Smith identifies as being essential to national identities.

The gardens were thus presented as English in form and likeness, but they simultaneously rejected the English ties; they were English in origin, which supplied them with cultural legitimacy, yet served as a place to assert American independence and nationalism through the display and practice of "symbols, memories, myths, and traditions." English forms were concurrently adopted and rejected within these sites, reflecting anxieties of the relationship between America and Britain witnessed in other cultural and social forms. This relationship was not the only binary to be tested in the new republic, however, and concerns surrounding the role of the country while industrialized cities expanded also played out within the pleasure gardens.

Rural/Urban and Agrarian/Industrial Visions

Tensions between rural simplicity and urban sophistication and between good, honest labor and rapid industrialization permeated early American society and culture. As Leo Marx discusses in his *The Machine in the Garden*, this tension was seen in American culture, with Americans seeking a middle ground between untamed nature and civilization.[29] Pleasure gardens brought the country to the city, giving city-dwellers the opportunity to indulge in nostalgia for the rural while remaining in the heart of ever-growing cities and allowing them to explore and test the tensions between these seemingly incompatible spaces.

The idea of the country was inextricably tied with understandings of the new nation, and the writings of Benjamin Franklin and Thomas Jefferson asserted the "honourable" and "virtuous" nature of agricultural pursuits. Thomas Bender similarly identifies agrarianism as "a political philosophy and a definition of a social ideal" in the early years of the United States.[30] These agricultural impulses were tied to Jeffersonian democracy, which saw the responsible use of land in support of natural industry as a patriotic and noble endeavor. As Tamara Thornton notes in her book *Cultivating Gentlemen*, involvement in agriculture through founding agricultural societies, writing essays on animal husbandry and agricultural practices,

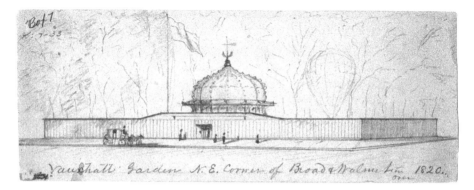

Figure 5.3. *Vauxhall Garden N. E. Corner of Broad and Walnut in 1820* (c. 1820), pencil. Historical Society of Pennsylvania.

and having physical ties to the countryside through owning land (ideally a working farm) were ways for individuals to show that their activities were practical and for the common good, and thus patriotic.[31] Yet these practices required wealth and leisure time, and associating oneself with the country by means of a country estate was only possible for the elite. Pleasure gardens gave their inferiors a chance to adopt a similar pose of landed independence and association with patriotic practices, while remaining in or near the city. It was this tension between the city and the country, between urbanization and agrarianism, and the relationship of these tensions to patriotism that was especially important within the operation of these gardens.

Philadelphia boasted a substantial number of pleasure gardens during the post-Revolutionary and antebellum periods, including Gray's Ferry (1789–92), Harrowgate (1789–91, 1810), Vauxhall (1813–25; figure 5.3), and McArann's Garden (1839–42).[32] Gray's Ferry (also known as "Lower Ferry") operated as a river crossing from 1747 to 1792 under the management of George and Robert Gray and was located about four miles southwest of the city.[33] In the opposite direction out of the city, Harrowgate (also known as Vauxhall) operated as a pleasure garden between 1789 and 1792 and was located four miles northeast of Philadelphia on the Frankford road.[34] These sites were located in the countryside but were close enough to the city to be easily accessible to city-dwellers.

Although the Philadelphia gardens initially drew a more elite clientele, lured by the prospect of rural enjoyments outside the city, the distance from the city and the cost involved in traveling to them were important factors determining the gardens' success (or lack thereof). The appeal of a rural retreat was a strong one to people of all levels of society, yet cost and distance were excluding a large proportion of the population, leading to "the creation of newer and nearer resorts and amusement centers."[35] More central venues such as Philadelphia's Vauxhall and McArann's gardens were more accessible than Gray's and Harrowgate, offering urban Americans the opportunity to participate in America's continued passion for rural culture with fewer restrictions. Gardens were increasingly found in more central locations, within the city limits, where they were more easily accessible to a wider range of people. The appeal of the rural was clear, but issues of location and accessibility increasingly shaped the decisions made by proprietors as they attempted to balance country and city, accessibility and exclusivity.

Baltimore hosted a variety of pleasure gardens both within and outside the city, including Jalland's Gardens, Gray's, Toon's, Spring Gardens, and the Columbian Gardens.[36] The garden known as Columbian Gardens began life as the "Rural Retreat" and was run by Margaret Myers beginning in 1789. Situated on the corner of Bond Street and Dulany Road, Myers offered patrons "recreation and refreshment" and "Boxes . . . for the Accommodation of Parties in the Summer Season."[37] Although the city of Baltimore was expanding, the gardens remained intact until Joshua K. Harrison's tenure in 1829.[38] These gardens operated just outside of Baltimore (Figure 5.4), allowing people without easy access to transportation to attend, and the fifteen-minute walk to the resort was advertised as part of its appeal.[39] Regularly described as affording a "partial retreat from the noise of the town," Baltimore's gardens sat on the cusp of rural and urban locations, and thus embodied the ideas of both.[40] However, this apparent solution of literally straddling country and city was not always easy to maintain. In New York, attempts to occupy the borders of town and country were hampered by the city's rapid growth. Delacroix's three Vauxhalls were located increasingly further north (Figure 5.5) as the city's expansion pushed him to relocate.[41]

The most common variety of pleasure garden, however, was the city center garden. These gardens were not the products of failed attempts to straddle the border between the city and the country; rather, they were designed to operate within the city. Niblo's in New York is a good example of this type.[42] Initially operating under the name "Sans Souci," the gardens were opened by William Niblo at the northwest corner of Broadway and Prince in 1828 and quickly became known simply as "Niblo's Garden,"

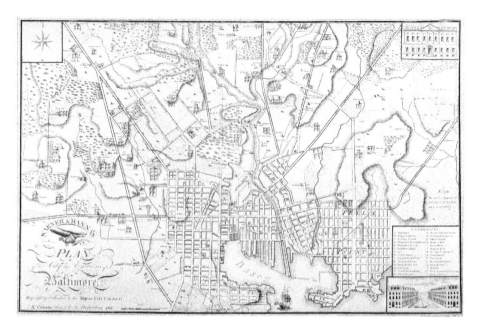

Figure 5.4. *Warner and Hanna's Plan of the City and Environs of Baltimore* (1801). Maryland Historical Society. The Columbian Gardens (also known as Rural Retreat) are located to the east of the city, immediately above the "FE" of "Fell's Point." Another pleasure garden, Gray's Garden, was located outside the city in the opposite direction. It appears to the west of the city, depicted here as a rectangle divided into eight squares.

offering concerts and illuminations.[43] The gardens were the site for the New York Horticultural Society's balls beginning in 1830, and the flowers were frequently commented on in the press, suggesting that the gardens themselves (both what was grown and what was brought to the site) were the focus in these early years of operation.[44] Indeed, allowing the rural aspects to thrive within the city's hustle and bustle could even become part of the gardens' appeal. One account from 1820s New York observes that "walks skirted with trees flowers and shrubs beside so much city confusion is delightful," and for many other sites it was this juxtaposition of country and city that was central to their success.[45] The bandbox shown in Figure 5.1 further demonstrates the perception of being removed from the city despite being within it; the backgrounds of each side are markedly different, and the focus is on the travel between the two "sides"; in reality, however,

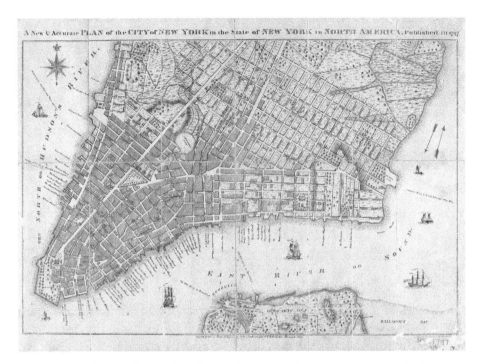

Figure 5.5. George Hayward, *A New and Accurate Plan of the City of New York* (1797), lithograph. The Lionel Pincus and Princess Firyal Map Division, The New York Public Library, Astor, Lenox and Tilden Foundations. Two of Delacroix's Vauxhalls are depicted: The 1796–97 site can be seen to the west of Broadway, four blocks up from the southern tip of Manhattan; and the later site of 1798–1805 is represented by a number of trees to the east of Broadway, four blocks north of Fresh Collect Pond.

this garden was not so much removed from the city as it was part of the city (simply by the water).

Other gardens found in the heart of their respective cities included Philadelphia's Vauxhall and McArann's Gardens, which were located near one another. McArann's was described as a "spacious and popular resort, capable of containing many thousand people" and opened around 1823 as a botanical garden run by John McArann (Figure 5.6).[46] McArann's was relaunched as a pleasure garden in June 1839 with a "series of concerts of vocal and instrumental music," and the Ravel family (actors, dancers, and acrobats), a magician, fireworks, and illuminations were soon added to the

Figure 5.6. Joseph Jackson, *McArann's Garden, Philadelphia* (1840), watercolor. The Historical Society of Pennsylvania, Kennedy Watercolours.

bill.[47] Clearly these entertainments were not the moneymaker McArann had hoped for, as he filed for bankruptcy in April 1842 and offered the contents of the gardens for sale in April and May 1843.[48] McArann's and Vauxhall were located within the city, close to the market houses, the Mint, the Exchange, and the prison. Similarly, Charleston's Vauxhall was located equidistant from several groups of public buildings, including City Hall, the Court House, and the Guard House (one and a half blocks to the east); the poor house, work house, and prison (one and a half blocks to the northwest); and the theater (one and a half blocks to the southeast). These gardens in Charleston and Philadelphia were thus operating on borders of morality, commerce, legislation, and pleasure.

All the gardens discussed here operated on one or more thresholds, with past and future, country and city, agriculture and technology all being accommodated in one space. Although the decisions proprietors made regarding location were largely made on the basis of economics, these gardens (and perceptions of them) spoke to wider concerns about what it meant to be American by being at once modern and nostalgic, rural and urban. Pleasure gardens allowed the desire for the country and city and the past and present to exist simultaneously for a time, but the eventual demise of the pleasure gardens suggests that the paradox could not be brought to a stable resolution. Despite many gardens eventually closing as a result of the growth of the city (and corresponding pressure on the land for development), the city cannot be seen to have "triumphed" in this battle. Even today, ideas of heartland and frontier compete with the major metropolitan areas in defining the image and essence of America.

Equality

Democracy and equality and the relation of these ideals to the realities of race relations and class structures have been (and probably always will be) important topics of debate in post-Revolutionary America. The idea that "all men are created equal" was a founding principle of the United States, yet racism and class-based prejudice persist today. In terms of the pleasure gardens, these inequalities were seen to be negotiated within the practices and regulations of the gardens and their proprietors in relation to race and class.

The patrons of the American pleasure gardens were overwhelmingly white. African Americans were frequently excluded from pleasure gardens, with the line "no admittance to persons of color" being a common feature in advertisements for such venues in both the north and south.[49] Chapter 6 discusses the role of race within the pleasure gardens in New Orleans in some detail. Here it is necessary simply to note that the vision of refined American culture, embodied by the gardens, while open to a certain degree of class mingling, was not so flexible with regard to skin color. There were, however, a small number of pleasure gardens that African Americans could patronize.

The African Grove in New York was a pleasure garden open specifically to accommodate African Americans and is the only such garden that has been reliably documented. Other pleasure gardens in New York open to African Americans included the Mead Garden (Manhattan, 1827), Mead Garden (Brooklyn, 1828), and Haytian Retreat (1829), though there is no study of these venues as yet (largely because of the scarcity of sources). Established in 1821 by William Brown in the backyard of his residence at 48 Thomas Street, for "fellow black stewards," the African Grove was open for only one month.[50] In *White People Do Not Know How to Behave*, Marvin McAllister explores the idea of an inclusive American identity that embraced Native and African identities, with pleasure gardens such as the African Grove being discussed as a forum for the experimentation with such a hybrid identity.[51] This "rehearsal space" allowed blacks to perform as American citizens and also presented a place in which to imitate white (assumed inherently superior) culture through a form of "whiteface minstrelsy." Yet, these largely undocumented gardens were the exception and not the rule, and African Americans were generally excluded from the main pleasure gardens of most cities. In addition to racial inequality, class prejudice was also seen in the United States and in the pleasure gardens.

The myth of an American society without class divisions is an enduring one: The early nineteenth-century Scottish travel writer James Flint identified America as not being "divided or formed into classes by the distinctions of title and rank";[52] a historian of New York's pleasure gardens describes antebellum New York as lacking "a rigid social structure" and as being "a classless society" in which "all but the extremes of the two ends mixed freely"[53] and, more recently, American historian Joyce Appleby notes, "a social homogeneity in which Americans began to take pride" after the Revolution.[54] Concepts of a "classless society" and "social homogeneity" were popular ideals that continue to be associated with the founding of the United States, despite their obvious falsehood.

London's Vauxhall has often been characterized as a place accessible to all levels of society, from the Prince of Wales to prostitutes, and everyone in between. Although the actual degree of social mixing may have been less than once thought, such social inclusion was much admired within Britain.[55] Given this popular conception of English pleasure gardens, one would expect American gardens to have provided the ideal site for the realization of that classless utopia with which the new nation sought to identify itself. If America was indeed fostering a society in which all classes could mingle without distinction or prejudice, this should have been evident in its pleasure gardens. Indeed, American gardens were occasionally noted as being distinctly "American" because they supposedly allowed for social mixing across traditional class lines. A Philadelphia newspaper contributor noted that Gray's gardens were "congenial with republican manners" due to his perception that class was not a primary concern at this site.[56]

The "middling sorts" of antebellum American cities constituted a substantial social group, and it was within this increasingly politically active segment of the population that anxieties of class were most clearly seen as they redefined, eroded, or blurred the boundaries between and among traditional lines.[57] As Richard Bushman argues, a "vernacular gentility" emerged in the late eighteenth and early nineteenth centuries, with outward markers of respectability being adopted by "middling people."[58] A heightened self-awareness was part of this development—one that saw people who were not previously identified as being "genteel" using dress and deportment to capitalize on these opportunities for social mobility.

Pleasure garden proprietors offered a refined space in which patrons could perform gentility, catering to a demand for respectable entertainment, untroubled by concerns of "prostitutes, drunkards, noisy spectators, and occasional riots, as well as risqué spectacles."[59] At the turn of the century, pleasure gardens were addressing an emergent desire of the "middling sorts" for "chaste entertainment" which "exclude[d] prostitutes and liquor and encourage[d] family attendance" in a manner that preempted the "minor revolution," which Bruce McConachie identifies as extending to the theaters in many American cities after 1845.[60]

Initially these spaces admitted anyone who could pay the admission charge and who was prepared to make an effort to ape gentility, even admitting those who could not afford to pay on certain days, so long as they were "decently dressed."[61] New York's Delacroix, for example, waived the admission fee every day of the week on which scheduled entertainment was not to take place (that is, evenings on which music might be performed but not a formal concert or fireworks).[62] Perhaps subscribing to the promotion of a "homogeneous" society, Delacroix wanted his gardens to be open to all.

Delacroix's admission policies changed in 1803, however, when he introduced a "refreshment ticket," which required all patrons to spend two shillings to enter the gardens on days without entertainment (whereupon they could redeem the ticket for refreshments up to that value).[63] Burrows and Wallace see this apparent shift from inclusivity to exclusivity as the "key to success" for the gardens.[64] Although Delacroix states in his newspaper announcement of the change that part of his motivation was to ensure a return on his investment, for the most part he focuses on the "genteel" nature of some (but not all) of his clientele. Delacroix observes that many who were "genteely dressed . . . were not genteel in character, [and] therefore not suited to the chief part of the company who frequented his gardens."[65] In order to assert a degree of exclusivity, Delacroix reintroduced the dividing line of price, enforcing a "refreshment ticket" on most days, acknowledging that his garden could not be classed as being genteel if "every person has an indistinct right of entrance."

Niblo's Garden was more pronounced in its attempts to be exclusive. It opened much later than the other resorts discussed here and, unlike them, aimed from the start to be exclusive. As Burrows and Wallace note, "After 1830 the upper classes deserted the déclassé Vauxhall and turned to William Niblo's new concern," which was described as surpassing "all others in elegance and respectability, its status sustained by high entrance fees, expensive food, and urbane entertainments."[66]

These attempts to become exclusive—as seen particularly in New York—were not especially successful, and despite the best efforts of the proprietors, problems were experienced with vandalism, theft, and "boisterous" behavior, which made it difficult for proprietors to maintain a genteel space. In Baltimore, for example, the destruction and theft of the lamps at Gray's was reported in 1794, along with several "disturbances" of the peace in 1794 and 1795. Perhaps a more common problem at many of the sites was pickpocketing, and numerous newspaper announcements requested the return of items stolen from persons at the gardens in Philadelphia and New York, among others. Attempts were made to regulate this behavior or to exclude the persons responsible through a variety of policies. The introduction of "officers" or constables was the most frequent practice, seen in Gray's Garden (Baltimore) from 1796, Vauxhall (New York) from 1799, Washington Gardens (Boston) from 1814, and Columbian Gardens (Baltimore) from 1832.[67] The Vauxhall of Charleston prohibited unaccompanied children from 1809, as Placide apparently considered them to be responsible for the depredations on his plants.[68] Few copies of the official rules and regulations of pleasure gardens survive, though we do have those for New York's Vauxhall.[69] These set out fines for picking flowers (four shillings), procedures for ejecting unruly persons from the gardens, and charges for breaking or damaging glasses or ornaments.

The result of such a situation was that the higher end of the "middling sorts" found their genteel space compromised by inappropriate behavior, while the lower end resented the restrictions presented by the imposition of codes of conduct. The mingling of classes in these gardens was not especially welcomed by many, and as the writer Asa Greene observed, it was considered "so vulgar . . . to be seen walking in the same grounds with mechanics, house servants, and laboring people."[70] The tensions among the class status, behavior, and expectations of the various patrons erupted at numerous sites in the form of violent riots, which led to the destruction of the grounds of at least four venues. Despite efforts to establish themselves as highbrow, genteel venues in the years between 1790 and 1820, pleasure gardens instead became decidedly lowbrow.[71]

Riots have been documented at pleasure gardens in Philadelphia (Gray's and Vauxhall), New York (Vauxhall), and Baltimore (Columbian Gardens). In those cases where a cause has been proposed, exclusion of certain persons through barriers or by an increase in admission fee is the most prevalent reason given. In Philadelphia, for example, the two documented riots transpired when people sought to gain entry without paying. At Gray's Ferry in 1791, a "disturbance" occurred when several people gained admission without paying the admission fee, only to meet with opposition from those who had paid.

According to a report in a local newspaper, several people gained entry to the gardens on the Fourth of July 1791 in order to join the Independence Day celebrations without paying the admission fee. After being ejected from the gardens by the constables, they "communicated their vindictive sentiments, on account of this treatment, to a number without the garden, who made a forcible attack with stones and clubs upon the door-keepers, and pulled down several fences and palings." Those inside the gardens are then described as "fighting for the right which their quarter of a dollar had purchased" by helping to force the offenders out of the gardens and returning the volley of stones and missiles. The fight (described as a "contest") ended without loss of life but with "hard knocks on both sides, and much injury to the house and gardens."[72]

The riot at the Vauxhall of Philadelphia (1819) arose from a similar instance of exclusion of individuals from a popular event—a balloon ascent, in this case. The increased admission charge levied led to a riot among the excluded viewers that ended in the destruction of the grounds. Those who were watching from outside the gardens were not able to see everything as "a high board fence enclosed Vauxhall Garden." The balloon took longer to inflate than expected, and eventually "the unruly mass went forward in a determined manner, tearing down the fence, ripping the balloon to shreds, sacking the wines and liquors in the garden;" they "threw stones, broke and tore everything with the balloon to pieces" and "complet[ed] the ruin by setting fire to the pavilion or theatre."[73]

Not only did the gardens initially encourage individuals of lower social classes to participate in a cultural form that presented itself as genteel, but there was a general belief in social equality (even if it were not a reality). By retracting this superficial equality through increased admission charges, the gardens brought about a riotous reaction that resulted in their appropriation by a less genteel public. Both the form of the gardens and the way in which they were represented changed. Embracing this change (or, perhaps, forced to do so for economic reasons), proprietors in turn changed the type of entertainment they offered, presenting such entertainment as minstrelsy, variety acts, and magic shows.

In 1802, for example, Columbian Gardens (then called Easton's Garden) offered fireworks, ice cream, and suppers. By 1805, mechanical representations of battles, songs (including one titled "The Learned Pig"), a ballet dance, a pageant, a hornpipe, and a "concert on the clarinet" were offered on one night.[74] McArann's garden opened with a focus on the plantings and the occasional concert, but by 1840 it was offering an enactment of the eruption of Mount Vesuvius, fireworks, minstrel performances, illuminations, and a concert—again, all on the same night.[75] Delacroix's early Vauxhalls offered evenings with simple concerts, fireworks, and refreshments, but by 1845 the gardens hosted minstrel performers, "the wonderful tattooed man," dancers, singers, and other variety acts, which were described as having "caught the attention of the Bowery people, who attend . . . in great numbers."[76]

In each example presented here, a shift can be seen toward increasingly eclectic acts as concert music and opera was cut back in favor of more popular variety performances.[77] Although the timing and duration of the shift varied, a change to lowbrow forms was seen in these venues between 1790 and 1820, with the pleasure gardens being almost universally considered to be lowbrow by the 1830s, and it is in this form that the gardens are most frequently depicted in literature. These sources describe a resort that was lowbrow but which nonetheless retained vestiges of its past as a place where distinction could be performed.

Chapter 29 of Cornelius Matthews's *The Career of Puffer Hopkins* (1842) is set in Vauxhall, New York, where the title character attends a ball organized by the fictional society the "Round-Rimmers."[78] The narrator presents the guests as struggling unsuccessfully to imitate a higher class. Dancing couples are described as "throwing out limbs," with gentlemen "thumping the floor with their heels at every descent," and ladies occasionally "losing balance" and dashing "headlong into the ruffles of one of the stationary young gentlemen." Even the speech of the guests (which is described as being "in a dialect which was in a great measure intelligible") is ridiculed.[79] The gardens are depicted as a site belonging to the lower classes who ineptly mimic their superiors and are openly mocked for doing so.

The gardens adopt a similar function in Benjamin Baker's *A Glance at New York* (1848), a play that focuses on the antics of Mose the Bowery b'hoy and his "gal" Eliza or "Lize."[80] The final scene takes place in Vauxhall, with "arches of variegated lamps" and dancing forming the setting. The scene is short but finds time to gently ridicule the characters. Lize for example orders "a cup of coffee, and nine doughnuts" for herself. The gardens are nonetheless presented as a relatively refined space where the men treat the women with courtesy. Although the rural and romantic elements of the gardens were maintained, the class of the focal figures had changed, and the idea that class could simply be performed there was openly mocked. Despite the persistent belief that class was not a defining element of one's identity in antebellum America, pleasure gardens reinforced a class hierarchy, restricting entry and aiming at elite status, before being reclaimed by those of a lower class, who in turn present a ludicrous contrast of lowbrow status and highbrow aspirations.

Conclusion

Far from being entertainment venues exclusively modeled on the English original, pleasure gardens provided a space for Americans to explore what it meant to be American. Were Americans merely displaced Brits, and did their culture replicate that of Britain? Or were they able to create their own distinctively American cultural form imbued with ideas of American nationalism? Did Americans thrive as an agricultural society, as Jefferson and Washington would have us believe, or were cities to be embraced as part of a forward-moving nation? Could ideals of equality be realized in American society, or were traditional prejudices and hierarchies still in place? In sum, could the ideals of independence, agrarianism, and equality actually be experienced in antebellum America?

The definition of America as being free (specifically, from Britain) was an important aspect of the American identity, yet culturally this was a highly problematic endeavor. While seeking a refined culture, Americans looked to Britain as a source of legitimacy even as they lamented their dependence on Britain. American pleasure gardens displayed numerous borrowings from the English venues (from the form and name, to the layout and kinds of entertainment offered), as well as rejections of English associations and assertions of American nationalism. In the pleasure gardens, American identity was communicated through neither a simple rejection nor a wholesale adoption of all things British but rather through a varied and complex negotiation of the relationship of the new nation to Britain.

Several of the Founding Fathers saw agrarianism as central to what it meant to be American. By accommodating the country within the city, pleasure gardens seemed to support this, with gardens established even in "corrupt," industrialized urban centers. Attempting to balance the rural ideal and nostalgia with the rapidly industrializing city of the future, pleasure gardens allowed Americans to indulge in a fantasy world where both existed, side by side. The speed of progress and the pressure on land led to the demise of pleasure gardens and might be read as signaling the triumph of the city in the American imagination, though the American heartland and honest labor remain central to notions of American identities.

The idea that Americans paid no heed to class structures is perhaps the most interesting proposition tested in the pleasure gardens. Although Britain had a formal class structure, the gardens were known for their mixture of classes. One would expect a new nation priding itself on democratic ideals to adopt this aspect wholeheartedly. What we have found is rather the opposite: distaste for the mingling of "fashionable society" and "toughs." Many of the gardens became a focal point for class tensions, with conflicts being played out in a very physical and violent manner. Attitudes toward class displayed within the space of the American pleasure gardens upset the popularly held belief that post-Revolutionary America supported a classless society, or at least one in which class status was not a defining aspect of one's identity.

Though individual ventures were often short-lived, pleasure gardens were found up and down the East Coast. They played an important role in American cultural identity and reveal much about cultural and national identities in the new nation. Within these establishments we find many elements reminiscent of the London Vauxhall. Yet these gardens offered more than merely a transplanted resort, providing a constellation of centrally located, public places for the exploration of what it meant to be American in post-Revolutionary America. Pleasure gardens were not, by any means, American creations, but the venues that emerged there were certainly unique.

Chapter 6

Pleasure Gardens in Nineteenth-Century New Orleans: "Useful for All Classes of Society"

LAKE DOUGLAS

British-born architect Thomas Kelah Wharton (1814–62) came to New Orleans in 1853 as superintendent for the construction of the Customs House, and for nine years, during a golden age of urban growth and prosperity, he wrote about contemporary life in the antebellum community.[1] On 2 May 1854, he described a rail excursion that he took with his family to Carrollton, a community several miles from downtown:

> The trip was delightful and the cool fresh breeze on the river bank quite invigorating after the heat and dust of a day in town. We met pleasant friends in the gardens and found every thing much changed, and not improved, since last May.
> The abrasions of the River have made a new Levee, far within the old one, absolutely necessary. Obliterating entirely one of the beautiful and far-famed gardens. The shade lane, too, of lofty oleander which last year was covered at this time with a perfect waste of blossoms. The pleasant walk on the river bank arched over with China trees.[2] The lovely alleys of Cape jessamines, and the white bell flowered Yucca, from which years ago I derived my first impressions of the exuberance of southern vegetation, all, all, have vanished and in their place nothing but a long, bald, earthy, embankment, a wind dusty road, immense piles of cord wood (for supplying the steamboats), with rail tracks in every direction to facilitate their transmission from point to point.[3] Stagnant pools of muddy water between

the old Levee and the new. In short, deformity for beauty, utility for poetry, but the grand river still redeems it all, and the fresh green woods on the distant bank, and the fresh pure air blowing across its restless current.[4]

At first, this account appears to be little more than a description of a nineteenth-century open space in New Orleans—perhaps a public park—that had deteriorated significantly within a year, much to Wharton's dismay. Neither the space nor its description seems to be of much significance for American urban history. What Wharton wrote about here, however, was Carrollton Gardens, a hotel in a landscaped setting created at the terminus of the streetcar line in the 1830s as an attraction to encourage the public to ride the streetcar and enjoy the refreshment and outdoor experiences the garden offered.[5] Such commercial spaces, together with similar examples elsewhere in the country, are unexplored opportunities to investigate how nineteenth-century Americans perceived and used open spaces.

Carrollton Gardens, in operation between 1835 and 1891, falls midway in a continuum of similar commercial open spaces in New Orleans that offered food, outdoor recreation, or amusements, the earliest of which dates from 1810. Sifting through seemingly unremarkable artifacts of everyday life such as newspaper advertisements, periodical articles, photographic images, and even sheet music, we find numerous references to open spaces similar to Wharton's description. Known over time in nineteenth-century newspaper advertisements as "pleasure gardens," "pleasure grounds," "houses and gardens of pleasure," and later as "amusement parks," these commercial ventures were scattered throughout the community. Spatially, however, they were situated in an ill-defined middle ground between the public sphere and private property. Accessible to the public, albeit on the owners' terms, these enterprises offered attractions their owners thought the public would embrace.

Early nineteenth-century pleasure gardens in America were versions of European examples from the seventeenth and eighteenth centuries. By the end of the nineteenth century, they had evolved into amusement parks, typological precedents for the "theme parks" found throughout the world from the mid-twentieth century on.[6] When one considers the wide variety of forms taken today by such amusement-oriented venues (not only theme parks but also waterparks, family entertainment centers, zoos, aquaria, "exploratoria," science centers, resorts, and casinos), the millions of people who have patronized them, and the revenues they generate, the significance of pleasure gardens as key precedents in the general evolution of these designed landscapes becomes clear.[7]

Substantial evidence, presented here for the first time, situates pleasure gardens in several major nineteenth-century American cities, and anecdotal evidence suggests examples may well have existed throughout America, in commnities large and small, coastal and inland. Investigations of these pleasure gardens have been initiated primarily by music and theater historians because such spaces, both in Europe (notably London) and later in America, primarily offered musical and theatrical entertainment; food, beverage, and leisure-related recreational activities were only of secondary importance. Pleasure gardens have been of marginal interest to landscape historians perhaps because the activities they offered are considered commonplace and therefore less worthy of study than more refined landscape expressions.[8]

Five factors have contributed to the marginal treatment of pleasure gardens in conventional discussions of American open space. The first is the absence of visual evidence. Examples—even plans—for pleasure gardens that predate late nineteenth-century amusement parks are largely nonexistent, and what documentation exists from earlier examples is mainly narrative rather than illustrative, describing activities rather than spatial order or design. Second, designers of these spaces (if we can even speak of them being "designed") remain anonymous. Third, pleasure gardens were private developments, not municipal features on public property; as such, they resemble other commodities in that their commercial success (and therefore longevity) was determined by market forces and fickle public tastes. Fourth, what was popular one season was often shunned the next. The raison d'être of pleasure gardens was the regularly programmed "entertainment" (including food, drink, theater, and music) that usually occurred during favorable weather conditions. Similar attractions may have been present in public parks on an occasional basis but were usually of less importance than the year-round active recreation and passive activities for which public parks were designed. Finally, a continuum leading from early pleasure gardens to more recent amusement parks is not well established or widely acknowledged. Early examples have long since vanished, the prevailing secondary literature neglects them in favor of more prominent public parks, and later amusement parks generally do not figure significantly in contemporary discourse of public open spaces.[9] As a consequence, pleasure gardens have gone largely unstudied and underappreciated as a landscape typology.

Nevertheless, a closer examination is warranted for several reasons. Pleasure gardens precede other examples of designed open spaces in America, and they occur much earlier than those well-documented efforts, found from the mid-nineteenth century onward, to build public parks in urban areas. They are different, in both form and content, from open spaces of the "rural cemetery" movement, and their purposes are distinct from the lofty appreciations of the landscape encouraged by the transcendentalists, intellectuals, and landscape painters of the nineteenth century. Finally, these early examples of the designed landscape are part of the evolution of American concepts of landscape architecture, recreation, and open-space usage that would later find expression in public projects as the profession of landscape architecture evolved from its mid-nineteenth-century origins.

Commercial pleasure gardens are one of at least five open-space models found in nineteenth-century New Orleans. As elsewhere, local pleasure gardens were commercial places of public amusement, eating and drinking, sport, and entertainment, precursors to later "concert saloons," brothels, theme and amusement parks, and even private country clubs because of the activities they offered (including amusements, sports, eating, and drinking) and the policies in place regarding admission.[10] The first notice of a pleasure garden appears in a newspaper advertisement from 1810 in a new residential area upriver from the colonial community; by the century's end, pleasure gardens had evolved into the suburban beer gardens, performance venues, and amusement parks of Spanish Fort and West End along the shores of Lake Pontchartrain, precedents for twentieth-century Pontchartrain Beach (for whites) and Lincoln Beach (for "coloreds").[11] Until now, New Orleans pleasure gardens have been discussed briefly, first as performance venues within the context of the community's nineteenth-century musical history, and later as places where "city people" went in the "expectation of pleasure."[12] Closer examination, however, reveals there is much more to learn here in terms of urban history.

Of the American cities one might take as the focus for an analysis such as that proposed here, New Orleans stands out for several reasons. This community's pleasure gardens demonstrate how local conventions of race and gender influenced access to and uses of these recreational spaces. They show European cultural influences on open-space design and recreational activities in an American community, demonstrating the persistence of such foreign influences through the nineteenth century. They also reveal how technology and rising middle-class aspirations encouraged access to and use of these open spaces, enabling them to become commodities of consumption in the local marketplace. The number of pleasure gardens found in nineteenth-century New Orleans—around twenty have been identified throughout the larger community thus far—indicate their public popularity; their importance as recreation and entertainment venues; their geographical place in the urban fabric; and the cultural, social, and economic roles they played in public life. In addition, their nineteenth-century trajectory demonstrates how external factors related to race, economics, and cultural heritage influenced organization, use, and content of these privately owned open spaces. Finally, information about local pleasure gardens, seen as part of the larger context of open spaces in other nineteenth-century American communities, adds significantly to a broader knowledge of the country's urban-landscape history.

The map (Figure 6.1) gives general locations for pleasure gardens in nineteenth-century New Orleans. Though many have come to light, it is difficult to know exactly how many there were in nineteenth-century New Orleans. Information about their contents and activities is inconsistent, and it is impossible to ascertain if all venues using the words "pleasure garden" or "garden" actually described open spaces or characterized theatrical attractions, musical entertainment, leisure activities, or decorative motifs instead.[13]

Notably, the names of well-known European pleasure garden precedents occur locally in different locations and at different times, suggesting both knowledge among locals of European precedents and specific interest in using nominal associations as a means of attracting customers.[14] Notices in the *New Orleans Emporium* occur in July 1832 for legal matters related to a Louisiana Vauxhall Gardens on Common Street; this may have been the predecessor to the New Vauxhall Garden, but no information exists as yet about its content or design. There were at least two New Orleans properties known as Tivoli: one is mentioned in 1808, location unknown; discussion on the other, found on the Carondelet Canal, follows.

As elsewhere, the unifying factor among local pleasure gardens is their entrepreneurial nature. These private spaces were open to the public as business ventures, and their existence and longevity responded to market forces of capital, location, opportunity, and clientele. Entrepreneurial characteristics explain their often short life spans and differentiate pleasure

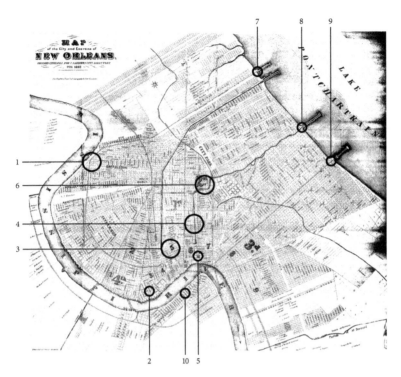

Figure 6.1. Recreation and amusement venues in New Orleans, with dates of documented existence. *C. Gardener's City Directory* (1867). Overlay by Micah Hargrove (2011). North is to the upper right of the map.
1. Carrollton Gardens (1853–91) at the terminus of St. Charles Avenue
2. Lower Garden District: Eliza Gardens (1810–30s); the Pleasure Garden in the suburb La Course on Tchoupitoulas Street and Orange Street; New Orleans Pleasure Garden, Delord and Magazine (1842); Fasnacht's Garden at Poeyfarre and Annunciation (1852)
3. American Sector: New Vauxhall Gardens (1853); Kossuth Gardens (1852)
4. Carondelet Canal: the Jardin du Rocher de Ste. Hélène (1844–48); Louisiana Tivoli (1840); Tivoli Garden, Roman St., and Carondelet Canal (1845–66); Vauxhall Gardens (1850–52)
5. Vieux Carré: Rasch's Garden on Chartre Street (1826); Mr. S. Vincent, St. Anthony Square (behind Cathedral, 1846)
6. Bayou St. John: Large Oaks (1812); an unnamed example (1830); the Magnolia Garden (1870–87)
7. West End (1880s–1920s)
8. Spanish Fort (1820s–1920s)
9. Milneburg (1880–1920s): Pontchartrain Beach (1920s–1980s)
10. Algiers (1843)

gardens from other nineteenth-century public open-space models such as neighborhood squares, levees, and public parks. Available evidence among pleasure gardens may be inconsistent, yet useful information about them emerges in four general categories: their administrative structures (admissions policies, conduct expected of patrons); the activities offered (sports, musical and theatrical events, spectacles); the accommodations provided (food and beverage); and their design (plant materials and structures). Pleasure gardens illustrate unique interpretations of public space in terms of organization, access, and content, and their characteristics demonstrate evolving local practices concerning consumption, leisure activities, social interaction, cultural influences, and open-space design, thereby giving new relevance to their importance in nineteenth-century urban life.

Social attitudes in nineteenth-century New Orleans based in racial and cultural identity are just now being explored through lenses of politics, culture, and music, and the practices that resulted from these attitudes are complicated, complex, and confusing.[15] Although legacies of these attitudes exist today, their impacts on publicly accessible spaces in nineteenth-century New Orleans remain, until now, largely unexplored.

Race and Gender: Eliza Gardens and Simon Lagnel, 1810–20s

An advertisement that appeared in a New Orleans newspaper in 1835 for the Vauxhall Gardens specifies "N.B. No colored persons admitted," a stipulation that appears in advertisements for pleasure gardens in Charleston (1799) and New York (1826).[16] However, notices of two earlier examples depict a more permissive attitude regarding race and gender, remnants of the community's colonial past.

On 11 July 1810 a three-sentence advertisement for the Eliza Gardens appeared in the *Louisiana Courier*. Several points are worth noting, first of which is the early date. Second is that on Wednesdays and Fridays the garden would receive "persons of color," a term that refers to the complicated social structure common in the colonial and post-colonial colony and its influence on spatial organization; clearly this term applies to African Americans, enslaved or not, but it could also apply to anyone of mixed blood ("creoles").[17] Third is its admission structure: a fee of "one bit" (a quarter of a dollar) was redeemable in liquid "refreshment," a common practice in the pleasure garden model. And finally is that children must have adult supervision and that those who might cause "injury . . . to the garden" will be held "accountable." This short notice suggests both the context in which patrons used a local pleasure garden and what can be learned about a local pleasure garden even if we are deprived of knowing its design.

We do know, however, its general location. According to architectural historian Sam Wilson Jr., this "amusement park of some sort" was located upriver from the Vieux Carré in a new residential neighborhood settled after the Louisiana Purchase. Wilson notes that it existed until 1831, and in 1832 lots were advertised for sale "being part of that fine property lately called *Eliza Gardens*."[18]

There was another pleasure garden nearby, and between July 1825 and April 1826 four lengthy advertisements for this enterprise appear, giving detailed and interesting information on both organizational structure and content. These notices are extraordinary glimpses into the social life of New Orleans in the mid-1820s and demonstrate how racial issues influenced urban life in general and spatial issues in particular.

In the first ad, subscribers—men only—are listed as those who financed this development and, judging from their names, they were of both French and non-French heritage.[19] Subscribers were encouraged to bring "friends of both sexes" together with children to what appears to have been an event held in their honor. Food (a "light collation" as well as "peaches, figs and raisins" for children) was provided with the admission fee of one dollar, together with musical entertainment and dancing. The entire family could attend, and the garden's operator engaged a skiff to ferry people from the Vieux Carré and the garden at a rate of twenty-five cents for the round-trip.

Later in the same week another advertisement appears, expanding on information provided in the previous announcement and outlining procedures for admission. The garden's operator wished to open his facility to "all classes of society" with three days for "white persons of both sexes," one day for "white gentlemen and free women of color,"[20] and one day for "free people of color of both sexes." As with Eliza Gardens, this venue's admissions structure arises from the intricate tripartite social structure that existed at the time in multiethnic New Orleans. Even on different days, all had access; the space was not divided into segregated sections as would happen a century later when segregationist laws were in full effect. Although divisions between races certainly existed, regulations here suggest accommodations that enabled all to maintain appropriate levels of separation where necessary but provided opportunities for union when convenient. This demonstrates that in the early decades of the nineteenth century open space was periodically a common ground allowing cross-cultural associations within existing social conventions and accepted practices regarding race and gender. Subscribers were urged to enlist their friends to join so that each day they would have crowds of people known to them. Games, "amusing" but not hazardous, were offered. In addition, the operator suggested the beneficial qualities to "inhabitants of the suburbs, nay even of the neighborhood[s] of the city, on both sides of the river . . . of having a place of re-union," and the advantages his venue offered "sick persons or convalescents." Finally, some plantings were mentioned, suggesting the garden then had fig and peach trees and grape arbors, and, "next spring," he hoped to have "a collection of the finest flowers."

In 1826 organizational rules and subscription policies were expanded and published. Subscribers would pay ten dollars per year; Saturdays are for "white subscribers" and Tuesdays for "free persons of color." On the first Sundays of the month there will be dinner and a ball for "parties of white persons;" the second Sunday, for "white gentlemen and free women of color." The other days are open to the public, and on days with no private parties, the fee is six and a quarter cents per person, "whatever age or sex." Subscribers could bring their families, as well as "all persons habitually living in the same house with him" (perhaps a reference to servants). On subscribers' days, there would be musicians, with the charge of "six and a quarter cents for each gentleman per cotillion or waltz." Games are provided, as are stables for subscribers' "horses and gigs," and the garden is open from sunrise to sunset.

Less than a month later, however, in April 1826, the pleasure garden's owner and its "keeper" offered this property, "well arranged and planted with a number of trees and flowers," for sale. We may conclude it was subdivided and sold off in response to increased pressure for new residential development.

Advertisements for both of these gardens provide evidence of an early use in America of designed open space as an attraction for which people would pay admission for recreation and entertainment and abide by the established codes of conduct. The admission rules, based on racial identity and gender, are remarkable, and their importance cannot be underestimated because they reveal important information about who had access and when and reflect the social order of the community.

An examination of local conventions of race and society reveals racial ambiguity with regard to the community's organization and uses of open space. Enslaved African Americans may have been routinely excluded from access to public accommodations (except as servants), but in these pleasure gardens days were designated for "people of color," and *plaçage* arrangements, recognized throughout all realms of the community, facilitated public social interaction among all racial groups. Such accommodations had existed since colonial times. New Orleans, unlike other communities in the South (Charleston, for instance), from the eighteenth century onward had at least three distinct racial groups: free (Europeans), enslaved (usually Africans), and those somewhere in between (often the progeny of the first two groups), known as free people of color and designated as FMC (free man of color) or FWC (free woman of color) in legal documents. If one includes Native Americans, the groups number four, and mingling of groups was not uncommon. According to historian Jerah Johnson, free people of color enjoyed a unique place in the colonial community because of their "unique social and legal standing, midway between the free and the slave sectors . . . and recognized as such in law." Consequently, he notes, "they tended to act with an exceptionally high degree of cohesiveness" and during the late eighteenth century and into the nineteenth century, they freely associated with everyone else, including Europeans, Native Americans, and Africans.[21] Although each group had distinct and well-established ideas about religion, education, and social structure, all groups met on the common ground of commerce, in public markets and gathering spaces, and through activities that involved horticulture, cuisine, and entertainment (notably music). As a result of these common associations, cultures intertwined and cultural boundaries blurred, and over time the community's unique multicultural character, social landscape, physical environment, cuisine, and musical heritage evolved.

As the nineteenth century progressed, the role race played in public negotiation of open spaces in New Orleans changed, and these changes are reflected to greater or lesser degrees in access to public spaces. With statehood the influence of the colonial "Code Noir" legal system decreased; yet race remained prominent well into the twentieth century when "Jim Crow" laws attempted to draw unequivocal lines of racial identity in all phases of life, notably in public accommodation. But while access to and use of open spaces may have changed for local residents over time, in practice those changes were not always strictly observed, as will be seen in late nineteenth-century venues along Lake Pontchartrain. Here, as elsewhere in the community, lines of racial separation were selectively drawn. They depended on circumstances more than laws, a reflection of racial attitudes from earlier in the century.

Technology: Carrollton Gardens

The Carrollton Gardens (1835–91), described in a contemporary written account as being "laid out in the English style,"[22] illustrate how an early transit initiative included leisure space as a commercial attraction, a business model that would be repeated in New Orleans and elsewhere in America. Early rail lines were horse-driven cars connecting downtown New Orleans with uptown communities of Lafayette and Carrollton, and as the nineteenth century progressed, rail lines became steam-powered, then electric. From the 1830s onward, these transit lines facilitated the development of popular "resorts" at their termini. Hotels, restaurants, amusement parks, and beer gardens enticed city residents to visit, encouraged their use of new transit systems, and contributed to real estate developments in adjacent areas.[23] By 1900 New Orleans had one of the country's most extensive networks of public rail transportation, with lines crisscrossing the city.[24]

In 1835 the New Orleans and Carrollton Railroad began service along St. Charles Avenue from Canal Street to Jackson Avenue. This line was then expanded to Carrollton, a community about five miles from the center of New Orleans. A depot was located at the end of the line, and shortly afterward a hotel with four acres of gardens was built nearby. There was a steamboat landing on the Mississippi River, and this destination soon became a popular attraction for locals and tourists. An account from the 28 September 1835 edition of the New Orleans *Bee/L'Abeille*, reporting on the opening of the attraction, noted that the streetcar route "passes through a level and beautiful country . . . affording one of the most pleasant drives in the southern states." The account then reported that "cultural and other improvements have been already made round the hotel; and a jet d'eau is placed in front. But when the gardens and walks are afforded and when refreshments can be given of all kinds throughout the day for visitors, we think this line must, as it should, acquire extensive support."

An image of the Carrollton Hotel property exists in the Notarial Archives, dated 25 March 1840, when the property of multiple lots was offered at public sale. At present the plan is unrestored and suffers from extensive tears and subsequent tape repairs that make it nearly illegible. It shows only the property for sale and not the location of the hotel or a design of its garden; however, it depicts the hotel structure with galleries, outbuildings, and the suggestion of the garden. Also shown are a steam rail car and a cluster of visitors, including adults and children, sitting on what appears to be a bench; in addition, there is an African American woman kneeling in front of the bench wearing the distinctive *tignon* customarily worn in public by women of color.

Subsequent advertisements in May, perhaps under new ownership, give "summer arrangements" for horse car and locomotive rail service, noting that expanded transit access on Sunday afternoons allowed visitors ample time "to enjoy the pleasant walks of one of the most beautiful gardens in the United States." And from 9 June 1840 is an account in the *Daily Picayune* that records the reporter's Sunday excursion to the garden:

> The galleries run all round the house and upon the side overlooking the garden the scene presented is much the same as in front. . . . But observe the beautiful flower garden below, where every variety of bud, blade, tint and odor that ever delighted the eye, ravished the nose, adorned the hair or the bosom of beauty, or the button hole of man, is flourishing in luxurious perfection. If the existence of this beautiful garden was known among European bees, there would be an immediate rage for emigration, and they would all become native Americans at once. Observe how the white shell paths contrast with the bright green grass, curving, winding and meandering like the walls of china, leading you into shade intricacies, where perhaps you stumble upon a pair of cooing lovers. . . . Every variety of description of tree and plant is around you. . . . Bowers, benches and alcoves, all redolent of sweets, are arranged with admirable elegance of taste all about the plants and flowers. . . . Upon the green in front of this gallery you see a large double swing in motion, and near it a fleet of ships are sailing in the air, making a successful voyage

around the pole. It was probably in such aerial vessels that Macbeth's witches were riding when they sung their delight "To sail in the air, When the moon shines fair."

The hotel burned in 1842, but it was rebuilt and its popularity continued. An account that appeared in 1851 reported on a "public garden about six miles from the city":

> It is a common resort, particularly on Sundays, when, as it is easily accessible by railroad, thousands flock to it to get a little fresh air and a nosegay. It is laid out in the English style, and is a pleasant place of retreat from the heat and stench of this dirtiest of all cities. It, however, possesses no horticultural or botanical attraction. The garden is a source of profit from its flowers, but I suspect more money is made from the sale of liquor in the hotel which is connected with it. It is owned by the railroad company, and is the only attraction at that terminus of the line.[25]

The "English style" the author mentions referred, in general, to the "natural" or "picturesque" manner in which large estates were arranged in England at the time: There were large expanses of grass; walks, if present, were curvilinear; and plantings were clustered in irregularly shaped beds. Often, the "French style" referred to seventeenth- and eighteenth-century precedents in which gardens were geometric, ordered, and controlled. By coincidence, the relative merits of both "English" and "French" styles, in relation to Louisiana examples, are discussed by Andrew Gordon, who noted that "the French style in the ornamental department of gardening is the most frequently adopted, particularly among the Creole portion of the population, and there are some very unique and judiciously arranged gardens laid out and kept according to that system, which, however much it may be repudiated by some, possesses a fascination under peculiar circumstances."[26] Both styles were artificial and highly structured; and in fact English and French gardens of the mid-nineteenth century were often quite similar in content and appearance. Comparing nineteenth-century English, French, and American manuals of garden theory, design, and practice, we see more similarities in designs than differences.[27]

From Wharton's description of 1854, we learn that the river significantly altered the garden's content, and although this altered the garden, as Wharton noted, evidently it did not diminish its popularity. Two engravings exist

Figure 6.2. A. T. Sears after Unknown Artist, *Carrollton Gardens* (c. 1889), wood print engraving. Courtesy The Historic New Orleans Collection, accession number 1974.25.29.61.

from 1875 and 1889 that depict the garden's lush and picturesque contents. In the later view (Figure 6.2), there are lush and varied plantings (Yucca, palms, tropical plants in planters, bananas, shrubs, and small trees) and garden features (paved walks, fountains, benches, and verandahs around the hotel for garden viewing), reminiscent of written descriptions from prior years.

The hotel survived until October 1891 when it and the adjacent streetcar station were demolished to accommodate the relocated Mississippi River levee.[28] Subsequently, the property was sold and redeveloped as a residential subdivision, thus ending a remarkable example of transit-based open space in New Orleans.

Cultural Heritage: Jardin du Rocher de Ste. Hélène and Tivoli Gardens

Strong European influences remain in pleasure gardens, as elsewhere in nineteenth-century New Orleans, long after the city became American in

1803, demonstrating the continued importance here of foreign traditions in both design and recreational activities. Musicologist Henry Kmen suggested a cultural association among pleasure gardens, music performed, and patrons: "If one preferred a French atmosphere, there was Rasch's Garden . . . Simon Laignel's Pleasure Garden . . . or the Louisiana Garden. . . . English tastes could be gratified at the Louisiana Vauxhall Gardens . . . the New Vauxhall Gardens . . . or the Vauxhall Gardens in the St. Charles Theater," but he neither elaborates nor gives citations.[29] Nevertheless, such cultural associations can be seen in pleasure gardens found on Bayou St. John, a natural waterway that extends to Lake Pontchartrain, and the Carondelet Canal, which was dug in the late eighteenth century to connect the lake with the Vieux Carré's back door.

Along Bayou St. John, venues for leisure activities occur as early as 1805 with an advertisement for "a new place called the Tivoli" where "men and ladies 'of the best families' trudge two miles and back to dance every Sunday through July and August."[30] Notice of a "house of pleasure" called Large Oaks being for sale on Bayou St. John appeared on 22 April 1812 in *The Courier*. Described as having "fine plants and trees," it also had "commodious rooms" for "pastime plays . . . and a good billiard table" and offered "every day and at every hour refreshments of every kind at moderate prices." Activities included "seesaws, bowling-greens, ninepins & c," and patrons could "shot [sic] at the wooden bird, and climb up the cocagne [sic] mast,[31] as it is practiced in France." Music was offered on Sundays, when "symphonies will be executed by a numerous and well selected orchestra." The proprietors could offer any food and entertainment, and assured their clientele that they would do their best to unite "conveniences with pleasure" and "secure good order and decency" in the activities offered. Here is an early description of a local pleasure garden that closely follows earlier European precedents in both activities (music, plays, games, refreshment) offered.

From later accounts in the 1840s, we see such cultural connections at the Jardin du Rocher de Ste. Hélène,[32] another Tivoli Gardens (1840–66), and the Vauxhall Gardens (1850s), all found on the Carondelet Canal. The Jardin du Rocher was a venue for those interested in maintaining their French heritage in the booming American city. Tivoli Gardens (not to be confused with the Tivoli on Bayou St. John from 1805), displayed German influences in offerings of entertainment and food and, in 1840, was the site of a public demonstration of the new daguerreotype process by a French free man of color. The nearby Vauxhall Gardens, according to Kmen, offered music and entertainment in the English taste.

All three pleasure gardens were on the Carondelet Walk, a paved promenade beside the canal that was popular for late afternoon strolls.[33] No doubt this walk, like the promenade along the Mississippi River levee, encouraged multicultural social interchange and facilitated the development and popularity of these commercial ventures.[34] The Jardin du Rocher and Tivoli provide examples of pleasure gardens being common ground on which those from different cultural backgrounds could associate.

The Jardin du Rocher de Ste. Hélène was offered for sale in September 1844, and a detailed description of its size and a plan of its spatial organization remain.[35] This development's name, the plan's notations of its features (in French), its design, and newspaper accounts of the activities that took place here all reflect a lingering French influence in the city. The plan shows a space of approximately 26,500 square feet—not large, about a half-acre—yet it has many features, organized generally into several horizontal bands. The front of the garden is enclosed by what appears to be an iron fence similar to those used around public squares separating this privately owned space from the public realm. Upon entry, the visitor would encounter a long reflecting pool with an island of grass in its center, in which a statue is placed; at the terminus of the canal axis is a raised platform, approximately six feet high, faced with rockery (perhaps representing the "Rock of St. Helena") with a statue. To either side of the entrance and along the sides is a small garden room ("cabinet") with tables and benches, enclosed by hedges, which seem to be less than waist high. Rectangular beds of lawn are punctuated with walkways leading to tables, statues, and benches. There are two identical buildings of two rooms each, with front and rear galleries and cisterns; in one building is a kitchen ("cuisinaire"). Between the structures is a large court area enclosed by a grass strip that includes a statue and a set of see-saws ("balançoires"). There is a three-lane pistol range ("tir au pistolet"), a long vine-covered arbor, an area with two unidentified elements (perhaps seesaws), a structure for billiards, and a small privy. Walkways and gathering spaces appear to be sand or rock. There is an absence of flowering plants and trees but the presence of hedges, vines, and grass. Recreational activities here are similar to those mentioned in the description of Large Oaks. The presence of enclosed structures suggests indoor activities, such as eating, games, perhaps even *les liaisons dangereuses*.

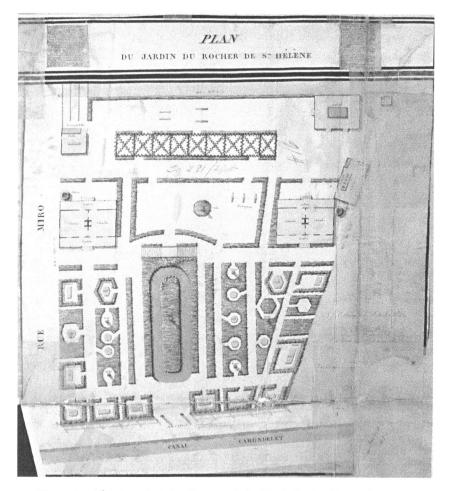

Figure 6.3. After Jean Antoine Bourgerol, *Jardin du Rocher Ste. Hélène* (1844), pen and ink with watercolor. Courtesy Clerk of Civil District Court, Notarial Archives Division, New Orleans, La. Plan Book 35.16.

After being sold in 1844 the garden continued in operation and figured prominently in events in the local French community in April 1848 that celebrated the birth of the Second Republic in France. Holding a political event here suggests a relationship between the local French community and this venue as well as a continuing French presence in the city more than four decades after it had become American.[36]

One of the earliest references to a pleasure garden in New Orleans is of a Tivoli on Bayou St. John; a later reference describes another Tivoli Garden on the Carondelet Canal.[37] It was here in 1840 that Jules Lion (c. 1810–66), a credible painter, lithographer, and French-born free man of color, gave a demonstration to the community of the nascent daguerreotype process (invented in France in the mid-1830s), one of the first such demonstrations in America. Lion came to New Orleans in 1837 and opened a studio in the Vieux Carré. Having spent the summer of 1839 in Paris, he returned to New Orleans with the city's first "Daguerreotype Instrument" and gave public demonstrations and lectures, for which he charged a dollar.[38]

An account in the Baton Rouge *Gazette* of 18 April 1840 reports Lion gave "an experiment performed by means of this wonderful and extraordinary machine at the Louisiana Tivoli near New Orleans." The reporter admits being "prepared to expect something wonderful" but declares, "Never has anything in my life caused me so much astonishment as to find nature so clearly delineated and copied by means of human invention." One might assume that the venue selected for this technology's introduction correlated with the drama of its presentation. It should be noted that Lion, a foreign-born free man of color, occupied and enjoyed a special place in New Orleans as a skilled artist, as did other artisans and tradesmen of his racial heritage. Lion secured Tivoli Gardens for his demonstration and was able to attract crowds who paid to witness it. He enjoyed commercial success, and the public enthusiastically accepted this new medium. One might conclude then that New Orleans played a small part in the birth of photography in America through Lion's daguerreotype demonstration at Tivoli Gardens. Also worth noting is that a presentation by a French-born free man of color was given in a pleasure garden to a receptive community more interested in seeing the latest invention than they were concerned about the race of the person who made the presentation.

An article in the New Orleans *Picayune* on 30 October 1849 indicates that Tivoli "fronted . . . the Old Canal in Faubourg Treme" and was

> a scale not often seen. . . . Nearest the city was the "Vauxhall Garden," across the street the largest, the "Tivoli Garden," and several squares on, an unnamed establishment[39] which charged a dime but gave a glass of refreshment to each guest. The gardens were thickly planted with choice trees and shrubbery beneath which were benches and tables, and amid which were latticed bowers and arbors. There were buildings for barrooms, ice cream cakes, coffee, etc. The capacious

ballrooms, bare of furniture, were almost entirely open at the sides. In galleries far above, musicians poured forth German waltzes, to which couples danced for a half dime each ten minutes. The gentlemen dancers mostly wore their hats; the ladies' attire was plain and modest.

Chilly winter did not eliminate attendance. German beer, quite bitter and strongly flavored with hops, was the favorite beverage, accompanied by a curious German Dough-nut, and ginger cakes. Good order, a spirit of mutual accommodation, and intense vivacity prevailed. Sunday afternoons and evenings drew the largest crowds, of old, young, and middle-aged—French, German, Irish, Spanish and Italian in race or extraction.

This description is the most detailed yet found with regard to both content and location. Noteworthy is the explicit mention of German content such as "waltzes" and "beer," indicating the German presence in the community and its influence on leisure activities.[40] Also noteworthy is the last sentence, suggesting that at least on one day of the week the entire community was welcome, regardless of age, "race," or "extraction."

Tivoli Garden is represented in a detailed view of a pleasure garden, a lithograph by Xavier Magny, circa 1850, later used on the cover of sheet music.[41] This image shows numerous well-dressed people (including children) enjoying various activities in the garden, perhaps on a Sunday afternoon. Nearly twenty tables are arranged under mature trees, occupied with people eating and drinking. There are at least three structures, including a hexagonal pavilion with lattice sides and bunting. A large rectangular structure has rooms that open out, apparently serving as a bar. Of significance is the association of the composition (through its title) with the pleasure garden itself, a musical connection similar to those found in eighteenth- and nineteenth-century English pleasure gardens and one that would occur later in the century with local lakefront attractions.

Music and refreshment were not the only activities this garden offered. An advertisement (in both French and English) from the *Courier*, 23 July 1852, invites the public "to witness the ascension of a Large and Magnificent Baloon [sic] 70 feet in circumference" two days hence. Such spectacles were often presented in local pleasure gardens, another connection with European examples.

According to occasional notices in the *Daily Picayune*, Tivoli Gardens was sometimes the site of mishap and mayhem. For instance on 5 December 1845 an old shed there collapsed "whilst a number of children were playing in it," resulting in bruises and a broken arm. Between 1847 and 1866, there were at least five reports of fighting and raucous behavior among both men and women, sending some to jail and others to the hospital. One such event involved a man who, having assaulted those who were trying to quiet him, "went to the bar-room in the garden . . . flung the glasses and decanters about, and after having been carried out by his mother, again returned to renew the disturbance, and was then arrested." Clearly, Tivoli Gardens was a lively place!

Over the course of the nineteenth century, cultural correlations between ethnic communities and physical spaces appear in open spaces, both privately owned and municipal. For instance, Congo Square, an early municipal space outside the ramparts that corresponded in size with the French colonial Place d'Armes, has, since colonial times, held significance for those of African descent. Such associations began to weaken by the nineteenth century's end because of increasing public mobility, a middle class with disposable income, and the emergence of new open-space concepts, notably large municipal parks such as Audubon Park and City Park. Looking at cultural connections in an evolutionary way, we see that different ethnic communities brought certain activities and uses into the open-space arena, and these patterns ultimately migrated into newer public spaces throughout the community. Activities were defined by both social customs and cultural traditions, and these characteristics existed long enough to make lasting contributions to local civic life. But as the community evolved and cultural boundaries dissolved, the culturally exclusive nature of these spaces began to erode. What started early in the nineteenth century as individual cultural threads woven through pleasure gardens became a whole fabric of open spaces by century's end. These new spaces are represented in the amusement parks on Lake Pontchartrain. Varied in both use and design, they were influenced by advancing technologies and governed by municipal laws and social custom as well as by the vagaries of the public marketplace.

Culminating Results on Lake Pontchartrain: Spanish Fort and West End, c. 1880–1920

Early settlers used Bayou St. John as a trade route between Lake Pontchartrain and the colonial settlement, a connection established by Native Americans, and with the creation of the Carondelet Canal in the 1790s, this route became the main connection to points beyond. By the late eighteenth century, swamps along Bayou St. John were cleared, and in the early decades of the nineteenth century, land was subdivided into plantations. Though sparsely populated, this area became a rural retreat from the urban community with the advent of rail transportation. Small settlements such as Milneburg, Spanish Fort, and West End developed on the southern shore of Lake Pontchartrain as places of recreation, amusement, and refuge from summer heat and seasonal yellow fever epidemics, and they were accessible by rail.

The first such connection between downtown and Lake Pontchartrain communities began in 1831 with a line to Milneburg,[42] followed by lines to West End (late 1860s) and Spanish Fort (early 1870s). Rowing and recreational sailing were common pastimes, and in 1849 the Southern Yacht Club was established at West End, with its clubhouse located on a pier over Lake Pontchartrain. After a decline of interest during the Civil War and Reconstruction years, interest in recreational boating had a revival in the 1870s. By the century's end, there were numerous lakefront recreation and amusement activities, all accessible by rail. Milneburg was known for its saloons, music venues, and family camps. Spanish Fort on Bayou St. John and West End adjacent to the New Basin Canal each had amusement parks that claimed to be the "Coney Island of the South" with hotels, restaurants, dance pavilions, amusement rides, and picnic areas.[43] In these venues, contemporary cultural, technological, and social influences converged to define local engagement with public space.

Like eighteenth-century English pleasure garden precedents, Milneburg, Spanish Fort, and West End were venues where early jazz musicians regularly appeared, and for this reason they are inextricably linked to this musical genre's evolution through participation from all strata of local economic, cultural, and racial groups (white, black, Creole). Writing about the origins of jazz and misconceptions of race, historian Jerah Johnson observed: "Jazz had its origins not in segregation, but in the assimilative tradition of easy interaction of peoples that prevailed in New Orleans, undiminished by the three Jim Crow laws of the 1890s. Jazz is a music of urban civilization and complexity, not a music of cultural isolation or of racial singularity. It is a music of freedom and joy, not a music of repression and sorrow. To understand its roots requires scholarly inquiry into the peculiar urban mix of late nineteenth-century New Orleans, for it was that unique mix that gave rise to the music."[44] A similar assessment of cultural diversity and assimilation could also describe urban pleasure gardens in New Orleans of the nineteenth century.

As in "Valse de Tivoli" from 1850, evidence of the community's multicultural character is found on the cover of F. Schleichardt's "Babes in the Woods," a composition from 1879 "Dedicated to Mr. M. Schwartz, President Spanish Fort Railroad" and "Performed by B. Moses' Band at Spanish Fort."[45] Here is music honoring the businessman who ran the railroad to Spanish Fort, where it was performed. Both composer and honorand are apparently of German heritage, and the music was performed, possibly by a mixed-race band, in the late nineteenth-century version of a pleasure garden, access to which was from advances in rail technology.

These lakefront venues, uncontested spaces defined more by recreation, pleasure, and performance than by separation by color or class, were also where musical techniques and ideas were regularly explored, shared, and celebrated. The spontaneous and improvisational nature of jazz was facilitated by the informal and unstructured nature of these spaces and encouraged by the audience's enthusiastic reception of what was offered. Many acknowledged milestones of early jazz—both musical composition and performers—are connected with these musical venues.[46] Among the many musicians who played here are Buddy Bolden (1877–1931), Joe "King" Oliver (1885–1938), and Louis "Satchmo" Armstrong (1900–1971), and important compositions include "Milenberg Joys" (composed jointly by two white men and one African American) and "West End Blues," among others.[47] Until World War I, performances by jazz musicians demonstrated that in these lakefront attractions, as indeed elsewhere in the community, ambiguity remained in use and access to public spaces, more or less as it had been in the nineteenth century.[48]

None of these lakefront sites remains. Periodic hurricanes and fires wreaked havoc on these flimsy structures, many of which were on piers in the lake. In the late 1920s and early 1930s, about five-and-a-half miles of water frontage, the site of earlier amusement venues (from West End to Milneburg) was wiped out when the lake's shore was extended for residential development. Nevertheless, venues at Spanish Fort and West End between the 1880s and 1920s are well documented in jazz history and in photographic images, and from both we may conclude that the lakefront was a lively and popular attraction among local residents.

The history of the lakefront attractions illuminates the nineteenth-century trajectory in New Orleans of pleasure gardens into amusement parks. Spanish Fort was on Lake Pontchartrain at the mouth of Bayou St. John, so named in the nineteenth century for its eighteenth-century colonial fortification. By the early nineteenth century, it had fallen into disrepair and was partially rebuilt by the U.S. War Department in 1808. It never saw action and fell into disrepair again when larger and more strategically located fortifications were built elsewhere. However, its prominent location at the intersection of public roads parallel to Lake Pontchartrain and crossing Bayou St. John made it attractive for redevelopment, and in the 1820s the fort was decommissioned and sold. A hotel and "garden" was built on its foundations, thus beginning a century of activities here related to leisure and recreation.

A plan exists from 1830 when the property changed hands, and it shows two small cabins and four structures: a stable with thirty-one stalls; a building with kitchen and seven rooms (a footprint of approximately 2,100 square feet); a larger building (a footprint of approximately 4,000 square feet) with eight rooms of varying sizes, one of which includes a billiard table, and a covered gallery overlooking a "Garden" that repeats the configuration of the "ancient Fortifications"; and a privy of six compartments. Two large planted areas are shown, one with linear green stripes and another with geometric beds. Several drainage ditches are shown together with indications of "yards" near the structures. These features suggest an attraction that could accommodate large groups for eating and other entertainment.

Over time, the property passed through several hands and was acquired by the Canal Street, City Park, and Lake Railroad Company, which had a line from downtown New Orleans to the lakefront hotel. The seven-and-a-half-mile trip took about twenty minutes and a round-trip ticket cost fifteen cents.[49] The property was sold in 1877 to Moses Swartz who opened an amusement park the next year.[50] At its terminus was the "amusement park" that included the hotel, as well as band pavilions, an "opera" house, an outdoor restaurant, and a beer garden named "Over the Rhine." Popular curiosities included an alligator pen and a Civil War-era submarine found submerged in Lake Pontchartrain near Bayou St. John in 1878.[51]

The other lakefront attraction was West End, dating from about 1880. It featured a wooden platform constructed over the water on which its attractions were built, including a roller coaster, Ferris wheel, music pavilions, hotels, and restaurants. It was here, in 1896, that the community's first moving picture was exhibited on an outdoor screen, powered with electricity from the streetcar line. Such an event must have been as novel as Lion's

Figure 6.4. George François Mugnier, *Opera House, Spanish Fort* (c. 1880–90), photograph. Louisiana Division/City Archives, New Orleans Public Library.

"extraordinary machine" and as exciting as the "ascension of a Large and Magnificent Baloon" [sic] at Tivoli Gardens decades before.

By the end of the nineteenth century, what had started in the 1820s as a lakefront hotel and grounds at Spanish Fort had evolved into two popular lakefront amusement parks, each at the terminus of a rail line.[52] Spanish Fort declined in popularity in the early 1900s in part because of competition from the larger amusement park at nearby West End, and its buildings subsequently burned. In 1911 the site was offered at public auction, and a plan from that sale shows changes from the earlier plan of 1830 in the subdivision of property, the subsequent loss of garden space, and the addition of structures.

The New Orleans Railway and Light Company purchased the property and revived the attraction with an expenditure of $200,000. Features included a new rail terminal, restaurants, a boardwalk, a water slide into Lake Pontchartrain, a carousel (now in City Park), and a rail line about a mile into Lake Pontchartrain.[53] The site's popularity returned, and once again Spanish Fort was a center for entertainment and recreation. For two days in September 1912, the New Orleans Railway and Light Company gave its annual "outing," and about 15,000 people, employees of the railway and the electric and gas departments, along with their families, were "entertained at the company's expense. The outing was successful."[54]

The rejuvenated attraction competed, as before, with nearby West End, which had more extensive attractions, including numerous pavilions, amusement rides, three hotels, restaurants, bathhouses, and the Southern Yacht Club. In 1926 Spanish Fort closed; shortly thereafter the leisure activities that had started there a century before ended, subsumed by a federal project that erased much of the community's cultural history as it created new residential neighborhoods by moving the southern shore about a half-mile northward into the lake.[55]

By the beginning of the second decade of the twentieth century, the popularity of Spanish Fort and West End had firmly established new concepts of open-space possibilities in the public consciousness, creating demand by offering convenient access, lively content, and numerous attractions. Audubon Park and City Park were both established as public parks, and in 1914 the city added a new municipal park related to Lake Pontchartrain to its inventory of public open spaces. Now known as West End Park (it was once called Lakeview Park) this new park—a rectangle with rounded ends—took advantage of established public connections between recreation and the lakefront and responded to public perceptions of government responsibility, expectations of civic life, and tenets of the "City Beautiful" movement popularized by the World's Columbian Exposition of 1896 in Chicago. The park featured a large fountain in its center animated with colored lights, but it had none of the structures or amusement activities of neighboring venues. Nevertheless it was a public open space and restaurants and bars soon opened nearby, offering food and drink to those who visited the park.

The shift from privately owned open space to city-owned open space, a subtle change of which few were aware, signaled the beginning of the end for commercially operated open spaces in the community. Providing venues for outdoor recreation, once offered in privately owned venues, now was a function of municipal government. The unprogrammed attractions offered in early twentieth-century public parks were different from features of late nineteenth-century amusement parks; by then, public open space in New Orleans had become less a commodity for commercial gain and more a product of civic responsibility.

The trajectory of recreation-oriented open spaces in nineteenth-century New Orleans begins with commercially driven pleasure gardens that evolve into amusement parks and then into municipal parks, and these local pleasure gardens, together with examples from elsewhere in America, suggest unrecognized cultural and economic motivations for American public open spaces. The less understood entrepreneurial and pleasure-driven motives of these spaces differ markedly from the reform agendas, moral concerns, and didactic motives that served as the stimuli for open-space awareness and examples such as New York's Central Park in nineteenth-century America. In fact, such didactic motivations, spiritual and moral issues, and urban reform agendas had little impact on open-space design in New Orleans, if, indeed any at all.[56] Perhaps this explains the emphasis thus far in American landscape history on other cities where these motives are more obvious instead of communities like New Orleans where open spaces evolved though different paths and less high-minded ideals.

In examining pleasure gardens of New Orleans, we see that these spaces were influenced by marketplace economics, social conventions relating to race, and popular culture. From the earliest examples onward, examples were widely scattered, suggesting that their existence and locations responded to market opportunities afforded by capital, demand, site, and technology. What started as small urban pleasure gardens in the early nineteenth century gave way, by the end of the century, to much larger amusement parks on the city's edges. Small urban pleasure gardens were susceptible to pressures of development as the city expanded and as real estate became too valuable to remain open space. Advancements in technology brought lakefront attractions within reach and provided novel amusements to the public, and these resorts' more elaborate features provided locals with more lively and interesting forms of entertainment. Finally, by the century's end, city authorities had recognized the value of urban parks, providing new open-space attractions for the city's residents to enjoy.

That pleasure garden examples are found in New Orleans is not surprising, given the community's reputation, expressed best in the local saying "laissez les bon temps rouler."[57] There is still much to learn about these venues, but there are enough similarities among them to hazard a few generalizations. These resorts were all commercial ventures, with access granted on payment of subscription or admission fees. Food and beverage service was common; entertainment included musical offerings, theatrical presentations, and other spectacles, together with games and individual sports. Pleasure gardens were spatially organized and embellished with horticultural features, though specifics remain largely unknown. Throughout the nineteenth century pleasure gardens were sites for multilayered social interactions. Some were marketed as "family attractions"; others were venues primarily for adult audiences where local racial accommodations (first *plaçage*; then apparent ambivalence with regard to racial integration) enabled unfettered association among different racial groups. Finally, it is worth noting that pleasure gardens emerged as private enterprises in the early nineteenth century, well before municipal efforts to create large-scale public parks at the century's end.[58]

With a broad perspective, the history of pleasure gardens suggests that the evolution of American concepts of open space should include previously ignored European influences and vernacular examples from nineteenth-century American cities, as well as culture-based factors related to economics, race, gender, recreation, and entertainment. A greater attentiveness to such factors represents a new approach to American landscape history and urban form from which there is much to gain.

Chapter 7

Night and Day:
Illusion and Carnivalesque at Vauxhall

DEBORAH EPSTEIN NORD

Few literary evocations of Vauxhall Gardens fail to mention the presence or absence of light, and why should it be otherwise in accounts of a place visited almost exclusively at night? Fanny Burney's 1778 heroine, Evelina, remarks on the "numerous lights" illuminating the scene at Vauxhall but ends by focusing her attention on the "dark walks," those avenues left unlit for courting couples and predatory gentlemen. Boz, Charles Dickens's alter ego of the 1830s, recalls an enchanted place "served up beneath the light of lamps" and "a few hundred thousand of additional [ones] dazzl[ing] our senses."[1] The narrator of *Vanity Fair* (1847–48) also comments on the "hundred thousand extra lamps" that light the park in the era of the Napoleonic Wars and then follows Dobbin down the "dark walk" to visit the famed hermit of the gardens.[2] The dark is occasionally pierced by firecrackers and fire-balloons; fountains sparkle by lamplight; certain walks are illuminated; and enough light is shed for visitors to view paintings, watch musicians, and feast on "burnt wine, *ham-shavings*, chickens, sherry, and a lively drop of arrack-punch."[3] The very meaning of Vauxhall, as experience and memory, revolves around the relationship between illumination and darkness and, ultimately, around their literal and metaphorical associations with illusion, deception, and exposure.

Vauxhall's nocturnal identity—its dependence on the play of light and dark—is one of the features that links it to a number of other nighttime phenomena of the eighteenth and early nineteenth centuries, among them public masquerades and the "noctambulisme" or gas-lit *flânerie* that Walter

Benjamin identifies with mid-century Paris. Terry Castle, in *Masquerade and Civilization: The Carnivalesque in Eighteenth-Century English Culture and Fiction*, and Benjamin, in *Charles Baudelaire: A Lyric Poet in the Era of High Capitalism*, associate certain cultural motifs with nocturnal fête and spectacle that help to identify the power, appeal, and ultimate fragility of the aura surrounding Vauxhall.[4] Most salient among these are utopian impulses, especially with regard to the mixing of social classes; sexual license, promiscuity, or danger; nocturnal carnival as urban microcosm or distillation of urban experience; and the promise and risk of illusion. In the essay that follows, I consider Burney's *Evelina*, Keats's sonnet "To a Lady Seen for a Few Moments at Vauxhall" (1818; pub. 1844), Pierce Egan's *Life in London* (1821), Dickens's *Sketches by Boz* (1839), and Thackeray's *Vanity Fair* with an eye to the connection between these motifs and patterns of light and dark. My analysis has two end points: Dickens's sketch "Vauxhall-Gardens by Day," in which Boz asks what happens to the pleasure garden when the contrast of light and dark is withdrawn, and Oscar Wilde's "Impression du Matin" (1881), a fin-de-siècle rendering of the moment when night grimly turns to day.

Utopian Impulse

Writing about the class composition of eighteenth-century masquerades, Terry Castle notes what she calls the "paradox of masquerade sociology."[5] Though known for and indeed advertised as possessing an aura of "fashionable exclusivity," masquerades nonetheless saw a mingling of classes, with men and women of all social ranks encountering each other, their precise social positions sometimes unknown to their fellow revelers or obscured by costume and mask.[6] The carnivalesque feature of disguise protected the identities of some high-born attendees in their desire, or at least willingness, to mix with the hoi-polloi (both the King and the Prince of Wales were reported to have attended a public soirée in disguise in 1727), and the relatively low price of tickets, at least in the early part of the century, ensured that some folks with very modest resources could attend too.[7] The "promiscuous Multitude" at a masquerade that Joseph Addison described in the *Spectator* outraged some observers but delighted others, who celebrated the rare social mixing of chimney sweeps, apprentices, loose women, and nobility.[8]

Walter Benjamin emphasizes this same kind of social heterogeneity in his evocation of the nocturnal city, especially the Paris arcades in gaslight, and he interprets this mixing of ranks as an expression of utopian aspirations. Every epoch, he writes, looks both backward and forward in forming its dreams of an ideal future. Although such dreams derive their "initial stimulus from the new," they also gain strength and shape from what must inevitably be fantasies of the past.[9] So, grasping at certain elements of "prehistory" (or fictions of prehistory), we fasten on the notion of a "classless society." The old, the new, and the dreams of the present combine to generate "the utopias which leave their traces in a thousand configurations of life."[10] For Castle, too, the idea of carnival, or masquerade, has what she calls "utopian impulses."[11] Like Benjamin, she sees utopian cultural forms giving way to an articulation of political and philosophical ideas, to literary expressions of the desire for an egalitarian or less socially fettered society.[12]

Turning to accounts of Vauxhall, we see frequent references to this utopian or anarchic strain. Richard Altick comments that, in the eighteenth century, the modest entrance fee of one shilling produced "a clientele notable ... for [Vauxhall's] democratic spread."[13] Like masquerade, the pleasure garden allowed for the mixing of nobility with commoners and even with servants and soldiers.[14] In his 1941 *Vauxhall Gardens: A Chapter in the Social History of England*, James Granville Southworth underscores the social diversity of an early nineteenth century Vauxhall crowd, alluding not only to a mixture of social ranks but also to varying degrees of respectability and even criminality: "Honest citizens with their wives, apprentices with their masters' daughters, women of easy virtue, their pimps . . . , pugilistic hoodlums, and all other concomitants of a public benefit—even a nobleman or two."[15] Pierce Egan's Regency swells celebrate this mingling at Vauxhall as an unqualified source of pleasure. "To me," declares Bob Logic, Oxonian companion of Tom and Jerry, "Vauxhall is the festival of LOVE and HARMONY, and produces a most happy mixture of society. . . . Every person can be accommodated."[16] Egan's swells even sound a utopian note. The "brilliancy" of Vauxhall strikes Jerry Hawthorne as so superior even to the wonders of Bath that he declares it a "NEW WORLD."[17] This London pleasure garden, with its eclectic and variegated group of sybarites, overtakes the attractions of Bath, the spa city so closely associated with the social season and watering habits of the upper classes (Figure 7.1).

The trope of class mixing is central to the well-known Vauxhall chapter in *Vanity Fair*, but Thackeray, as we might expect, enlarges and complicates

Figure 7.1. George Cruikshank, "Tom, Jerry and Logic, Making the Most of an Evening at Vauxhall" from Pierce Egan, *Life in London* (1821), hand-colored engraving.

the trope in ways that reverberate through the rest of the novel. The episode of Jos Sedley's inebriation after imbibing too much arrack punch and his subsequent declaration that Becky Sharpe is his "dearest, diddle-diddle darling" is no mere comic set piece.[18] By the time the reader turns to chapter 6, called simply "Vauxhall," the novel has already established class distinction and social mobility as salient themes. The narrative has carefully identified the precise class position and trajectory of each character: Becky, the penniless art master's daughter; Dobbin, the grocer's son, now a successful military man; Amelia Sedley, whose parents have risen in the world; and George Osborne, whose father is a wealthy merchant with the pretensions of a well-born gentleman. The question comically though pointedly posed by the Vauxhall chapter is whether Becky Sharpe, invited to stay with her school-friend Amelia before she enters the world as a governess, will snag Jos Sedley, a civil servant in India (and the collector of Boggley Wallah), and coax a proposal from him at Vauxhall. Will there be something or someone to save her from her governess's fate?

The possibility of class mixing and even social anarchy is shadowed in the chapter by the theme of miscegenation. The Sedley parents can see that Becky has designs on their hapless son but console themselves with the fact that at least Jos hasn't brought them a "black daughter-in-law" from India or arranged for them to have "a dozen or so of mahogany grandchildren" in Boggley Wallah.[19] Britain's colonial ventures might produce such heirs, just as they have produced Becky and Amelia's schoolmate Miss Swartz, "the rich woolly-headed mulatto from St. Kitts."[20] Here, the colonies, with their opportunities for unpredictable mingling of black and white, form a strange analogue to Vauxhall, a place where it might be hard to discern the class or even the color of a fellow reveler. Even belowstairs in the Sedley home, far from the unpredictable climes of empire, "black Sambo" is in love with the (presumably white) cook.

Anticipating Jos's proposal to the déclassé Becky (the addled Jos thinks she's "distinguée"), Amelia and Mrs. Sedley are reconciled to the match, partly as the result of a sage reminder by the housekeeper, Mrs. Blenkinsop, that "we was only grocers when we married Mr. S . . . and we hadn't five hundred pounds among us."[21] Not only are the Sedleys open to this alliance but, when the Vauxhall outing ends in Jos's drunkenness, neither the demure Amelia nor Becky herself is deterred by his behavior. Indeed, they await Jos's proposal the following morning, Amelia dreaming of her bridesmaid's dress. It is George Osborne who scuttles the deal: He was "not overwell pleased that a member of a family into which he, George Osborne . . . was going to marry, should make a *mésalliance* with a little nobody—a little upstart governess."[22] George's snobbery, his unfounded sense of his family's own superiority ("You always were a Tory," Dobbin teases him, "and your family's one of the oldest in England"),[23] and his barely hidden disdain for the Sedleys's "low" status lead him to embarrass Jos so badly about his behavior that the collector of Boggley Wallah abandons his matrimonial plans and skips town. Mrs. Blenkinsop, now that any chance of a marriage has passed and Becky Sharpe is about to leave the Sedley home to make her own living, reverses herself and declares to the maid, Pinner, that she never did trust governesses anyhow, with their "hairs and hupstarts" and "wages . . . no better than you nor me."[24]

One way to read this Vauxhall chapter is to see the possibility for class mixing confined to the pleasure garden, the nighttime carnival of obscured identities and social mingling that provides a brief opening for Jos Sedley to marry an "upstart governess," but Thackeray is up to something a bit more satiric here and perhaps even a bit more serious. We know that in the rest of the novel Becky Sharpe will marry into the aristocratic family of Sir Pitt Crawley; Mr. Sedley will lose his money; George Osborne will be disowned by his father because he marries Amelia anyway; Jos will leave his life insurance to Becky; and, most significant, George, the snob, and Becky, the upstart, will enter into an intense, adulterous flirtation. Rather than providing a break from the strictures of English society, Vauxhall, with its upending of social morés and class hierarchies under the cover of night, may signal the unpredictable future of the Napoleonic era and beyond. Jos and Becky's carnivalesque encounter at Vauxhall might have been aborted before they could reach the altar, but deviation from conventional class arrangements is the order of the day in *Vanity Fair*.

Sexual License, Sexual Danger

Yet another way to look at Thackeray's Vauxhall episode is to see Becky Sharpe as a demi-mondaine, the courtesan she is destined to become or, more precisely, as a woman whose sexual status is ambiguous and up for grabs. Prostitutes were a common feature of Vauxhall, as of eighteenth-century masquerades and the Parisian streets Benjamin elegizes.[25] Masks, disguises, and the obscuring powers of dark—or gaslight—could make it difficult, however, to distinguish proper women from harlots. Unescorted women of the respectable classes might be taken for women of the night. Sexual danger, as well as the frisson of sexual freedom, might await all women in the gardens. Castle, emphasizing the libratory aspects of eighteenth-century masquerade, treats it as "a kind of collective foreplay—the Dionysiac preliminary to indiscriminate acts of love."[26] Thackeray, a Victorian writer chronicling a pre-Victorian world, balances his narrative between license and propriety. For him, Becky is and isn't a prostitute, Vauxhall is and isn't a "Dionysiac preliminary."

It was Fanny Burney, in her epistolary novel *Evelina*, who exploited this aspect of Vauxhall most fully, and she did so from a distinctly gendered perspective. In Letter XLVI, the innocent heroine, raised in a sheltered, rural world and now exposed to the corrupt ways of London society, gives an account of finding herself in a party on its way to Vauxhall. The only part of the journey that pleases her, she writes to her guardian Mr. Villars, is the Thames crossing. She finds the gardens themselves pretty but too formal, though she concedes she might have found them "enchanted ground" had she been in congenial company. But distaste turns to terror after her companions, the feckless Branghton sisters, decide to "take a turn in the dark walks," the site of assignations and illicit encounters.[27] There the young women are trapped by a party of drunken gentlemen who encircle them, jeering and hallooing, and seize Evelina, until she struggles free and runs off, straight into a second band of men. This next group grabs her too, and she is "almost distracted with terror" until she realizes that one of them is Sir Clement Willoughby, the man who has been pursuing her persistently throughout London.[28] Regarding him in this context as an ally and a potential savior, she begs him to help her, and he obliges, only to proceed to assault her himself. Evelina eludes him by walking forcefully away from the "dark walks" and toward the light. Sir Willoughby manages an apology, but she leaves Vauxhall nonetheless, declaring the experience of the pleasure garden a "disagreeable . . . evening's adventure!"[29]

This episode, which some have speculated had its origins in one of Samuel Pepys's 1667 diary entries, suggests that not only did respectable, unmarried women walk alone (however foolishly) in Vauxhall but they also risked being mistaken for women of easy virtue.[30] One of Evelina's assailants declares that she has the voice of the "prettiest little actress I have seen this age," whereupon Evelina vehemently responds, "No,—no,—no—*I am no actress*—pray let me go."[31] The interchangeability of women's bodies—the impossibility of distinguishing between a respectable woman and a prostitute (or an actress), especially in the dark—was a trope of writing about the nocturnal city, and sometimes the city *tout court*, throughout the nineteenth century. Was the woman walking alone on the street an independent spirit (later, a "new woman") or a streetwalker looking for customers? When, at the end of the Vauxhall episode in *Vanity Fair*, Mrs. Blenkinsop reminds us that Becky Sharpe is a wage earner, she signals something not only about the young adventuress's future as a disreputable woman but also about the risks attendant upon a woman who makes her own way in the world.

Urban Microcosm

Observers habitually compared nocturnal phenomena like public masquerades and Paris "noctambulisme" to the quintessential experience of the modern city. Terry Castle focuses on the "'strange Medley' of persons" that mimics the mixture of types in the "protean City itself."[32] For Benjamin, the covered shopping streets of Paris—the arcades—are "a world in miniature," navigable during the night because of gaslight.[33] "An arcade is a city," he writes, emphasizing the display of goods to be savored and consumed, as well as the sensory stimulation the nighttime *flâneur* might experience while walking under glass on marble floors.[34] Vauxhall, too, seemed to epitomize, to concentrate within a circumscribed space, metropolitan pleasures, opportunities, and, as we have seen, dangers. "If *enjoyment* is your *motto*," Egan's Bob Logic declares, "you may make the most of an evening in these Gardens more than at any other place in the Metropolis."[35] Evelina meets with the risks of the urban *flâneuse* exposed to the unwanted attentions of men; and Thackeray's Vauxhall party flirts with and then abandons the social anarchy and disorientation of metropolitan carnivalesque.

Each of these settings allows for distinctly *public* kinds of interaction. Similarly, the cultural forms that represent the city, the arcade, and the masquerade celebrate, or at least evoke, a particular set of emotions and sensations that inhere in public experience. Among these "public" forms, Castle includes the picaresque, a literary tradition that follows the hero on a journey outside the private sphere.[36] Benjamin focuses on other forms: *physiologies*, small paper volumes of graphic sketches representing an array of urban types, from criminal to dandy, and *feuilletons*, running sections of the newspaper that featured tidbits of news of the city.[37] Pierce Egan's *Life in London* combines the picaresque with elements of the literary sketch; and Thackeray's Vauxhall chapter is a novelistic set piece that borrows from urban sketches of the 1820s and 1830s, like Dickens's *Sketches by Boz*. The novel generally makes what Castle calls a "topographic shift" into the private sphere in the nineteenth century, when public, nocturnal entertainment ceases to figure prominently in narrative fiction. It is worth noting in this context that Benjamin describes the arcade as a cross between interior and exterior space (with the arcade, he writes, the "street becomes a dwelling for the *flâneur*").[38] The public masquerade and the pleasure garden share something of this inside and outside character and make of the city a more circumscribed and confined space.

These literary and popular forms—sketch, physiology, *feuilleton*, picaresque—emphasize fleeting, temporary exposure to urban life. One of the quintessential experiences of the crowd they capture is the momentary encounter, the fleeting glance of a desirable but anonymous figure, an attraction kindled in passing. Related to but distinct from the motif of sexual danger, these meetings or, more accurately, glimpses depend on the play of light and dark, the briefly illuminated face and subsequent disappearance into the night. Benjamin offers Baudelaire's sonnet "A une passante" as a poem about just such an urban occurrence, what Benjamin calls love "at last sight."[39] The poet's object of interest and desire is not obviously a woman of the streets but a woman "with majesty," "Graceful, noble, with a statue's form," dressed in mourning, who, as she passes, raises "in her poised hand" the flounces of her dress.[40] He sees her for but an instant:

> A flash—then night!—O lovely fugitive,
> I am suddenly reborn from your swift glance;
> Shall I never see you in eternity?

Is this "flash" (in French, "éclair") a literal moment of gaslight or lightning? the illumination of her glance? or, rather, a moment of revelation, of sudden lucidity? Has she passed, fully visible, beneath a lamp, only to vanish again into the dark? The *flâneur*'s sudden rebirth, the result of the woman's returned glance, animates him, and his last sight of her is a source of both bereavement and elation:

> Somewhere, far off! too late! *Never*, perchance!
> Neither knows where the other goes or lives;
> We might have loved, and you knew this might be!

The joys and pains of meeting *en passant* derive from the pure potential and the impossibility of love. The "pleasure that kills," Baudelaire calls it, naming the twinned feelings of unexpected delight and poignant loss.

This peculiar mix of pain and pleasure, associated with a wordless, brief encounter between male poet and female object of longing, also dominates a Vauxhall poem by John Keats, "To a Lady Seen for a Few Moments at Vauxhall." In this sonnet by a poet not typically identified with the nocturnal frissons of London life, the speaker recalls an occurrence—not an occurrence, really, but a sight—that haunts him still, five years later:

> Time's sea hath been five years at its slow ebb,
> Long hours have to and fro let creep the sand,
> Since I was tangled in thy beauty's web,

And snared by the ungloving of thine hand.
And yet I never look on midnight sky,
But I behold thine eyes' well memory'd light;
I cannot look upon the rose's dye,
But to thy cheek my soul doth take its flight.
I cannot look on any budding flower,
But my fond ear, in fancy at thy lips
And hearkening for a love-sound, doth devour
Its sweets in the wrong sense:—Thou dost eclipse
Every delight with sweet remembering,
And grief unto my darling joys dost bring.[41]

The sonnet's title emphasizes the painfully short-lived nature of the encounter—"Seen for a Few Moments"—and places it at the pleasure garden, though this setting is never mentioned in the body of the poem. Indeed, we would have no sense at all of the sonnet's context without the title, and we get no hint of urban entertainments or a noctambulist crowd. In Baudelaire's "*A une passante*," Benjamin points out, "the crowd is nowhere named in either word or phrase," and yet, he asserts, "the whole happening hinges on it."[42] The same could be said of Keats's sonnet: The very terms of the poet's longing and lingering entanglement in the memory of this woman's beauty depend on anonymity and a complete absence of words exchanged or introductions made, though the poem neither mentions surrounding company nor indicates a populated place. Indeed, Keats's sonnet scrupulously avoids urban imagery and is filled, instead, with references to natural phenomena: sea, sand, sky, "rose's dye," "budding flowers." His memory of the Vauxhall scene and the lady's beauty—her eyes, her cheeks, her lips—is triggered, somewhat perversely, by any and all glimpses of these aspects of the natural world. The remembering is compulsive—"I never look on," "I cannot look upon," "I cannot look on"—and always linked to a setting absent any marks of the city or the crowd.[43]

The occasion or moment Keats remembers, however, is classically urban: a love "at last sight," what decades later Arthur Symons would call one of the "chance romances of the streets," made possible by the fleeting, anonymous encounters of city life.[44] Like Baudelaire's *passante*, this "lady" silently engenders a type of intimacy between herself and the smitten walker. "I was tangled in thy beauty's web, / And snared by the ungloving of thine hand" he declares, suggesting that she had enticed, seduced, or even, spiderlike, set a trap for him. The image of the naked hand or, rather, the hand as it is undraped, conveys the sexual charge of this moment—wordless, anonymous, but indelible. This exposure of the hand—a kind of unmasking, perhaps akin to the intrigues of identity in the masquerade—focuses on one of the parts of the body that also draws the eye of Baudelaire's *flâneur*. His *passante* raises the flounce of her gown "in her poised hand." Eyes, too, attract both walkers. Baudelaire's speaker drinks, like a "trembling . . . madman," from his woman's eyes. Five years after the episode he recalls, Keats is still reminded of the lady's eyes whenever he looks at "midnight sky." Without any exchange of words and with the woman's body mainly concealed, hands and eyes become primary modes of communication: expressive, enticing, capable of conveying desire. Here, we have none of the sexual danger or predation remarked by many Vauxhall observers but rather a silent exchange of signals or, perhaps, the projection of the poet's longing onto the limbs and glances of the woman he passes.[45]

Despite the absence, except in its title, of direct reference to Vauxhall, Keats's poem takes its place with other evocations of the pleasure garden and, indeed, other urban nocturnes through its emphasis on the play of light and dark. The lady's eyes are no mere organs of flirtation but sources of light, and the poet is reminded of them by way of their opposite, the dark skies:

And yet I never look on midnight sky,
But behold thine eyes' well memoried light.[46]

The poet so deeply associates the "midnight sky," presumably a reminder of the nighttime visit to Vauxhall, with the light he remembers emanating from this woman's eyes, that he cannot see one without thinking of the other. The contrast and interplay between light and dark, so crucial to experiences and literary accounts of Vauxhall, here infuse the memory of this momentary attraction. The lights of the pleasure ground—the thousands of lanterns and lamps—are displaced onto the eyes of the woman glimpsed but "for a few moments." This close relationship of light to dark and its important role in the process of remembering returns at the poem's end. In the twelfth line the sonnet takes a discordant turn: the poet's ear "devours" the "sweets" of the lady's imagined voice ("in fancy at thy lips / And hearkening for a love-sound") "*in the wrong sense*" (emphasis added). We cannot know exactly what this "wrong sense" means until, perhaps, we get to the last lines. Now, the lady is no source of light but rather of shadow: "Thou dost eclipse / every delight with sweet remembering." Does the memory of past pleasure darken present joy, overshadow loves of the moment, interfere with the possibility of new passions? The last line, picking up the cue of the jarringly absolute "wrong sense," tells us that this shadowing or eclipse of "sweet remembering" amounts to "grief." The light and dark that, for the most part, remains a visual pattern in Vauxhall imagery, here coincides with what Baudelaire calls "the pleasure that kills," the mixture of pleasure and pain that inevitably accompanies a "love at last sight."

Illusion

Dark skies, gaslight, and scattered lanterns allow not just for spectacle but also for illusion, what Walter Benjamin refers to as "phantasmagoria."[47] Optical illusion, *trompe l'oeil*, and shadow act as forms of disguise and distortion. Respectable women are taken for women of the night, whores can pass as respectable women, and the ambiguity of their identities adds either an extra frisson or an element of danger to sexual or potentially sexual encounters. For Benjamin, the "phantasmagoria of the *flâneur*" is inseparable from gaslight, which seemed to transform the arcade (where the first gas lamps burned) from an exterior space or street to an interior one, creating a form of spatial and geographical illusion. In Vauxhall, as in the Paris of the mid-nineteenth century and the public masquerades of the eighteenth, illusion and its more insidious manifestation, deception, abound: fantasy, reverie, dream, sleepwalking, distorted vision, exteriors experienced as interiors, imagined utopias, and alternative and enhanced ways of perceiving material and social realities that may not bear scrutiny in the light of day. Visual tricks, aided by lanterns and nightfall, made Vauxhall: strips of tin "shimmering in the light of concealed lamps" created the appearance of a waterfall, while *trompe-l'oeil* paintings at the ends of long vistas charmed visitors into believing they approached the Temple of Neptune or the ruins of Palmyra.[48]

The illusions that delight Evelina's guides to Vauxhall strike her as vexing dissemblance, predictive, perhaps, of the assaults she will encounter as the evening wears on. Even before her companions lead her down the dark walks, however, she is struck by the inherent falseness of what she sees: "They led me about the garden," she writes, "purposely to enjoy my first sight of various other deceptions."[49] Her sex, her innocence, and her rectitude make Burney's Evelina an exception to the general acceptance and, indeed, savoring of illusion that visitors to Vauxhall in the eighteenth and early nineteenth centuries record. For the most part, the pleasure of typical nighttime visits, though sometimes inseparable from the lingering pain of aborted desire, centered precisely on the delight of being deceived. A sketch by Dickens, published first in the *Morning Chronicle* in 1836 and later in *Sketches by Boz* (1836), confronts the matter of illusion at Vauxhall head-on. In "Vauxhall-Gardens by Day" he meditates on the relationship between illusion and light—both gaslight and daylight—and makes the pleasure garden into the very emblem of our desire, even our need, for what Burney's heroine calls "deception."

Dickens's sketch, in which Boz, his urban-rambler persona, records impressions of Vauxhall in the noonday sun, marks the official daytime opening of the gardens in 1836. The words "disenchantment" and "disappointment" are repeated over and over again in the sketch, as Boz compares this unveiled Vauxhall to "a gas-light without gas."[50] The nighttime glitter and glory of the gardens, "served up beneath the light of lamps," has been replaced by shabbiness and a kind of grim nakedness.[51] Like Jonathan Swift's nymph, Corinna, getting ready for bed, stripping herself of one adornment after another—artificial hair, glass eye, fake eyebrows, false teeth—until she is left an unrecognizable form of "Lumps" and "Hollows," this Vauxhall is utterly exposed and all pretense of its beauty shed.[52] Mortification replaces mystery. Artifice jettisoned, a male singer whose imposing image Boz had seen lithographed on sheet music, looks "particularly small."[53] A fountain that had "sparkled so showily by lamplight" now looks like a "water-pipe that had burst."[54] With the sun, rather than gaslight, shining on the spangled dresses of rope-dancers, their "evolutions were about as inspiring and appropriate as a country dance in a family-vault."[55] "How different people *do* look by daylight," Boz declares, "and without punch, to be sure!"[56] Among the former delights of Vauxhall Boz mentions are the cosmoramas, scenes of natural beauty or historical importance enhanced and magnified for the viewer through lighting, peepholes, and lenses.[57] We can easily take the cosmorama as a metonym for the entire nocturnal experience of the gardens—an experience of illusion, heightened

Figure 7.2. George Cruikshank, frontispiece to Charles Dickens, *Sketches by Boz* (1836), engraving. Mary Evans Picture Library.

reality, enchantment, and what Jonathan Conlin calls "willed disbelief."[58] Daylight threatens this experience and the pleasures of deception enthusiastically embraced by Vauxhall crowds. What, if anything, will replace these now that the pleasure garden has been stripped of the disguising garments of dark and gaslight?

Boz expands on the unveiling of mundane Vauxhall realities as his sketch proceeds, but he concludes not with the thwarting of the human need for illusion but with new possibilities for gratifying it. One reason for opening Vauxhall during the day was to enable Charles Green to attract larger crowds to the launch of his "Royal Vauxhall" balloon (Figure 7.2).[59] Boz observes the crowd rushing toward the launch, primed for a miraculous sight. From the start, though, he takes a debunking tone. A little man in faded black with a dirty face touts the balloonist with inflated rhetoric. Then a member of the House of Lords ascends with Green. The little man in black confides that if his lordship becomes frightened and tries to climb out, Green will crack him over the head with a telescope and "stun him till they come down again" so as to maintain the illusion of equanimity and calm.[60] Boz remarks that a military band plays so raucously to accompany the launch that any man, no matter how timid, would be "only too happy to accept any means of quitting that particular spot of earth" and go up in a balloon to escape the din.[61] By the light of day, the launch, like the gardens themselves, seems more mundane than sensational. But, Boz informs us, his view of the scene does not square with the account he reads of it in the newspapers the following day. There he finds a glowing and much exaggerated rendering of the whole proceedings: It was the finest day imaginable, "gorgeously picturesque," and the ascent was mysterious, even miraculous. The amazing Green, suspended miles above the earth, claims to have been able to hear a man in a rowboat beneath him exclaim "My eye!" all by virtue of the echoing effects of the balloon.[62] Some mumbo-jumbo about the refraction of the sun's rays, atmospheric heat, and "eddying currents of air" add to the elevated tone of the newspaper account. A combination of mystification and bogus science helps to hype the launch and encourage readers to attend another the following week.

Ready for a new illusion, the press and the crowd welcome the miracle of the "Royal Vauxhall" balloon. Daylight, Boz suggests, might offer only a temporary setback, a momentary stripping away of the garments of enchantment. Gaslight may no longer shed its transformative glow, but the hawkers of fantasy can try to reinvent wonder, and some customers will always be ready to be deceived. The sunlit world of the 1830s may not signal the decline of the carnivalesque: Other outlets for utopian aspiration and clandestine pleasures might be found, and the need for fantasy—for deception—fulfilled in other ways. And the press, as Dickens notes, could perform its own alchemy, changing the tawdry to the glamorous, all on its own.

In Dickens's sketch, then, the harsh light of day certainly exposes Vauxhall and its shabby realities to a clear-eyed view, but it does not stifle the desire for illusion or completely preclude its fulfillment. What, then, of the other textual endpoint of this essay, Oscar Wilde's 1881 "Impression du matin," a poem about the city at the very moment when night turns to day? A fin-de-siècle lyric, influenced by Whistler's London paintings of the 1870s and by the Impressionist painters to whom the poem's title pays tribute, Wilde's "Impression" is not about Vauxhall or any other London pleasure garden.[63] In its echoes of some themes and imagery of Vauxhall representation, however, it suggests what is lost in the noctambulism of the late century and highlights, by contrast, what the illusions of the pleasure garden offered its visitors and memorialists.

Wilde's poem inevitably owes something to Wordsworth's "Composed Upon Westminster Bridge" (1802), a sonnet that catches the city as it awakens, wearing "the beauty of the morning."[64] But the similarities between the two poems serve only to underscore their striking differences. Wordsworth's London is undefiled, pure, "smokeless," calm, and, as yet, unpeopled.[65] The sight he describes is as fair as any place on earth, the sun that rises over the metropolis never shone more beautifully on any "valley, rock, or hill."[66] In Wilde's poem, the "blue and gold" of night—of the "Thames nocturne" that is now ending—have turned to a "Harmony in grey," and "chill and cold" accompany the yellow fog that creeps along the river, wharves, and bridges.[67] The aesthete's palette of ochre, yellow, and grey muddies the crystalline atmosphere of Wordsworth's London. The walls of Wilde's houses seem "changed to shadows," unlike Wordsworth's structures and edifices, which are all "open unto . . . the sky."[68] In "Impression," it is the dome of St. Paul's, not the blessed sun, that looms over the city. Wilde's morning brings no clarity but rather a city struggling, straining to awaken in the fog, shadow, and chill of the new day.

Wilde's poem culminates in a verse that introduces one figure to this, thus far, uninhabited scene, diverging further from the pristine, peopleless view from Westminster Bridge:

> But one pale woman all alone,
> The daylight kissing her wan hair,
> Loitered beneath the gas lamp's flare,
> With lips of flame and heart of stone.[69]

The coloration of the woman initially extends the dull palette of the city: pale, wan. But she is, nonetheless, out of place, a creature of night that has remained on the street beyond the hour of dawn. She "loiters," as if her habitual stance at the lamppost refers also to her ill-advised and prolonged lingering into day. A victim, as it were, of sunrise, she is at a disadvantage as the object of a dual and harsh illumination. The daylight "kiss[es]" her hair, the poem making that caressing act into a chilling punishment, and the gaslight exposes her garish lips—not pale but "of flame"—and, more devastating, her hardened soul. In the light of day, Boz's Vauxhall appears tawdry, commonplace, and distinctly unenchanted. Wilde's daylight reveals the muddy hues of a quotidian scene and a lone prostitute who has overstayed her welcome, if welcome she ever had.

Gone, then, is all illusion. The longed-for and willingly believed deception of Vauxhall and its nighttime encounters has simply become impossible in Wilde's fin-de-siècle London. Daylight's stripping away of pretense and disguise does not lead to other forms of distortion or deception—the newspaper, for instance, as in Boz's sketch—but to unredeemable disenchantment or, perhaps, to a vision of the city that never admitted illusion. No "love at last sight" or "chance romance of the streets," this encounter between the noctambulist poet, who has likely been out all night, and a prostitute, who is both sordid and pathetic, claims no mystified status of any kind. Unlike the disguised celebrants of masquerade, the mysterious *passantes* of Paris streets, and the obscurely glimpsed women in Vauxhall's dark walks, Wilde's "pale woman" cannot be mistaken for a respectable one. The poem admits no ambiguity about her occupation or social status, and it is precisely ambiguity that makes possible the atmosphere of carnivalesque, the tantalizing chaos of confusions of rank, the utopian possibility of class mixing, and the fantasy of cross-class romance. If, as Miles Ogborn has phrased it, "Vauxhall's pleasures had always been about experimenting with social roles" and about the "malleability of identity," this poem precludes the very possibility of experimentation, at least for the woman beneath the lamp—and her identity is fixed.[70]

Vauxhall ultimately stands as an instance of the need for fantasy and a world turned briefly upside down—a need that will be answered by other cultural forms as the modern age proceeds. The phantasmagoric spaces of modern spectacle in the eighteenth and early nineteenth centuries—masquerades, pleasure gardens, and arcades—would give way in later decades to the light-and-dark extravaganzas of department stores, moving pictures, and the underground, and to ever new *frissons* of urban rambling.[71] It is not that the world Wilde inhabits provides no opportunities for the lovers of illusion but rather that it signals a weakening resolve to sustain illusion and to fall for it, to take the dark for light and the woman of the streets for a duchess. Cosmoramas, nighttime shows under lantern light, and gaslit promenades in streets that are not streets all make use of light and dark, day and night, to trick the eye and foster fantasies, even utopian dreams of camaraderie and classlessness. Wilde registers the moment of dis-illusion and exposure, when the fog rolls in and the whore looks sad and grotesque. But then, so do Thackeray and Dickens: Once the arrack punch has worn off, Becky Sharpe is an unmarriageable, penniless social climber and governess, and, when Vauxhall is opened during the day, glittering fountains appear as burst water pipes and imposing tenors seem "particularly small." If the aim of Vauxhall is to deceive, the role of satire—going back at least to Swift—is to expose. Wilde adds a new gloss, however, for in his vision, exposure carries with it its own delights.

Chapter 8

"Strange Beauty in the Night": Whistler's Nocturnes of Cremorne Gardens

ANNE KOVAL

> It is the surprises and paradoxes of beauty in realism that he [Whistler] loves; he wagers to find charm in the modern town and modern fashion; a fairy vision at night from squalid facts, the fiery jewelry that is the accident of a vulgar fete, chimneys that are like campaniles, phantoms of moderns that are almost like princes.
> —D. S. MacColl, *Nineteenth Century Art* (1902)

The American painter James McNeill Whistler's series of nocturnal paintings, particularly the paintings of Cremorne Gardens, has gained historical significance as one of the key markers for early modernism, where the site—the spectacle at Cremorne—intersects with its avant-garde representation. As a popular pleasure garden in Victorian London, Cremorne can be seen as a site for modernity, the visual equivalent, of the café and cabaret life depicted by Whistler's contemporaries, the French Impressionists.

As the Impressionists sought out popular sites of urban leisure, Whistler found at Cremorne a suitable subject that could be immediately recognized as a controversial site for spectacle, one of the dominating features of modernity. The advent of Impressionism was arguably a visual response to the critic Charles Baudelaire's 1863 essay "The Painter of Modern Life," in which he encouraged the artist to look for subjects suitable for modernity—the ephemeral, the fleeting, the underworld—to "distill the eternal from the transitory" in depicting the subjects of the modern city.[1]

By the 1870s when Whistler painted and exhibited his nocturnes of Cremorne in Chelsea, Cremorne had long been established as a place of dubious reputation, associated with the mixing of classes, the swell or the dandy, and most significantly the prostitute. It is prostitution that came to be the downfall of Cremorne, leading to its closure in 1877, the same year that Whistler exhibited his most famous painting *Nocturne in Black and Gold: The Falling Rocket*, a work that led to the notorious *Whistler v. Ruskin* trial of the following year.

This chapter will examine the intersections of the site and spectacle of Cremorne Gardens as envisioned through the nocturnes of Whistler. By revisiting Whistler's nocturnes of Cremorne, arguably his most abstract and modern work, this chapter will examine the history of these pleasure gardens, particularly Cremorne's demise and the trial that hastened its closure in 1877, against Whistler's own agency of producing work that can be regarded as part of the larger avant-garde movement of Modernism.

One key feature of early Modernism and the rise of Impressionism was the controversy over the subjects depicted, many portraying the nightlife of Paris and prostitution. As Griselda Pollock has argued, prostitution became a marker for modernism: "Modernity is presented as far more than a sense of being 'up to date'—modernity is a matter of representations and major myths—of a new Paris for recreation, leisure and pleasure, of nature to be enjoyed at weekends in suburbia, of the prostitute taking over and of fluidity of class in the popular spaces of entertainment. The key markers in this mythic territory are leisure, consumption, the spectacle and money."[2] Although Pollock is speaking of Paris and the French Impressionists, the same can be said of Whistler and his decision to paint the pleasure gardens at Cremorne. Much of the city, as a site for modernity, involved the commodity of exchange, and the pleasure gardens functioned within the nexus of leisure activities brought on by these shifts in mid-century economic relations. Linked to this was the fact that Cremorne was a sought-out tourist destination, not only for visitors to the city but also for the urban dweller as a place for leisure and recreation. Dean MacCannell in *The Tourist: A New Theory of the Leisure Class* classifies tourism as a form of modernity, formed fundamentally through leisure and culture, in major city centers like London and Paris.[3]

Cremorne Gardens as a site occupied a liminal space, being neither city nor country. The gardens were situated within the village of Chelsea outside the metropolis of London, located along the Thames River but easily accessible by cab, omnibus, or steamer. Chelsea had been a working-class artisan

Figure 8.1. James Abbott McNeill Whistler, *Nocturne in Black and Gold: The Falling Rocket* (1875), oil on panel. Detroit Institute of Arts, USA. Gift of Dexter M. Ferry Jr./Bridgeman Art Library.

village and attracted a culture of bohemia with its mixture of artisans, intelligentsia, and the working-classes, including the historian Thomas Carlyle, the Pre-Raphaelite Dante Gabriel Rossetti, the poet A. L. Swinburne, and later Oscar Wilde. As early as 1860 Whistler chose to live in Chelsea and resided at different locations until his death in 1903.[4]

With the shifting demographics of class and urban planning what came to be known as Old Chelsea was replaced in the 1870s with the building of the Thames embankment and new property developments.[5] Gradually Chelsea was absorbed by greater London and all vestiges of the pleasure garden were erased by the housing estates that replaced it.

The Spectacle of Cremorne

The most complete history of Cremorne Gardens was written by Warwick Wroth in 1907.[6] The book opens with an etching by Whistler's most devoted pupil Walter Greaves and shows the grand entrance gates to Cremorne Gardens in Chelsea.[7] This set of gates is all that remains today of the once-fashionable Cremorne Gardens.[8] Originally the grounds that came to be known as Cremorne Gardens were the private estate of Cremorne House and Farm. By 1830 the estate had been purchased by Baron Charles de Berenger who opened the grounds to the public as Cremorne Stadium in 1832, which was used as a sports facility for shooting, fencing, swimming, and rowing until 1843. Gradually the facility began to include the galas, fireworks, and balloon displays that came to characterize Cremorne Gardens. In 1846 the grounds were purchased by Thomas Bartlett Simpson whose interest in the theater transformed the site into what is typically known as Cremorne Gardens. By 1850 more acreage and Ashburnham House were added to extend the gardens, which included avenues of mature trees, laid-out lawns, and extensive flower gardens with fountains, bowers, and ponds.[9] The Ordnance Survey map of 1865 shows that the pleasure garden included a marionette theater, circus, diorama, shooting gallery, bowling saloon, hermit's cave, gypsy's grotto (where fortunes were told), a garden maze, a fireworks gallery, two large halls, a stereorama, and a large Chinese dancing pagoda. The dancing platform was magnificently lit by flickering gaslight and came alive in the evenings. In addition, spectacular events were held, such as balloon ascents, acrobatics, tightrope walking across the Thames by the female Blondin, tournaments and fêtes, performances by the man-frog, the flying man, human curiosities such as the Russian dog-men, puppet shows, ballets such as *Giselle*, operettas, and seriocomic singers. By the 1860s Cremorne Gardens had become a full-blown commercial enterprise with over one hundred employees and its popularity surpassed the now-defunct Vauxhall as a place of entertainment. The contemporary journalist Edmund Yates in his book *The Business of Pleasure* noted this aspect of the gardens: "Here must be large capital involved, very many people engaged, constant supervision exercised, and all for the production of Pleasure."[10] Although a seasonal enterprise, the gardens employed hundreds of people, from the fifteen gardeners; to stage-set carpenters; to the corps de ballet and other performers; to the twenty-five-member orchestra and two bands, multiple waiters and barmaids, and cooks; to the fireworks master with his seven assistants. Yates describes the mixture of sounds he encountered at Cremorne, which provides a better understanding of the range of activities: "What do people hear at Cremorne? The band and the peripatetic brass instruments (which indeed are rather too much heard), and the rumble of the bowls in the American Saloon, and the crack of the rifles discharged by the sportsmen at the little tin beasts which slowly revolve, and the whizzing rush of the rockets, and the roar of the final firework explosion (which must be so comforting to a neighbour suffering with sick-headache, and just in his first sleep); and sometimes, I am given to understand, there may be heard by young couples at Cremorne the voice of love!"[11] This circus-like atmosphere was also noted by Wroth, "The gardens had a tendency to become congested with side-shows, flaring stalls and shooting galleries, too much suggesting a fair; but, unlike Earl's Court and the later Vauxhall, Cremorne remained a garden."[12] All these attractions reflect the commercial aspect of the gardens, an indication of the popularity and commodity culture it attracted. Cultural historian Lynda Nead describes Cremorne Gardens at mid-century as "a hybrid blend of rural retreat and theme park."[13] As a place of amusement or recreation, Cremorne was continually updating its offerings, intending to offset novelty with respectability.

The fairground or carnivalesque atmosphere attracted a mixture of classes from the working classes on their day off to the middle-class families who frequented the grounds in the late afternoon. Admittance to Cremorne was only a shilling, a cost that could be easily absorbed by the aspiring middle-class patron. The demographics of class and clientele varied, depending on the time of the day. Middle-class families would enjoy the gardens and attractions from the late afternoon to the early evening. Gradually shopgirls and workers would join the crowds to partake in the dancing that began in the evening and lasted well into the night. It was the nocturnal Cremorne where an open-air quality permeated with the outdoor dancing platform, the gardens, and the nightly fireworks as shown in this music sheet cover (Figure 8.2) of dancers performing the "Cremorne Quadrille."[14] Inherent in the dancing—many dances choreographed specifically for Cremorne—was the exchange of glances between the swirling partners. With the spectacle of fireworks scheduled for 10 P.M., the crowds would change again, and afterward the revelers took on another noted demographic. The cascade of fireworks signaled to the local prostitutes, commonly known as "gay women," to enter the gardens from their nearby brothels and abodes.[15] To most Londoners this temporal aspect at Cremorne was well known and certainly recognized in Whistler's painting *Nocturne in Black and Gold: The Falling Rocket*. Although this work is the most abstract of Whistler's paintings, its subject, the fireworks at Cremorne take on a loaded meaning. Using MacCannell's observation that "a spectacle is a simion (cluster of associated signs) ultimately based on iconic representation,"[16] this complexity of meaning can be read into Whistler's painting. The indicators are all present, from the title "The Falling Rocket" signifying the fireworks at Cremorne to the illuminated bandstand and spectators in the background. Although shown indistinctly, the figures in the foreground are single women, thus signaling their identity as prostitutes.[17] It is no wonder that the moral arbiter of taste, John Ruskin, took such offense when he first observed the painting on display at the newly opened Grosvenor Gallery in the summer of 1877. I will examine the proceedings and outcome to the ensuing *Whistler v. Ruskin* trial later in this chapter; first, though, I wish to further explore the visual culture and iconography that associated prostitution with Cremorne.

Prostitution was a common reality of the urban center and part of the history of Vauxhall and other pleasure gardens in London and Paris.[18] Cremorne was not unique as a complex and shifting site for the different classes. As Nead observes: "Cremorne was a mutable social space. To an extent, it gave people what they wanted to find. It was part of the moral geography of 'fast' London. It was on the circuit of night-spots in bachelors' guides to the city and it turned up regularly in fast-life fiction and journalism."[19] The visibility of the prostitute at Cremorne was ever-present in the

Figure 8.2. Alfred Concanen, Cover from *Marriott's Cremorne Quadrilles* (c. 1860s), chromolithograph. Royal Borough of Kensington and Chelsea, Family and Children's Service.

popular press. In *The Days' Doings*, the caption reads: "The Derby Carnival—Keeping It Up and Making a Night of It" (Figure 8.3) and depicts a number of revelers after a day of gambling at the Derby, engaging in heavy drinking with the "Gay women" of Cremorne. Such impropriety is shown by the drunken swell under the table with his head leaning against the silken skirts of a well-dressed prostitute. The looseness of morals and libation came to popularize Cremorne, known for its cheap champagne and restorative sherry. Cremorne Gardens was infamous for its sherry and the cobblers were particularly popular among the women clients, as can be seen in an engraving (Figure 8.4) titled "Life at Cremorne." The caption reads: "Now waiter, look sharp, and bring Sherry cobblers for two."[20] The public would have immediately identified the dubious status of these women, with their exposed ankles and undergarments. In the background, a gentleman-*flâneur* functions as the voyeur. The perpetuation of images of the prostitute in the popular press and her ubiquitous presence at Cremorne led to its eventual demise. Historian Wroth commented on a number of petitions, started as early as 1857, by the Chelsea Vestry, against the gardens for the "immoral character of its female frequenters [prostitutes], and its detrimental influence generally on the morals (and house property) of the neighbourhood."[21] These local brothels added to the angst of the Chelsea Vestry, as they decreased the value of property in the area and were another motive to bring down Cremorne. Wroth commented that as Cremorne aged, the rowdy and wanton element increased.[22]

The Last Days of Cremorne

By the 1870s the new proprietor of Cremorne was John Baum, notable for his associations with the theater. Part of his revamping of Cremorne was to bring various types of entertainment, such as comic-singers, operettas, and the ballet. Despite his valorous attempts to make the gardens more fashionable and respectable, his efforts were challenged by the rowdy crowds, and heavy drinking, though profitable, would spell the end for Cremorne. With a rising debate on places of public entertainment, including fairs, music halls, and pleasure gardens, Cremorne was one of many sites that suffered the fate of closure.[23] Reflecting this moral climate of the 1870s, with numerous petitions being signed against Cremorne, in 1872 Baum was refused the dance license from the Chelsea Vestry.[24] This was a serious economic loss

Figure 8.3. Unknown artist, "The Derby Carnival—Keeping It Up and Making a Night of It," from *The Days' Doings*, 27 May 1871. Private collection.

LIFE AT CREMORNE.—Now waiter, look sharp, and bring Sherry cobblers for two.

Figure 8.4. Unknown artist, "Life at Cremorne" (c. 1870s). Royal Borough of Kensington and Chelsea, Family and Children's Service.

and the increasing restrictions were making it difficult for Baum to operate Cremorne efficiently. Toward the end of 1876 a pamphlet was distributed titled *The Trial of John Fox, or Fox John, or the Horrors of Cremorne*. It was signed A.B., Chelsea, and was discovered to be Alfred Brandon, a Baptist minister and tailor from Chelsea. As an indictment of Cremorne, described as a "nursery of every kind of vice," the doggerel verse spelled out for anyone in the know the goings-on and ruin of reputation at Cremorne. The money-grubbing "John Fox," was meant to be John Baum, who regarded the pamphlet as libelous for defamation of character.

The libel action of *Baum v. Brandon* took place in May 1877 and proved to be popular in the press. A lengthy press clipping is preserved in a collection of papers relating to the history of Cremorne in the Kensington Library. In this press clipping on the proceedings of the trial the testimony of witnesses for Brandon is given, including previous employees from Cremorne, a local builder, a city missionary, and, most pertinent, a reformed prostitute. The first witness for the defendant was a young man called Fredrick Young who had been employed as check taker at Cremorne and reported that "gay women frequented the gardens—50 or 60 a night, more or less." Another witness for Brandon was John Munn, a waiter employed at the hotel in Cremorne Gardens, who spoke of the private rooms as being used largely by prostitutes:

> I was employed in May and June last year as waiter in the hotel. The four private rooms are well frequented indeed—(laughter)—I mean by young unfortunate ladies. They had companions. There are cabinets in the gardens, which are much frequented on Sunday nights by ladies. They have curtains which can be drawn. . . . There are dark places which can be frequented at night—the shrubberies. I have seen couples go there. They are most frequented on Sundays. The young ladies wore dresses with attraction—they were swell women. I have seen them paint their faces at the cash bar—it is called "making up." (Laughter).

Munn's account of "swell" women is telling about the clientele who came to the gardens and the popularity of the place on Sundays, in particular, as it was the working man's day off.

A Chelsea builder named Charles Haye testified as a witness to the quality of the housing in the neighboring vicinity of Cremorne: "In half a dozen streets near the gardens there was not one respectable house in ten, and yet they were well built. They were occupied by gay women." Another witness, a missionary called James Mercer, spoke of the "gay women" who frequented the Cremorne and who "on leaving the gardens went with men to houses in the neighbourhood." The most pertinent witness for Brandon was a reformed prostitute called Lucy Davis, who was the inmate of a reformatory. She had frequented Cremorne for three years, going by cab to the gardens. Her madam had a season ticket and her girls went up three or four times a week. Notably their arrival to the pleasure garden was generally around 10 P.M., when they "sought the company of men." The reporter wrote further: "Witness had committed acts of immorality in the gardens."[25]

Such reports filled the press and Cremorne's notoriety doubled. Despite the excellent witnesses for Brandon, Baum was able to claim victory but was only awarded a farthing in damages with each side paying their own costs.[26] With the rising costs of running a now-declining establishment and mounting pressures from his landlady, the widow of Simpson the previous proprietor and owner, Baum withdrew his application for his license and the contents of the gardens were auctioned off the following April. The owner, Mrs. Simpson, lost no time in leasing the land to developers and within the next year, much of Cremorne Gardens had become terraced housing for the middle classes. The *Daily Telegraph* reported of this inevitable end to Cremorne, pointing out that the impending economics of urban development had closed many earlier pleasure gardens: "Cremorne Gardens, like old Marylebone, old Ranelagh, and old Vauxhall, had become absorbed by London the irrepressible and the insatiable. Thirty years ago Battersea was to most intents and purposes a sequestered little village, and Cremorne was, comparatively speaking, in the country."[27] Examining the Ordnance Survey Map of 1865 of Chelsea and comparing it with a map of approximately thirty years later, the sprawl of urban London is most apparent. Little remains of Cremorne Gardens, with only the road named after it. The working-class and bohemian Old Chelsea was replaced by new housing for the middle classes. This development continued into the next century when the *Daily Chronicle* reported: "The entire face of historic Chelsea is undergoing a change and street after street of artisan dwellings has been and continues to be leveled as though swept down by an enemy's guns, and blocks of fashionable mansions are springing up in their place. Hundreds of small traders have seen their businesses swept away at a blow, while thousands of working people have been shipped off to all parts of London in search of other homes."[28] Approximately 20,000 working-class inhabitants were displaced during the 1870s to the turn of the century. Despite this gradual exodus, Chelsea was growing in population, from 40,000 inhabitants in 1841 to double that number in 1881 and rising to 95,000 by 1901, signifying the increasing middle-class demographic of greater London.

The Artist-*Flâneur*

It was the disreputable Cremorne of the 1870s that Whistler capitalized on in his representations of the pleasure gardens. This is where he is closest to his French contemporaries, the Impressionists, in his representation of popular culture. As Cremorne degenerated and became less appealing to bourgeois respectability it became a suitable and contentious subject for the painter. Whistler was not alone in seeking out questionable subject matter

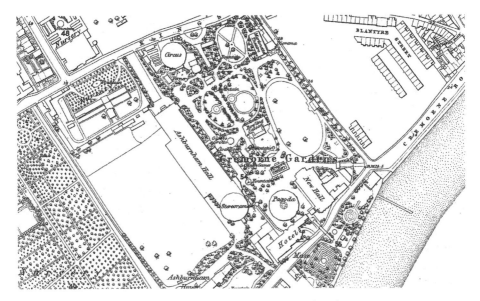

Figure 8.5. Cremorne Gardens, Ordnance Survey Map (1865).

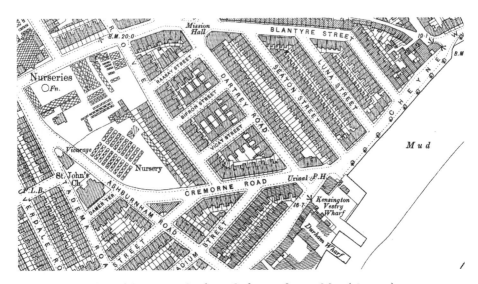

Figure 8.6. Site of Cremorne Gardens, Ordnance Survey Map (1894–95).

for representation, and his alignment with Impressionism at this time is most evident. Trained in Paris he quickly came to be associated with the French avant-garde, including Gustave Courbet, Edouard Manet, Edgar Degas, and others, who soon would be recognized as the Impressionists. As early as 1862 Whistler's etchings of the Thames found favor with the important critic Charles Baudelaire who described them as "the profound and intricate poetry of a vast capital."[29] The following year Baudelaire published his key essay "The Painter of Modern Life" in *Le Figaro*, where he described the role of the modern painter as the *flâneur*: "For the perfect flâneur, for the passionate spectator, it is an immense joy to set up house in the heart of the multitude, amid the ebb and flow of movement, in the midst of the fugitive and the infinite. To be away from home and yet feel oneself everywhere at home; to see the world and to be the centre of the world and yet remain hidden from the world—such are a few of the slightest pleasures of those independent, passionate, impartial natures which the tongue can but clumsily define. The spectator is a *prince* and everywhere rejoices in his incognito."[30] Although Baudelaire was speaking of Paris, his words could equally apply to London where Whistler sought out the urban subject for his paintings of the seventies. In London Whistler, as artist-*flâneur*, sought out suitable subject matter, looking for the equivalent of the Impressionist café-cabaret life of Paris. To Whistler, living in Chelsea, the nearby Cremorne Pleasure Gardens served as such a site for modernity. In the evening Whistler could stroll along the new Chelsea Embankment to the south entrance of the gardens where he would be greeted with the nocturnal spectacle of Cremorne.

One of Whistler's pupils, Walter Greaves, produced an etching (Figure 8.7) depicting Whistler the suitably dressed *flâneur*, strolling within the grounds of Cremorne Gardens, with the easily recognized bandstand rising behind him. Shown to the right is the infamous hotel with a questionable woman leaning against a doorframe. Although Greaves sets the scene in daylight, he is showing a more typical late-evening representation of Cremorne, when the revelers come out and the prostitute was the norm. The body language of the woman standing against a doorframe with one hand on her hip suggests solicitation and is not typically the gesture of what is considered a respectable woman. Whistler is clearly depicted by Greaves as the artist-*flâneur*, witness to the colorful scenarios of Cremorne before him. Griselda Pollock further conceptualizes the *flâneur* as belonging to—but still apart from—the crowd: "One of the key figures to embody the novel

Figure 8.7. Walter Greaves, *The Dancing Platform, Cremorne Gardens* (c. 1866), etching with drypoint. © The Trustees of the British Museum.

forms of public experience of modernity is the flâneur or impassive stroller, the man in the crowd who goes, in Walter Benjamin's phrase 'Botanizing on the asphalt.' The flâneur symbolizes the privilege or freedom to move about the public arenas of the city observing never interacting, consuming the sights through a controlling but rarely acknowledged gaze, directed as much at other people as at the goods for sale. The flâneur embodies the gaze of modernity which is both covetous and erotic."[31]

This covetous but distanced gaze of the *flâneur* can be seen in Whistler's own paintings of Cremorne Gardens at night. Notably all of his paintings of Cremorne are depictions of the night. In *Cremorne Gardens, no. 2*, Whistler shows a crowd scene at night after the fireworks at 10 P.M. The nocturne of *Cremorne Gardens, no. 2*, situates two lavishly dressed women at the center of the composition being greeted by a man who lifts his top hat to the women. Other unattached women drift about the gardens and to the right of the composition two men are seated at a table imbibing a few drinks. The painting acts as homage to the Baudelairian concept of modernity where the city becomes the site for spectacle: "The pageant of fashionable life and the thousands of floating existences—criminals and kept women—which drift about in the underworld of a great city."[32] The moody, even mysterious quality of Whistler's nocturne conjures up the very personification of night at Cremorne. This is a modern painting about the contemporary social and sexual relations between men and women taking place at Cremorne once the fireworks were spent, when the atmosphere at Cremorne transformed. Although Whistler depicts the women as elegant and Watteau-like in their trailing dresses to a discriminating Victorian audience the subject was not difficult to discern.[33]

Art for Art's Sake

For the sake of argument it is worth examining a work by the Victorian artist Phoebus Levin against Whistler's painting (Figure 8.8), *Cremorne Gardens, No. 2*. Both artists depict separate locales within the pleasure garden and share the subject of a mixed crowd, yet the paintings couldn't be more different. Levin's crowd scene (Figure 8.9) has a greater affinity to the genre paintings of William Powell Frith than to the Whistler.[34] As in Frith's paintings, the scene is a recognizable landmark, in this case the famous dancing platform at Cremorne. The picture is laden with anecdotal details

Figure 8.8. James Abbott McNeill Whistler, *Cremorne Gardens, No. 2* (c. 1870), oil on canvas. Metropolitan Museum of Art, New York. John Stewart Kennedy Fund, 1912. © Photo SCALA, Florence.

Figure 8.9. Phoebus Levin, *The Dancing Platform at Cremorne Gardens* (1864), oil on canvas. © Museum of London.

that the Victorian audiences admired. Particular classes and types are represented that would be immediately recognized by the viewer familiar with Cremorne. To the left, the infamous dining cabinets display an amorous couple, with the woman throwing flowers on the crowd below. Also included for narrative interest are the numerous soldiers, beggar children, performers, demimondes, and potential criminals, dependent on their costume, physiognomy, or gestural expression for a clear visual reading. The painting is laden with visual cues as to how to interpret the colorful life within. Little ambiguity is left for the beholder to speculate or even meditate on the image. All is spelled out in unambiguous visual representation.

Whistler's image is quite different, full of atmosphere and mystery, speculative in the theory of art for art's sake, where all is suggestion.[35] One artist is all about description; the other is all about interpretation. Where one artist mimics nature as closely as possible, the other interprets nature. As Whistler poetically wrote: "The imitator is a poor kind of creature. If the man who paints only the tree, or flower, or other surface he sees before him were an artist, the king of artists would be the photographer. It is for the artist to do something beyond this."[36] Many of these ideas evolve from the writings of Baudelaire and the concept of "Art for Art's Sake" that also influenced the work of Manet and the Impressionists. One key difference between Whistler and Levin is in their treatment of paint and surface. Levin's work falls into the category of high finish where the surface reflects little of the brushwork or personal calligraphy of the artist's hand. Whistler's work by comparison lacks finish or detail, allowing for a more allusive or ambiguous reading of what is actually represented. We see the painterly brush of the Impressionist painter who allows the surface of the canvas and the paint to speak for itself. Here is "Art for Art's Sake" where the painting is not an illustration for a narrative, as so many Victorian paintings were, but existed for its own sake. It is in Whistler's nocturnes where his affinity to the ideology of the French Impressionists is most apparent and where his aesthetic theory is in alignment with his painterly practice.

Notably the Aesthetic Movement, with Walter Pater's claim that all art aspires to the condition of music, was a current ideology when Whistler was creating his nocturnes and producing musical titles for his paintings.[37] By subjecting his work to a musical title such as "nocturne" Whistler was able to focus attention on the painting itself and away from the constraints of subject or narrative as the overriding concern. The artist was fully aware of these innovations when he wrote to a friend in Paris of his objectives:

"They are not merely canvasses having interest in themselves alone, but intended to indicate slightly to 'those whom it may concern' something of my theory in art. The science of color and 'picture pattern' as I have worked it out for myself during these years."[38] Whistler's awareness of having worked out a "science of color" and "picture pattern" is critical to understanding his theoretical leanings at this time. His mention in the letter of "those whom it may concern" refers to his French artist colleagues who would be privy to the Whistler exhibition currently on view at the Durand-Ruel Gallery in Paris.

Whistler further articulates his arguments on "Art for Art's Sake" on the eve of his 1878 trial with Ruskin. Whistler in a letter to *The World* states: "As music is the poetry of sound, so is painting the poetry of sight, and the subject-matter has nothing to do with harmony of sound or of colours." He argues: "Art should be independent of all clap-trap—should stand alone, and appeal to the artistic sense of eye or ear, without confounding this with emotions entirely foreign to it, as devotion, pity, love, patriotism, and the like. All these have no kind of concern with it; and that is why I insist on calling my works 'arrangements' and 'harmonies.'"[39] According to Whistler, art should be regarded as autonomous from society, in direct opposition to the Ruskinian notion of attaching moral and ethical values to art.

Whistler v. Ruskin Trial

In the summer of 1877 Whistler was invited to exhibit work at the inaugural opening of Grosvenor Gallery, considered the major venue for the Aesthetic artists of the late 1870s and early 1880s. Of the eight works that Whistler displayed, only one painting was for sale, listed under the title, *Nocturne in Black and Gold: The Falling Rocket*. The listing price of 200 guineas was not a high price for an established artist. It was this painting that became the target for Ruskin's often-quoted criticism published in the summer issue of *Fors Clavigera*: "For Mr. Whistler's own sake, no less than for the protection of the purchaser, Sir Coutts Lindsay ought not to have admitted works into the gallery in which the ill-educated conceit of the artist so nearly approached the aspect of wilful imposture. I have seen, and heard, much of cockney impudence before now; but never expected to hear a coxcomb ask two hundred guineas for flinging a pot of paint in the public's face."[40]

Whistler, for his part, was clearly courting controversy when he chose to exhibit his *Nocturne in Black in Gold: The Falling Rocket* at the Grosvenor Gallery in the aftermath and with the publicity of the *Baum v. Brandon* trial held in May 1877. The current notoriety of Cremorne was implicitly linked to Ruskin's criticism, a criticism that led inevitably to the lawsuit *Whistler v. Ruskin*, in which the artist sued the critic for libel.

Ruskin's attack on Whistler's work can be read as a very complex response. On the one hand, the more abstract, nonnarrative painting that the artist was producing, what Ruskin perceived as a daub in paint produced in a few hours, was the antithesis of the detailed, labor-intensive paintings of the pre-Raphaelites and other artists he supported. According to Ruskin, labor equaled cost.

The two-day trial took place in November 1878 when Ruskin's counsel, well prepared by Ruskin who was too ill to attend, focused their inquiries on the concept of labor equaling cost.[41] Another line of questioning related more closely to the specificity of site. Whistler's *Nocturne in Black and Gold: The Falling Rocket* was seen as an incarnation of the sins at Cremorne, the signaling fireworks and single female figures embodying the temporal reality of prostitution. This specific site of Cremorne Gardens was a key aspect of the questioning by Ruskin's counsel, well versed by their client. Under cross-examination, Sir John Holker, as Ruskin's defense, asked Whistler to define the subject of the picture *Nocturne in Black and Gold: The Falling Rocket*. Whistler's reply, "It is a nightpiece and represents the fireworks at Cremorne Gardens," piqued Holker to further ask: "Not a view of Cremorne?" Whistler responded, "If I called it a 'View of Cremorne' it would certainly bring about nothing but disappointment on the part of the beholders. It is an artistic arrangement. That is why I call it a 'nocturne.'" When asked to define a nocturne, Whistler spoke with characteristic eloquence: "I have, perhaps meant rather to indicate an artistic interest alone in the work, divesting the picture from any outside sort of interest which may have otherwise attached to it. It is an arrangement of line, form and colour first; and I made use of any incident of it which shall bring about a symmetrical result. Among my works are some night pieces; and I have chosen the word Nocturne because it generalises and simplifies the whole set of them."[42] Whistler's primary concern was not with narrative but with the formal problems of line, form, and color.

Later in the trial, Ruskin's defense returned to the notoriety of Cremorne Gardens: "Passing to the Cremorne Nocturne, I do not know what the ladies would say to that, because it has a subject they would not understand—I hope they have never been to Cremorne—(laughter)—but men will know more about it."[43] Ruskin's lawyer was alluding to the sexual politics at Cremorne where respectable women were rarely seen. According to Pollock: "To enter such spaces as the masked ball or the café-concert constituted a serious threat to a bourgeois woman's reputation and therefore her femininity. The guarded respectability of the lady could be soiled by mere visual contact for seeing was bound up with knowing. This other world of encounter between bourgeois men and women of another class was a no-go area for bourgeois women."[44] These sexualized spaces of the city were off limits to the bourgeois woman. Likewise the pleasure garden was forbidden territory, as Wroth recorded in his account of Cremorne: "It was not, for one thing, a place that ladies (in the strict sense of the word) were in the habit of visiting, unless, perhaps, (as Mr. Sala puts it) 'in disguise or on the sly,' or, at any rate, under the safe conduct of a husband or brother. Ladies of some sort were, no doubt, considerably in evidence there, though we are not to think of Cremorne as so entirely given over to 'drink, dancing and devilry' as its sterner critics declared."[45] Whistler's dubious association with Cremorne as witnessed during the *Whistler v. Ruskin* trial undoubtedly affected the eventual outcome of the trial. Although the artist won the trial, he was only awarded a farthing in damages and both sides were required to pay court costs, the same outcome as *Baum v. Brandon*. The comparison to the Cremorne trial of the previous year was not lost on Whistler or the press.[46]

The Legacy of Whistler's Cremorne

> If we wish to know the extent of Whistler's legacy, we must ask ourselves to what has he opened our eyes. . . . The revelation may be a mere pattern of form and colour—"such stuff as dreams are made of"— . . . or unveil, like Whistler, strange beauty in the night.[47]
> —*Frank Rutter,* James McNeill Whistler: An Estimate and a Biography *(1911)*

In the nocturnes, Whistler turned to a less descriptive and more interpretive representation of nature, in allegiance with French Impressionism.

Arguably his greatest innovation, the nocturnes, allowed the artist to expound his theories on art. In the *Whistler v. Ruskin* trial the witness box provided the artist with a platform to inform the public of his aesthetic theories concerning painting. It was in his later "Ten O'Clock Lecture" given in London in 1885, notably at ten o'clock at night, where Whistler fully articulates his theoretical concerns.[48] Although Cremorne Gardens had been closed for nearly a decade, its memory was conjured up in the public's mind when Whistler poetically stated: "And when the evening mist clothes the riverside with poetry, as with a veil, and the poor buildings lose themselves in the dim sky, and the tall chimneys become campanili, and the warehouses are palaces in the night, and the whole city hangs in the heavens, and fairy-land is before us."[49] As the industrial Thames is transformed into art so too is the tawdry aspect of Cremorne at night where, gaudy spectacle is re-imagined, "and fairy-land is before us." Although Cremorne Gardens had long been sold off, subdivided and replaced by new housing, the memory lingered on, forever, in Whistler's atmospheric nocturnes and poetic statements. Whistler as preservationist, contrary to Ruskin's beliefs, immortalized Cremorne and paradoxically preserved it as a site for modernity. As the theorist Guy Debord once speculated: "The spectacle is not a collection of images; rather, it is a social relationship between people that is mediated by images."[50] Whistler's nocturnes of Cremorne Gardens function within this relational aesthetic by disrupting the conventional perception of spectacle and creating a "fairyland" from squalid facts. "In a world which really is topsy-turvy, the true is a moment of the false."[51] By applying Debord's use of détournement, whereby spectacular images or language disrupt the fluidity of spectacle, the practice of the avant-garde as seen by Whistler's nocturnes of Cremorne takes on new meaning.

Chapter 9

Edwardian Amusement Parks: The Pleasure Garden Reborn?

JOSEPHINE KANE

In early 1907, the *Manchester Evening Chronicle* made an intriguing announcement. Manchester's Royal Botanical Gardens, opened in 1829 at Old Trafford, were undergoing a radical transformation. Under the direction of American businessman John Calvin Brown, the plant houses, fruit trees, flower beds, and rockeries were to be swept away, and many of the old architectural features of the gardens, including the "tunnel-alcove," ivy-covered archways, and music stands, demolished. In their place, the White City Amusement Park—"such as are to be found all over the United States"—was being created at a reported cost of £50,000.[1] The plans for the twenty-acre site were on "a most lavish scale," with a "huge tower, pavilions, lakes, gondolas, switchback runs, side shows of every variety, new band stands and refreshment rooms, and the place will blaze with . . . over 60,000 electric lights."[2] The centerpiece of the park would be a giant Water Chute and one of the first Scenic Railway roller coasters in England.[3] The intention is clear: Manchester was to have a new kind of outdoor entertainment landscape.

The reinvention of the Botanical Gardens was greeted with more than a hint of dismay from some quarters. In March, the amusement industry trade newspaper, the *World's Fair*, reported: "The hustling American, so to speak, is 'right here,' and his strong-armed satellites are hard at work driving stakes into the grounds of romance. . . . The well-kept garden paths, with their fringes of green and their background of budding plants, are reverenced no longer; the 'modern' artistic eye is on them, and now they

Figure 9.1. *White City, Manchester* (1910), postcard. Private collection.

are being walked upon by heavy-booted navvies, digging and hammering everywhere."[4] But, despite the ambiguity toward the new manager, it is clear that the dramatic rebirth of the gardens was understood as a sign of the times, a process that—although periodically troublesome—was an inevitable part of progress. The report went on to concede that "the great object of the organisers of this dazzling pleasure ground-to-be is to banish dullness, and they are sparing no effort to secure the biggest novelties and the newest features which the active American mind can suggest."[5]

The creation of an amusement park at Old Trafford proved very profitable. During its first season, more than 750,000 visitors flowed through the White City's ornate entrance gates, and profits were reinvested in new rides and attractions (Figure 9.1).[6] In the autumn of 1907, buoyed by his success, Calvin Brown announced plans to build a chain of amusement parks across the country, starting with Leeds and New Brighton.[7] Two years later, he also controlled the amusements at London's Earl's Court exhibition ground and at two newly built parks on the Continent: La Rabassada Park in Barcelona and Magic City in Paris.[8] In December 1910, Brown announced a plan to organize an international chain of amusement parks, with a one-guinea season-ticket plan for unlimited admission to Earl's Court and the White Cities at Paris and Manchester. He had even begun negotiating for reciprocal arrangements with American amusement parks. "It is quite probable," commented the *World's Fair*, "that before Mr. Brown ceases developing his idea there will be practically a world-wide interchangeability of amusement park season tickets."[9]

Calvin Brown was far from a solitary visionary. The Edwardian era produced a number of wealthy entrepreneurs who recognized the huge potential for amusement parks as new forms of commercial entertainment. The earliest parks had begun evolving in England around the turn of the twentieth century, but the opening of Manchester's White City coincides with the beginning of a frenzied phase of investment in American-style amusement parks across the country, a period that—though short lived—would have a lasting impact on British popular entertainment. Brown's international scheme never materialized, but it reveals the energy and optimism that infused the amusement-park world in 1910.

Springing up in urban centers and seaside resorts all over Britain, amusement parks enjoyed startling success, with huge numbers of visitors seeking out the pleasurable mix of fast-flowing crowds, thrilling rides, and spectacular landscapes they offered. Amusement parks were the magpies of the entertainment world, selecting the most popular and profitable amusements and combining them within one site for the first time. Their appeal transcended age, gender, and class boundaries, attracting children and adults, men and women from varied backgrounds in vast numbers. Between 1906 and 1914, more than thirty major amusement parks operated across the country and, by the outbreak of World War I, millions of people visited these sites each year.[10] The amusement park had become a key component in the pleasurescape of twentieth-century Britain.

Calvin Brown and his peers proclaimed themselves pioneers of modern entertainment, providers of "ideal outdoor amusement resorts" and "castles in the air."[11] But did the experiences on offer really mark a significant break with the past? Or were they simply a new expression of the spectacular entertainment and social mixing that had made the pleasure gardens of the eighteenth and nineteenth centuries so successful? Focusing on the Edwardian heyday, this chapter begins by sketching the phenomenon of the early amusement parks, tracing their emergence and the characteristics that came to define them, before turning in more detail to the particular kinds of experiences they provided. In doing so, this chapter considers the extent to which the Edwardian amusement parks preserved the legacy of earlier pleasure gardens.

Figure 9.2. *Entrance to Dreamland, Coney Island, N.Y.* (c. 1906), postcard. Private collection.

Early History

The concept of an enclosed and a permanent amusement park originated at Coney Island, New York—a small island directly south of Brooklyn, which began attracting visitors in the early 1800s. By the end of the century Coney was famous as a popular resort for the New York masses and it soon became synonymous with the enormously successful amusement parks that had developed there.[12] Its three parks—Steeplechase, Luna, and Dreamland, opened between 1897 and 1904—contained reenactment spectacles, native villages, fairground booths and refreshments, novelty games and, in particular, a variety of the latest roller coasters and other mechanical rides. The parks were characterized by large flamboyant buildings decked with electric lights to create an otherworldly atmosphere. Day-trippers converged on Coney in their millions during the summer season.[13] More important, the amusement-park formula established there was replicated throughout America. By 1906 more than 1,500 parks were in operation across the *United States*.[14]

Britain was not far behind. Roller coasters and similar devices in fact predated the amusement parks, as they had done in the United States. Early

Figure 9.3. Jean Nicolas Lerouge after Louis Garneray, *Promenades Aériennes Jardin Beaujon*, (1817), etching. Mary Evans Picture Library.

incarnations of thrill rides can be traced back to the medieval trade fairs of Europe and, from the early 1800s, to the Montagnes Russes (essentially giant slides) installed in French pleasure gardens. Two such slides opened in Paris in 1817: the Montagnes Russes at Belleville and the Promenades Aeriennes at Beaujon Gardens (Figure 9.3). But the first recognizable roller coaster was La Marcus Thompson's Gravity Pleasure Switchback Railway, built at Coney in 1884.[15] The ride appeared in Britain at Skegness just one year later and thereafter roller-coaster-type rides proliferated. Interestingly, many of the early switchbacks of the late 1880s were built on sites of natural beauty, such as at Matlock Baths, in Derbyshire, at Devil's Dyke in Sussex, and on Folkestone's much-admired sea front.[16]

Britain's first amusement park opened on Blackpool's South Shore in 1896. By 1903 the collection of rides and stalls was referred to as an "American amusement park," and the title of Pleasure Beach first appeared in advertisements in 1905.[17] On the eve of World War I, the Bank Holiday crowd at the Pleasure Beach reached 200,000.[18] As the largest and longest-serving amusement park in Britain, Blackpool Pleasure Beach cast the die

Figure 9.4. Blackpool Pleasure Beach from the Sea (c. 1920), photograph. © Blackpool Pleasure Beach. By kind permission of the Thompson Family, Pleasure Beach Resort, Blackpool.

for a growing number of successful competitors, including the parks that became a standard element of London exhibition grounds, such as Earl's Court, White City (Shepherd's Bush), and Kensington's Olympia.

Amusement parks quickly began appearing around the country. In particular, the years 1907 to 1912 witnessed a wave of daring schemes, championed by an experienced group of promoters and businessmen, including Charles Blake Cochran, the internationally renowned Kiralfy brothers and, as we have seen, John Calvin Brown. These men were the leaders of the Edwardian amusement-park world, drawn from the worlds of theater, advertising, and engineering. Their high-profile success spawned numerous imitators, but, in an atmosphere of fierce competition, many ventures proved short-lived. The National Archives holds the records of hundreds of failed schemes, which were launched as public liability ventures during this period.[19] The Manchester White City, despite huge visitor numbers, ran for just seven years.[20] Nevertheless, an impressive number did survive, including parks at Liverpool, Edinburgh, Birmingham, Rhyl, Newport, Morecombe, Southend, Douglas, Whitley Bay, Southport, Great Yarmouth, Skegness, Cleethorpes, and Scarborough. As a result, by 1914 the vast majority of Britons would have had firsthand experience of an amusement-park landscape.

Figure 9.5. *Wiggle-Woggle and Racing Toboggan, Great White City, London* (1908), postcard. © Hammersmith and Fulham Archives and Local History Centre.

Edwardian amusement parks are related to but distinct from the Disney-inspired theme parks of the later twentieth century and the amusement parks that operate today. In current usage, "amusement park" refers to small and often rundown permanent fairgrounds—a very different prospect to the hugely profitable and spectacular Edwardian parks. The postwar theme parks, pioneered by Disney, offered similar attractions to their amusement-park predecessors but are distinguished by a more coherent and corporate-themed experience; out-of-town locations necessitating private-car ownership; and a more narrowly defined suburban, family audience. Walt Disney himself was quick to distance his ventures from the amusement-park tradition, loudly asserting the novelty of his 1955 Disneyland.[21]

Though far from uniform, these sites adhered to a recognizable formula. First, the new parks were operated as enclosed and controlled zones developed by a single business interest (individual ownership or, more often, a small group of investors) rather than by a shifting collective of concessionaires. Blackpool Pleasure Beach, for example, was run by William Bean and John Outhwaite, who in 1903 secured a £30,000 mortgage to develop thirty acres of shorefront into an amusement park.[22] The big rides

Figure 9.6. R. B. Mather, The Casino, Blackpool Pleasure Beach (c. 1913), watercolor. © Blackpool Pleasure Beach. By kind permission of the Thompson Family, Pleasure Beach Resort, Blackpool.

were generally run by companies controlled by the park owners and established specifically for that purpose, while concessionaires were invited to run the smaller attractions, in return for rent and a percentage of gross profits.[23]

Second, in contrast to their itinerant fairground cousins, the amusement parks were fixed-site installations, which had major ramifications for the style and scale of the attractions they offered. Alongside American-style thrill rides, which demanded substantial initial investment, most parks drew on a wide range of popular entertainment traditions, featuring battle reenactments, cinema, dancing venues, theaters, concession stalls and booths, landscaped gardens, and often a zoo. As permanent sites, the amusement parks were able to provide cafés, bars, and restaurants (Figure 9.6) to suit a range of budgets, and visitor facilities such as toilets and drinking fountains. It also made them accountable to the local authorities who granted annual licenses for everything from basic refreshments to dancing and music.

Third, their target audience was urban, adult, and socially all-encompassing. It ranged "from the young to the middle aged, and from those who could just afford an annual day trip, to the curious middle classes for whom the crowd itself was an essential part of the spectacle."[24] In the interest of minimizing disreputable behavior (and thereby maximizing their potential appeal) park managers imposed their own controls on behavior, such as employing wardens to police the grounds and installing floodlights to banish opportunities for shady dealings in the most literal sense.[25] Some parks levied a small entrance fee at the gates in addition to individual ride charges.[26]

The parks were conceived and promoted as a specifically American form of entertainment, no doubt drawing on the established appeal of American-styled novelties, including the American Bowling Saloon at London's Vauxhall Gardens in the 1840s and Buffalo Bill's Wild West shows at Earl's Court from 1887.[27] Brown's park at New Brighton Tower, for example, promoted itself as "absolutely the First American Free Amusement Park on this side of the Atlantic."[28] Many park owners used their strong personal ties to the United States to validate claims of American authenticity. In doing so, the parks exploited the growing popularity of American culture in Britain at the turn of the twentieth century.[29]

Many of these characteristics would have been familiar to first-time visitors to the new parks. They drew heavily on the tried and tested entertainment of the circus, music hall, and fairground. But one key element marks the amusement parks as something unique: their dependence on large-scale mechanized amusement. The parks were dominated by machines for fun, and it was this aspect that signified a decisive break with the past. Amusement parks were, in the words of Arwen Mohun, "technologically intensive entertainments" in which "the use of machinery . . . proved enormously effective at commodifying leisure."[30] Nowhere was this better exemplified than in the phenomenon of the roller coaster, which became the defining characteristic of the amusement park and enjoyed phenomenal success.[31]

Moreover, the composite visual landscape of the parks was quite unlike anything that had come before. Architectural eclecticism ruled. Amusement parks combined familiar styles—the exoticism and grandeur of international exhibitions and seaside piers, and the faux luxury and scenic realism of theatrical design—with the "tober" layout of traditional fairgrounds.[32] With a single sweep of the eye, the visitor might encounter in quick succession the imposing industrial skeleton of a roller coaster, a tin-roofed hoop-la stall, the towering molded concrete fortress of a battle reenactment show, a mock Tudor house, and an Indian-style tea room. This seemingly ad hoc jumble was, however, underpinned by the visual language of machines, and it was this technological aesthetic—of mechanical rides in motion and multicolored electric lights—that set the amusement-park experience apart. The "Ferris wheels, rollercoasters, aerial swings, and other rides, often in concert with fanciful architecture and existing landforms," observes Brenda Brown, "made amusement park skylines unique."[33]

The Edwardian amusement park had complex and somewhat ambiguous historical roots, and it is not surprising that the details of its heritage are often rather hastily skimmed over.[34] Many of the smaller attractions, for example, were imported straight from the traveling fairground (with its own ancient and intricate practices), while elements of the circus tradition—freak shows, acrobatics, and performing animals—were also incorporated.[35] Perhaps even more influential, in terms of the scale and layout of the new parks, were the great exhibitions of the nineteenth century. This link is made explicitly in histories of American amusement parks, where the Chicago Exposition of 1893 is credited as the key impetus for their emergence.[36] But a close connection can also be identified in Britain. Following in the wake of the iconic Great Exhibition of 1851, a series of major events (such as the American Exhibition at Earl's Court in 1887) established a legacy of respectable pleasure—characterized by fast-flowing crowds, visual wonders, consumption, and architectural spectacle—which British amusement parks undoubtedly exploited.[37]

These interconnections are explained to a degree by the personal histories of the men behind the amusement-park phenomenon. It was not uncommon for leading entrepreneurs to have worked in the wider world of popular entertainment before becoming involved in amusement parks, and this broad body of experience was clearly brought to bear on the emerging park formula. Charles B. Cochran (1872–1951), for example, cut his teeth as a promoter in the music halls of London, managing Harry Houdini and the celebrity wrestler Hackenschmidt before establishing Olympia's Fun City in 1906. Imre Kiralfy (1845–1919) drew on his early experiences of exhibitions on both sides of the Atlantic to develop his own amusement parks at London's White City.[38] These networks echoed the careers of earlier pleasure garden promoters, but the clear identification of an "amusement industry"—defined by trade newspapers such as the *World's Fair* (first published in 1904)—emerges as a new element in the Edwardian period.

Pleasure Gardens and the Early Amusement Parks

Part of the problem that scholars have faced in trying to pin down where the amusement parks came from is that they brought together multiple types of entertainment in or near an outdoor space that often had a pre-history as a pleasure garden or commercial park of some sort. The lines between pleasure garden and amusement park become especially blurred on the Continent, where a number of gardens survived through the nineteenth and twentieth centuries, offering many of the same rides and types of entertainment as later amusement parks. At Copenhagen's Tivoli Park (which opened in 1841) visitors tried their luck at coconut shies and other games of chance. A switchback railway was added in 1843. A second roller-coaster ride, the Bjergrutschebanen (mountain roller coaster) was built in 1914.[39] The survival of successful pleasure gardens on the Continent and their diversification into thrill rides shows how definitions and terminology might be challenged.

A similar though less well-documented process can be seen in Britain. Shipley Glen, West Yorkshire, was an ever-popular Victorian pleasure ground featuring one of the earliest switchback railways in England (1887), an Aerial Flight (1889), a Cable Tramway (1895), a giant camera obscura, a Toboggan Slide (1897), and an Aerial Glide (c. 1900).[40] From 1871 Raikes Hall Pleasure Gardens delighted Blackpool visitors with its "double-arched entrance gateway for carriages, its grand statuary avenue, its skating rink and conservatory, monkey house, boating pool, pavilion theatre (and concert hall), open-air dancing platform, . . . its magnificent firework displays,"[41] and even an early switchback railway.[42] Interestingly, the decline of Raikes Hall happened just as the Pleasure Beach was establishing itself on Blackpool's South Shore. Crossover sites such as these have led several historians to draw a direct trajectory between the late pleasure garden and the early amusement park.[43] Despite the presence of roller coasters, however, Raikes Hall and Shipley Glen lacked the enclosed spatial boundaries and the single ownership that would have lent them the coherence of an American-style amusement park.

Figure 9.7. *From the Grand Hall by the Sea* (1913), souvenir. © Bill Evans Collection.

Margate's Hall by the Sea—a late Victorian entertainment complex that survived into the twentieth century—helps to clarify the interconnections and distinctions between the last pleasure gardens and the arrival of the amusement parks. In 1874 famed circus showman "Lord" George Sanger (1825?–1911) took charge of an ailing seafront music and dancing venue in Margate, with twenty acres of adjoining land, including a stream and swamp.[44] He quickly transformed Hall by the Sea into a profitable music hall, offering a fully licensed bar, restaurant, and refurbished ballroom, in which well-known London acts performed. In 1898 the main building was replaced by a narrow single-story building (Figure 9.7) with a seating capacity of 1,400, and space for 3,000 dancers. The rough land behind the hall was landscaped to provide a pleasure garden, complete with ornamental ponds and fountains, a medieval folly, classical statuary, and a bandstand. The gardens included an amusement section, reflecting Sanger's showman connections. Among the diversions on offer during the 1890s were swings, shooting galleries, a waxwork exhibition, a roller-skating rink, a steam-powered roundabout, and an impressive menagerie.[45] Sanger created a new program of balls and concerts, charging visitors a single gardens admission fee of sixpence and a combined entry to the Hall of one shilling.[46]

The combination of music-hall or circus-style entertainment with fairground rides at the Hall was typical of numerous late nineteenth-century establishments in cities and thriving resorts. Birmingham's Casino Theatre of Varieties and Pleasure Grounds offered a similar range of indoor and outdoor entertainment aimed at the popular market.[47] But, according to the definition of amusement parks used here (mechanized amusements in a permanent enclosed zone, controlled by a single business interest, and targeting a heterogeneous adult audience), the absence of large-scale mechanized rides at the Hall by the Sea is decisive. There is no evidence that Sanger envisaged his venue as anything more than a complex of different types of entertainment aimed at snaring the widest possible market. This was neither a pleasure garden nor an early amusement park but perhaps something in-between. By 1900 the Hall by the Sea, like many other ventures across the country, bridged the gap between Victorian pleasure gardens and the first American-style amusement parks.

The transformation into full-fledged amusement park came a little later. Sanger died in 1911; a year later, the showman Pat Collins (1859–1943) announced his intention to establish a "White City" on the grounds.[48] In 1912 Collins's use of the term "white city" must be seen as an intentional reference to the thriving amusement parks at Manchester and London. A souvenir program from 1913 includes "The Great Fun City" among the attractions, together with an illustration of a Joy Wheel. Though little other evidence of mechanical amusements survives, this tantalizing visual reference suggests that Collins harbored notions of updating the Hall by the Sea with an ambitious "re-brand" in acknowledgment of the amusement-park phenomenon, which by 1913 was well-established.

The promotion of the Joy Wheel is especially significant. It was one of a new generation of highly publicized American rides, introduced at Coney Island, that proved extremely popular in Britain following its demonstration at Kensington Olympia (as the "Human Roulette Board") in 1908, at Great Yarmouth in 1909, and then at Blackpool Pleasure Beach in 1910.[49] It consisted of a polished wooden circular platform on which riders sat or lay so that, as the platform revolved, they were thrown outward by centrifugal force. The idea was to engineer a total loss of bodily control among the riders—men and women of all ages—for the entertainment of a gallery of onlookers. One journalist described the effect: "You may go feet first, head first, or sideways like a crab. You may go on your elbows, your ankles, the knuckles of your hands, the broad of your back, the pit of your stomach; you may go even on your eyebrows or on one ear. . . . The world is full of flying arms and legs and spinning bodies until the Joy Wheel is spinning empty and triumphant [and] the arena is rocking with laughter."[50] This was a far cry from the sedate and genteel diversion offered by the Hall's newest competitor in Margate—the recently opened Winter Gardens—and is suggestive of a new direction at the Hall by the Sea. The war in 1914 put an end to Collins's plans at Margate but not to the arrival of the amusement park. When the new owner John Henry Iles (a successful roller-coaster entrepreneur since 1906) reopened the site as Dreamland Amusement Park in 1920, he maintained the landscaped gardens and much of the original format. Two key changes completed the transformation into an amusement park. First, the installment of an American manager Mr. C. C. Bartram (born in Michigan, 1873), underlining the idea that this would be an American-style park, inspired by its Coney Island namesake.[51] And, second, the strategic addition of a Scenic Railway roller coaster at the center of the grounds.

Amusement parks which—like Dreamland—launched on sites associated with defunct or failing pleasure gardens were able to take advantage of ready-made visitor markets and incorporate garden features that might lure more visitors and, once through the gates, keep them occupied for longer. In 1901, for example, the Kursaal opened on the pleasure ground at Southend's Marine Park, gradually augmenting its nineteen acres of landscaped gardens and entertainment program of dancing and music (Figure 9.8) with an amusement area complete with a switchback, an aerial flight, and an illusion show.[52] Manchester's Belle Vue—a popular commercial pleasure ground and zoo from the 1840s—acquired fairground rides in the early 1900s and hosted a full-fledged American amusement park from the 1920s.[53] Similar patterns were repeated across Britain.

Although thrill rides were the main attraction of the new amusement parks, the pleasure garden tradition of providing more sedate recreation was often continued. In an attempt to appeal to the broadest market, parks that preserved or invested in landscaped gardens heavily promoted the suggestion of a quiet escape to nature. Plans for the White City at Old Trafford drawn up in 1907 may have centered on securing "the biggest novelties," but Calvin Brown retained the ornamental lake and many of the trees and plants from the old Botanical Gardens, insisting that "the picturesque is not to be overlooked."[54] Likewise, an early plan of Dreamland shows that the gardens created by Sanger were largely preserved, operating as a liminal space of greenery that separated the bustling seafront road outside from the chaos of the amusements within.[55] Gardens and quiet retreats could

Figure 9.8. Poster for the Kursaal and Gardens, Southend-on-Sea (c. 1912). © Southend Museum.

enhance the visitors' experience of otherworldliness within the amusement park—an important tool for maximizing visitors' time and spending, and a key lesson learned from the pleasure gardens.

Thrill, Risk, and Respectable Pleasures

Thrill was *the* defining experience of the amusement park. Adventure and excitement had, of course, been key features of earlier pleasure gardens. As Neil Harris puts it, their appeal "lay precisely in the atmosphere of (controlled) risk they contained, the casual and unpredictable encounters they offered," an appeal that was certainly incorporated by the amusement parks.[56] But the new parks became synonymous with thrilling encounters of a rather different kind. The amusement park was, above all, a landscape of machines designed to bump, shake, and startle the body in constantly new and apparently enjoyable ways. People paid for the excitement of being hurled through the air at breakneck speeds then delivered safely back to a loading bay. As the long history of riding devices illustrates, this kind of thrill-seeking was not in itself new in 1900.[57] But the amusement parks provided for the first time a smorgasbord of cheap, machine-produced, commodified thrill, which was widely recognized as fun. These parks, in effect, inaugurated the socially inclusive culture of mechanized thrill-seeking that is so familiar to us today.

In 1908 a journalist explained the universal appeal of the roller-coaster ride, providing a glimpse of Edwardian attitudes to thrill. The writer describes a complex state, producing visceral and mental transformations. Thrill is an "ecstasy of excitement" that "stirs his blood, excites his brain," offering transcendent possibilities. On the Scenic Railway roller coaster, we are told that even the "mildest of men" becomes a "reckless hero" and "staid old ladies . . . frisky maidens." The perception of danger and speed is an essential determinant of this momentary catharsis, enabling the individual to take "the brake off himself" or to "relieve her feelings." For the journalist, the roller-coaster experience is part of living in modern times, "a psychological revelation" in which "the modern man . . . enjoys primitive emotions in a scientific fashion."[58]

But the perception of thrill as an enjoyable experience depended entirely on the trust placed in the safety of the rides themselves. New attractions were expected to deliver the sensation of *ersatz* danger and patrons were repeatedly reassured that no real risk was involved.[59] Although serious and sometimes fatal mishaps frequently *did* occur at amusement parks, newspaper reports reveal surprisingly naive attitudes to safety and risk-taking among amusement-park patrons.[60] The overwhelming majority of accidents were caused by passengers misusing rides—standing up in cars or leaning out—perhaps in an attempt to add variation and excitement, or simply because they were unaware of the potential hazards.[61] The caution demanded in daily life on the construction site, the factory floor, or a traffic-filled street was not translated to the amusement park. Thrill machines were disassociated from their industrial counterparts and the dangers they posed.[62]

Concepts of danger at the amusement park—as at the pleasure gardens—were more commonly expressed in terms of moral safety and linked to attitudes toward class and social mixing. Local opposition to amusement parks was often quick to point out the lowering of social tone that accompanied a new venture. Critics of Blackpool Pleasure Beach, for example, voiced fears about the influx of working-class visitors into the middle-class South Shore district. One resident noted with horror the growing prevalence of "men standing in the gardens on Sunday at noon minus coat, vest, collar, and tie, and shirt sleeves rolled up and smoking clay pipes."[63]

It is important to note, however, that finding evidence of *actual* moral transgressions is very difficult indeed. Critics were generally concerned with the *potential* problem of mass entertainment and, by and large, newspaper coverage emphasizes the orderly and respectable behavior of amusement-park patrons. *The Times*, for example, reported that "the utmost order and decorum prevailed" among the massive bank holiday crowd at London's White City in 1908.[64] In 1907 only two cases of drunkenness were reported at Manchester's White City during a season in which more than 750,000 people visited.[65] Describing the crowds at Blackpool for a London readership in 1906, one journalist rhapsodized: "The behaviour, the conduct, the general demeanour of Lancashire mill hands when let loose with money in both pockets in Blackpool is simply amazing. I lack words with which to express my admiration for Tom and Mary at the business of pleasuring."[66] Unruly behavior undoubtedly manifested itself at popular holiday resorts such as Margate, Southend, and Blackpool, but it is much easier to locate in the liminal spaces of the beach, pubs, and ramshackle seafront entertainment than in the carefully regulated amusement parks.[67] A letter published in *John Bull* in 1909, for example, expressed outrage at the behavior of "hobbledehoys and wenches . . . in the lanes, in the shelters, on the sandhills" of Blackpool but made no mention of the Pleasure Beach.[68]

The restrained behaviour of amusement park crowds was in large part because the permanent nature of the amusement parks brought accountability. The licensing system, which required parks—like pleasure gardens—to reapply on an annual basis to local magistrates for licenses to provide music, dancing, and refreshments, meant that they were answerable to local complaints and were subject to far more exacting standards of health and safety than their fairground cousins.[69] In 1913 Imre Kiralfy's London White City was granted a restricted license to sell alcohol on the strict proviso that noise from fireworks be reduced and that free and plentiful "sanitary accommodation," fountains and drinking posts, and seating should be provided.[70] Visitors to the parks were invariably noisy. The *World's Fair* regularly published details of court actions brought by local residents complaining about the noise of rides and screaming visitors.[71] But brightly lit avenues, toilets, drinking water, and limited alcohol supply all seem to have done their bit to keep visitors in line.

Furthermore, park owners went to great lengths of their own to deter disreputable behavior. They did so, first and foremost, by policing their premises and encouraging a family presence. Measured against American counterparts and itinerant fairgrounds, freak shows and the more daring sideshow novelties were notably lacking at British amusement parks.[72] Second, attractions were marketed as healthy, invigorating, and transformative, appropriating the language of (and thus deflecting potential criticism from) the rational recreation movement.[73] A new ride at the Pleasure Beach, for example, was promoted as being "splendid for the liver."[74] Third, the owners themselves became high-profile figures, cultivating public images that emphasized their education, philanthropy, and commitment to local affairs. The career of William Bean, co-founder of the Pleasure Beach, illustrates how successful such a strategy could be. Initial opposition to the Pleasure Beach was quelled by a brilliant public relations campaign waged in the press and by Bean's prominent role in local politics.[75]

Finally, the mechanical nature of the big attractions was, in itself, an important factor in establishing respectability. Rides were presented as the products of pioneering technology and science, conferring on them an exalted status. In addition to providing a novel experience, for example, the Great Wheels at Earl's Court (1896–1907) and Blackpool (1896–1928) were viewed as a testament to the engineering prowess of modern Britain. As the

World's Fair observed, "The Great Wheel [Earl's Court] was almost as much of a landmark for London as the Eiffel Tower is to Paris."[76] At the Shepherd's Bush White City, the impressive dimensions and novel motion of the Flip Flap (Figure 9.9) won special praise from *The Times*. With its "two gigantic steel arms 150 ft. long," which carried as many as forty passengers "through the air to a height of 200 ft. and deposited [them] upon the ground again at a distance of 300 ft. from the starting point," the extraordinary Flip Flap was considered a "mechanical marvel."[77]

The amusement parks' status as symbols of progress and modernity was cemented in 1909 by a royal visit to Kiralfy's White City at Shepherd's Bush. Queen Alexandra and Princess Victoria, after passing through the Empire Exhibition pavilions, were given a tour of the amusement park and, to the delight of onlookers, sampled several rides. The *London Daily Telegraph* reported that the Princess rode the Witching Waves (an early incarnation of the dodgems imported from America), while the Queen took a trip on the Scenic Railway and two winning runs on the Miniature Brooklands racetrack.[78] It was a promotional master stroke and amusement parks across the country reaped the benefits. Just as Buffalo Bill's well-publicized performance for Queen Victoria at Earl's Court in 1887 ensured massive and lasting popular success for similar Wild West shows,[79] so Queen Alexandra's endorsement signalled the amusement parks' arrival as a respectable popular entertainment.[80]

The amusement parks thus struck a careful balance between safe, respectable entertainment and the promise of visceral thrill and simulated danger. They owed a great deal to technology. The landscape was dominated by rides that combined the body and machine in new ways and required passengers to suspend the rules of bodily restraint that operated in everyday life. The Brooklyn Cakewalk, for example, was an oscillating platform over which patrons attempted to walk. The result was a comically exaggerated version of the popular American dance after which it was named. The *Blackpool Gazette News* described the effect on a group of elderly ladies attempting the Cakewalk at the Pleasure Beach in 1908: "Everyone who steps aboard this contrivance is bound to cake walk. There is positively no escape. To see a number of portly dames going through the 'graceful' movements of this popular 'walk' is too grotesque for words. It has entertained thousands during the week-end and will entertain thousands more."[81] Attractions like these, which threw the body into awkward and undignified positions, can be seen as part of a general shift in attitudes

Figure 9.9. *The Flip-Flap, Franco-British Exhibition, London* (1908), postcard. Private collection.

Figure 9.10. Max Cowper, "Witching Waves Ride, White City" (1909), from the *Illustrated London News*. © Mary Evans Picture Library.

to the body and social etiquette. But the popularity of "body in chaos" rides also reflects a discourse of childlike adult play, which emerged in Britain at the turn of the century. The "Peter Pan ethos"—the idea that adults (in particular, middle-class men) were grown-up children, desiring simple, sensuous fun—was first and most vociferously promoted by the new consumer cultures of America from the later 1890s. But amusement-park owners in Britain were quick to seize on the idea.[82] By providing profit-driven, thrilling, and playful rides, amusement parks commodified the freedom and exuberance of childhood. The parks were thus cast as adult playgrounds where the return to childhood was sanctioned by the use of sophisticated "man-made" technologies.[83] The Peter Pan ethos conveniently obscured any hint of sexual titillation and provided amusement-park owners with an effective defense against charges of encouraging risqué behavior. Men and women could mix freely in these engineered playgrounds without threatening masculine authority and female decency—the cornerstones of Edwardian society. As Calvin Brown put it in 1912, "Last year, both in London and Paris the most popular amusement I provided was the helter-skelter with a bowl at the bottom into which people were swept and had to be hauled out. It is probably the silliest kind of entertainment ever devised. But it helped revive the boyish feeling in middle-aged men. . . . It appeals to inner desires, often hidden desires."[84] Park owners were quick to understand the benefits of using the Peter Pan ethos as a promotional strategy. It was the perfect foil for encouraging respectable middle-class families to visit the amusement parks and to spend money freely. The Velvet Coaster roller coaster—according to its designer—could be both "the highest development known to engineering science" and "merely an elaboration of the boy's trick of sliding down the balustrade."[85] The mechanical framing of childlike play embodied a paradox central to the success of the parks: The body was both out of control (compared to normative social etiquette) and highly disciplined (by the predictable, rhythmic motion of the ride machinery, and the limits of pay per ride).

Sociability and Informality

The throngs of people who patronized the amusement parks were as important in defining the experiences on offer as the technologically dependent rides and shows. Southend's Luna Park (also known as the Kursaal) reported a crowd of more than 100,000 during the Easter holiday of 1911 alone.[86] In 1913 Edinburgh's Marine Gardens claimed 500,000 patrons.[87] For one journalist writing about Blackpool Pleasure Beach in 1907, the attractions themselves were overshadowed by the sheer volume of people. "The spectacle was simply bewildering," he reports. "One gazed in amazement, and wondered where all the people came from."[88] Just as the taking of refreshments at a pleasure garden had been an opportunity to observe the crowds at play, the tea gardens at Manchester's White City were carefully positioned so that its patrons were "enabled to watch the constantly moving and changing human panorama as it passes along the promenade."[89]

The scale of the amusement-park crowds was partly a consequence of their broad social appeal. Rides and shows at the Pleasure Beach generally cost between one and three pence, ensuring a core wage-earning clientele.[90] Even at London's White City—where rides cost between six pence and a shilling—a large proportion of the Bank Holiday crowd in 1908 was made up of a spectrum of industrial workers. The *Times* reported: "The Cooperative Societies of Newcastle, Manchester, Liverpool, Derby, Lincoln, Retford, and Hucknell each sent large parties, and, in addition, there were parties of engineers from Newcastle and Bristol, gasworkers from Cardiff, steelworkers from Sheffield, foundry-workers from Birmingham, and railway employés [sic] from several centres."[91] Although the wage-earning masses made up a core component of the crowd, it is clear that the amusement parks were not exclusively male, adult, or working class. A colorful description from 1907 shows the eclectic mix enjoying the Pleasure Beach sideshows, ranging from "the bewildered miner" to "smirking young ladies, awkward hobbledehoys, self-conscious matrons, reluctant papas, and uneasy family groups."[92] In 1911 a party of elderly ladies were reported enjoying the delights of the amusement park with "youthful enthusiasm." "Two giddy old dames of over 70 years of age" were whirled off the Joy Wheel, while another eighty-five-year-old "derived the keenest enjoyment from the thrilling rush round the Velvet Coaster."[93]

It is especially significant that women formed a major and highly visible element of the crowd. Far from taking a backseat by sticking to the quieter gardens or more sedate attractions—and contrary to the expectations of the time—female visitors of all ages were as likely to head for the large-scale thrill rides as men. In 1910 the *Times* reported a Lord Mayor's Court action to recover damages for injuries sustained on the Spiral Railway at White City, Shepherd's Bush. The plaintiff, Blanche Dunn, was the wife of a veterinary surgeon from Poplar, London. There is no hint in the report that Mrs. Dunn, as a respectable middle-class woman patronizing a mechanical thrill ride, was considered exceptional.[94] Indeed, by 1912 the manager at White City could confidently state that "women far exceed men in the numbers patronizing the newer sensations" such as the Screamer, the Flip-Flap, and the Mountain Railway. "Their attitude to these novelties suggests that women are certainly more enterprising than men in collecting new sensations."[95] Given the highly restricted nature of commercial recreations available to "respectable" women in the late Victorian and Edwardian periods, it is hardly surprising to find that women made up a significant portion of the amusement park's clientele. Indeed, the amusement parks, like the cinema, may be seen as part of a wider process in which commercialized entertainment increasingly catered to the female consumer.

For both men and women, the amusement parks promised release from the demands and constraints of everyday life, and they played host to a mass of individuals joined together in the pursuit of fun. To be part of such a collective could be uplifting, liberating, and exciting—a far cry from the indifference and distrust attributed to urban crowds by sociologist Georg Simmel in *The Metropolis and Mental Life* (1903).[96] As the *Manchester Sunday Chronicle* put it: "You wander in search of adventure, and you find it in canvas booths, in the shower of sand, in the rumble of wheels, in the glad cry of the triumphant tripper, in the shrieks of maidens, in the glorious crescendo of a summer crowd climbing to the knowledge of holiday happiness."[97]

Cross and Walton have called this the "playful crowd," a phenomenon that, they argue, represented a modernized expression of preindustrial saturnalia, or carnivalesque.[98] "In place of traditional aggressive games and the mocking of authority," they suggest, the crowds "sought the thrill of rides, simulated encounters with others' misfortune, and the playful ridicule of modern machines."[99] And yet—as we have seen—there is strikingly little evidence of the wild and hedonistic behavior associated with the Bakhtinian crowd.[100] The amusement-park landscape, with its myriad of attractions, created an atmosphere of collective freedom in which the formality of official, working life was relaxed. But, far from representing "a second life,"[101] the crowds' experience was framed by familiar rhythms of sociability, celebration, and consumption. The sense of collectivity imparted by the crowd, does not—as Bakhtin would have it—produce an inevitable dissolution of individual self.[102] Rather than turning the "world inside out,"[103] the amusement parks magnified the positive and festive features of everyday life. Thanks to new mechanical forms of pleasure, crowds enjoyed the "holiday mood," rather than the carnival spirit.

The freedom of bodily movement, social mixing, and compulsory screaming that occurred at the amusement park—but would have been quite unacceptable in everyday life—might be seen as elements of carnival had they not been regulated by the rhythm and movement of the mechanical rides and, to a great extent, by the crowds themselves. Bakhtin states that carnival "is not a spectacle seen by the people; they live in it, and everyone participates."[104] And yet, at the amusement park, spectatorship was a key element of the amusements on offer. Members of the crowd were encouraged to be both actors in, and spectators of, the entertainment, just as they had been at Vauxhall and Ranelagh. Archive photographs show how crowds gathered to watch mechanical rides in operation. The Joy Wheel was designed with a large raised circular gallery on which people could stand to watch and laugh at the fate of those being spun around.[105] New Brighton Tower's water chute provided "almost as much amusement to the onlookers as to the passengers themselves."[106] A visit to the amusement park offered its own set of coded behaviors, ritual practices that lay somewhere between the everyday and the liminality of the beach or fairground.

Novelty and Transience

Novelty lay at the very heart of the amusement-park experience. Success was seen to depend on satisfying an insatiable popular appetite for new sensations and experiences. The *World's Fair* observed in 1912 that "Blackpool hungers and thirsts for novelty. . . . The immense popularity of Blackpool's big pleasure beach provides striking proof of this."[107] The most profitable parks were thus defined by their "up-to-dateness," an ability to adapt to popular demands, to rapidly absorb and then shed a range of attractions as their profitability waxed and waned, often on an annual basis. Flexibility translated directly to the visual landscapes of the parks, which were characterized by frequent overhauls and redesigns. This was especially true during the first two decades of the twentieth century, as the attractions at amusement parks were constantly augmented and renovated in an attempt to capture new audiences and secure loyalty among existing ones.

The constant modification and adaptation of entertainments by incorporating the latest invention (notably motor cars and flying machines) or sporting themes during popular crazes was a key element of the amusement-park formula borrowed from the pleasure gardens and, more recently, from the music halls.[108] In the 1900s, for example, roller skating became an almost national obsession and was quickly added to the list of essential amusement-park attractions. But, after a rush of investment across the country in 1909, costly rink enterprises plummeted into bankruptcy and, by 1910, the craze had subsided.[109] Amusement parks exploited this latest craze while it lasted. The Pleasure Beach built an expensive new rink accommodating up to a thousand skaters and then, once interest had waned, transformed it into an alternative venue for film, pageants, and exhibitions, thereby substituting a once-fashionable attraction with something even more up to date.[110]

Similarly, the popularity of winter sports grew steadily from the 1890s, thanks partly to British enthusiasts such as Arthur Conan Doyle and Sir Henry Lunn, who organized the first package ski tour in 1898.[111] Early travelogue films depicting bob-sleigh runs, skating lakes, and ski slopes stoked popular interest in an otherwise elite pastime.[112] The amusement parks were again quick to capitalize on this interest, with toboggan slides appearing across the country and even, in 1914, the launch of a skiing simulator ride, providing "all the pleasurable sensations of ski-ing; of swift descent over gleaming snow, without difficulty or fatigue."[113]

That a novelty such as this was operated as a concession is significant. The system of temporary leasing at the amusement parks was underpinned by the drive to appear fresh and new. The stalls and booths, which operated side by side with the big rides, were—underneath their highly decorative facings—little more than makeshift sheds. Vanderdecken's Haunted Cabin, documented in a suitably ghostly photograph of the Pleasure Beach in 1906, was a simple wooden structure with painted canvas frontage, which lasted only a few years.[114] Cheap building materials facilitated transport and remodeling but also perpetuated the ephemerality of the landscape. Highly flammable wood, staff, and hessian frontages regularly succumbed to fire and storm damage, which in turn generated more rebuilding.[115] A storm that swept through Blackpool in March 1907 caused thousands of pounds of damage on the Pleasure Beach, destroying most of its wooden sideshows.[116] Yet, just three months later, an elaborate Spanish-themed street was erected to house concessionaires and create a new attraction in its own right.[117]

The flimsy nature of many of these structures, the ad hoc evolution of layout, the flowing crowds, and the momentary pleasures on offer all contributed to the transience of the amusement-park experience, a reflection perhaps of the instability and dynamism of the early twentieth century. For Baudelaire, modernity was defined by "the transient, the fleeting, the contingent."[118] The innate transitoriness of the amusement-park world was, in a sense, a metaphor for the wider experience of modernity as contemporaries perceived it.

As sites that touted their novelty and up-to-dateness, it is perhaps surprising to find that historical narratives also played an important role in the amusement-park experience. Through the architecture and the entertainment provided, the parks presented visitors with a romanticized version of the past *alongside* glimpses of the future.[119] In this way, visitors to the Pleasure Beach in 1910 could experience both a nostalgic re-creation of naval history in the Monitor and Merrimac Naval Spectatorium (which depicted an American Civil War battle between two ironclad warships in 1862) and a utopian glimpse of the future on Voyage on a Submarine (a pseudoscientific simulation of the latest underwater technology).[120] Drawing on a formula established by the international exhibitions, amusement parks thus located modern technologies like the submarine, airplane, and car, in a clear chronological line of patriotic progress.

The historical theming of architecture at the amusement parks further underlined a patriotic notion of ever-improving Britishness. Shakespeare's England—a large-scale reproduction of Elizabethan London, shown at Earl's Court in 1912—was received with enormous enthusiasm by the public.[121] The same year, the Pleasure Beach transformed its Spanish Street into Ye Olde Englyshe Street. The Moorish frontages of the concessions arcade were remodeled into "traditional" houses, with "quaint medieval architecture cleverly imitated in fibre plaster . . . reminiscent of the buildings in ancient Chester." Proudly claiming to recapture an authentic premodern Englishness, no hint of irony is evident in the combination of salvaged doors and roof tiles ("some of it really is antique"!) and varicolored electric illuminations.[122] Similarly, "Lord" George Sanger installed a medieval folly in the ornamental gardens of the Hall by the Sea, which remained as a highly publicized feature of Dreamland after 1920.

This was not theming of the scale or coherence that operated later at Disney's parks. But it perhaps reflects a fundamental element of life in Britain at this time. On the one hand, the amusement-park landscape represented a romanticized vision of modern life—visceral, intense, and stripped of the banality of everyday industrial labor. On the other hand, it recaptured a highly popular rose-tinted version of the past. Rieger has shown how historical narratives—as a response to, and an expression of, ambivalence toward modernity—were used to explain the present as a culmination of continuous progress, while at the same time identifying and underlining the fundamental division between past and present.[123] In this sense, the juxtaposition of historic-themed structures and modern mechanical amusements might be seen as a reflection of the temporal confusion felt by many living through the early twentieth century.[124]

This chapter set out to consider the extent to which the Edwardian amusement parks preserved the legacy of earlier pleasure gardens. Neil Harris describes the amusement park, theme park, and pleasure garden as "siblings" that offered the same mix of "illusion, excitement, myth-making and role-playing," and a number of important historical continuities are clearly evident.[125] Like the pleasure gardens of Victorian Britain, visitors flocked to the amusement parks in search of spectacular otherworldly entertainment, for experiences that promised thrills and excitement without posing a serious threat to the social and cultural mores of the day. The colorful promoters, the faux-scientific entertainment, the surprise encounters, and the sanctioning of childlike pleasures that characterized the delights of Vauxhall all found their counterparts in the amusement-park phenomenon.

In terms of the designed landscape, however, places like Blackpool Pleasure Beach represented a distinct form of visual and physical encounter to the commercial gardens of the previous century. Drawing on the legacy of modern spectacle inaugurated by the exhibitions, department stores, and Coney Island, the amusement parks in Britain created their own eclectic and highly popular formula of fantasy, noise, color, and movement. Most important, the new parks were defined by their machine landscapes and the technologically produced sensations they offered. This chapter began with a provocative description of Calvin Brown's "modern" eye "driving stakes into the grounds of romance" at Manchester's Botanical Gardens. It was in many ways an astute observation. Amusement parks looked and felt dramatically different from anything that had come before. Moreover, this novelty was understood as entirely in keeping with the pervading sense felt among Britons that they were living through an era defined by permanent and "man-made" change.[126]

In a more metaphorical sense, however, the reporter failed to grasp the fundamental aspect that underpinned the success of the amusement-park phenomenon: that American-style fast rides and sparkling electric lights held a powerful romantic allure of their own. The arrival of the White City did not signal the end of romance but rather its reinvention. Amusement-park landscapes celebrated a utopian vision of technology, transience, and bodies in motion. Like the burgeoning cinema, they catered for a shared desire for sensuous and immediate engagement with life, a desire that has been viewed as a key point of tension in the last century.[127]

Amusement parks catered for a seemingly perennial desire to escape the everyday, but they did so in a manner that reflected the preoccupations and characteristics of the Edwardian world into which they were born. The amusement-park formula survived World War I. The Empire Exhibition at Wembley in 1924 featured a forty-acre amusement zone costing £1.7 million, but it proved in many ways to be the swan song of the Edwardian model.[128] By the 1930s the respectability of the amusement-park experience had been seriously undermined by new ideas about mass leisure. The "modern spirit" sweepingly rejected all that had been associated with the Victorian and Edwardian years and, though popular as ever, amusement parks were increasingly viewed with disdain by the cultural elite. J. B. Priestley famously identified the patrons of Blackpool's attractions as "less intelligent," "passive and listless."[129]

Increasingly the respectable pleasures of public amusements were challenged by the pleasures of personal consumption—of food, holidays, films, cars, and other newly available commodities. The enthusiasm for simulated technologies and exotic locations lost its edge as more people became able to afford their own firsthand experiences. The interwar amusement parks found themselves competing with new forms of mass recreation, such as cinema, holiday camps, and even foreign travel. The visceral pleasures of the early amusement parks did not simply disappear. In the 1950s, they were to make a comeback under the guise of ultra-controlled, all-inclusive theme parks, exemplified by the Disney experience.

Notes

Introduction

1. Thomas Myers Garrett, "A History of Pleasure Gardens in New York City, 1700–1865," Ph.D. diss., New York University, 1978, 11. In the seventeenth century "Spring Garden" (the name of the first pleasure garden in London, described below) seems to have been used in a similar fashion, to refer to pleasure gardens in general. For an example of this usage, taken from Celia Fiennes's account of a 1698 visit to Newcastle, see Alicia Amherst, *A History of Gardening in England* (London: Bernard Quaritch, 1895), 214.

2. Warwick Wroth, *The London Pleasure Gardens of the Eighteenth Century* (London: Macmillan, 1896).

3. For a discussion of how many parties might visit a relatively well-known pleasure ground such as Hackfall, see Edward Harwood, "Rhetoric, Authenticity, and Reception: The Eighteenth-Century Landscape Garden, the Modern Theme Park, and Their Audiences," in *Theme Park Landscapes: Antecedents and Variations*, ed. Terence Young and Robert Riley (Washington, D.C.: Dumbarton Oaks Research Library and Collection, 2002), 57–58.

4. Madame de Scudéry's account of the visit of a group of courtiers to another, grander royal garden (Versailles) noted how "in praising Versailles they came naturally to speak of the King." Cited in John Dixon Hunt, "'Lordship of the Feet': Towards a Poetics of Movement in the Garden," in *Landscape Design and the Experience of Motion*, ed. Michel Conan (Washington, D.C.: Dumbarton Oaks Research Library and Collection, 2003), 201.

5. Though Frederick, Prince of Wales, did have his own pavilion for entertaining within Vauxhall, and the Duchy of Cornwall was ground-landlord, the Prince was not a host but a distinguished visitor. Such royal patronage continued at Vauxhall in the nineteenth century, but the "Royal" added to the title in 1822 was nothing more than a marketing exercise. Suzannah Fleming, "Frederick as Apollo at Vauxhall: A 'Patriot Project'?" *London Gardener* 13 (2007–8): 46–66.

6. William Knowler, ed., *The Earl of Strafforde's Letters and Dispatches*, 2 vols. (London: William Bowyer, 1739), 1:262.

7. Garrett, "Pleasure Gardens in New York," 4.

8. Confusingly, Therese O'Malley's recent work does not discuss pleasure gardens under "pleasure garden" but under "public garden/public ground." She notes "the two senses of the phrase . . . one indicating an improved site open to the citizenry, the other referring to a commercial establishment designed for entertainment." Therese O'Malley, *Keywords in American Landscape Design* (New Haven, Conn.: Yale University Press, 2011), 547. Compare James Stevens Curl, *A Dictionary of Architecture and Landscape Architecture*, 2nd ed. (Oxford: Oxford University Press, 2002), 586–87; James Fleming, Hugh Honour, and Nikolaus Pevsner, *The Penguin Dictionary of Architecture and Landscape Architecture*, 5th ed. (London: Penguin, 1998), 441.

9. Although it does little to categorize the leading traits of each type of resort, James Stevens Curl's *Spas, Wells, and Pleasure-Gardens of London* (London: Historical Publications, 2010) is useful, as is his somewhat more analytical "Spas and Pleasure Grounds of London, from the Seventeenth to the Nineteenth Century," *Garden History* 7, no. 2 (Summer 1979): 27–68.

10. John Dixon Hunt, "Approaches (New and Old) to Garden History," in *Perspectives on Garden Histories*, ed. Michel Conan (Washington, D.C.: Dumbarton Oaks Research Library and Collection, 1999), 77–90.

11. John Evelyn, *Fumifugium, or the Inconveniencie of the Aer and Smoak of London Dissipated* (London: Gabriel Bedel and Thomas Collins, 1661), 24–25.

12. Lawrence Gowing, "Hogarth, Hayman and the Vauxhall Decorations," *Burlington Magazine* 95 (January 1953): 4–19; Brian Allen, "Francis Hayman and the Supper-Box Paintings for Vauxhall Gardens," in *The Rococo in England*, ed. Michael Snodin (London: Victoria and Albert Museum, 1986), 113–33; David Solkin, *Painting for Money: The Visual Arts and the Public Sphere in Eighteenth-Century England* (New Haven, Conn.: Yale University Press, 1992).

13. The paintings are little more than noted in David Coke and Alan Borg, *Vauxhall Gardens: A History* (New Haven, Conn.: Yale University Press: 2011), 119–20.

14. Kathleen Wilson, *The Sense of the People: Politics, Culture, and Imperialism in England, 1715–1785* (Cambridge: Cambridge University Press, 1995).

15. Gary S. Cross and John K. Walton, *The Playful Crowd: Pleasure Places in the Twentieth Century* (New York: Columbia University Press, 2005), 31.

16. Jonathan Conlin, "Vauxhall on the Boulevard: Pleasure Gardens in London and Paris, 1764–1784," *Urban History* 35, no. 1 (2008): 24–47; Wolfang Cillessen, *Exotismus und Kommerz: Bäder- und Vergnügungswesen im Paris des späten 18. Jahrhunderts* (Frankfurt: Peter Lang, 2000); Charles Gruber, "Les 'Vauxhalls' Parisiens au XVIIIe siècle," *Bulletin de la Société de l'Histoire de l'Art Français* 65 (1971): 125–43. See also Michael R. Lynn, "Sparks for Sale: The Culture and Commerce of Fireworks in Early Modern France," *Eighteenth-Century Life* 30, no. 2 (Spring 2006): 86–87.

17. R. J. Arnold is currently researching these resorts at Birkbeck, University of London. I am grateful to him for this information.

18. Archives générales du royaume, Bruxelles: Conseil privé, Periode autrichienne. A 124, Requêtes à Joseph II, File 1346. I am grateful to Professor Derek Beales for this reference.

19. In 1766 Joseph II ordered that the "Bratter" [Prater] promenade was to be open to all, for walking, riding, and ball games. Géza Hajós, "Die Stadtparks der österreichischen Monarchie von 1765 bis 1867 im gesamteuropäischen Kontext," in Hajós, ed, *Stadtparks in der österreichischen Monarchie, 1765–1918* (Vienna: Bohlau, 2007), 25, 28–33. Vauxhall and its Parisian imitators are referenced here (25) as "eine spezielle Form der öffentlichen Grüngestaltung," but the distinction between commercially operated public gardens and public parks is overlooked.

20. Hans E. Pappenheim, "In den Zelten—durch die Zeiten: Kulturgeschichte am Tiergartenrand 1740–1960," *Jahrbuch für brandenburgische Landesgeschichte* 14 (1963): 113.

21. Jonathan Conlin, "Vauxhall Revisited: The Afterlife of a London Pleasure Garden, 1770–1859," *Journal of British Studies* 45 (2006): 735–38. Jacob Larwood, *The Story of the London Parks*, 2 vols. (London: John Camden Hotten, 1874), 2:18, 272.

22. Jacob Henry Burn, "Historical Collections Relative to Spring Garden at Charing Cross . . . and to Spring Garden, Lambeth . . . Since Called Vauxhall Gardens," British Library, Cup.401.k.7–8; Oxford, Bodleian Library, G.A. Surrey c.21–5; "Vauxhall Miscellany," Lewis Walpole Library, Farmington, Conn. Jacob Henry Burn, *A Descriptive Catalogue of the London Traders, Tavern and Coffee-House Tokens Current in the Seventeenth Century*, 2nd ed. (London: Corporation of London, 1855). Warwick Wroth, "Tickets of Vauxhall Gardens," *Numismatic Chronicle*, 3rd ser. (1898): 73–92.

23. The same year also saw the publication of H. A. Rogers, *Views of Some of the Most Celebrated By-Gone Pleasure Gardens of London* (privately printed, 1896; reprinted, Basingstoke: Macmillan, 1979).

24. James Granville Southworth, *Vauxhall Gardens: A Chapter in the Social History of England* (New York: Columbia, 1941); Lawrence Gowing, "Hogarth, Hayman and the Vauxhall Decorations," *Burlington Magazine* 95 (January 1953): 4–19; W. S. Scott, *Green Retreats: The Story of Vauxhall Gardens, 1661–1859* (London: Odhams, 1955); Mollie Sands, *The Eighteenth-Century Pleasure Gardens of Marylebone* (London: Society for Theatre Research, 1987); Sarah Jane Downing, *The English Pleasure Garden, 1660–1860* (Oxford: Shire, 2009); Curl, *Spas, Wells, and Pleasure Gardens of London*; Richard D. Altick, *The Shows of London* (Cambridge, Mass.: Harvard University Press, 1978), 94–98, 319–22.

25. Larwood, *Story of London Parks*, 2:18, 272.

26. Peter Borsay, *The English Urban Renaissance: Culture and Society in the Provincial Town, c. 1660–1770* (Oxford: Clarendon, 1989). That Borsay's 1981 Lancaster Ph.D. dissertation had been subtitled "Landscape and Leisure" instead of the subsequent book's "Culture and Society" is itself indicative of shifts in academic discourse.

27. Cyril Ehrlich, *The Music Profession in Britain Since the Eighteenth Century: A Social History* (Oxford: Oxford University Press, 1985); Simon McVeigh, *Concert Life*

in London from Mozart to Haydn (Cambridge: Cambridge University Press, 1993); Michael Talbot, ed., *The Business of Music* (Liverpool: Liverpool University Press, 2002).

28. John Brewer, *The Pleasures of the Imagination: English Culture in the Eighteenth Century* (New York: Farrar, Straus Giroux, 1997), 377–78.

29. Jürgen Habermas, *The Structural Transformation of the Public Sphere*, trans. Thomas Burger (Cambridge, Mass.: MIT Press, 1989), 166.

30. John Brewer, Neil McKendrick, and J. H. Plumb, *The Birth of a Consumer Society: The Commercialization of Eighteenth-Century England* (London: Europa, 1982).

31. Habermas's refusal to give the "private domestic sphere" as much attention as the "formation of the public sphere" made his work a "lopsided account of cultural consumption and the making of a culture-consuming public." Anne Bermingham, "Introduction," in Anne Bermingham and John Brewer, eds., *The Consumption of Culture: Image, Object, Text* (London: Routledge, 1995), 1–22 (10).

32. Though he mentioned them only in passing, Lewis Mumford had defined the development of pleasure gardens in similar terms. Lewis Mumford, *The Culture of Cities* (New York: Harcourt Brace, 1938), 112.

33. The 12,000 figure came from the account in the April 1749 issue of the *Gentleman's Magazine*.

34. Brewer, *The Pleasures of the Imagination*, 28.

35. Tom Williamson, *Polite Landscapes: Gardens and Society in Eighteenth-Century England* (Baltimore: Johns Hopkins University Press, 1995), 107.

36. L. D. Schwartz, *London in the Age of Industrialization: Entrepreneurs, Labour Force and Living Conditions, 1700–1850* (Cambridge: Cambridge University Press, 1992); M. Hunt, *The Middling Sort: Commerce, Gender and the Family in England 1680–1780* (Berkeley: University of California Press, 1996); Penelope J. Corfield, ed., *Language, History, and Class* (Oxford: Blackwell, 1991), chap. 5.

37. The 3,500 figure was first proposed by David Hunter. David Hunter, "Rode the 12,000? Counting Coaches, People, and Errors en Route to the Rehearsal of Handel's *Music for the Royal Fireworks*," London Journal 37.1 (forthcoming, March 2012): 13–26. Even historians aware of the "mythology" of this episode seem surprisingly unwilling to question the 12,000 figure. See Coke and Borg, *Vauxhall Gardens*, 151.

38. Lockman, "The Charms of Dishabille," in Rogers, *Pleasure Gardens of London*, 47.

39. Such as "A German Prince" [Hermann, Fürst von Pückler-Muskau], *Tour in England, Ireland, and France* (Philadelphia: Carey, Lee and Blanchard, 1833), 157.

40. David Hunter, "The Real Audience at Vauxhall, 1729–59," unpublished paper delivered at "Vauxhall Revisited," Tate Britain, July 2008.

41. Hannah Greig, "'All Together and All Distinct': Social Exclusivity and the Pleasure Gardens of Eighteenth-Century London," *Journal of British Studies* 51 (January 2012): 50–75. I am grateful to Hannah Greig for permitting me to read a draft of

this article, itself based on a paper delivered to the 2008 "Vauxhall Revisited" conference, and for drawing the Mrs. Cary/Lady Bunbury episode (discussed below) to my attention.

42. Lady Sarah Lennox to Lady Susan O'Brien, 9 January 1766. Countess of Ilchester and Lord Stavordale, *The Life and Letters of Lady Sarah Lennox 1745–1826*, 2 vols. (London: Murray, 1901–2), 1:177.

43. Conlin, "Vauxhall Revisited."

44. Marvin Edward McAllister, *White People Do Not Know How to Behave at Entertainments Designed for Ladies and Gentlemen of Colour: William Brown's African and American Theater* (Chapel Hill: University of North Carolina Press, 2003), 27, 29. I am grateful to Naomi Stubbs for this reference.

45. Craig Koslofsky, *Evening's Empire: A History of the Night in Early Modern Europe* (Cambridge: Cambridge University Press, 2011).

46. Richard Quaintance, "Who's Making the Scene? Real People in Eighteenth-Century Topographical Prints," in *The Country and the City Revisited: England and the Politics of Culture, 1550–1850*, ed. Gerald Maclean, Donna Landry, and Joseph P. Ward (Cambridge: Cambridge University Press, 1999), 134–59.

47. Fanny Burney, *Cecilia, or Memoirs of an Heiress*, 5 vols. (London: T. Cadell, 1782), vol. 2, chap. 12; William Harrison Ainsworth, *The Miser's Daughter*, 3 vols., 2nd ed. (London, 1843), 2: 257–75; Georgette Heyer, *The Masqueraders* (London: William Heinemann,1928).

48. Emma Griffin, *England's Revelry: A History of Popular Sports and Pastimes, 1660–1830* (Oxford: Oxford University Press, 2005), 4.

49. Griffin, *England's Revelry*, 36.

50. Douglas A. Reid, "Weddings, Weekdays, Work and Leisure: The Decline of Saint Monday Revisited, 1791–1911," *Past and Present* 153, no. 1 (1996): 135–63.

51. For a discussion of such campaigns, see M. J. D. Roberts, *Making English Morals: Voluntary Association and Moral Reform in England, 1787–1886* (Cambridge: Cambridge University Press, 2004).

52. For an image of Castle Garden (1848), see O'Malley, *Keywords*, 546.

53. Charles Sedley, *The Mulberry-Garden, a Comedy as It Is Acted by His Majestie's Servants at the Theatre Royal* (London: H. Herringman, 1675), 9.

54. John Dixon Hunt's *Vauxhall and London's Garden Theatres* (London: ProQuest, 1985) was an important exception. See also John Dixon Hunt, "Theaters, Gardens and Garden Theaters" in John Dixon Hunt, *Gardens and the Picturesque: Studies in the History of Landscape Architecture* (Cambridge, Mass.: MIT Press, 1988).

55. Williamson, *Polite Landscapes*, 1.

56. Evelyn, *Fumifugium*, 24.

57. [Balthasar] Monconys, *Journal des Voyages de Monsieur de Monconys*, 3 pts. (Lyon: Horace Boissat and George Remeus, 1665–66), pt. 2 (1666), 16–17.

58. For an example from 1681, see Coke and Borg, *Vauxhall Gardens*, Figs. 14–15.

59. Brian Allen, "Jonathan Tyers' Other Garden," *Journal of Garden History* 1, no. 3 (1981): 215–38.

60. Mark Laird, *The Flowering of the Landscape Garden: English Pleasure Grounds, 1720–1800* (Philadelphia: University of Pennsylvania Press, 1999).

61. Hunt, *Vauxhall and London's Garden Theatres*, 23, 25; Hunt, "Theatres, Gardens, and Garden Theaters," 50.

62. "Alexander le Blond" [Antoine-Joseph Dézallier d'Argenville], *The Theory and Practice of Gardening*, trans. John James, 2nd ed. (London: Bernard Linton, 1728), 2. For an earlier use of "garden of pleasure," see Andrew Mollet, *The Garden of Pleasure* (London: for John Martyn, 1670), 1.

63. Sue Berry, "Pleasure Gardens in Georgian and Regency Seaside Resorts: Brighton, 1750–1840," *Garden History* 28, no. 2 (Winter 2000): 226. A shrubbery was, admittedly, added to the remote corner of Vauxhall Gardens in 1786. Coke and Borg, *Vauxhall Gardens*, 241.

64. Stephen Switzer, *Ichnographia Rustica*, 3 vols. (London: D. Browne, 1718), 1:60.

65. Switzer, *Ichnographia Rustica*, 1:52.

66. Horace Walpole, *The History of the Modern Taste in Gardening* [1782] (New York: Ursus, 1995), 43.

67. Michael Leslie, "History and Historiography in the English Landscape Garden," in *Perspectives on Garden History*, ed. Michel Conan (Washington, D.C.: Dumbarton Oaks Research Library and Collection, 1999) 103.

68. Alicia Amherst, *A History of Gardening in England* (London: Bernard Quaritch, 1895), 259.

69. Heath Schenker, "Pleasure Gardens, Theme Parks, and the Picturesque," in Young and Riley, *Theme Park Landscapes*, 85; Schenker, *Melodramatic Landscapes* (Charlottesville: University of Virginia Press, 1999).

70. Anonymous 1856 correspondent to *Tribune* cited in Roy Rosenzweig and Elizabeth Blackmar, *The Park and the People: A History of Central Park* (Ithaca, N.Y: Cornell University Press, 1992), 105.

71. O'Malley, *Keywords*, 546–47.

72. Walpole, *History of the Modern Taste*, 59, 50.

73. Switzer, *Ichnographia Rustica*, 1:65.

74. [D'Argenville], *Theory and Practice of Gardening*, 51. Writing in 1670, Mollet agreed that "the Garden-Alleys, which are the chiefest Ornaments of a Garden, and where *England* excelleth other Countrys, as well as by its art in Turffing." André Mollet, *Garden of Pleasure* (London: John Martyn, 1670), 9.

75. Gregory Nosan, "Pavilions, Power, and Patriotism: Garden Architecture at Vauxhall," in *Bourgeois and Aristocratic Cultural Encounters in Garden Art, 1550–1850*, ed. Michel Conan (Washington, D.C.: Dumbarton Oaks Research Library and Collection, 2002), 114. The arches are incorrectly dated to c. 1751 in Coke and Borg, *Vauxhall Gardens*, 212. A 1732 account refers to one of Vauxhall's walks "wonderfully improv'd by the *Triumphant Arches* now rais'd." *Universal Spectator*, 3 March 1732, 1.

76. See the images in Downing, *English Pleasure Garden*, 44–45. Here I am using the categories outlined by John Dixon Hunt in his essay "Lordship of the Feet," 188.

77. Laurent Turcot, *Le Promeneur à Paris aux dixhuitième siècle* (Paris: Gallimard, 2007), 153.

78. Christopher Morris, ed., *Illustrated Celia Fiennes* (London: Macdonald, 1982), 126n. See also Monconys, *Journal*, pt. 2, 21; Larwood, *Story of London Parks*, 1: 58–60.

79. A footnote in the original explains that the word *square* refers to "that part of the garden, where the company walk mostly, in which are the organ, the tent, the pavillions, Handel's statue, &c. 'To Molly,'" *Gentleman's Magazine* 13 (August 1743): 439.

80. For a mock-heroic 1716 celebration of such pedestrianism, see Clare Brant and Susan Whyman, eds., *Walking the Streets of Eighteenth-Century London: John Gay's Trivia: or, the Art of Walking the Streets* (Oxford: Oxford University Press, 2007).

81. See Jonathan Conlin, "'Mr. What-d'ye-call-him': À la recherche du flâneur à Paris et à Londres au dixhuitième siècle," in *Les Histoires de Paris*, ed. Thierry Belleguic and Laurent Turcot (Paris: Editions Hermann, 2012).

82. Charles Dufresnoy, cited in Turcot, *Le Promeneur à Paris*, 72.

83. Benjamin Baker, *A Glance at New York* (New York: Samuel French and Sons, 189?), II, sc. 5.

Chapter 1. Theaters of Hospitality

I am most grateful to Michael Leslie for a careful reading and commentary on a first draft of this chapter and for posing some challenging questions about my argument and for suggesting some fresh references.

1. *The Elements of Architecture*, opening of Part Two: here from *Reliquiae Wottonianæ* (London: R. Marriot and G. Bedel, 1651), 271.

2. Or mocked, if grotesquely handled. See Pope's lines perhaps on Cannons ("Timon's Villa") in his *Epistle to Burlington*; also see "Timon and the Duke of Chandos," in the Twickenham edition of *Epistles to Several Persons*, ed. F. W. Bateson (London: Methuen, 1951), Appendix B, 170–74.

3. There is a particular heavy, jargon-filled discussion of this in Peter de Bolla, *The Education of the Eye* (Stanford, Calif.: Stanford University Press, 2003), 72–103.

4. From "The Pleasures of the Imagination," *Spectator*, 411, 21 June 1712.

5. All Walpole quotations, unless otherwise noted, are to *The Yale Edition of Horace Walpole's Correspondence*, ed. W. S. Lewis et al., 48 vols. (New Haven, Conn.: Yale University Press, 1937–84), 13:103 and 9:42, respectively. I am grateful to my graduate students, Sarah Katz, in particular, and Charly Nelson for help with trawling these volumes for Walpole's commentary on public gardens and their visitation.

6. *Walpole's Correspondence*, 9:105–10.

7. There is some hesitation as to whether the Lambeth site was constituted of two gardens or one. Pepys seems to imply that he walked a short distance from one to the other, which would mean that his reference to "the Old Spring Garden" could not

refer to the site near Charing Cross. See Warwick Wroth, *The London Pleasure Gardens of the Eighteenth Century* (London: Macmillan, 1896; reprint, London: Macmillan, 1979), 286 ff; David Coke and Alan Borg, *Vauxhall Gardens: A History* (New Haven, Conn.: Yale University Press, 2011), 19; and Kerry Downes, *Sir John Vanbrugh: A Biography* (London: Sidgwick and Jackson, 1987), Appendix F ("Spring Garden"), for remarks on the different sites called by that name. The Lambeth site had long been divided into two adjacent parcels, which may explain Pepys's remark about them; for a brief rehearsal of the site's ownership, see Linda Dawn Glazier, "Vauxhall Gardens," master's thesis, California State University, 2000, 21.

8. A "variety of singing birds" was imitated also at the temple of Flora, near Westminster Bridge; see Wroth, *The London Pleasure Gardens*, 266. Obviously this particular birdsong evinced a strong sense of countryside.

9. Jonathan Swift, *Journal to Stella*, ed. A. Williams (Oxford: Oxford University Press, 1948), 272; Joseph Addison, *Spectator* 383 (1712); *Walpole's Correspondence*, 10:279. For the bird imitations, see Rudolph Ackerman, William Pyne, and William Combe, *Microcosm of London*, 3 vols. (London: R. Ackermann, 1808–11), vol. 3.

10. *Walpole's Correspondence*, 4:239.

11. I have reviewed some of these theatrical perspectives in John Dixon Hunt, "Theaters, Gardens, and Garden Theaters" in *Gardens and the Picturesque: Studies in the History of Landscape Architecture* (Cambridge, Mass.: Harvard University Press, 1988), 49–74. See also an even earlier example: Richard Brome's comedy *The Sparagus Garden* (1635), set in a real market garden in Lambeth marshes. (I am grateful to Michael Leslie for this reference.)

12. Quoted in W. S. Scott, *Green Retreats: The Story of Vauxhall Gardens 1661–1859* (London: Odhams, 1955), 15.

13. Scott, *Green Retreats*, 67ff.

14. John Timbs, *Romance of London: Strange Stories, Scenes, and Remarkable Persons of the Great Town*, 3 vols. (London: Richard Bentley, 1865; reprint, Detroit, Mich.: Singing Tree Press, 1968), 3:36. Quoted in Glazier, "Vauxhall Gardens," 30.

15. T. J. Edelstein, *Vauxhall Gardens: A Catalogue* (New Haven, Conn.: Yale Center for British Art, 1983), 20.

16. Richardson, *Arcadian Friends, Inventing the English Landscape Garden* (London, Bantam, 2007), 385. For plays, see note 8.

17. Stephen Switzer, *Ichnographia Rustica*, 3 vols. (London: D. Browne, 1718), 2:187 and 1:87, respectively. At Vauxhall such "mazes" did indeed afford promiscuous opportunities of another sort (see Fig I.4).

18. The whole painting is reproduced by John Harris, *The Palladian Revival: Lord Burlington, His Villa and Garden at Chiswick* (New Haven, Conn.: Yale University Press, 1994), 56.

19. There is a brief discussion of Evelyn's references to "well painted perspective[s]" "as large as the real" in B. Sprague Allen, *Tides of English Taste (1619–1800): A Background for the Study of Literature*, 2 vols. (Cambridge, Mass.: Harvard University Press, 1937), 1:137–38. On those at Vauxhall, see Allen, *Tides of English Taste*, 1:157.

20. For Bath, see Brenda Snaddon, *The Last Promenade. Sydney Gardens Bath* (Bath, Millstream Books2000), 21; for Smollett, the passages reprinted in John Dixon Hunt, *Vauxhall and London's Garden Theatres* (Cambridge: Chadwyck-Healey, 1985). Both cascades were removed in the 1820s. Cascades were an important feature in gardens from the Italian renaissance to the picturesque and thus virtually de rigueur; and if we think Sydney or Vauxhall Gardens are a touch absurd, we might recall that in the 1780s the German garden theorist Hirschfeld was urging the example of Niagara Falls as a model for waterfalls in public parks.

21. Brian Allen, "Jonathan Tyers's Other Garden," *Journal of Garden History* 1 (1981): 215–38.

22. See John Dixon Hunt, *William Kent: Landscape Garden Designer* (London: Zwemmer, 1987), 159 (cat. 90).

23. There seems to be no surviving imagery of this work; see Richardson, *Arcadian Friends*, 464–46.

24. *The Ambulator, or the Stranger's Companion in a Tour Round London* (1782), 195. De Bolla, *The Education of the Eye*, 87–89, provides other citations in which "pleasure" is the keynote.

25. See, for example, the extracts from visitors' accounts reprinted in Hunt, *Vauxhall and London's Garden Theatres*.

26. *Walpole's Correspondence*, 17:434.

27. *Walpole's Correspondence*, 13:102.

28. Of course, almost all of the graphic record shows Vauxhall in the daylight, which presumably is when artists could see to paint it. Many of the smaller gardens, especially tea gardens and places attached to eating establishments were open only during the day. By contrast, the illuminations of Vauxhall relied, for their best effect, upon darkness.

29. *Walpole's Correspondence*, 18:485.

30. *Walpole's Correspondence*, 39:133; he also told Fox that "the trees at Vauxhall and purling basins of goldfish, never inspire one" (30:100).

31. *Walpole's Correspondence*, 10:314–16.

32. It is interesting that what is "acted out" at Vauxhall—after all, most of its attractions were scenery and theater, does not seem to work when—as Walpole puts it—"a small Vauxhall was *acted* for us" at Stowe. However, it is not the case that private gardens did not host entertainment or illuminate their grounds for such purposes; it was rather than Vauxhall did it to successful excess.

33. I owe to Sarah Katz the recognition of these Walpolean neologisms: see Sarah Katz, "Horace Walpole's Landscape at Strawberry Hill," *Studies in the History of Gardens and Designed Landscapes* 28 (2008): 179.

34. *Walpole's Correspondence*, 10:127.

35. *Walpole's Correspondence*, 10:278–79.

36. See his remarks in the thirteenth discourse to Royal Academy students in December 1786.

37. *The Complete Letters of Lady Mary Wortley Montagu*, ed. Robert Halsband, 3 vols. (Oxford: Clarendon Press, 1965–67), 2:12.

38. Linda Colley, *Britons: Forging the Nation 1707–1837*, 2nd ed. (New Haven, Conn.: Yale University Press, 2005), xvi.

39. This quotation is taken from Walpole's manuscript notes to Mason's *Heroic Epistle*, in William Mason, *Satirical Poems: Published Anonymously by William Mason with Notes by Horace Walpole Now First Printed from His Manuscript*, ed. Paget Toynbee (Oxford: Clarendon Press, 1926), 43–44.

40. Colley, *Britons*, xi.

41. Quoted in Edelstein, *Vauxhall Gardens*, 26. A foreigner could applaud both the "luxury of the English" Vauxhall and Ranelagh in a letter to "a friend in Paris," quoted Glazier, "Vauxhall Gardens," 44.

42. *Walpole's Correspondence*, 13:102.

43. Lockman, quoted in Edelstein, *Vauxhall Gardens*, 18; anonymous author from "A Description of Vaux-Hall Gardens," 355, quoted in Edelstein, *Vauxhall Gardens*, 22; quoted in Scott, *Green Retreats*, 76.

44. Kent, though, had inserted a Gothic Triumphal Arch as an eyecatcher at Rousham. There was also at Vauxhall the feature that Walpole considered the masterstroke of English gardening, the ha-ha.

45. "A Description of Vaux-Hall Gardens," 420. See also Gregory Nosan's essay charting the "spectacular, patriotic environment that celebrated and commemorated both British royalty and great British artists." Gregory Nosan, "Pavilions, Power, and Patriotism: Garden Architecture at Vauxhall," in *Bourgeois and Aristocratic Cultural Encounters in Garden Art 1550–1850*, ed. Michel Conan, 101–22 (Washington, D.C.: Dumbarton Oaks, 2002).

46. Quoted in Wroth, *The London Pleasure Gardens*, 292. Michael Leslie, in *A Cultural History of Gardens*, ed. John Dixon Hunt, 6 vols. (Oxford: Berg, forthcoming, 2012), argues that such references were simply a code for the sex.

47. *Champion*, 5 August 1742.

48. *Walpole's Correspondence*, 10:156.

49. See Giuseppe Tassini, *Curiosità Veneziane* (Venice: Filippi, 1999), 548.

50. Venice continued to exert its charms: As late as June 1847 a vast picture model of the city was exhibited at Vauxhall, see Scott, *Green Retreats*, 104. On the theatrical landscapes of Venice, see "Garden, Theatre, and City" in John Dixon Hunt, *The Venetian City Garden: Place, Typology and Perception* (Basel: Birkhäuser, 2009), 116–35.

51. Stella Rudolph, "Dai diari inediti di Giannantonio Selva: il viaggio in Inghilterra," *Labyrinthos* 5, no. 6 (1984): 228–29. It is perhaps also important to note that Selva's enthusiasm for the "new" and naturalistic "English" landscape style was by no means overwhelming.

52. *Walpole's Correspondence*, 17:434 (writing in May 1742 OS). However an east wind made the river journey more irksome (17:421).

53. *The World* 59, 14 February 1754. The author is unknown.

54. Quoted in Richardson, *Arcadian Friends*, 182.

55. See Richard Clary, "Making Breathing Room: Public Gardens and City Planning in Eighteenth-Century France," in *Tradition and Innovation in French Garden Art: Chapters of a New History*, ed. John Dixon Hunt and Michel Conan (Philadelphia: University of Pennsylvania Press, Studies in Landscape Architecture, 2002), 68–81, to which I am principally indebted. Also Marcel Poëte, *La Promenade à Paris au XVIIe siècle* (Paris: Colin, 1913).

56. Promenading is still deemed a particularly French activity: Alain Finkielkraut, a philosopher and supporter of President Nicolas Sarkozy, opined that "Western civilization, in its best sense [by which of course he meant French] was born with the promenade"; reported in *New York Times* [International section], 22 July 2008, 8.

57. See Harris, *The Palladian Revival*, Appendix 1, 267. For Stowe, see Peter Willis, *Charles Bridgeman and the English Landscape Garden: Reprinted with Supplementary Plates and a Catalogue of Additional Documents, Drawings, and Attributions* (Newcastle-upon-Tyne: Elysium, 2002), especially the frontispiece and plates 129–43.

58. Harris, *The Palladian Revival*, 47, 102, 202, 229, and 256, respectively.

59. Richard Quaintance, "Who's Making the Scene? Real People in Eighteenth-Century Topographical Prints," in *The Country and the City Revisited: England and the Politics of Culture, 1550–1850*, ed. Gerald Maclean, Donna Landry, and Joseph P. Ward (Cambridge: Cambridge University Press, 1999), 134–59.

60. This is a criticism that Harris levels frequently at Rigaud's work: Harris, *The Palladian Revival*, 47, 102, 104; for what he calls the "fictionalized views," 175, 190.

61. Harris, *The Palladian Revival*, 233, 238.

62. See Jacques Carré, *Lord Burlington (1694–1753): le connoisseur, le mécène, l'architecte*, 2 vols. (Clermont-Ferrand: Editions Adosa, 1993), 1:57.

63. Quoted in John Harris, *The Palladian Revival: Lord Burlington, His Villa and Garden at Chiswick* (New Haven: Yale University Press, 1994), p.267, citing Vertue's *Notebooks* published by the Walpole Society, III (1934), 69 and VI (1955), 194.

64. *Walpole's Correspondence*, 10:316.

65. *The World* 15, 12 April 1753.

Chapter 2. Pleasure Gardens and Urban Culture
in the Long Eighteenth Century

1. Quoted in Rosamond Bayne-Powell, *Travellers in Eighteenth-Century England* (London: John Murray 1951), 82, from Pierre Jean Grosley, *A Tour to London*, trans. T. Nugent (1772).

2. Peter Borsay, *A History of Leisure: The British Experience Since 1500* (Basingstoke: Palgrave, 2006), 1–8.

3. Lewis Mumford, *The City in History* (1961; reprint, Harmondsworth: Penguin Books, 1975), 431–34.

4. Lawrence E. Klein, "The Polite Town: Shifting Possibilities of Urbanness, 1660–1715," in *The Streets of London: From the Great Fire to the Great Stink*, ed. Tim Hitchcock and Heather Shore (London: Rivers Oram Press, 2003), 30–31.

5. John Brewer, "'The Most Polite Age and the Most Vicious': Attitudes Towards Culture as a Commodity, 1660–1800," in *The Consumption of Culture, 1660–1800: Image, Object, Text*, ed. Ann Bermingham and John Brewer (London: Routledge, 1997), 346.

6. Peter Borsay, *The English Urban Renaissance: Culture and Society in the Provincial Town, 1660–1770* (Oxford: Clarendon Press, 1989).

7. Warwick Wroth, *The London Pleasure Gardens of the Eighteenth Century* (1896; reprint, Hamden, Conn.: Archon, 1979), 5–7.

8. For exceptions, see Helen Conway, *People's Parks: The Design and Development of Victorian Parks in Britain* (Cambridge: Cambridge University Press, 1991); Robert Scott, *A Breath of Fresh Air: The Story of Belfast's Parks* (Belfast: Blackstaff Press, 2000); Todd Longstaffe-Gowan, *The London Town Garden, 1700–1840* (New Haven, Conn.: Yale University Press, 2001); Katy Layton-Jones and Robert Lee, *Places of Health and Amusement: Liverpool's Historic Parks and Gardens* (Swindon: English Heritage, 2008).

9. *The A to Z of Georgian London*, introductory notes by Ralph Hyde (Lympney Castle, Kent: Harry Margary, 1981), maps 1, 17, 19; Andrew Davies, *The Map of London from 1746 to the Present Day* (London: B.T. Batsford, 1987), 10–12, 20, 42, 44.

10. Laura Williams, "'To Recreate and Refresh Their Dulled Spirites in the Sweet and Wholesome Ayre': Green Space and the Growth of the City," in *Imagining Early Modern London: Perceptions and Portrayals of the City from Stow to Strype, 1598–1720*, ed. Julia F. Merritt (Cambridge: Cambridge University Press, 2001), 186.

11. Zacharias Conrad von Uffenbach, *London in 1710 from the Travels of Zacharias von Uffenbach*, trans. and ed. W. H. Quarrell and Margaret Mare (London: Faber and Faber, 1934), 12–13, 15, 21 36, 52, 91, 96, 114, 116, 120, 126, 130–32, 139–40, 153–54, 156, 161.

12. *A Companion to All the Principal Places of Curiosity and Entertainment in and about London and Westminster*, 8th ed. (London, 1795), 198.

13. Borsay, *English Urban Renaissance*, 162–72, 350–54; Mark Girouard, *The English Town* (New Haven, Conn.: Yale University Press, 1990), 145–54.

14. John Money, *Experience and Identity: Birmingham and the West Midlands, 1760–1800* (Manchester: Manchester University Press, 1977), 80, 83; Jonathan Barry, "The Cultural Life of Bristol, 1640–1775," D.Phil. diss., University of Oxford, 1985, 168–69; *Victoria County History: Warwickshire*, vol. 8, ed. W. B. Stephens (London: Oxford University Press, 1969), 224; John Brand, *History and Antiquities of the Town and County of Newcastle-upon-Tyne*, 2 vols. (London, 1789), 2:538; Angela Dain, "An Enlightened and Polite Society" in *Norwich Since 1550*, ed. Carole Rawcliffe and Richard Wilson (London: Hambledon and London, 2004), 205–7; Trevor Fawcett, *Music in Eighteenth-Century Norwich and Norfolk* (Norwich: Centre for East Anglian Studies, 1979), 29.

15. Trevor Fawcett, *Bath Entertain'd; Amusements, Recreations and Gambling at the Eighteenth-Century Spa* (Bath: Ruton, 1998), 57–62.

16. Thomas Benge Burr, *A History of Tunbridge Wells* (London, 1766), 56–59.

17. [William Matthews], *The New History, Survey and Description of the City and Suburbs of Bristol* (Bristol, 1794), 51; John Wood, *A Description of Bath*, 2nd ed. (1749, reissued 1765; reprint, Bath: Kingsmead Reprints, 1969), 345.

18. Samuel Rudder, *A New History of Gloucestershire* (Cirencester, 1779), 596; William Hutton, *A History of Birmingham to the End of the Year 1780* (Birmingham, 1781), 249.

19. Celia Fiennes, *The Journeys of Celia Fiennes*, ed. Christopher Morris (London: Cresset Press, 1947), 211; H. Bourne, *The History of Newcastle upon Tyne; or the Ancient and Present State of That Town* (Newcastle upon Tyne, 1736), 137–38; J. V. Pickstone and S. V. Butler, "The Politics of Medicine in Manchester, 1788–1792: Hospital Reform and Public Health Services in the Early Industrial City," *Medical History* 28 (1984), 229.

20. Fiennes, *Journeys*, 215–16; Daniel Defoe, *A Tour Through the Whole Island of Great Britain*, ed. G. D. H. Cole and D. C. Browning, 2 vols. (1724–26; reprint, London: Everyman, 1962), 1:46.

21. Fiennes, *Journeys*, 227; Paul Stamper, *Historic Parks and Gardens of Shropshire* (Shrewsbury: Shropshire Books, 1996), 38–39.

22. Burr, *Tunbridge Wells*, 56, 101–2; Fiennes, *Journeys*, 133–34.

23. Ralph Thoresby, *Ducatus Leodiensis; or, the Topography of the Ancient and Populous Town and Parish of Leedes* (London, 1715), 96, 102.

24. Wroth, *London Pleasure Gardens*, see map; Felix Barker and Peter Jackson, *The Pleasures of London*, ed. Ann Saunders and Denise Silvester-Carr (London: London Topographical Society, 2008), 58–59.

25. John Hutchins, *The History and Antiquities of the County of Dorset* (London, 1774), 1:731; Fiennes, *Journeys*, 249; James Spershott, *The Memoirs of James Spershott*, ed. Francis W. Steer, Chichester Papers, no. 30 (1962), 17–18; Ralph Hyde, *A Prospect of Britain: The Town Panoramas of Samuel and Nathaniel Buck* (London: Pavilion Books, 1994), plate 31.

26. Hyde, *Prospect of Britain*, plate 15; Tenby Museum, Borough of Tenby Order Book, f. 18, 30 March 1781; Oliver Creighton and Robert Higham, *Medieval Town Walls: An Archaeology and Social History of Defence* (Stroud: Tempus, 2005), 241–42.

27. Hyde, *Prospect of Britain*, plates 1, 46, and 73; Francis Drake, *Eboracum: or, the History and Antiquities of the City of York* (1736; reprint, East Ardsley: EP Publishing, 1978), map opp. 244 ; Fiennes, *Journeys*, 238; [Matthews], *New History . . . of Bristol*, 53–54; Thoresby, *Ducatus Leodiensis*, 92, 96; Benjamin Donn, "A Plan of the City and Suburbs of Exeter," in *A Map of the County of Devon* (1765; reprint, Devon and Cornwall Record Society, 1965).

28. Wood, *A Description of Bath*, 225; Mary Chandler, *The Description of Bath* (London, 1734), 16.

29. Richard Pococke, *The Travels through England*, ed. J. Joel, Camden Society, 2nd ser., 2 vols. XLII, XLIV (1888–49), 2:5.

30. Peter Borsay, "Le développement des villes balnéaires dans l'Angleterre Géorgienne," in *Les Villes Balnéaires d'Europe Occidentale du XVIIIe Siècle à Nos Jours*, ed. Yves Perret-Gentil, Alain Lottin, and Jean-Pierre Poussou (Paris: PUPS, 2008), 24–26.

31. Lybbe Powys, *Passages from the Diaries of Mrs. Lybbe Powys*, ed. E. J. Climenson (London: Longmans, Green and Co., 1899), 69, 79; Hyde, *Prospect of Britain*, plate 25. See also Wood, *A Description of Bath*, 351, for a view from the Grand Parade at Bath.

32. Walter Harrison, *A New and Universal History, Description and Survey of the Cities of London and Westminster* (London, 1775), 512; see also H. Chamberlain, *A New and Compleat History and Survey of the Cities of London, Westminster, the Borough of Southwark and Parts Adjacent* (London, 1770), 574.

33. Jonathan Conlin, "Vauxhall on the Boulevard: Pleasure Gardens in London and Paris, 1764–1784," *Urban History* 35, no. 1 (2008): 35; Tom Williamson, *Polite Landscapes: Gardens and Society in Eighteenth-Century England* (Stroud: Alan Sutton, 1995).

34. Girouard, *English Town*, 270.

35. Mollie Sands, *The Eighteenth-Century Pleasure Gardens of Marylebone, 1737–1777* (London: Society for Theatre Research, 1987), 42 and plates 4–5.

36. Quoted in David Coke, "Vauxhall Gardens," in *Rococo: Art and Design in Hogarth's England*, ed. Michael Snodin and E. Moncrieff (London: Trefoil Books/Victoria and Albert Museum, 1984), 88.

37. Williamson, *Polite Landscapes*, 35–47.

38. *London in Miniature: Being a Concise and Comprehensive Description of the Cities of London and Westminster* (London, 1765), 243; Chamberlain, *New and Compleat History*, 179–80; *Companion to all the Principal Places*, 193–96.

39. *A Companion to Every Place of Entertainment in and About London and Westminster* (London, 1767), 177; John Lockman, *A Sketch of the Spring-Gardens* (1752), 2, quoted in Miles Ogborn, *Spaces of Modernity: London's Geographies, 1680–1780* (New York: Guilford Press, 1998), 120.

40. *The Bull-Finch*, 2nd ed. (London, [1760]), 123.

41. *The A to Z of Regency London*, introduction by Paul Laxton (Lympney Castle: Harry Margary, 1985), map 33.

42. *A Complete Guide to All Persons Who Have Any Trade or Concern with the City of London and Parts Adjacent* (London, 1763), 193.

43. Penelope Corfield, *Vauxhall and the Invention of the Urban Pleasure Gardens* (London: History and Social Action Publications, 2008), 11–13.

44. Donald Burrows and Rosemary Dunhill, ed., *Music and Theatre in Handel's World: The Family Papers of James Harris, 1732–1780* (Oxford: Oxford University Press, 2002), 893; Yale University, Beinecke Rare Book and Manuscript Library, Osborne Shelves, f.c.80, Diary of Edward Pigott (1770–83), 2 vols., 1 May 1776.

45. Susan E. Whyman, "Sharing Public Spaces" in *Walking the Streets of Eighteenth-Century London: John Gay's Trivia (1716)*, ed. Clare Brant and Susan E.

Whyman, 43–61 (Oxford: Oxford University Press, 2007), 53–56; Susan E. Whyman, *Sociability and Power in Late-Stuart England: The Cultural World of the Verneys, 1660–1720* (Oxford: Oxford University Press, 2002), 100–107; Mark Jenner, "Circulation and Disorder: London Streets and Hackney Coaches, c. 1640–c. 1740," in *Streets of London*, ed. Hitchcock and Shore, 40–53.

46. James Boswell, *Boswell's London Journal, 1762–3*, ed. Frederick Albert Pottle (Harmondsworth: Penguin Books, 1966), 275–76, 279, 303–4.

47. *Old Bailey Proceedings Online (OBP)* [cited on 6 July 2009]. Available from www.oldbaileyonline.org: 29 June 1785, trial of Joseph Bossey (t17850629-23), 28; 26 June 1773, trial of Robert Straham (t17730626-18), 15; *Companion to All the Principal Places*, 196.

48. Von Uffenbach, *London*, 16, 130–31.

49. *The London Guide, Describing the Public and Private Buildings of London, Westminster and Southwark* (London, [1782]), 5–6.

50. C. Pope, *The New Bath Guide: Or, Useful Pocket-Companion*, 5th ed. (Bath, [1768]), 36.

51. Sands, *Marylebone*, 31; *London Guide* ([1782]), 5.

52. Sylas Neville, *The Diary of Sylas Neville, 1767–1788*, ed. Basil Cozens-Hardy (London: Oxford University Press, 1950), 10.

53. Carl Philip Moritz, *Journeys of a German in England: Carl Philip Moritz, a Walking Tour in England in 1782*, trans. R. Nettel (London: Eland Books, 1983), 44–45, 47.

54. *OBP*, 28 June 1769, trial of Joseph Trippet and James Fannen (t17690628-30), 32.

55. *Scots Magazine*, quoted in Coke, "Vauxhall Gardens," 77.

56. For the Pantheon at Spa Fields, see Wroth, *London Pleasure Gardens*, 25–28.

57. Norman Scarfe, ed., *Innocent Espionage: The La Rochefoucauld Brothers' Tour of England in 1785* (Woodbridge: Boydell Press, 1995), 207; Beinecke Library, Diary of Edward Pigott, 1, May 1776; *Companion to Every Place* (1767), 180–81; Harrison, *New and Universal History* (1775), 617; *Companion to All the Principal Places*, 196.

58. Moritz, *Journeys*, 45–46; Boswell, *London Journal*, 279; Tobias Smollett, *Humphry Clinker*, ed. Angus Ross (1771; reprint, Harmondsworth: Penguin Books, 1967), 120.

59. *The London and Westminster Guide, Through the Cities and Suburbs* (London, 1768), 15.

60. Mark Girouard, *Life in the English Country House* (Harmondsworth: Penguin Books, 1980), 119–212.

61. Moritz, *Journeys*, 46.

62. Ogborn, *Spaces of Modernity*, 151; Peter de Bolla, "The Visibility of Visuality: Vauxhall Gardens and the Siting of the Viewer," in *Vision and Textuality*, ed. Stephen Melville and William Readings (Basingstoke: Macmillan, 1995), 289; Defoe, *A Tour Through the Whole Island of Great Britain*, 1:126–27.

63. Williams, "'To Recreate and Refresh Their Dulled Spirites,'" 194.

64. Conlin, "Vauxhall on the Boulevard," 35.

65. Moritz, *Journeys*, 46–47.

66. Wroth, *London Pleasure Gardens*, preface; Corfield, *Vauxhall*, 13; Brewer, "'Most Polite Age,'" 348; David Solkin, *Painting for Money: The Visual Arts and the Public Sphere in Eighteenth-Century England* (New Haven, Conn.: Yale University Press, 1992), 123.

67. Wroth, *London Pleasure Gardens*, 8.

68. *Companion to Every Place* (1767), 177, 180–81; Burrows and Dunhill, *Music and Theatre*, 935; Moritz, *Journeys*, 46–47; Conlin, "Vauxhall on the Boulevard," 25; Solkin, *Painting for Money*, 110; Sands, *Marylebone*, 12, 30–31.

69. Corfield, *Vauxhall*, 14; Sands, *Marylebone*, 12, 67, 106; Coke, "Vauxhall Gardens," 91.

70. Sands, *Marylebone*, 25–26, 119; Solkin, *Painting for Money*, 114.

71. J. Nicolson, *Vauxhall Gardens, 1661–1859* (London: Vauxhall Society and St. Peter's Heritage Society, 1991), 11.

72. York City Archives, House Book of the Corporation, 28 April 1742, 14 July 1742.

73. Jonathan Conlin, "Vauxhall Revisited: The Afterlife of a London Pleasure Garden, 1770–1859," *Journal of British Studies* 45 (2006), 718–43.

74. Corfield, *Vauxhall*, 14, 16.

75. *Companion to Every Place* (1767), 180; *London Guide* ([1782]), 5.

76. Corfield, *Vauxhall*, 13; Ogborn, *Spaces of Modernity*, 120.

77. Von Uffenbach, *London*, 130–31; *OBP*, 5 July 1732, trial of Thomas Gardon (t17320705-30), 21; 28 June 1738, trial of Ann Holden (t17380628-32), 18; 16 January 1745, trial of Henry Simms (t17450116-15), 11.

78. Moritz, *Journeys*, 42; *OBP*, 18 July 1753, trial of Margaret and Carbery Hasley (t17530718-36), 30–32; 29 June 1785, trial of Joseph Bossey (t17850629-23), 28; 13 September 1785, trial of Dove Ash (t17750913-28), 23–24.

79. *OBP*, 13 September 1785, trial of Dove Ash (t17750913-28), 23–24; 23 Oct 1771, trial of Charles Lyon (t17711023-50), 29.

80. *Spectator*, no. 383, 20 May 1712; *OBP*, 16 Jan 1745, trial of Henry Simms (t17450116-15), 11.

81. *OBP*, 28 June 1738, trial of Ann Holden (t17380628-32), 18.

82. *OBP*, 8 September 1773, trial of Catherine Duffey and Elizabeth Davis (t17730908-83), 67.

83. Burrows and Dunhill, *Music and Theatre*, 102.

84. *OBP*, 11 July 1781, trial of Joseph Brassey and William Huggins (t17810711-10), 112.

85. *OBP*, Ordinary's Account, 5 October 1744 (OA17441005), 9.

86. *OBP*, 11 July 1759, trial of James Toms (t17590711-15), 16; 9 September 1772, trial of Lewis Williams (t17720909-3), 3; 11 July 1781, trial of William Gough (t17810711-4), 100; 29 June 1785, trial of Samuel Champness and Edward Crowder (t17850629-59), 65.

87. Sands, *Marylebone*, 26–27, 31, 58–59, 70–71; Wroth, *London Pleasure Gardens*, 8–9; *OBP*, 10 April 1771, trial of Thomas Boyce (t17710410–25), 11.

88. Solkin, *Painting for Money*, 108–15; John Brewer, *The Pleasures of the Imagination: English Culture in the Eighteenth Century* (London: HarperCollins, 1997), 65–66; Sands, *Marylebone*, 31; Wroth, *London Pleasure Gardens*, 10; Dagmar Kift, *The Victorian Music Hall: Culture, Class and Conflict* (Cambridge: Cambridge University Press, 1996), 146–47.

89. Wroth, *London Pleasure Gardens*, 301; Laura J. Williams, "Rus in urbe: Greening the English Town, 1660–1760," Ph.D. diss., University of Wales, 1998, 241–42.

90. Ogborn, *Spaces of Modernity*, 123, 128–33, 152–53.

91. Terry Castle, *Masquerades and Civilization: The Carnivalesque in Eighteenth-Century English Culture and Fashion* (London: Methuen, 1986), 6; Coke, "Vauxhall Gardens," 97–98; Sands, *Marylebone*, 30, 120; Vic Gatrell, *City of Laughter: Sex and Satire in Eighteenth-Century London* (London: Atlantic Books, 2006), 204–8.

92. *OBP*, 5 July 1732, trial of Thomas Gardon (t17320705–30), 21.

93. *Apollo's Lyre: Being a Selection of the Most Approved Songs, Including Those Sung at Vauxhall, Theatres Royal, &c.* (London: Silvester Sikes & Co, 1795), 48.

94. Robert Shoemaker, *Gender in English Society, 1650–1850: The Emergence of Separate Spheres?* (Harlow: Longman, 1998), 317.

95. *Jubilee Masquerade Balls, at Ranelagh Gardens, a Bad Return for the Merciful Deliverance from the Last Earthquake* (London: W. Owen, 1750), 18, 21.

96. Paul Langford, *Englishness Identified: Manners and Character, 1650–1850* (Oxford: Oxford University Press, 2000), 102.

97. Wroth, *London Pleasure Gardens*, 7; *Companion to All the Principal Places*, 187, 197.

98. *The Improved Bath Guide; or, Picture of Bath and Its Environs* (Bath, [1812]), 103.

99. York City Archives, House Book of the Corporation, 7 December 1732.

100. Quoted in Sands, *Marylebone*, 60.

101. Wood, *A Description of Bath*, 437–38.

102. Pope, *New Bath Guide*, 36; R. Crutwell, *The New Bath Guide: Or, Useful Pocket Companion* (Bath, [1772]), 37; John Penrose, *Letters from Bath, 1766–1767*, ed. Brigitte Mitchell and Hubert Penrose (Gloucester: Alan Sutton, 1983), 70, 96, 98; Sands, *Marylebone*, 15, 19.

103. Wood, *A Description of Bath*, 439, 442; Beinecke Library, Diary of Edward Pigott, 1, March 1777, refers to the company gathering on the Parades at Bath at 2 p.m.

104. Wroth, *London Pleasure Gardens*, 6–7, 16.

105. Conlin, "Vauxhall on the Boulevard," 35.

106. *Companion to All the Principal Places*, 187; Conlin, "Vauxhall Revisited," 729; von Uffenbach, *London*, 12, 36; Wroth, *London Pleasure Gardens*, 7, 25–28.

107. *Companion to Every Place* (1767), 179, 180–81; *Companion to All the Principal Places*, 187, 192.

108. Burrows and Dunhill, *Music and Theatre*, 444.

109. Neville, *Diary*, 10.

110. Beinecke Library, Diary of Edward Pigott, 1, May 1776.

111. Scarfe, *Innocent Espionage*, 207.

112. Jane Fiske, ed., *The Oakes Diaries: Business, Politics and the Family in Bury St. Edmunds, 1778–1827*, 2 vols. (Woodbridge, Suffolk: Boydell Press, 1990–91), 1:271.

113. *OBP*, 29 June 1785, trial of Samuel Champness and Edward Crowder (t17850629-59), 65; 23 May 1787, trial of Samuel Toomes and William Ellicott (t17870523-11), 18.

114. Sands, *Marylebone*, 26, 119.

115. M. Falkus, "Lighting in the Dark Ages of English Economic History: Town Streets Before the Industrial Revolution," in *Trade, Government and Economy in Pre-Industrial England*, ed. Donald Cuthbert Coleman and Arthur H. John (London: Weidenfeld & Nicolson, 1976), 248–73.

116. Beinecke Library, Diary of Edward Pigott, 1 May 1776.

117. *Companion to Every Place* (1767), 180; Nicolson, *Vauxhall Gardens*, 10; *Ambulator: Or a Pocket Companion in a Tour Round London*, 4th ed. (London, 1792), 251.

118. Moritz, *Journeys*, 46–47.

119. Sands, *Marylebone*, 86–96; Conlin, "Vauxhall on the Boulevard," 43–44.

120. *Improved Bath Guide* [1812], 104.

121. Brant and Whyman, *Walking the Streets*; Mark Hallett and Christine Riding, *Hogarth* (London: Tate Publishing, 2006), 130–35; *Companion to All the Principal Places*, 193–96.

122. Fanny Burney, *Evelina*, ed. E. A. Bloom (London: Oxford University Press, 1968), 39.

123. *London Guide* ([1782]), 6–7; Burney, *Evelina*, 195.

Chapter 3. Guns in the Gardens

1. [Joseph Addison], *The Spectator*, no. 383 (20 May 1712), quoted in T. J. Edelstein, "The Gardens," in *Vauxhall Gardens*, ed. T. J. Edelstein (New Haven, Conn.: Yale University Press, 1983), 12. See also David Bindman, "Roubiliac's Statue of Handel and the Keeping of Order in Vauxhall Gardens in the Early Eighteenth Century," *Sculpture Journal* 1 (1997): 22–31.

2. T. J. Edelstein, "The Paintings," in Edelstein, *Vauxhall Gardens*, 25; Brian Allen, "Francis Hayman and the Supper-Box Paintings for Vauxhall Gardens," in *The Rococo in England: A Symposium*, ed. Charles Hind (London, 1986), 113–33; David Coke, "Vauxhall Gardens" in *Rococo: Art and Design in Hogarth's England*, ed. Michael Snodin and E. Moncrieff (London: Trefoil Books/Victoria and Albert Museum, 1984), 77–80.

3. Allen, "Francis Hayman," 128. See also Martin Eidelberg, "Watteau Paintings in England in the Early Eighteenth Century," *The Burlington Magazine* 117, no. 870

(September 1975): 576–83; Craig Hanson, "Dr. Richard Mead and Watteau's 'Comédiens Italiens,'" *Burlington Magazine* 145, no. 1201 (April 2003): 265–72.

4. David Solkin, *Painting for Money: The Visual Arts and the Public Sphere in Eighteenth-Century England* (New Haven, Conn.: Yale University Press, 1992), 110.

5. Edelstein, "The Paintings," 31–32; Allen, "Francis Hayman," 125; Suzannah Fleming, "Frederick as Apollo at Vauxhall: A 'Patriot' Project?" *London Gardener* 13 (2007–8): 46–66.

6. In 1762, for example, one colonnade of supper boxes had *The Taking of Porto Bello* at one extreme and *The Taking of the St. Joseph* at the other, bookending *Mlle. Catherina, the Famous Dwarf, Ladies Angling, Bird-Nesting, Falstaff's Cowardice Detected*, and *The Play at Bob-Cherry: A Description of Vaux-Hall Gardens Being a Proper Companion and Guide for All Who Visit That Place* (London, 1762), 8.

7. Alan Russet, "Peter Monamy's Marine Paintings for Vauxhall Gardens," *Mariner's Mirror* 80, no. 1 (February 1994): 79–84; F. B. Cockett, *Peter Monamy 1681–1749 and His Circle* (Woodbridge: Antique Collectors Club, 2000), 24, 85–86.

8. See Kathleen Wilson, *The Sense of the People: Politics, Culture, and Imperialism in England, 1715–1785* (Cambridge: Cambridge University Press, 1998), 140–65; Gerald Jordan and Nicholas Rogers, "Admirals as Heroes: Patriotism and Liberty in Hanoverian England," *Journal of British Studies* 28 (July 1989): 201–24.

9. David Coke and Alan Borg, *Vauxhall Gardens: A History* (New Haven, Conn.: Yale University Press, 2011), 120.

10. Lawrence James, *The Rise and Fall of the British Empire* (London: Little, Brown, 1994), 58–61; Christine Gerrard, *The Patriot Opposition to Walpole: Politics, Poetry, and National Myth, 1725–1742* (Oxford: Clarendon, 1994), 6–7.

11. Wilson, *Sense of the People*, 142.

12. Jordan and Rogers, "Admirals as Heroes," 202–3; Richard Harding, "Vernon, Edward (1684–1757)," *Oxford Dictionary of National Biography* (Oxford: Oxford University Press, 2004); online edition, January 2008. http://www.oxforddnb.com/view/article/28237, accessed 17 December 2010.

13. Vernon to Newcastle, 31 October 1739, The National Archives (UK) [hereafter TNA]: SP 42/85, f. 31, quoted in Harding, "Vernon, Edward."

14. J. K. Laughton, "Hosier, Francis (bap. 1673, d. 1727)," rev. J. D. Davies, *Oxford Dictionary of National Biography* (Oxford: Oxford University Press, 2004); online edition, January 2008. http://www.oxforddnb.com/view/article/13833, accessed 17 December 2010.

15. For a full description of the action, see Cyril Hughes Hartmann, *The Angry Admiral: The Later Career of Edward Vernon Admiral of the White* (London: William Heinemann, 1953), 16–35.

16. *London Magazine*, 13 March 1740; Hartman, *The Angry Admiral*, 17. Rentones's role in piloting the fleet won him the honor of bringing the news back to England in one of the captured Spanish vessels.

17. *London Magazine*, 13 March 1740.

18. Wilson, *Sense of the People*, 147; Jordan and Rogers, "Admirals as Heroes," 204. Evidence of Vernon's popularity persists in the naming of pubs; in the eighteenth century, signs for pubs named "Admiral Vernon" or "Portobello" were another form through which visual representations of the event were disseminated.

19. "On the Taking of Porto Bello," *Vernon's Glory, Containing Fifteen Songs, Ocassion'd by the Taking of Porto Bello and Fort Chagre* (London: n.p., 1740).

20. A. Marvell Jr. [pseud.], *Satyrical and Panegyrical Instructions to Mr. William Hogarth, Painter, on Admiral Vernon's Taking Porto Bello with Six Ships of War Only* (London: H. Goreham, 1740), 4.

21. Kathleen Wilson, "The Good, the Bad, and the Impotent: Imperialism and the Politics of Identity in Georgian England" in *The Consumption of Culture 1600–1800: Image, Object, Text*, ed. Anne Bermingham and John Brewer (London: Routledge, 1995), 238.

22. Charles Harrison-Wallace, "Peter Monamy," *Société Jersiase: Annual Bulletin* 23, no. 1 (1981): 101.

23. Coke and Borg, *Vauxhall Gardens*, 119.

24. Similar plans were available in several of the London and provincial newspapers, as well as at print sellers. Wilson, *Sense of the People*, 143.

25. *The London Evening Post*, 13–15 March 1740.

26. Anne Bermingham, introduction to Bermingham and Brewer, *The Consumption of Culture*,15.

27. Geoff Quilley, "Missing the Boat: The Place of the Maritime in the History of British Visual Culture," *Visual Culture in Britain* 1, no. 2 (December 2000): 79–92. See also Kathleen Wilson's reference to "the broad social basis within Britain of investment in the imperial project, from the financing of ships, investment in cargoes, and colonial land speculation to the distribution, consumption, and population patterns which spread colonial and British goods across regions, oceans, and nations." Wilson, "The Good, the Bad, and the Impotent," 238.

28. See Richard Hill, *The Prizes of War: The Naval Prize System in the Napoleonic Wars 1793–1815* (Stroud: Royal Naval Museum Publications, 1998), 7–8.

29. N. A. M. Rodger, *The Wooden World: An Anatomy of the Georgian Navy* (London: Collins, 1986), 129. For a full explanation of the naval system of ranks and ratings, see 16–29.

30. Rodger, *The Wooden World*, 19.

31. Rodger, *The Wooden World*, 256.

32. Hill, *The Prizes of War*, 7.

33. Rodger, *The Wooden World*, 135.

34. *Scots Magazine* (1739), 481.

35. *Gentleman's Magazine and Historical Chronicle* 9 (November 1739): 602.

36. Unknown source, 1777, quoted in David Coke, *The Muse's Bower: Vauxhall Gardens 1728–1786* (Sudbury: Gainsborough House Museum, 1978), n.p.

37. Edelstein, "The Paintings," 27–31.

38. Solkin, *Painting for Money*, 147.

39. Edelstein suggests that this parody "indicates the extent to which Vauxhall had passed into popular consciousness." Edelstein, "The Gardens," 14.

40. James Anthony Gardner, *Above and Under Hatches: Being Naval Recollections in Shred and Patches with Strange Reflections*, ed. Christopher Lloyd (London: Batchworth, 1955), 25.

41. British Library (UK) [hereafter BL]: *Broadsides Relating to Invasion*, f. 41.

42. Susan's inclusion at Vauxhall complicates the assertion that Monamy's paintings for Vauxhall "may have resulted from a perceived requirement for some specifically masculine spaces as a counterbalance to Hayman's undeniably gentler pleasures." Coke and Borg, *Vauxhall Gardens*, 119.

43. See Eleanor Hughes, "The Palmer Collection," in *Art for the Nation*, ed. Geoff Quilley (Greenwich: National Maritime Museum, 2006), 93–94.

44. George Vertue, *Notebooks: Walpole Society* 22 (1933–34): 145.

45. Linda Colley, *Captives: Britain, Empire, and the World 1600–1850* (London: Pimlico, 2003), 47.

46. *London Magazine and Monthly Chronologer* (1740), 148–49. Later in the century the willingness of English sailors to rescue their drowning enemies would become a trope of national self-definition in the wars against the French.

47. Collection of songs bound in 1830. BL, 171621.e.2.

48. Jürgen Habermas, *The Structural Transformation of the Public Sphere: An Inquiry into a Category of Bourgeois Society*, trans. Thomas Burger and Frederick Lawrence (Cambridge, Mass.: MIT Press, 1989), 41.

49. Solkin, *Painting for Money*, 190.

Chapter 4. Performance Alfresco

1. H. Edmund Poole, ed., *Music, Men, Manners in France and Italy 1770. Being the Journal Written by Charles Burney During a Tour Through Those Countries Undertaken to Collect Material for* A General History of Music. *Transcribed from the Original Manuscript in the British Museum*, Additional Manuscript 35122 (London: Folio Society, 1969), 21 (21 June 1770).

2. Statistics from Edward Croft-Murray and Simon McVeigh, "London, §V: Pleasure Gardens," *Grove Music Online, Oxford Music Online*, http://www.oxfordmusiconline.com, accessed 9 July 2008. This source lists the thirty-eight London pleasure gardens known to have provided their clientele with music. On further comparisons and general relationships between English and Continental "vauxhalls" at this time, including Torré's Wauxhall, see Jonathan Conlin, "Vauxhall on the Boulevard: Pleasure Gardens in London and Paris, 1764–1784," *Urban History* 35 no. 1 (2008): 24–47.

3. At Vauxhall, one thousand silver tickets were also put up for sale at the beginning of each season, priced at 25 shillings, to admit two people every night.

4. Tobias Smollett, *The Expedition of Humphry Clinker*, ed. O. M. Brack Jr. (Athens: University of Georgia Press, 1990), 92, quoted in Paul F. Rice, "Musical Nationalism and the Vauxhall Gardens," *Lumen: Selected Proceedings from the Canadian Society for Eighteenth-Century Studies* 19 (2000): 69.

5. Among the outcomes of this research are the facsimile edition *Johann Christian Bach: Favorite Songs Sung at Vauxhall Gardens, Originally Published in London 1766–1779*, Introduction by Stephen Roe, with General Introduction to the Pleasure Gardens by Christopher Hogwood, Music for London Entertainment 1660–1800, Series F, Vol.1 (Tunbridge Wells: Richard Macnutt, 1985), recorded on *J. Chr. Bach: Vauxhall Songs Complete*, Mária Zádori/Capella Savaria/Pál Németh, Hungaroton Classic, HCD 31730 (1998); Peter Holman, "The Sadler's Wells Dialogues of Charles Dibdin," in *Art and Ideology in European Opera: Essays in Honour of Julian Rushton*, ed. Rachel Cowgill, David Cooper, and Clive Brown (Woodbridge: Boydell & Brewer, 2010), 148–75; Charles Dibdin, *The Sadler's Wells Dialogues (1772–1780)*, Centre for Eighteenth-Century Music, Massey University, Series 1, no. 3, ed. Peter Holman (Wellington, NZ: Artaria, 2007); *Three Operas by Charles Dibdin* [*The Brickdust Man*, *The Grenadier*, and *The Ephesian Matron*], Opera Restor'd/Peter Holman, Hyperion, CDA66608 (1992).

6. See Hogwood, "General Introduction to the Pleasure Gardens," in *Johann Christian Bach: Favorite Songs*.

7. The most useful study of Marylebone to date is Mollie Sands, *The Eighteenth-Century Pleasure Gardens of Marylebone 1737–1777* (London: Society for Theatre Research, 1987), although the sources are not referenced. Current work on Ranelagh includes Berta Joncus, "'To Propagate Sound for Sense': Music for Diversion and Seduction at Ranelagh Gardens," *London Journal* 38, no. 1 (2013). Research on music-making in London's pleasure gardens benefits from substantial collections of primary-source material, including, among others, the Vauxhall collections at the Minet Library, Lambeth Archives; material on Cremorne Gardens in the Local Studies section, Central Library, Royal Borough of Kensington and Chelsea; and scrapbooks for Bagnigge Wells and Marylebone Gardens at the Centre for Performance History, Royal College of Music, London. These collections have not, to date, been mined to their full potential, and the ongoing digitization of the British Library's Newspaper collection offers further scope for new research. For a study that considers pleasure garden music in the context of London concert life generally, see Simon McVeigh, *Concert Life in London from Mozart to Haydn* (Cambridge: Cambridge University Press, 1993).

8. On the notion of "soundscape," which finds its roots in the work of R. Murray Schafer and the World Soundscapes Project at Simon Fraser University in the 1960s and 1970s, as well as in the work of Scandinavian musicologists at this time, see John M. Picker, *Victorian Soundscapes* (Oxford: Oxford University Press, 2003).

9. *The Diary of Samuel Pepys: A New and Complete Transcription*, ed. Robert Latham and William Matthews, 11 vols. (London: Bell, 1970–83), 8:240.

10. *Weekly Register*, 17 June 1732, quoted in *Gentleman's Magazine* 2 (1732): 802–3.

11. Miles Ogborn, "The Pleasure Garden," in his *Spaces of Modernity: London's Geographies 1680–1780* (New York: Guilford Press, 1998), 118, 122; see also Roy Porter,

"Material Pleasures in the Consumer Society," in *Pleasure in the Eighteenth Century*, ed. Roy Porter and Mary Mulvey Roberts (Basingstoke: Macmillan, 1996), 19–35.

12. For a facsimile of Rocque's map, see *The A-Z of Georgian London*, introductory notes by Ralph Hyde (Lympne Castle and London: Harry Margary and Guildhall Library, 1981).

13. The orchestra was first used at the opening of the season on 2 June 1735; see *Daily Advertiser*, 2 June 1735. Tyers's innovation was clearly successful, for Cuper's Gardens and Marylebone hired bands soon afterward.

14. "The Prince, who, lately form'd the Nation's Delight, and is now the just Subject of their unfeigned Sorrow, has ennobled this *Salon* by his Presence; His Royal Highness, attended by many distinguish'd Persons of both Sexes, sometimes supping in it, and closing the Night with Country Dances. Hence the *Portico*, before this *Salon*, is usually stiled the *Prince of Wales's Pavillion*." [John Lockman], *A Sketch of the Spring-Gardens, Vaux-Hall* (London: G. Woodfall, [1751]), 4–5.

15. Nebahat Avcıoğlu, *Turquerie and the Politics of Representation, 1728–1876* (Farnham: Ashgate, 2011), 97–138.

16. Of the Rotunda, Lockman writes: "The Roof or Cieling [sic] is adorned with grand painted Festoons of Flowers, terminating in a Point; and looks like the Dome, if I may so speak, of a most august, royal Tent." *A Sketch of the Spring-Gardens, Vaux-Hall*, 9.

17. Avcıoğlu, *Turquerie*, 98. On Mary Wortley Montagu, see note 25.

18. Ibid., 124.

19. *The Ladies Delight, Containing . . . IV. Ridotto al'Fresco. A Poem. Describing the Growth of This Tree* [the arbor vitae] *in the Famous* Spring Gardens *at* Vaux-Hall (London: W. James, 1732), 22–23.

20. *Universal Spectator, and Weekly Journal*, 3 June 1732.

21. See Matthew Head, *Orientalism, Masquerade and Mozart's Turkish Music* (London: Royal Musical Association, 2000).

22. Avcıoğlu, *Turquerie*, 100.

23. [Lockman], *A Sketch of the Spring-Gardens, Vaux-Hall*, 26 and 28 (with references also to Eden and Arcadia).

24. *A Description of Vaux-Hall Gardens. Being a Proper Companion and Guide for All Who Visit That Place* (London: S. Hooper, 1762), 36. For a discussion of this statue and its significance for our understanding of Handel's reception, see Suzanne Aspden, "'Fam'd Handel Breathing, Tho' Transformed to Stone': The Composer as Monument," *Journal of the American Musicological Society* 55 (2002): 39–90.

25. [Lockman], *A Sketch of the Spring-Gardens, Vaux-Hall*, 13. One is reminded here of an account of the Turkish court penned by Lady Mary Wortley Montagu in a letter of 19 May 1718: "Thus, you see, Sir, these people are not so unpolished as we represent them. 'Tis true, their magnificence is of a very different taste from ours, and perhaps of a better. I am almost of opinion that they have a right notion of life. They consume it in music, gardens, wine, and delicate eating, while we are tormenting our

brains with some scheme of politics, or studying some science to which we can never attain . . . Considering what short-liv'd, weak animals men are, is there any study so beneficial as the study of present pleasure?" *Letters of the Right Honourable Lady M—y W——y M——e; Written During her Travels in Europe, Asia, and Africa, to Persons of Distinction, Men of Letters, &c., in Different Parts of Europe* (London, 1790), 43. Her comments coincided with the "tulip period" in Ottoman history (1718–30), during which the Ottomans imitated European practices (for example, by constructing gardens in the French style), thereby creating an occidentalist counterpoint to an orientalist position. John Morgan O'Connell deals with some of these themes in "In the Time of Alaturka: Identifying Difference in Musical Discourse," *Ethnomusicology* 49 no. 2 (2005): 177–205.

26. Avcıoğlu, *Turquerie*, 148–50.

27. See David Hunter, "Rode the 12,000? Counting Coaches, People, and Errors En Route to the Rehearsal of Handel's *Music for the Royal Fireworks* at Spring Gardens, Vauxhall in 1749," *London Journal* 37 no. 1 (2012), 13–26.

28. Avcıoğlu, *Turquerie*, 148–50. The prince's appropriation of Handel in the 1730s and 1740s predates later Georgian appropriation of him in support of the Hanoverian monarchy's position in Britain, although William Weber warns against reading Handel's canonic position in the 1770s and 1780s back into the earlier period in his *The Rise of Musical Classics in Eighteenth-Century England: A Study in Canon, Ritual and Ideology* (Oxford: Clarendon Press, 1996). Suzanne Aspden had discussed Roubiliac's statue of Handel for Vauxhall Gardens in relation to general ideas of Britishness and the construction of national heroes; see Aspden, "The Composer as Monument."

29. *General Advertiser*, 16 April 1751.

30. *A Solemn Dirge, Sacred to the Memory of His Royal Highness Frederic Prince of Wales, as It Was Sung by Mr. Lowe, Miss Burchell, and others, at Vaux-Hall. Written by Mr. Smart. The Music Compos'd by Mr. Worgan, M.B.*, 2nd ed. (London: T. Carnan, 1751). The music, unfortunately, does not appear to have survived.

31. Avcıoğlu, *Turquerie*, 110, 112.

32. See *A Description of Vaux-Hall Gardens*, 10, 22, and Jonathan Conlin, "Vauxhall Revisited: The Afterlife of a London Pleasure Garden, 1770–1859," *Journal of British Studies* 45 (October 2006): 725.

33. *A Description of Vaux-Hall Gardens*, 19.

34. See Lawrence Gowing, "Hogarth, Hayman, and the Vauxhall Decorations," *Burlington Magazine* 95 (January 1953): 4–17, 19.

35. *A Description of Vaux-Hall Gardens*, 19–20.

36. Ibid., 20. See also Jacob Henry Burn, "Historical Collections Relative to Spring Garden at Charing Cross . . . and to Spring Garden, Lambeth . . . Since Called Vauxhall Gardens," British Library, Cup.401.k.7, f. 445 (letter to editor signed "Surriensis" and dated [ms] October 1826, clipped from an unidentified newspaper).

37. Bodleian Library, Oxford. Gough Adds. Surrey C.21, item 75/2. As John Dixon Hunt notes in Chapter 1 of this book, Vauxhall's birds were a long-established part of the garden soundscape.

38. J. Pellet to E. Parker, Browsholme Letters, Browsholme Hall, Clitheroe, Lancashire (uncataloged), 7 July 1743, quoted in Amanda Vickery, *The Gentleman's Daughter: Women's Lives in Georgian England* (New Haven, Conn.: Yale University Press, 1998), 248.

39. James Boswell, *Life of Johnson*, 3 vols., 2nd ed. (London: Henry Baldwin, 1793), 3:94, note 4.

40. *A Brief Historical and Descriptive Account of the Royal Gardens, Vauxhall* (London: for the proprietors, 1822), 43.

41. McVeigh, *Concert Life in London*, 41.

42. John Rosselli, "Incledon, Charles (bap. 1763, d. 1826)," *Oxford Dictionary of National Biography* (Oxford: Oxford University Press, 2004) http://www.oxforddnb.com, accessed 17 October 2011.

43. "Weichsel, Mrs. Carl Friedrich, Fredericka, née Weirman," *A Biographical Dictionary of Actors, Actresses, Musicians, Dancers, Managers and Other Stage Personnel in London, 1660–1800*, ed. Philip H. Highfill, Kalman A. Burnim, Edward A. Langhans, 15 vols. (Carbondale: Southern Illinois University Press, 1973–93), 15:331–32.

44. *Gazetteer and New Daily Advertiser*, 21 March 1778.

45. *A Brief Historical and Descriptive Account of the Royal Gardens, Vauxhall*, 24. On the "tin cascade," as it became known, see *A Description of Vaux-Hall Gardens*, 8–9. It seems to have disappeared by the 1820s.

46. *A Brief Historical and Descriptive Account of the Royal Gardens, Vauxhall*, 33.

47. Hogwood, General Introduction to the Pleasure Gardens. For more on scoring, see Cudworth, "The Vauxhall 'Lists,'" *Galpin Society Journal* 20 (March 1967): 27.

48. Mark Argent, ed., *Recollections of R. J. S. Stevens, an Organist in Georgian London* (Basingstoke: Macmillan, 1992), 3–4.

49. William Parke, *Musical Memoirs: Comprising an Account of the General State of Music in England*, 2 vols. (London: H. Colburn and R. Bentley, 1830), 1:106.

50. Brian Robins, ed., *The John Marsh Journals: The Life and Times of a Gentleman Composer (1752–1828)* (Stuyvesant, N.Y.: Pendragon, 1998), 131 (June 1775).

51. Michael Kassler, ed., *Charles Edward Horn's Memoirs of His Father and Himself* (Aldershot: Ashgate, 2003), 13–14.

52. Cudworth, "The Vauxhall 'Lists,'" 24–42. See also Pamela McGairl, "The Vauxhall Jubilee, 1786," *Musical Times* 127 (November 1986): 611–15.

53. Cudworth, "The Vauxhall 'Lists,'" 30.

54. Robins, ed., *The John Marsh Journals*, 77 (June 1770).

55. Just four years later, the magistrates faced complaints that the gardens were not fully emptied of members of the public until 4.30 A.M., see letter to editor signed "Surriensis" and dated [ms] October 1826. Burn, "Historical Collections Relative to Spring Garden at Charing Cross," Cup.401.k.7, f. 445. Fireworks had been introduced at the gardens in 1798.

56. *Il Barbiere di Seviglia* [sic] *as represented at the Royal Gardens, Vauxhall, June, 1829* (London: for the proprietors, [1829]); *La cenerentola* [...] *as represented at the*

Royal Gardens, Vauxhall, June, 1829 (London: for the proprietors, [1829]); *Songs, Duets, Trios, Choruses, &c. &c., In Actors al fresco* [...] *first produced at the Royal Gardens, Vauxhall, 4th June, 1827* (London: by the proprietors, [1827]); *Songs, Duets, Trios, and Choruses, in the New Vaudeville, called The Statue Lover* [...] *first performed at the Royal Gardens, Vauxhall, June 2d, 1828* (London: By the Proprietors [1828]).

57. The extensive diary of Frederick Gye Jr. is held at the Royal Opera House Archives, Covent Garden, but was not available for consultation during this project. On his career in opera management, see also Gabriella Dideriksen and Matthew Ringel, "Frederick Gye and 'The Dreadful Business of Opera Management,'" *Nineteenth-Century Music* 19 (Summer 1995): 3–30.

58. *Songs, Duets, Trios, &c. &c. in the New Operetta, Called The Magic Fan; or, A Fillip on the Nose.* (London: for the proprietors, [1832]); for the score, see Royal College of Music, MS 57/1–2.

59. On this act, see Dominic Shellard and Steve Nicolson, *The Lord Chamberlain Regrets . . . : A History of British Theatre Censorship* (London: British Library, 2004), pt. I.

60. See Holman, "The Sadler's Wells Dialogues of Charles Dibdin."

61. *A Description of Vaux-Hall Gardens*, 22; [Lockman], *A Sketch of the Spring-Gardens, Vaux-Hall*, 9.

62. *A Brief Historical and Descriptive Account of the Royal Gardens, Vauxhall; Particulars of Vauxhall-Gardens . . . which will be sold by auction . . . April 14, 1818* (London: W. Smith, [1818]). There was some lack of clarity whether the licenses issued in 1818 and from 1822 onward permitted social dancing rather than the ballet, see Gye and Hughes's discussion with magistrates over the granting of the licence, Burn, "Historical Collections Relative to Spring Garden at Charing Cross," Cup.401.k.7, f. 446 and Figure 7.1. The magistrates advised Gye that "dancing" only referred to the ballet, but certainly by the 1840s, in fact probably earlier, social dancing was an important part of Vauxhall's attractions; see *The Times*, 15 July 1848.

63. Robins, ed., *The John Marsh Journals*, 268 (July 1782), and 559 (July 1794).

64. *A Description of Vaux-Hall Gardens*, 9.

65. Ibid., 49.

66. Burn, "Historical Collections Relative to Spring Garden at Charing Cross," Cup.401.k.7, f. 349 (unidentified news clipping dated 23 July).

67. See, for example, ibid., f. 335 (unidentified news clipping dated [ms] 11 July 1796).

68. Gowing, "Hogarth, Hayman, and the Vauxhall Decorations."

69. Burn, "Historical Collections Relative to Spring Garden at Charing Cross," Cup.401.k.7, f. 84.

70. *A Description of Vaux-Hall Gardens*, 44–45.

71. [Lockman], *A Sketch of the Spring-Gardens, Vaux-Hall*, ii.

72. See, for example, Croft-Murray and McVeigh, "London, §V: Pleasure Gardens."

73. *Season 1837. Songs, Duets, Trios, Glees, &c. As sung in the Concert of the Royal Gardens, Vauxhall* (London: the proprietors, [1837]).

74. See the Journal of Receipts and Expenditure for Vauxhall (1822–59). Lambeth Borough Archives, Minet Library, IV/162/7. This offers a summary of each season's musical programming.

75. See Adam Carse, *The Life of Jullien, Adventurer, Showman-Conductor and Establisher of the Promenade Concerts in England, Together with a History of Those Concerts up to 1895* (Cambridge: W. Heffer, 1951), 54.

76. See Michael Musgrave, *The Musical Life of the Crystal Palace* (Cambridge: Cambridge University Press, 1995), and photographs of South Kensington and the Crystal Palace in Gavin Stamp, *The Changing Metropolis: Earliest Photographs of London, 1839–79* (Harmondsworth: Penguin, 1994).

77. Ken Gay, *Palace on the Hill: A History of Alexandra Palace and Park*, 2nd ed. (London: Hornsey Historical Society, 1994); Janet Harris, *Alexandra Palace: A Hidden History* (Stroud: Tempus, 2005).

78. J. R. Thackrah, *The Royal Albert Hall* (Lavenham: Terence Dalton, 1983).

79. See, for example, Leanne Langley, "Building an Orchestra, Creating an Audience: Robert Newman and the Queen's Hall Promenade Concerts, 1895–1926," in *The Proms: A New History*, ed. Jenny Doctor and David Wright (London: Thames & Hudson, 2007), 34.

80. Cudworth, "The Vauxhall 'Lists,'" 26, 29–30.

Chapter 5. Pleasure Gardens of America

1. *People's Friend*, 6 June 1807.

2. Anthony D. Smith, *Chosen Peoples: Sacred Sources of National Identity* (Oxford: Oxford University Press, 2003), 24–25.

3. In 1800 these cities were the top five in terms of population size. See Campbell Gibson, "Population of the 100 Largest Cities and Other Urban Places in the United States: 1790–1990," Population Division, U.S. Bureau of the Census, Washington, D.C., June 1998. Available from http://www.census.gov/population/www/documentation/twps0027/twps0027.html, accessed 4 May 2010.

4. Royall Tyler, *The Contrast: A Comedy in Five Acts* (1787; reprint, Boston: Houghton Mifflin, 1920), 20.

5. Joel J. Orosz, *Curators and Culture: The Museum Movement in America, 1740–1870* (Tuscaloosa: University of Alabama Press, 1990); Tim Barringer, "The Course of Empires: Landscape and Identity in America and Britain, 1820–1880," in *American Sublime: Landscape Painting in the United States 1820–1880*, ed. Andrew Wilton and Tim Barringer (Princeton, N.J.: Princeton University Press, 2002); and Jeffrey H. Richards, *Drama, Theatre and Identity in the American New Republic* (Cambridge: Cambridge University Press, 2005).

6. The difficulty in uncovering names, dates, and locations of pleasure gardens (many only lasting weeks), coupled with the sheer size of the United States, means it

is very difficult to identify a precise number, though there were certainly more than a hundred such venues. Thomas Garrett identifies forty-seven sites in his survey of New York's venues, noting there were certainly more than this but that sources are scarce. Thomas M. Garrett, "A History of Pleasure Gardens in New York City, 1700–1865," Ph.D. diss., New York University, 1978, 599.

7. The three other Vauxhalls in New York that have been identified operated for a very brief time, and little is known of them besides isolated advertisements. Samuel Francis operated a site formerly known as Bowling Green from 1765, while a Mr. Miller attempted to open a garden under the name of Vauxhall on Great-George Street in June 1793. Edwin G. Burrows and Mike Wallace, *Gotham: A History of New York City to 1898* (New York: Oxford University Press, 1999), 176; *Daily Advertiser*, 27 June 1793. Another short-lived Vauxhall was established by Peter Thorn at 5 Pearl Street in 1797. This venture closed later the same year. *Minerva*, 23 May 1797; *Daily Advertiser*, 26 July 1797.

8. I. N. Phelps Stokes, *The Iconography of Manhattan Island, 1498–1909* (New York: Robert H. Dodd, 1928), 5:1352; D. T. Valentine, *The Manual of the Corporation of the City of New York* (New York: McSpedon and Baker, 1856), 627; *Minerva*, 20 May 1797; O. H. Holley, *A Description of the City of New York* (New York: J. Disturnell, 1847), 53.

9. The Nashville site hosted balls and dinners, and it served turtle soup. See various advertisements in the *National Banner and Nashville Whig*, 7 April 1834 through 2 December 1836. The Richmond venue was open on Monday, Thursday, and Saturday evenings by Mr. Raphael, offering illuminations and music and charging a fifty-cent admission. See the *Richmond and Manchester Advertiser*, 12 May through 2 June 1802. It is not clear if the New Orleans site ever opened, but plans were put forward in 1837. See *The Picayune*, 31 March and 5 April 1837.

10. *Columbian Centinel*, 10 and 24 February 1798. These gardens failed to ever open.

11. The last of these sites was depicted in an image in Valentine's *Manual of the Corporation of the City of New York*, 1866, but this is problematic as it was apparently etched from memory and was not a pleasure garden at the time the engraver was in New York. Baron de Montlezun, "A Frenchman Visits Charleston, 1817," ed. Lucius Gaston Moffat and Joseph Médard Carrière *South Carolina Historical and Genealogical Magazine* 49, no. 3 (1948): 147; Garrett, "A History of Pleasure Gardens in New York City," 281.

12. It should be noted here that the layout of Vauxhall, London, was not typical of the English school of garden design at this time. See Chapter 1 for further discussion.

13. See various newspaper advertisements in the *City Gazette* and *Charleston Courier*, 1799–1812. After Placide's death in 1812, the garden passed through the hands of a variety of managers, none of whom met with any great success. After being sold in 1816, in 1817, and in 1821, the garden closed its doors to entertainment and became a school for young boys. *City Gazette*, 23 February 1816, 13 January 1817, 3 January 1821, 28 April 1821, and 18 December 1821.

14. *Poulson's American Daily Advertiser*, 15 May 1819; *Franklin Gazette*, 26 May 1819. The "velocipede" was essentially a form of bicycle; the *Lecture on Heads* was a popular series of satirical monologues based on various character "types," using busts as props. See Gerald Kahan, *George Alexander Stevens and the Lecture on Heads* (Athens: University of Georgia Press, 1984) for more on this piece. *New-York Chronicle*, 22–29 June 1769, 63, and 14–21 September 1769, 165.

15. *Columbian*, 11 June 1811.

16. See, for example, the lyrics for "Thrifty Wife" sung by Dignum (*Federal Orrery*, 26 November 1795), "Homeward Bound" (*Pennsylvania Packet*, 29 September 1785), and "Queen of the May" sung by Mr. Vernon (*Federal Gazette*, 28 April 1789).

17. *Daily Advertiser*, 22 June 1805.

18. The drama of the period provides us with excellent displays of the assumption that European culture was considered to be more refined, with the plays *Fashion* (Anna Cora Mowatt, 1845) and *The Contrast* (Royall Tyler, 1787) openly mocking the general acceptance of the superiority of French and English culture.

19. *New-York Packet*, 18 August 1785; *New-York Mercury*, 9 November 1767.

20. *Spectator* (New York), 23 September 1833.

21. *Columbian Centinel*, 7 July 1819. [Italics in original.]

22. These fairs were held here each year until 1853 when they moved to New York's Crystal Palace.

23. See, for example, *Spectator*, 9 September 1839.

24. See, for example, *Franklin Gazette* (Philadelphia), 6 July 1819; *National Gazette* (Philadelphia), 7 July 1827; *Boston Daily Advertiser*, 3 July 1815; *City Gazette* (Charleston), 6 July 1801; and *Commercial Advertiser* (New York), 1 July 1805.

25. *Commercial Advertiser*, 1 July 1817.

26. *Columbian*, 30 June 1820.

27. Michael R. Lynn, "Sparks for Sale: The Culture and Commerce of Fireworks in Early Modern France," *Eighteenth-Century Life* 30, no. 2 (Spring 2006): 75.

28. The first fireworks display in Boston to mark the Fourth of July took place on Boston Common on 4 July 1777. James R. Heintz, "The First Fireworks on the Fourth of July." Available from http://www1.american.edu/heintze/fireworks.htm, accessed 13 November 2010; *New-York Daily Advertiser*, 6 July 1818; *Mercantile Advertiser*, 6 July 1820.

29. Leo Marx, *The Machine in the Garden: Technology and the Pastoral Ideal in America* (Oxford: Oxford University Press, 1967).

30. Albert Henry Smyth, introduction to *The Writings of Benjamin Franklin* (New York: Haskell House, 1970), 148; Merrill D. Peterson, ed., *Thomas Jefferson: Writings* (New York: Library of America, 1984), 301; Thomas Bender, *Towards an Urban Vision: Ideas and Institution in Nineteenth Century America* (Baltimore: Johns Hopkins University Press, 1975), 4.

31. Tamara Thornton, *Cultivating Gentlemen: The Meaning of Country Life Among the Boston Elite, 1785–1860* (New Haven, Conn.: Yale University Press, 1989).

32. Others include Lombardy Gardens, Lebanon Gardens, Tivoli Gardens, and the Labyrinth Gardens. See Harold Donaldson Eberlein, and Cortlandt Van Dyke Hubbard, "The American 'Vauxhall' of the Federal Era." *Pennsylvania Magazine of History and Biography* 57 (1944): 167, and Geraldine A. Duclow, "Philadelphia's Early Pleasure Gardens," *Performing Arts Resources* 21 (1998): 1–17.

33. Gray's Ferry was by the time the pleasure gardens opened (1789) a floating bridge. Joseph Jackson, *Encyclopedia of Philadelphia* (Harrisburg, Pa.: National Historical Association, 1932), 3:650, 668; David John Jeremy, ed., *Henry Wansey and His American Journal: 1794* (Philadelphia: American Philosophical Society, 1970), 112.

34. Duclow, "Philadelphia's Pleasure Gardens," 5; *Independent Gazetteer*, 15 May 1790.

35. F. H. Shelton, "Springs and Spas of Old-Time Philadelphians," *Pennsylvania Magazine of History and Biography* 47 (1923): 216.

36. See Barbara Wells Sarudy, *Gardens and Gardening in the Chesapeake, 1700–1805* (Baltimore: Johns Hopkins University Press, 1998), chap. 9, for a cursory discussion of the variety of outdoor entertainment venues in Baltimore and neighboring areas during this time frame.

37. *Maryland Journal*, 7 July 1789 and 8 February 1791.

38. *American and Commercial Daily Advertiser*, 4 July 1827.

39. *Democratic Republican*, 30 June 1802. These gardens could be found at today's East Baltimore Street, between S. Dallas and N. Bond Streets. George W. McCreary, *Street Index*, 68 and 187.

40. *Federal Gazette*, 30 January 1800; Mary Ellen Hayward, and Frank R. Shivers, eds., *The Architecture of Baltimore: An Illustrated History* (Baltimore: Johns Hopkins University Press, 2004), 12; *American and Commercial Daily Advertiser*, 3 August 1801.

41. *New York Gazette*, 25 May 1798; *Evening Post*, 13 June 1820.

42. Although Niblo retained a portion of the garden (a strip of land 257 feet long, running between the hotel and theater), after 1849 Niblo's ceased to be a pleasure garden while keeping the name "Niblo's Garden."

43. W. Harrison Bayles, *Old Taverns of New York* (New York: Frank Allaben Genealogical Company, 1915), 456; *New York Morning Herald*, 29 June 1830 and 5 July 1830; *Weekly Herald*, 24 July 1841.

44. See, for example, *Spectator*, 10 September 1830 and 19 July 1831.

45. Diaries, 1821–24, New York Historical Society (New York, 10 May 1822).

46. Antonio Blitz, *Fifty Years in the Magic Circle* (San Francisco: A. L. Bancroft, 1871), 171; Thomas Meehan, "An Early Philadelphia Nursery," *Gardener's Monthly and Horticulturist* 29, no. 347 (November 1887): 346.

47. *Philadelphia Inquirer*, 11 June 1839.

48. *North American*, 12 April 1842.

49. See, for example, *City Gazette* (Charleston), 29 July 1799, and the *New York American*, 4 May 1826.

50. Marvin Edward McAllister, *White People Do Not Know How to Behave at Entertainments Designed for Ladies and Gentlemen of Colour: William Brown's African*

and American Theater (Chapel Hill: University of North Carolina Press, 2003), 27, 29. Brown went on to open the African Theatre the following year—a theater famous for the "Shakespeare riots" and for seeing African American actors Ira Aldridge and James Hewlett on the stage.

51. McAllister, *White People Do Not Know How to Behave*, chap. 1.

52. James Flint, *Letters from America, Containing Observations on the Climate and Agriculture of the Western States, the Manners of the People, the Prospects of Emigrants, &c., &c.*, ed. Reuben Gold Thwaites (Cleveland, Ohio: Arthur H. Clark, 1904), 292.

53. Garrett, "A History of Pleasure Gardens in New York City," 614.

54. Joyce Appleby, "The Social Consequences of the American Revolutionary Ideals in the Early Republic," in *The Middling Sorts: Explorations in the History of the American Middle Class*, ed. Burton J. Bledstein and Robert D. Johnston (New York: Routledge, 2001), 39.

55. This generally held truth was questioned most recently by Hannah Greig. Hannah Greig, "'All Together and All Distinct': Public Sociability and Social Exclusivity in London's Pleasure Gardens, ca. 1740–1800 ," *Journal of British Studies* 51.1 (January 2012): 50–75.

56. *Pennsylvania Packet*, 28 May 1789.

57. Although the precise makeup of the middling sorts and the development of internal hierarchies fluctuated with time and from city to city, this study covers too many cities and too long a time period to allow for an in-depth study of the changing composition and organization of this large group. Instead, for my purposes here, what matters is that this group was undergoing constant renegotiation of relative status and definition.

58. Richard Bushman, *The Refinement of America: Persons, Houses, Cities* (New York: Vintage, 1993), xiii.

59. Bruce A. McConachie, *Melodramatic Formations: American Theatre and Society, 1820–1870* (Iowa City: University of Iowa Press, 1992), 157.

60. McConachie, *Melodramatic Formations*, 158.

61. Such as Vauxhall, New York, and Harrowgate. See *Daily Advertiser*, 2 May 1803, and Jeremy, *Henry Wansey and His American Journal*, 95.

62. The music offered at the pleasure gardens varied from military marches and airs by American composers such as James Hewitt to various pieces sung at Vauxhall, London.

63. *Daily Advertiser*, 2 May 1803.

64. Burrows and Wallace, *Gotham*, 585.

65. Burrows and Wallace, *Gotham*, 585.

66. Burrows and Wallace, *Gotham*, 585, 642.

67. *Federal Gazette*, 10 September 1796; *Daily Advertiser*, 4 July 1799; *Boston Daily Advertiser*, 1 August 1814; *Baltimore Gazette and Daily Advertiser*, 18 February 1832.

68. *City Gazette*, 7 April 1809.

69. *New-York American*, 4 May 1826.

70. Asa Greene, *Glance at New York: Embracing the City Government, Theatres, Hotels, Churches, Mobs, Monopolies, Learned Professions, Newspapers, Rogues, Dandies, Fires and Firemen, Water and Other Liquids, &c. &c.* (New York: A. Green, 1837), 216–17.

71. This progression from "classless" to highbrow to lowbrow could be seen within the various cities along the East Coast, and although the precise dates varied, the pattern remained constant and largely contained within this thirty-year period.

72. *General Advertiser*, 6 July 1791.

73. Ibid., 295; Alan S. Downer, ed., *The Memoir of John Durang: American Actor, 1785–1816* (Pittsburgh: University of Pittsburgh Press, 1966), 141. It should be noted that there were no reports of such violent riots in the London sites—this element of the gardens appears to be unique to the American sites.

74. *American and Commercial Daily Advertiser*, 13 July 1805.

75. *Public Ledger*, 5 June 1840.

76. *New York Herald*, 17 August 1845.

77. I use the term "popular" here to refer to both the breadth of the appeal of their performance and the lowbrow associations of the entertainment that began to be offered.

78. Cornelius Matthews, *The Career of Puffer Hopkins* (1842; reprint, New York: Garrett Press, 1970).

79. Matthews, *The Career of Puffer Hopkins*, 217–18, 223.

80. Benjamin Baker, *A Glance at New York* (1848), in *On Stage America!*, ed. Walter J. Meserve (New York: Feedback Theatrebooks and Prospero Press, 1996). Bowery boys (or "b'hoys") were typically American-born apprentices (often to butchers) and were a New York phenomenon in the 1840s and 1850s. Tyler Anbinder, *Five Points: The Nineteenth-Century New York City Neighborhood That Invented Tap Dance, Stole Elections, and Became the World's Most Notorious Slum* (New York: Free Press, 2001), 180–81.

Chapter 6. Pleasure Gardens in Nineteenth-Century New Orleans

1. Sam Wilson Jr., Patricia Brady, and Lynn D. Adams, eds., *Queen of the South: New Orleans, 1853–1862: The Journal of Thomas K. Wharton* (New Orleans: The Historic New Orleans Collection, 1999).

2. Chinaberry (*Melia azedarach*).

3. Likely Wharton means cape jasmine or gardenia (*Gardenia jasminoides*); the yucca was either "Adam's Needle" (*Y. filamentosa*) or "Spanish-dagger" (*Y. gloriosa*).

4. Wilson, Brady, and Adams, *Queen of the South*, 25.

5. Incorporated in 1833, the St. Charles Avenue streetcar line was one of the first passenger railroads in the United States and remains the oldest continuously operating streetcar in the world.

6. Various sources estimate there were between 1,500 and 2,000 amusement parks in the United States by 1919.

7. According to the International Association of Amusement Parks and Attractions (IAAPA), the American theme-park industry generated over $11.2 billion revenue in approximately 600 "amusement/theme parks & attractions" in 2005, with attendance estimated at 335 million.

8. For London examples, see Warwick Wroth, *The London Pleasure Gardens of the Eighteenth-Century* (London: Macmillan, 1896), and Penelope J. Corfield, *Vauxhall and the Invention of the Urban Pleasure Garden* (London: History and Social Action Publications, 2008). For New York, see Thomas M. Garrett, "A History of Pleasure Gardens in New York City, 1700–1865," Ph.D. diss., New York University, 1978; Heath Schenker, "Pleasure Gardens, Theme Parks, and the Picturesque," in *Theme Park Landscapes: Antecedents and Variations*, ed. Terence Young and Robert Riley (Washington, D.C.: Dumbarton Oaks Research Library and Collection, 2002), 69–90; Heath Schenker, *Melodramatic Landscapes: Urban Parks in the Nineteenth Century* (Charlottesville: University of Virginia Press, 2009), 117–30; and Patrick Taylor, ed., *The Oxford Companion to the Garden* (Oxford: Oxford University Press, 2006), 336, 386. For New Orleans, see Lake Douglas, *Public Spaces, Private Gardens: A History of Designed Landscapes in New Orleans* (Baton Rouge: Louisiana State University Press, 2011); little is known of Charleston examples; Garrett, "A History of Pleasure Gardens" (613) claims in his investigation of New York examples that pleasure gardens existed in "Newport, New Haven, Philadelphia, Baltimore, Norfolk, Charleston and other cities up and down the [east] coast . . ." but gives no supporting information and cites only an unpublished reference to an example in New Haven, Connecticut. Elizabeth Barlow Rogers, *Landscape Design: A Cultural and Architectural History* (New York: Harry N. Abrams, 2001), gives a brief discussion of pleasure gardens "in eighteenth-century England" in her Glossary (518). More extensive discussions are given of American twentieth-century theme parks (461–69).

9. Elizabeth Barlow Rogers in *Landscape Design* discusses amusement parks in some detail. Note that "disneyfication" has entered the design lexicon as a term of derision and unrealistic perfection.

10. Such activities, particularly those of a sexual nature, are a subtext in accounts of English pleasure gardens. Schenker notes these connections among New York examples. Schenker, "Pleasure Gardens, Theme Parks, and the Picturesque," 73, 89. For detailed explanations of local "concert saloons" and the community's rich heritage of related activities, see Alecia Long, *The Great Southern Babylon: Sex, Race, and Respectability in New Orleans, 1865–1920* (Baton Rouge: Louisiana State University Press, 2004), 60–101. Kenneth Jackson's discussion of the origin of country clubs does not include discussion of pleasure gardens. Kenneth Jackson, *Crabgrass Frontier: The Suburbanization of the United States* (Oxford: Oxford University Press, 1984).

11. Pontchartrain Beach (1928–83), originally opposite Spanish Fort, moved to Milneburg in 1940. Lincoln Beach (1939–65) was located a few miles to the east.

12. Henry A. Kmen, *Music in New Orleans: The Formative Years, 1791-1841* (Baton Rouge: Louisiana State University Press, 1966), 9, 211, 212; Mary P. Ryan, *Civic Wars* (Berkeley: University of California Press, 1998), 45. Kmen's work, like Garrett's investigation of New York examples, is uninformed by landscape architectural history. Ryan's work focuses on "public life" in nineteenth-century New York, New Orleans, and San Francisco but mentions pleasure gardens only once, in general terms, as being "private parks accessible for a small admission price and the cost of refreshments" (9). Discussion of individual examples in either New York or New Orleans is not given.

13. The St. Charles Theater opened in New Orleans in late 1835, and it was the largest theater in America. When its interior was decorated to resemble a garden, it was called "Vauxhall Gardens." It should not be confused with the Louisiana Vauxhall Garden and New Vauxhall Garden elsewhere in the city. Kmen, *Music in New Orleans*, 9.

14. For the use of the Vauxhall name in an American context, see Chapter 5.

15. See Arnold R. Hirsch and Joseph Logsdon, eds., *Creole New Orleans: Race and Americanization* (Baton Rouge: Louisiana State University Press, 1992); Gwendolyn Midlo Hall, *Africans in Colonial Louisiana: The Development of Afro-Creole Culture in the Eighteenth Century* (Baton Rouge: Louisiana State University Press, 1992); Sybil Kein, ed., *Creole: The History and Legacy of Louisiana's Free People of Color* (Baton Rouge: Louisiana State University Press, 2000); Jerah Johnson, "Jim Crow Laws of the 1890s and the Origins of New Orleans Jazz: Correction of an Error," *Popular Music* 19, no. 2 (2000): 243–51.

16. An advertisement appeared in the *South-Carolina Gazette* of 1 July 1799, for Charleston's Vauxhall Garden, noting entertainment (an "illumination"), dining ("cold suppers prepared at a minute's warning"), and admission restrictions ("No admittance for people of color"). Garrett ("A History of Pleasure Gardens in New York City," 490) maintains that African Americans were regularly excluded from New York City pleasure gardens, but the first specific mention of this practice ("no admittance for coloured people") occurs in 1826. The first pleasure garden exclusively for African Americans, the African Grove, is mentioned in two articles from 1821 that remarked on how this tea garden's patrons (blacks) imitated the manners and attitudes of their white owners or employers (491, 492). The Mead Garden was advertised in 1827 in New York's first black newspaper for the "accommodation of genteel and respectable persons of colour," and there is mention in 1829 of the Haytian Retreat ("a place of resort for colored people"), though nothing is known of its history. Garrett suggests there were others, too, "probably more than are known of" (494–95).

17. For general discussion of free black society in colonial New Orleans, see Kimberly S. Hanger, *Bounded Lives, Bounded Places: Free Black Society in Colonial New Orleans, 1769–1803* (Durham, N.C.: Duke University Press, 1997).

18. Sam Wilson Jr., "Early History of the Lower Garden District" in *New Orleans Architecture*, vol. 2, *The Lower Garden District* (Gretna, La.: Pelican Press, 1971), quotes the 1810 advertisement (14) without giving a citation or quoting the complete advertisement; likewise, he fails to give a citation for the 1832 advertisement.

19. Many of the names listed in this advertisement were prominent men in the community: M. T. Mossy was a real estate auctioneer; Barthelomy Grima was from a prominent French Creole family and fathered a child with a free woman of color; Grima's brother Felix was an prominent jurist; Joseph Pilié (1789–1846), from St. Domingue, was a civil engineer, architect, and city surveyor who drew many plans now found in the Notarial Archives.

20. This clearly is a reference to *plaçage*, an arrangement recognized by all parties involved that openly allowed men of European descent to establish families and maintain relationships with women—particularly those of African American and mixed-race origin—other than their wives.

21. Jerah Johnson, "Colonial New Orleans: A Fragment of the Eighteenth-Century French Ethos," in Arnold R. Hirsch and Joseph Logsdon, eds., *Creole New Orleans* (Baton Rouge: Louisiana State University Press, 1992), 53.

22. Alexander Gordon, "Remarks on Gardening and Gardens in Louisiana," *Magazine of Horticulture, Botany, and All Useful Discoveries and Improvement in Rural Affairs* 15 (1849): 245–49.

23. J. L. Guilbeau, *The Saint Charles Street Car or the New Orleans and Carrollton Rail Road* (New Orleans, 1975), 1–5.

24. New Orleans in 1900 had approximately two hundred miles of urban street and interurban rail lines, by far the most extensive network in the state (Shreveport was next, with nine miles). Louis C. Hennick and E. Harper Charlton, *The Streetcars of New Orleans*, 2 vols. (Shreveport, La.: Louis C. Hennick, 1965), 2:367, 368.

25. "Sylvanus," "Random Notes on Southern Horticulture," *Horticulturist, and Journal of Rural Art and Rural Taste* 6 (1851): 220–24.

26. Andrew Gordon, "Remarks on Gardening and Gardens in Louisiana," *Magazine of Horticulture, Botany and All Useful Discoveries and Improvements in Rural Affairs* 15 (1849): 245–49.

27. See, for instance, Humphry Repton, *Observations on the Theory and Practice of Landscape Gardening Including Some Remarks on Grecian and Gothic Architecture* (London: J. Taylor, 1803); L. E. Audot, *Traité de la composition et de l'ornement des jardins* . . . (1859; reprint, Paris: LVDV Inter-livres, n.d.); and Andrew J. Downing, *A Treatise on the Theory and Practice of Landscape Gardening*, 4th ed. (New York, 1849).

28. Guilbeau, *The Saint Charles Street Car*, 41.

29. Kmen, *Music in New Orleans*, 9, 211, 212.

30. Kmen, *Music in New Orleans*, 8–9.

31. "Cocagne [sic]" a variant of Cockaigne, was an imaginary medieval land of luxury and pleasure. In Latin cultures, a cockaigne pole (or, as here, a "mast") was a popular festival event that involved a horizontal or vertical pole, covered with a slippery substance such as soap or grease, with a prize at one end. To the amusement of the assembled crowd, contestants try to navigate the slippery pole and claim the prize.

32. The Rocher de Ste. Hélène is the island in the south Atlantic off the western coast of Africa where Napoleon was exiled in 1815. New Orleans residents sympathetic

to Napoleon's cause planned to rescue him and bring him to New Orleans; Nicholas Girod (mayor from 1812 through 1815) supposedly offered his residence as a refuge. The plan did not materialize, and Napoleon died on the island in 1821.

33. The appellation "Carondelet Walk" existed on survey and municipal maps well into the twentieth century.

34. See Thomas Ashe, *Travels in America Performed in 1806 for the Purpose of Exploring the Rivers Alleghany, Monongahela, Ohio and Mississippi, and Ascertaining the Produce and Condition of Their Banks and Vicinity* (London: Richard Phillips, 1808), 272–74, for a particularly detailed account of such activities.

35. The official description of the sale in both English and French is affixed to the plan.

36. Lengthy descriptions of the events were reported in the *Courier* from 10 April: "a number of French residents and others . . . met on the Place d'Armes, and repaired in a body to the Garden of St. Helena . . . to partake of the banquet." From 11 April, the report of a "splendid repast" awaited the crowd of "about 400 gentlemen" and the day was "entirely devoted to the glorification of the events which have just transpired in France." Another such event was announced for 15 April and was designed to "bring together all citizens of France residing in this place." Historian Caryn Cossé Bell discusses these events in detail as evidence of local interest among members of the French community (many of whom were renegade Freemasons), Catholics, and Afro-Creoles in republican and antislavery ideals in their struggle against the emerging power of Louisiana's planter autocracy. Caryn Cossé Bell, *Revolution, Romanticism, and the Afro-Creole Protest Tradition in Louisiana 1718–1868* (Baton Rouge: Louisiana State University, 1997), 145–86.

37. Using "Tivoli" as a place name first appeared in New Orleans in 1807 when engineer Barthelemy Lafon drew subdivision plans for the Delord-Sarpy plantation property above Canal Street in the Faubourgs, Ste. Mary, and Annunciation. He created the Place du Tivoli, encircled first by the Tivoli Canal and then by a paved street; this traffic circle was renamed in honor of General Robert E. Lee in the 1870s. Another use of *Tivoli* occurs with a plantation and garden on nearby Bayou St. John from 1808 through 1824, previously discussed. Some may conflate these two examples into one location, an understandable conclusion because early notices of Tivoli plantation mention garden features, and the Carondelet Canal is an extension of Bayou St. John.

38. Margaret Denton Smith and Mary Louise Tucker, *Photography in New Orleans: The Early Years* (Baton Rouge: Louisiana State University Press, 1982), 18.

39. This "unnamed establishment" undoubtedly was the Jardin du Rocher de Ste. Hélène.

40. This German influence continued throughout the nineteenth century, finding expression elsewhere in the city's river commerce, infrastructural improvements, and architecture.

41. "Valse de Tivoli" sheet music, The Historic New Orleans Collection, New Orleans. 86.1788-RL.

42. This was the first rail line west of the Alleghenies.

43. Catherine Campanella, *Lake Pontchartrain* (Charleston, S.C.: Arcadia Publishing, 2007), 51.

44. Johnson, "Jim Crow Laws," 249.

45. Found at the William Ransom Hogan Archive of New Orleans Jazz, Tulane University Special Collections. At present, information about the composer, band, or honorand is unknown.

46. Pioneer jazz musicians were white, Hispanic, Creole, and black; many most likely would have identified themselves as Creole.

47. Note the misspelling: *Milneburg* became *Milenberg*, an appellation that remains with many locals.

48. Following World War I, more stringent Jim Crow laws were enacted, and many black and Creole musicians left the city for Chicago, New York, and Europe. Some never returned.

49. Hennick and Charlton, *The Streetcars of New Orleans*, 2:170.

50. Joseph H. De Grange, "Historical Data of Spanish Fort," *Louisiana Historical Quarterly* 2, no. 3 (July 1919): 269–70.

51. The origin of this maritime curiosity is uncertain. For many years it was thought to be the *Pioneer*, built in New Orleans in 1861 to counter the Union blockade of the mouth of the Mississippi River, but recently discovered maritime documents disprove this assumption. The vessel likely predates the *Pioneer*, but how or why it sunk is unknown. The vessel is the property of the Louisiana State Museum and is on display in Baton Rouge.

52. The similarity between the Spanish Fort attraction and Carrollton Hotel and Gardens should not escape notice.

53. "Spanish Fort Park of the New Orleans Railway and Light Company," 20 July 1912, *Electric Railway Journal* 40, no. 12 (July–December 1912): 91–92.

54. "Annual Outing of New Orleans Employees," 21 September 1912, *Electric Railway Journal* 40, no. 12 (July–December 1912): 464.

55. Hennick and Charlton, *The Streetcars of New Orleans*, 2:180; see also Campanella, *Lake Pontchartrain*, 37.

56. New Orleans, unlike other major American cities, had few nineteenth-century champions of urban reform and certainly no one to advance parks and civic improvements.

57. As Long notes in *The Great Southern Babylon* (231), "New Orleans's reputation as an exotic, erotic hot spot grew out of the demographic, social, and economic conditions that prevailed in the city in the colonial and antebellum periods."

58. Small neighborhood-oriented urban "squares" (including Jackson, Congo, Washington, Lafayette, Coliseum, and Annunciation) follow urban development from the colony's inception in 1720 onward; some were "designed," but most were simply open spaces, like New England village greens, that could accommodate multiple activities. Their governance, from the nineteenth and early twentieth centuries, was not

from city government but rather from adjacent property owners. City Park and Audubon Park (designed by the Olmsted Brothers office), the major urban public parks in New Orleans, date from the end of the nineteenth century and the early decades of the twentieth century.

Chapter 7. Night and Day

1. Charles Dickens, "Vauxhall-Gardens by Day," in *Sketches by Boz*, ed. Dennis Walder (1839; reprint, Harmondsworth, Middlesex: Penguin, 1995), 153.

2. William Makepeace Thackeray, *Vanity Fair* (1847–48; reprint, Harmondsworth, Middlesex: Penguin, 1968), 92.

3. Pierce Egan, *Life in London; or, The Day and Night Scenes of Jerry Hawthorne, Esq., and His Elegant Friend Corinthian Tom, Accompanied by Bob Logic, the Oxonian, in Their Rambles and Sprees Through the Metropolis* (London: Sherwood, Nealy & Jones, 1821), 369.

4. Terry Castle, *Masquerade and Civilization: The Carnivalesque in Eighteenth-Century English Culture and Fiction* (Stanford, Calif.: Stanford University Press, 1986); Walter Benjamin, *Charles Baudelaire: A Lyric Poet in the Era of High Capitalism*, trans. Harry Zohn (London: New Left Books, 1973).

5. Castle, *Masquerade and Civilization*, 28.

6. Castle, *Masquerade and Civilization*, 28.

7. Castle, *Masquerade and Civilization*, 29.

8. *Spectator*, vol. 8, 9 March 1711.

9. Benjamin, *Charles Baudelaire*, 159.

10. Benjamin, *Charles Baudelaire*, 159.

11. Castle, *Masquerade and Civilization*, 344.

12. "The great nineteenth-century tracts on political economy," Castle writes, "the writings of socialism, feminism, and other new forms of libertarian thought, embody what one might call carnivalesque wishes in a new discursive and rationalized imaginative form" (*Masquerade and Civilization*, 344).

13. Richard Altick, *The Shows of London* (Cambridge, Mass.: Harvard University Press, 1978), 94.

14. Altick, *The Shows of London*, 94.

15. James Granville Southworth, *Vauxhall Gardens: A Chapter in the Social History of England* (New York: Columbia University Press, 1941), 3.

16. Egan, *Life in London*, 366.

17. Egan, *Life in London*, 368.

18. Thackeray, *Vanity Fair*, 93.

19. Thackeray, *Vanity Fair*, 67, 89.

20. Thackeray, *Vanity Fair*, 42.

21. Thackeray, *Vanity Fair*, 89.

22. Thackeray, *Vanity Fair*, 96.

23. Thackeray, *Vanity Fair*, 97.

24. Thackeray, *Vanity Fair*, 99.

25. Richard Altick comments on Vauxhall's "developing reputation for occasional riotousness and licentiousness" in the nineteenth century. It became a "summer retreat," he writes, "for a class of women then known by the erudite euphemism of 'Paphians.'" Altick, *The Shows of London*, 320.

26. Castle, *Masquerade and Civilization*, 38.

27. Fanny Burney, *Evelina; or, The History of a Young Lady's Entrance into the World* (New York: Norton, 1965), 180.

28. Burney, *Evelina*, 181–82.

29. Burney, *Evelina*, 191.

30. Samuel Pepys, *The Diary of Samuel Pepys*, ed. Henry B. Wheatley, 11 vols. (1664–67; reprint, London: G. Bell and Sons, 1924), 322.

31. Burney, *Evelina*, 181. [Italics my own.]

32. Castle, *Masquerade and Civilization*, 28.

33. Benjamin, *Charles Baudelaire*, 158.

34. Benjamin, *Charles Baudelaire*, 158.

35. Egan, *Life in London*, 367.

36. Castle, *Masquerade and Civilization*, 342–43.

37. Benjamin, *Charles Baudelaire*, 35.

38. Benjamin, *Charles Baudelaire*, 37.

39. Benjamin, *Charles Baudelaire*, 125.

40. Quoted in Benjamin, *Charles Baudelaire*, 124–25. The poem is published in its entirety in both French and English in Benjamin.

41. John Keats, "To a Lady Seen for a Few Moments at Vauxhall," in *Selected Poems and Letters*, ed. Douglas Bush (1844; reprint, Boston: Houghton Mifflin, 1959), 136. Richard Monckton Milnes in his 1848 edition of Keats's works and letters, John Keats, *Life, Letters, and Literary Remains of John Keats*, 2 vols., ed. Richard Monckton Milnes (London: Edward Moxon, 1848), titles this sonnet "To _____" and adds this explanatory note: "A young lady whom he saw for some few moments at Vauxhall" (2:297). Sidney Colvin's 1917 biography of Keats, *John Keats: His Life and Poetry, His Friends, Critics, and After-Fame* (New York: Charles Scribner, 1917), nicely refers to the episode that inspired the poem as "a momentary impression of a woman's beauty received one night at Vauxhall, and so intense that it continued to haunt his memory for years" (23). Colvin indicates that the Woodhouse Transcripts are the source for this (259).

42. Benjamin, *Charles Baudelaire*, 124.

43. Keats, "To a Lady Seen for a Few Moments at Vauxhall," 136.

44. Arthur Symons, "Stella Maris," in *Silhouettes and London Nights* (Oxford: Woodstock Books, 1993), 40.

45. The description and cataloguing of a beloved's physical features, especially facial features, is familiar, of course, from the Elizabethan blazon. For a particular focus on hands in the nineteenth century, see Dante Gabriel Rossetti's portraits of women.

46. Keats, "To a Lady Seen for a Few Moments at Vauxhall," 136.
47. Benjamin, *Charles Baudelaire*, 50.
48. Altick, *The Shows of London*, 95.
49. Burney, *Evelina*, 179.
50. Dickens, "Vauxhall-Gardens by Day," 153, 155.
51. Dickens, "Vauxhall-Gardens by Day," 153.
52. Jonathan Swift, "A Beautiful Young Nymph Going to Bed," *The Poems of Jonathan Swift*, 2 vols., ed. Harold Williams (Oxford: Oxford University Press, 1958), 2:582: "Proceeding on, the lovely Goddess / Unlaces next her Steel-Rib'd Bodice; / Which by the Operator's Skill, / Press down the Lumps, the Hollows fill."
53. Dickens, "Vauxhall-Gardens by Day," 156.
54. Dickens, "Vauxhall-Gardens by Day," 156–57.
55. Dickens, "Vauxhall-Gardens by Day," 157.
56. Dickens, "Vauxhall-Gardens by Day," 156.
57. Altick, *The Shows of London*, 211ff.
58. Jonathan Conlin, "Vauxhall Revisited: The Afterlife of a London Pleasure Garden, 1770–1859," *Journal of British Studies* 45 (2006): 743.
59. Altick, *The Shows of London*, 322.
60. Dickens, "Vauxhall-Gardens by Day," 158.
61. Dickens, "Vauxhall-Gardens by Day," 158.
62. Dickens, "Vauxhall-Gardens by Day," 159.
63. Richard Ellmann, *Oscar Wilde* (New York: Vintage, 1988), 131, 262.
64. William Wordsworth, "Composed Upon Westminster Bridge, September 3, 1802," in *Selected Poems and Prefaces*, ed. Jack Stillinger (Boston: Houghton Mifflin, 1965), 170 (stn. 1, line 5).
65. Wordsworth, "Composed Upon Westminster Bridge, September 3, 1802," 170 (stn. 1, line 8).
66. Wordsworth, "Composed Upon Westminster Bridge, September 3, 1802," 170 (stn. 1, line 10).
67. Oscar Wilde, "Impression du matin," *The Complete Works of Oscar Wilde*, ed. Bobby Fong and Karl Beckson (1881; reprint, Oxford: Oxford University Press, 2000), 1:153 (stn. 2, lines 1–4).
68. Wilde, "Impression du matin," 1:153 (stn. 1, line 7).
69. Wilde, "Impression du matin," 1:153 (stn. 2, lines 13–16).
70. Miles Ogborn, "Locating the Macaroni: Luxury, Sexuality, and Vision in Vauxhall Gardens," *Textual Practice* 11 (1997): 452.
71. For a discussion of underground spaces and their "mysteries," see David L. Pike, *Metropolis on the Styx: The Underworld of Modern Urban Culture,1800-2001* (Ithaca, N.Y.: Cornell University Press, 2007), 158-312.

Chapter 8. "Strange Beauty in the Night"

Note to epigraph: D. S. MacColl, *Nineteenth Century Art* (Glasgow: James MacLehose and Sons, 1902), 154.

1. Charles Baudelaire, "The Painter of Modern Life," originally published in *Le Figaro*, 26 and 28 November, 3 December 1863, reprinted in Charles Baudelaire, *Art in Paris 1845–1862*, trans. Jonathan Mayne (London: Phaidon, 1964), 12.

2. Griselda Pollock, *Vision and Difference: Femininity, Feminism and Histories of Art* (London: Routledge, 1988), 52.

3. Dean MacCannell, *The Tourist: A New Theory of the Leisure Class* (Berkeley: University of California Press, 1999).

4. Whistler resided in Chelsea for nearly forty years. His early addresses are 7a Queen's Road, West Chelsea, followed by 7 and 2 Lindsey Row (96 Cheyne Walk). By 1878 he had moved briefly to the "White House," on Tite Street. On his return from Venice he lived at 13 Tite Street then the "Pink Palace" at 2 The Vale. He moved to 14 Upper Cheyne Row briefly, then returned to Tower House, Tite Street. His last Chelsea residence was 74 Cheyne Walk.

5. The Chelsea Embankment was built between 1871 and 1874 and restructured the riverfront along the Thames, allowing for more direct access to central London. For further discussion on this aspect of urban renewal, see Robin Spencer, "London as Seen by James McNeill Whistler," in *The Image of London: Views by Travellers and Emigrés, 1520–1920*, ed. Malcolm Warner (London: Barbican Art Gallery, 1987), 61–65.

6. For Wroth, see the Introduction to this volume. The Royal Borough of Kensington and Chelsea Library houses a "Collection of Prints and Printed Matter Concerning Cremorne Gardens," donated by Wroth.

7. Warwick Wroth, *Cremorne and the Later London Gardens* (London: Elliot Stock, 1907), frontispiece with caption reading "*Waterside Entrance, Cremorne*, from an etching by W. Greaves, 1871."

8. These gates apparently stood on Kings Road and not at the waterside entrance to Cremorne. They now stand at the entrance to a small garden named after Cremorne Gardens at Worlds End, Chelsea, at the original site of the pleasure gardens.

9. Wroth, *Cremorne and the Later London Gardens*, 1–6.

10. Edmund Yates, *The Business of Pleasure*, 2 vols. (London: Chapman and Hall, 1865), 1:12.

11. Yates, *The Business of Pleasure*, 1:10–11.

12. Wroth, *Cremorne and the Later London Gardens*, 7.

13. Lynda Nead, *Victorian Babylon: People, Streets and Images in Nineteenth-Century London* (New Haven, Conn.: Yale University Press, 2000), 113.

14. Nead discusses at length the dancing at Cremorne. Nead, *Victorian Babylon*, 122–28.

15. The term "gay women" signifies prostitute and was used frequently at the time.

16. Dean MacCannell, *Empty Meeting Ground: The Tourist Papers* (London: Routledge, 1992), 236.

17. David Park Curry, *James McNeill Whistler at the Freer Gallery of Art* (New York: Smithsonian Institution with W.W. Norton, 1984), 75–76, 85–86. Here Curry discusses the pyrotechnic skills displayed at Cremorne Gardens.

18. See Lynda Nead, *Myths of Sexuality: Representations of Women in Victorian Britain* (Oxford: Blackwell, 1988), on the spread of prostitution in Victorian London.

19. Nead, *Victorian Babylon*, 130.

20. Unidentified woodcut from Walter Sidney Scott, *Bygone Pleasures of London* (London: Marsland Publications, 1948), 126.

21. Wroth, *Cremorne and the Later London Gardens*, 11.

22. Wroth, *Cremorne and the Later London Gardens*, 11.

23. The 1871 Fairs Act resulted in more than 700 fairs being closed in England. Peter Stallybrass and Allon White, eds., *The Politics and Poetics of Transgression* (London: Methuen & Co., 1986), 8.

24. Wroth, *Cremorne and the Later London Gardens*, 17.

25. All these accounts were from an unidentified press clipping in the *Papers upon the History of Cremorne Gardens, Chelsea, 1840–1878*, Royal Borough of Kensington and Chelsea Library.

26. Wroth, *Cremorne and the Later London Gardens*, 22.

27. *Daily Telegraph* (London), 6 October 1877, press clippings from *Papers upon the History of Cremorne Gardens, Chelsea, 1840–1878*, Royal Borough of Kensington and Chelsea Library.

28. Cited in William Gaunt, *Chelsea* (London: B.T. Batsford, 1954), 180. The population survey of Chelsea records: 40,000 for 1841; 88,000 for 1881; 95,000 for 1901.

29. Charles Baudelaire, "Painters and Etchers," originally published in *Le Boulevard*, 14 September 1862, in Charles Baudelaire, *Art in Paris 1845–1862*, 220.

30. Baudelaire, "The Painter of Modern Life," 119.

31. Pollock, *Vision and Difference*, 67.

32. Charles Baudelaire, "On the Heroism of Modern Life" (1846), from Baudelaire, *Art In Paris*, 119.

33. Whistler, although not interested in the public morality concerning prostitution, did plan a painting of a prostitute in what came to be known as *Wapping*, 1860–64. In reworking the painting, he made the subject less obvious and more ambiguous. However, still the subject of solicitation appears to be present.

34. I am thinking of William Powell Frith's *The Railway Station* (1862) or *Derby Day* (1858), in particular.

35. This reflects Stéphane Mallarmé's statement on poetry: "To name an object is to suppress three quarters of the enjoyment of the poem, which is made to be divined bit by bit: to suggest it, that is the dream."

36. J. M. Whistler, "Red Rag," in Whistler, ed., *The Gentle Art of Making Enemies*, 2nd ed. (London: William Heinemann, 1892; reprint, Mineola, N.Y.: Dover, 1967), 128.

37. Whistler was indebted to his patron Frederick Leyland (an amateur pianist with a fondness for playing Chopin's *Nocturnes*) for the concept of using the musical term "nocturne" to describe his "moonlights."

38. J. A. Mahey, "The Letters of James McNeill Whistler to George A. Lucas," *Art Bulletin* 49, no. 3 (1967): 252–53.

39. Whistler, "Red Rag," 127–28.
40. John Ruskin, *Fors Clavigera*, Letter 79, July 1877.
41. For more on the trial aspect of "labour equally cost," see Linda Merrill, *A Pot of Paint: Aesthetics of Trial in Whistler v. Ruskin*, (Washington, D.C.: Smithsonian Press, 1992), 147–48.
42. Anonymous, *Daily News*, 26 November 1978. Glasgow University Library, press clipping, BPII 29/28.
43. Merrill, *A Pot of Paint*, 167.
44. Pollock, *Vision and Difference*, 76.
45. Wroth, *Cremorne and the Later London Gardens*, 11.
46. Such court decisions were usually in response to the validity of the plaintiff's brief in bringing the libel to court in the first place. Although legally correct, such actions were regarded as superfluous by the court and a waste of their resources.
47. Frank Rutter, *James McNeill Whistler. An Estimate and a Biography* (London: Grant Richards, 1911), 144.
48. Whistler's *Ten O'Clock Lecture*, given on 20 February 1885 at Prince's Hall, Piccadilly, London was published as a pamphlet in 1888 and reprinted in Whistler, ed., *The Gentle Art of Making Enemies* (London: William Heinemann, 1892).
49. J. M. Whistler, "Ten O'Clock Lecture," in Whistler, ed., *The Gentle Art of Making Enemies*, 144.
50. Guy Debord, *The Society of the Spectacle* (1967), fourth thesis. http://www.marxists.org/reference/archive/debord/society.htm.
51. Debord, *The Society of the Spectacle*, ninth thesis.

Chapter 9. Edwardian Amusement Parks

1. "Americanising Old Trafford," *Manchester Evening Chronicle*, 21 January 1907. Clipping from William Bean Scrapbook, Blackpool Pleasure Beach Archive (hereafter cited as BPBA). "The White City," *World's Fair*, 2 March 1907, 1.
2. "The White City," *World's Fair*, 2 March 1907, 1.
3. "White City Schemes," *World's Fair*, 14 February 1908, 4.
4. "The White City," *World's Fair*, 2 March 1907, 1.
5. "The White City," *World's Fair*, 2 March 1907, 1.
6. "White City Schemes" and "The White City Make Another Application for a Drink License," *World's Fair*, 15 February 1908, 4–5.
7. "American Enterprise," *World's Fair*, 14 September 1907, 7; advertisement, *World's Fair*, 21 March 1908, 12.
8. "Earl's Court," *The Times*, 17 September 1910, 11.
9. "Tickets for Amusement Parks," *World's Fair*, 10 December 1910, 12.
10. This figure is based on a survey of parks featured in *World's Fair* from 1906 to 1939, and on the comprehensive lists of Robert Preedy in *Rollercoasters: Their Amazing History* (Leeds: Robert Preedy, 1992), and *Rollercoaster: Shake, Rattle and Roll!* (Leeds: Robert Preedy, 1996). Reliable visitor statistics are scarce, but a sense of numbers can

be gleaned from newspaper reports and other contemporary sources. It is estimated that 200,000 people visited Blackpool Pleasure Beach on a typical bank holiday weekend in 1914. See Gary Cross and John K. Walton, *The Playful Crowd: Pleasure Places in the Twentieth Century* (New York: Columbia University Press, 2005), 47.

11. "Fair Ground Novelties," *Blackpool Times*, 20 February 1907, BPBA.

12. John F. Kasson, *Amusing the Million: Coney Island at the Turn of the Century* (New York: Hill & Wang, 1978), 29. Coney owed its fame in Britain to the reports of London newspapers' New York correspondents and especially to the show *The Belle of New York*, with its signature song, "Take Me Down to Coney Island." *Belle* reached London in spring 1898 and ran for 697 performances; between 1899 and 1901 a second production toured the country, playing at every major town and seaside resort in Britain. Gustave Kerker, *The Belle of New York: A Musical Comedy in Two Acts*, vocal score with words by Hugh Morton (London: Hopwood and Crew, 1898), 217–22.

13. By 1910 Coney Island claimed twenty million day trippers per year. John K. Walton, "Popular Playgrounds: Blackpool and Coney Island, c.1880–1970," *Manchester Region History Review* 17, no. 1 (2004): 52.

14. "Park Notes," *Billboard*, 3 February 1906, 20. Quoted in Lauren Rabinovitz, *For the Love of Pleasure: Women, Movies and Culture in Turn-of-the-Century Chicago* (London: Rutgers University Press, 1998), 139.

15. For histories of early riding devices, see Robert Cartmell, *The Incredible Scream Machine* (Bowling Green, Ohio: Bowling Green State University Popular Press, 1987), 19–33; Todd Throgmorton, *Rollercoasters of America* (Osceola, Wisc.: Motorbooks International, 1994), 12–13; and Frederick Fried, *A Pictorial History of the Carrousel* (New York: Barnes, 1964).

16. Between the 1890s and 1940, more than seventy roller coasters were built around the country. Preedy, *Rollercoaster: Shake, Rattle and Roll!*, 2, 5, and *Rollercoasters: Their Amazing History*, 56. Ann Andrews provides a detailed online history of Switchback patents in the 1880s and, in particular, the example at Matlock Bath: http://dialspace.dial.pipex.com/town/terrace/pd65/matlock/pix/matlockbath_derwentgardens01_switchback.htm, accessed 1 March 2012.

17. Peter Bennett, *Blackpool Pleasure Beach: A Century of Fun* (Blackpool: Blackpool Pleasure Beach, 1996), 18.

18. Cross and Walton, *The Playful Crowd*, 47.

19. National Archives Board of Trade: Companies Registration Office records. The companies registered to build amusement parks or to run concessions were predominantly funded by shareholders in limited-liability joint stock companies. The majority either never began trading because of the lack of investors or traded for very short periods before being wound up, liquidated, or taken over. See, for example, Rome International Amusement and Construction Company Ltd., September 1910. The National Archives [hereafter cited as TNA], BT 31 13372/111618.

20. "Manchester White City Disappears," *World's Fair*, 6 June 1914, 18.

21. For the distinctions between theme parks and amusement parks, see Raymond Weinstein, "Disneyland and Coney Island: Reflections on the Evolution of the Modern

Amusement Park," *Journal of Popular Culture* 26, no. 1 (Summer 1992): 131–64; Brenda J. Brown, "Landscapes of Theme Park Rides: Media, Modes, Messages," in *Theme Park Landscapes: Antecedents and Variations*, eds Terence G. Young and Robert B. Riley (Washington, D.C.: Dumbarton Oaks Research Library and Collection, 2002), 263–64; Isabelle Auricoste, "Leisure Parks in Europe: Entertainment and Escapism," in *The History of Garden Design*, ed. Monique Mosser and Georges Teyssot (London: Thames & Hudson, 1991), 483, 490; and Karal Ann Marling, ed., *Designing Disney's Theme Parks: The Architecture of Reassurance* (New York: Flammarion, 1997). Neil Larry Shumsky's definitions for "amusement parks" and "theme parks" appear in the *Encyclopedia of Urban America: The Cities and Suburbs* (1998): http://www.credoreference.com/entry/abcurban/amusement_parks and http://www.credoreference.com/entry/abcurban/theme_parks, accessed 1 March 2012.

22. Bennett, *Pleasure Beach*, 18.

23. The Sir Hiram Maxim Captive Flying Machine Company, which built and operated Flying Machines at amusement parks across the country, for example, was registered at Southport in 1904 with an initial capital of £30,000 in £1 shares. "Captive Flying Machines an Unsuccessful Venture," *World's Fair*, 27 June 1914, 13.

24. Walton, "Popular Playgrounds," 54.

25. At Blackpool Pleasure Beach, for example, gambling and gypsies were banned and the grounds were "policed in accordance with the requirements of the Chief Constable." *Blackpool Gazette News*, 12 April 1907, BPBA.

26. Calvin Brown levied a sixpence admission fee on the White City. "Americanising Old Trafford," *Manchester Evening Chronicle*, 21 January 1907, BPBA.

27. An "American Bowling Saloon" opened at London's Vauxhall in 1849. Lambeth Borough Archives, Minet Library. Vauxhall Scrapbooks IV/162/7; John Glanfield, *Earl's Court and Olympia: From Buffalo Bill to the "Brits"* (Stroud: Sutton Publishing, 2003), 18.

28. Advertisement, *World's Fair*, 27 April 1907, 2.

29. Murray Fraser and Joe Kerr, *Architecture and the "Special Relationship": The American Influence on Post-War British Architecture* (London: Routledge, 2007), 78–81; Ross McKibbin, *Classes and Cultures: England 1918–1951* (Oxford: Oxford University Press, 1998), 391–94.

30. Arwen P. Mohun, "Design for Thrills and Safety: Amusement Parks and the Commodification of Risk, 1880–1929," *Journal of Design History* 14, no. 4 (2001): 295.

31. See J. M. Neil, "The Rollercoaster: Architectural Symbol and Sign," *Journal of Popular Culture* 15, no. 1 (1981): 108–15.

32. "Tober" is a term used to describe the site occupied by the fair.

33. Brown, "Landscapes of Theme Park Rides," 241.

34. See, for example, Karen R. Jones and John Wills, *The Invention of the Park: Recreational Landscapes from the Garden of Eden to Disney's Magic Kingdom* (Cambridge: Polity, 2005), 92–100. Cross and Walton provide a useful overview of the diverse historical influences on amusement parks in Britain and America. Cross and Walton, *Playful Crowd*, 31–39.

35. Vanessa Toulmin, *Pleasurelands* (Sheffield: National Fairground Archive, 2003); Jones and Wills, *The Invention of the Park*, 93.

36. Rem Koolhaas, *Delirious New York: A Retroactive Manifesto for Manhattan* (New York: 010, 1994), 33; Woody Register, *The Kid of Coney Island: Frederick Thompson and the Rise of American Amusements* (Oxford: Oxford University Press, 2001), 92; David Nasaw, *Going Out: The Rise and Fall of Public Amusements* (Cambridge, Mass.: Harvard University Press, 1993), 79.

37. Rabinovitz discusses the relationship between concepts of pleasure at American exhibitions and the emerging amusement parks. Lauren Rabinovitz, "Urban Wonderlands: Siting Modernity in Turn-of-the-Century Amusement Parks," *European Contributions to American Studies* 45 (2001): 89. Also see Ray MacLeod, "Weltausstellungen—Weltbilder—Geschichtsbilder: Reflections on Exhibitions and their History 1851–2001," in *The Great Exhibition and Its Legacy*, eds Franz Bosbach and John R. Davis (Munich: G. R. Saur, 2002), 353; Paul Greenhalgh, *Ephemeral Vistas: The Expositions Universelles, Great Exhibitions and World's Fairs 1851–1939* (Manchester: Manchester University Press, 1988); Lieven de Cauter, "The Panoramic Ecstasy: On World Exhibitions and the Disintegration of Experience," *Theory, Culture and Society* 10, no. 4 (1993): 5–6; Glanfield, *Earl's Court and Olympia*.

38. For the careers of Cochran and Kiralfy, see Sam Heppner, *Cockie* (London: Leslie Frewin, 1969), 17–35, 57; James Harding, "Cochran, Sir Charles Blake (1872–1951)," *Oxford Dictionary of National Biography* (Oxford: Oxford University Press, September 2004), online edition, May 2005. http://www.oxforddnb.com/view/article/32471, accessed 8 September 2010; "The Champion Showman," *World's Fair*, 25 January 1908, 8; Javier Pes, "Kiralfy, Imre (1845–1919)," *Oxford Dictionary of National Biography* (Oxford: Oxford University Press, September 2004), online edition, May 2005, http://www.oxforddnb.com/view/article/53347, accessed 1 March 2012.

39. Jones and Wills, *The Invention of the Park*, 92–93; "History: Amusements" http://www.tivoli.dk/composite-6379.htm, accessed 1 March 2012.

40. Nick Laister and Mike Short, "Spot Listing of the Aerial Glide Static Fairground Ride, Shipley Glen" (unpublished submission to the Secretary of State for Culture, Media, and Sport), 26 October 2003, 4–6; Preedy, *Rollercoaster: Shake, Rattle and Roll!* 52–53. A short film held by the Yorkshire Film Archive documents these attractions, *Easter on Shipley Glen* (1912). John Outhwaite—who established Blackpool Pleasure Beach with William Bean—was originally from Shipley, and may well have been inspired by the large-scale amusements there. "Pleasure Beach Pioneer," *Blackpool Herald*, 14 March 1911, BPBA; *World's Fair*, 1 October 1910, 3.

41. Allen Clarke, *The Story of Blackpool* (London: Palatine Books, 1923), quoted in Gary Cross, *Worktowners at Blackpool: Mass-Observation and Popular Leisure in the 1930s* (London: Routledge, 1990), 199.

42. Bennett, *Pleasure Beach*, 4. Preedy, *Rollercoasters: Their Amazing History*, 8, 5–6.

43. John K. Walton, *Riding on Rainbows: Blackpool Pleasure Beach and Its Place in British Popular Culture* (St. Albans: Skelter Publishing, 2007), 4–5; Jones and Wills, *The Invention of the Park*, 93.

44. "Hall-by-the-Sea," *The Isle of Thanet Gazette and East Kent Times*, 29 November 1919; Nick Evans, *Dreamland Remembered: 140 Years of Seaside Fun in Margate* (Whitstable: Nick Evans, 2003), 5–6.

45. Evans, *Dreamland Remembered*, 7–8.

46. "Hall By the Sea," Poster. Margate: Printed by D. & J. Allen, Lithographers, William St. South, Belfast, c. 1880; John K. Walton, *The English Seaside Resort: A Social History, 1750–1914* (Leicester: Leicester University Press, 1983), 172.

47. Advertisement, *World's Fair*, 26 May 1906, 2.

48. "The Hall By the Sea," *World's Fair*, 13 April 1912, 6. Pat Collins was a successful fairgrounds impresario and bioscope exhibitor before making several forays into the amusement-park world at Blackpool and Margate. He was a keen rival of the Pleasure Beach owners, Bean and Outhwaite, having been outbid on the South Shore Site at Blackpool in 1903. "Pleasure Beach," *West Lancashire Evening Gazette*, 12 June 1929, BPBA. Also see "Bioscope Presenters: Pat Collins," http://www.nfa.dept.shef.ac.uk/history/bioscopes/presenters/collins.html, accessed 1 March 2012; Vanessa Toulmin, "Collins, Patrick (1859–1943)," in *Oxford Dictionary of National Biography* (Oxford: Oxford University Press, 2004); online edition, January 2008. http://www.oxforddnb.com/view/article/73080, accessed 1 March 2012.

49. "Showmen in the City," *World's Fair*, 21 November 1908, 8.

50. "Blackpool's Carnival of Sensations," *Sunday Chronicle* (Manchester), 31 July, 1910, 2.

51. "Margate Merger," *World's Fair*, 14 February 1920, 1.

52. Crowe, *Kursaal Memories: A History of Southend's Amusement Park* (St. Albans: Skelter Publishing, 2003), 3–5; H. Darbyshire, *Darbyshire's Guide to Southend-on-Sea* (1901), reprinted in Sylvia Everritt, *Southend Seaside Holiday* (London: Phillimore & Co., 1980), 117.

53. See Robert Nicholls, *The Belle Vue Story* (Manchester: Neil Richardson, 1992).

54. "The White City," *World's Fair*, 2 March 1907, 1.

55. See Dreamland site plan, 1920. From prospectus for Dreamland, Margate Ltd. (1921). TNA BT 31/26750/176510.

56. Neil Harris, "Expository Expositions: Preparing for the Theme Parks," in *Designing Disney's Theme Parks: The Architecture of Reassurance*, ed. Karal Ann Marling (New York: Flammarion, 1997), 20.

57. Jeffrey T. Schnapp provides a thought-provoking "prehistory of the modern anthropology of speed and thrill" in "Crash (Speed as Engine of Individuation)," *Modernism/Modernity* 6, no. 1 (1999): 3–4.

58. "A Fortune in a Thrill," *Sunday Chronicle* (Manchester), 23 August 1908, BPBA.

59. See, for example, the description of the Water Chute in the *Souvenir of the White City* (1909), 11. Copy held by the Manchester Archives at the Manchester Room and County Record Office, acc. 791 M24.

60. See, for example, the inquest into the death of Alfred Butts reported in "Figure 8. Roller Accident at Cleethorpes," *World's Fair*, 4 June 1910, 7.

61. See the inquest report into a fatality on a scenic railway in Doncaster, "Ill-Fated Bravado," *World's Fair*, 25 April 1914, 6.

62. Mohun, "Design for Thrills and Safety," 292.

63. "The Fairground," *Blackpool Herald*, 8 February 1907, BPBA.

64. "Bank Holiday," *The Times*, 9 June 1908, 8.

65. "The White City Make Another Application for a Drink License," *World's Fair*, 15 February 1908, 5.

66. "A Day in Breezy Blackpool," *London Herald*, 24 August 1906, BPBA.

67. Shields locates the carnivalesque on the beaches of Brighton and Margate. Blackpool's Golden Mile, with its wax works and freak shows, offered visitors graphic inversions of social norms—see Gary Cross, "Crowds and Leisure: Thinking Comparatively Across the Twentieth Century," *Journal of Social History* 39, no. 3 (Spring 2006): 635–36.

68. "The Morals of Blackpool," *John Bull*, 1 May 1909, BPBA.

69. "The White City Make Another Application for a Drink License," *World's Fair*, 15 February 1908, 5; "The White City License," *World's Fair*, 5 March 1910, 12.

70. "'White City' License Granted," *The Times*, 2 May 1913, 3.

71. For example, see cases against Manchester's White City in *World's Fair*, 4 July 1908, 10; against Earl's Court in *World's Fair*, 1 August 1908, 10; and against Kursaal in *World's Fair*, 14 March 1914, 10–11.

72. Cross and Walton provide a useful comparison highlighting the differences between the amusements at Coney Island and Blackpool in the early twentieth century. See "Making the Popular Resort" in Cross and Walton, *The Playful Crowd*, 34–35, 55.

73. When William Bean advertised Pleasure Beach as offering "Good Health, Good Air, and Open Sea," he was consciously referencing the combined tenets of the rational recreationalists that had fueled civic park movements in England and America in the nineteenth century and, more recently, an enthusiasm for camping, and the Boy Scout movement. Advertisement, *Blackpool Gazette News*, 29 March 1907; Pamela Horn, *Pleasures and Pastimes in Victorian Britain* (Stroud: Sutton Publishing Ltd., 1999), 13; Colin Ward and D. Hardy, *Goodnight Campers! The History of the British Holiday Camp* (London: Mansell Publishing, 1986), 4–8.

74. "The 'Rainbow' Pleasure Wheel," *Blackpool Gazette News*, 20 February 1912.

75. Meticulously kept scrapbooks held at the Pleasure Beach Archive document the almost weekly press releases, charity-event reports, and articles penned by the owners, and they reveal how important local support was considered to be for the success and reputation of Pleasure Beach. Bean was elected as councillor in 1907 and remained on the council until 1925, when he became an alderman. "Our New Councillor," *Blackpool Herald*, 26 November 1907.

76. *World's Fair*, 15 February 1908, 1.

77. "Bank Holiday . . . at the Franco-British Exhibition," *The Times*, 9 June 1908, 8.

78. "Visit of the Queen to White City," *London Daily Telegraph*, 15 July 1909, BPBA.

79. Glanfield, *Earl's Court and Olympia*, 18.

80. Not until the interwar period did concerns about the social dangers of mechanized entertainment begin to make a more visible impact, reflected in commercial films like Maurice Elvey's *Hindle Wakes* (Gaumont British Picture Corporation, 1927), which depicted the heady mix of flowing crowds and thrill rides at Blackpool Pleasure Beach as a hothouse for illicit romance. The film was based on a Stanley Haughton stage play written in 1912, which made no reference to an amusement park.

81. "The Pleasure Beach," *Blackpool Gazette News*, May Bank Holiday 1908, BPBA.

82. Woody Register provides a fascinating account of the relationship between shifting gender identities and attitudes to consumption and pleasure in early twentieth-century America. He places the Coney Island showman Frederick Thompson, who created the iconic Luna Park in 1903, at the center of this phenomenon, presenting him as one of the most influential agents of the commercial culture of Peter Pan. Woody Register, "Everyday Peter Pans," *Men and Masculinities* 2, no. 2 (1999): 202–4; Register, *The Kid of Coney Island*.

83. For example, Blackpool Pleasure Beach was described as a "playground" in 1907, "Blackpool and Its Fairground," *World's Fair*, 28 December 1907, 4. London's White City used the term during an unsuccessful application for a drink license in 1908. "The White City," *World's Fair*, 15 February 1908, 5.

84. "Big Show Organiser and the Secret of Success," *World's Fair*, 31 August 1912, 8.

85. "The Velvet Coaster," *Gazette News* (Blackpool), 6 April 1909, BPBA.

86. Advertisement, *World's Fair*, 9 July 1910, 2; Crowe, *Kursaal Memories*, 15.

87. Advertisement, *World's Fair*, 21 March 1914, 5.

88. "Bank Holiday," *Blackpool Herald*, 6 August 1907, BPBA.

89. *Souvenir of the White City*, 30.

90. "On the Pleasure Beach," *Blackpool Times*, 24 August 1907, BPBA.

91. "Bank Holiday . . . at the Franco-British Exhibition," *The Times*, 9 June 1908, 8.

92. "Blackpool: On the Seafront at Holiday Time," *Lancashire Daily Post*, 16 August 1907, BPBA.

93. "Old Folks Become Young Again," *Blackpool Gazette News*, 16 September 1911, BPBA.

94. "A White City Accident," *The Times*, 10 May 1910, 12.

95. "The Taste for 'Thrills,'" *World's Fair*, 17 August 1912, front page.

96. Originally published as "Die Großstadt und das Geistesleben," 1903. English translation reprinted in Donald N. Levine, ed., *On Individuality and Social Forms* (Chicago: University of Chicago Press, 1971), 324–40.

97. "Blackpool's Carnival of Sensations," *Sunday Chronicle* [Manchester], 31 July 1910, 2.

98. Cross and Walton, *The Playful Crowd*, 4–5, 61.

99. Cross and Walton, *The Playful Crowd*, 62.

100. My understanding of the carnivalesque is based on a reading of Mikhail Bakhtin's *Rabelais and His World*, trans. Hélène Iswolsky (Bloomington: Indiana University Press, 1984).

101. Bakhtin, *Rabelais*, 6, 9.

102. Bakhtin, *Rabelais*, 255.

103. Bakhtin, *Rabelais*, 11.

104. Bakhtin, *Rabelais*, 7.

105. "Blackpool's Carnival of Sensations," *Sunday Chronicle*, 31 July 1910, 2.

106. "New Brighton Tower," *World's Fair*, 5 March 1910, 14.

107. "Rainbow Pleasure Wheel," *World's Fair*, 24 February 1912, 8.

108. As Horrall has shown, the concept of "up-to-dateness" was a defining characteristic of the halls. Andrew Horrall, *Popular Culture in London c. 1890–1918: The Transformation of Entertainment* (Manchester: Manchester University Press, 2001), 1–4.

109. "Pleasures of Today," *World's Fair*, 26 February 1910, 12. Sean Creighton, "The Edwardian Roller Skating Boom," *British Society of Sports History Bulletin* 11 (1991), 65–82.

110. "The Pleasure Beach," *Blackpool Gazette News*, 28 May 1909, BPBA.

111. E. John B. Allen, *The Culture and Sport of Skiing* (Amherst: University of Massachusetts Press, 2007), 90–100; Stella Wood, "Lunn, Sir Henry Simpson (1859–1939)," *Oxford Dictionary of National Biography* (Oxford: Oxford University Press, 2004), online edition, September 2004. http://www.oxforddnb.com/view/article/34633, accessed 1 March 2012.

112. A list of bioscope travelogues distributed by the Charles Urban Trading Co. Ltd. in February 1905 includes an "International Winter Sports" series featuring Canada, Norway, Sweden, and Switzerland (68–70). Original catalog reprinted in Stephen Herbert, ed., *A History of Early Film*, 3 vols. (London: Routledge, 2000), 1: 79–414.

113. "Switzerland in England," *World's Fair*, 30 May 1914, 14.

114. Vanderdecken's Haunted Cabin, or the Flying Dutchman. Pleasure Beach, 1906. Image available at the Pleasure Beach Private Archive.

115. Staff was a malleable gypsum compound that could be plastered onto the surfaces of basic wood or steel structures and then molded and spray painted to resemble extravagant stone or marble façades at a fraction of the cost of stone or marble. It was used widely at the Columbian International Exhibition, Chicago 1893. Register, *The Kid of Coney Island*, 42.

116. See "Buried Under Tons of Sand," *Manchester Daily Dispatch*, 18 March 1907, BPBA; "Scenes at Blackpool," *Lancashire Daily Post*, 18 March 1907; "Havoc at the Fairground," *Blackpool Herald*, 19 March 1907, BPBA.

117. "A Whirl of Wonders," *Gazette News*, 1 May 1907, BPBA.

118. Charles Baudelaire, "The Painter of Modern Life," quoted in O'Shea, "English Subjects of Modernity," in *Modern Times: Reflections on a Century of English Modernity*, ed. Alan O'Shea and Mica Nava (London: Routledge, 1996), 19.

119. Rieger has shown how historical narrative—as a response to and an expression of ambivalence toward modernity—were used in a variety of contexts to explain the present as a culmination of continuous progress, while at the same time identifying and underlining the fundamental division between past and present. Bernhard Rieger, *Technology and the Culture of Modernity in Britain and Germany, 1890–1945* (Cambridge: Cambridge University Press, 2005), 10.

120. "Blackpool's Newest Entertainment," *World's Fair*, 20 August 1910, 14. The Monitor and Merrimac reenactment arena was imported from America, where it had been an attraction at the Jamestown Exposition of 1907, held near the original battle site. "Pleasure Beach Novelties," *Blackpool Herald*, 31 May 1912; "On the Pleasure Beach, by a Visitor," *Blackpool Times*, 24 August, 1907.

121. "The Park of Amusements at Earl's Court," *World's Fair*, 25 May 1912, 1.

122. "Pleasure Beach Novelties," *Blackpool Herald*, 31 May 1912, BPBA.

123. Rieger, *Technology and the Culture of Modernity*, 10.

124. Martin Daunton and Bernhard Rieger, eds., *Meanings of Modernity: Britain from the Late Victorian Era to World War II* (Oxford: Berg, 2001), 5.

125. Harris, "Expository Expositions," 20.

126. Rieger, *Technology and the Culture of Modernity*, 10.

127. Shea, "English Subjects of Modernity," 20, 22; Marshall Berman, *All That Is Solid Melts into Air* (New York: Simon & Schuster, 1982), 5.

128. "Cleaning up at Wembley," *The Times*, 22 April 1924, 7.

129. See J. B. Priestley, *English Journey* (London: W. Heinemann, 1934), 267–68. Quoted in Cross, *Worktowners at Blackpool*, 9.

Select Bibliography

Allen, Brian. "Francis Hayman and the Supper-Box Paintings for Vauxhall Gardens." In *The Rococo in England: A Symposium*, ed. Charles Hind, 113–33. London: Victoria and Albert Museum, 1986.
Altick, Richard. *The Shows of London*. Cambridge, Mass.: Harvard University Press, 1978.
Barringer, Tim. "The Course of Empires: Landscape and Identity in America and Britain, 1820–1880." In *American Sublime: Landscape Painting in the United States 1820–1880*, ed. Andrew Wilton and Tim Barringer, 39–65. Princeton, N.J.: Princeton University Press, 2002.
Baudelaire, Charles. *Art in Paris 1845–1862*, trans. Jonathan Mayne. London: Phaidon, 1964.
Bender, Thomas. *Towards an Urban Vision: Ideas and Institution in Nineteenth Century America*. Baltimore: Johns Hopkins University Press, 1975.
Bermingham, Anne, and John Brewer, eds. *The Consumption of Culture 1600–1800: Image, Object, Text*. London: Routledge, 1995.
Berry, Sue. "Pleasure Gardens in Georgian and Regency Seaside Resorts: Brighton, 1750–1840." *Garden History* 28, no. 2 (Winter 2000): 222–30.
Borsay, Peter. *A History of Leisure: The British Experience Since 1500*. Basingstoke: Palgrave, 2006.
———. *The English Urban Renaissance: Culture and Society in the Provincial Town, 1660–1770*. Oxford: Clarendon Press, 1989.
Brewer, John. *The Pleasures of the Imagination: English Culture in the Eighteenth Century*. London: HarperCollins, 1997.
Castle, Terry. *Masquerades and Civilization: The Carnivalesque in Eighteenth-Century English Culture and Fashion*. London: Methuen, 1986.
Coke, David. "Vauxhall Gardens." In *Rococo: Art and Design in Hogarth's England*, ed. Michael Snodin and E. Moncrieff, 74–98. London: Trefoil Books/Victoria and Albert Museum, 1984.
———. *The Muse's Bower: Vauxhall Gardens 1728–1786*. Sudbury: Gainsborough's House Museum, 1978.
Coke, David, and Alan Borg. *Vauxhall Gardens: A History*. New Haven, Conn.: Yale University Press, 2011.

Conlin, Jonathan. "Vauxhall on the Boulevard: Pleasure Gardens in London and Paris, 1764–1784." *Urban History* 35, no. 1 (2008): 24–47.

———. "Vauxhall Revisited: The Afterlife of a London Pleasure Garden, 1770–1859." *Journal of British Studies* 45 (2006): 718–43.

Conway, Helen. *People's Parks: The Design and Development of Victorian Parks in Britain*. Cambridge: Cambridge University Press, 1991.

Corfield, Penelope. *Vauxhall and the Invention of the Urban Pleasure Gardens*. London: History and Social Action Publications, 2008.

Cross, Gary. "Crowds and Leisure: Thinking Comparatively Across the Twentieth Century." *Journal of Social History* 39, no. 3 (Spring 2006): 635–36.

Cross, Gary, and John K. Walton. *The Playful Crowd: Pleasure Places in the Twentieth Century*. New York: Columbia University Press, 2005.

Curl, James Stevens. "Spas and Pleasure Grounds of London, from the Seventeenth to the Nineteenth Century." *Garden History* 7, no. 2 (Summer 1979): 27–68.

de Bolla, Peter. *The Education of the Eye*. Stanford, Calif.: Stanford University Press, 2003.

———. "The Visibility of Visuality: Vauxhall Gardens and the Siting of the Viewer." In *Vision and Textuality*, ed. Stephen Melville and William Readings, 282–95. Basingstoke: Macmillan, 1995.

Douglas, Lake. *Public Spaces, Private Gardens: A History of Designed Landscapes in New Orleans*. Baton Rouge: Louisiana State University Press, 2011.

Eberlein, Harold Donaldson, and Cortlandt Van Dyke Hubbard. "The American 'Vauxhall' of the Federal Era." *Pennsylvania Magazine of History and Biography* 68 (1944): 150–174.

Edelstein, T. J., ed. *Vauxhall Gardens: A Catalogue*. New Haven, Conn.: Yale Center for British Art, 1983.

Garrett, Thomas M. "A History of Pleasure Gardens in New York City, 1700–1865." Ph.D. diss., New York University, 1978.

Girouard, Mark. *The English Town*. New Haven, Conn.: Yale University Press, 1990.

Greig, Hannah. "'All Together and All Distinct': Social Exclusivity and the Pleasure Gardens of Eighteenth-Century London." *Journal of British Studies* 51.1 (January 2012): 50–75.

Habermas, Jürgen. *The Structural Transformation of the Public Sphere: An Inquiry into a Category of Bourgeois Society*, trans. Thomas Burger and Frederick Lawrence. Cambridge: Polity, 1989.

Hunt, John Dixon. "Theaters, Gardens, and Garden Theaters." In *Gardens and the Picturesque: Studies in the History of Landscape Architecture*. Cambridge, Mass.: MIT Press, 1992.

———. *Vauxhall and London's Garden Theatres*. Cambridge: Chadwyck-Healey, 1985.

Hunter, David. "Rode the 12,000? Counting Coaches, People, and Errors en Route to the Rehearsal of Handel's Music for the Royal Fireworks at Spring Gardens, Vauxhall in 1749." *London Journal* 37, no. 1 (2012).

Joncus, Berta. "'To Propagate Sound for Sense': Music for Diversion and Seduction at Ranelagh Gardens." *London Journal* 38, no. 1 (2013).

Klein, Lawrence E. "The Polite Town: Shifting Possibilities of Urbanness, 1660–1715." In *The Streets of London: From the Great Fire to the Great Stink*, ed. Tim Hitchcock and Heather Shore, 27–39. London: Rivers Oram Press, 2003.

Koslofsky, Craig. *Evening's Empire: A History of the Night in Early Modern Europe*. Cambridge: Cambridge University Press, 2011.

McConachie, Bruce A. *Melodramatic Formations: American Theatre and Society, 1820–1870*. Iowa City: University of Iowa Press, 1992.

McVeigh, Simon. *Concert Life in London from Mozart to Haydn*. Cambridge: Cambridge University Press, 1993.

Nead, Lynda. *Victorian Babylon: People, Streets and Images in Nineteenth-Century London*. New Haven, Conn.: Yale University Press, 2000.

Nosan, Gregory. "Pavilions, Power, and Patriotism: Garden Architecture at Vauxhall." In *Bourgeois and Aristocratic Cultural Encounters in Garden Art 1550–1850*, ed. Michel Conan, 101–22. Washington, D.C.: Dumbarton Oaks Research Library and Collection, 2002.

Ogborn, Miles. *Spaces of Modernity: London's Geographies, 1680–1780*. New York: Guilford Press, 1998.

———. "Locating the Macaroni: Luxury, Sexuality, and Vision in Vauxhall Gardens." *Textual Practice* 11 (1997): 445–61.

Picker, John M. *Victorian Soundscapes*. Oxford: Oxford University Press, 2003.

Pollock, Griselda. *Vision and Difference: Femininity, Feminism and Histories of Art*. London: Routledge, 1988.

Richardson, Tim. *The Arcadian Friends: Inventing the English Landscape Garden*. London: Bantam, 2007.

Snodin, Michael, and E. Moncrieff, eds. *Rococo: Art and Design in Hogarth's England*. London: Trefoil Books/Victoria and Albert Museum, 1984.

Solkin, David. *Painting for Money: The Visual Arts and the Public Sphere in Eighteenth-Century England*. New Haven, Conn.: Yale University Press, 1992.

Williams, Laura. "'To Recreate and Refresh Their Dulled Spirites in the Sweet and Wholesome Ayre': Green Space and the Growth of the City." In *Imagining Early Modern London: Perceptions and Portrayals of the City from Stow to Strype, 1598–1720*, ed. Julia F. Merritt, 185–213. Cambridge: Cambridge University Press, 2001.

Williamson, Tom. *Polite Landscapes: Gardens and Society in Eighteenth-Century England*. Stroud: Alan Sutton, 1995.

Wilson, Kathleen. *The Sense of the People: Politics, Culture, and Imperialism in England, 1715–1785*. Cambridge: Cambridge University Press, 1995.

Wroth, Warwick. *Cremorne and the Later London Gardens*. London: Elliot Stock, 1907.

———. *The London Pleasure Gardens of the Eighteenth Century*. 1896. Reprint, London: Macmillan, 1979.

Young, Terence, and Robert Riley. *Theme Park Landscapes: Antecedents and Variations*. Washington, D.C.: Dumbarton Oaks Research Library and Collection, 2002.

Contributors

Peter Borsay is Professor of History at Aberystwyth University. His 1989 book *The Urban Renaissance: Culture and Society in the Provincial Town, 1660–1770* as well as his 1990 reader *The Eighteenth-Century Town* have had a lasting impact on the study of the early modern town. His most recent book is *A History of Leisure: The British Experience Since 1500* (2006).

Jonathan Conlin is Senior Lecturer in Modern History at the University of Southampton. A cultural historian of modern Britain who has published articles on Victorian Vauxhall and Parisian "Wauxhalls" in the *Journal of British Studies* and *Urban History*, he is the author of *The Nation's Mantelpiece: A History of the National Gallery* (2006) and *Civilisation* (a study of the 1969 television series, 2009).

Rachel Cowgill is Professor of Musicology at the University of Cardiff. She has published widely on Mozart reception; opera and politics; British musical cultures from 1760 through 1940; blackface minstrelsy; and gender, sexuality, and identity in music. She co-edited *Europe, Empire, and Spectacle in Nineteenth-Century British Music* (with Julian Rushton, 2006) and *Music in the British Provinces, 1690–1914* (with Peter Holman, 2007). She edits the *Journal of the Royal Musical Association*.

Lake Douglas is Associate Professor at the Robert Reich School of Landscape Architecture at Louisiana State University. He has written extensively for academic journals, popular magazines, books, and professional publications in America and Europe and curated two groundbreaking exhibitions in New Orleans: *In Search of Yesterday's Gardens: Landscapes of Nineteenth-Century New Orleans* (2001) and *Plants of the Louisiana Purchase* (2003). Among his books are *Gardens of New Orleans: Exquisite Excess* (2001) and *Public Spaces, Private Gardens: A History of Designed Landscapes in New Orleans* (2011).

Eleanor Hughes is Associate Curator and Head of Exhibitions and Publications at the Yale Center for British Art. She is currently working on an exhibition and related book on eighteenth-century British marine painting.

John Dixon Hunt teaches at the University of Pennsylvania's School of Design, where he is Professor Emeritus of the History and Theory of Landscape. Before joining Penn in 1994 he served as Director of Studies in Landscape Architecture at Dumbarton Oaks. He is the author of numerous articles and books on garden history and theory, including a catalog of the landscape drawings of William Kent, *Garden and Grove* (1986), *Gardens and the Picturesque* (1992), *The Picturesque Garden in Europe* (2002), and *The Afterlife of Gardens* (2004). He edits *Studies in the History of Gardens and Designed Landscapes* and was founding editor of *Word & Image*.

Josephine Kane is currently British Academy Post Doctoral Fellow in the Department of Architecture at the University of Westminster, London. Her special interest is the relationship among the experience of pleasure, modernity, and the architectural landscape in twentieth-century Britain. She has previously held posts as Research Associate at the University of Hertfordshire and Associate Lecturer at Central St. Martin's School of Art and Design. She has also worked for Historic Royal Palaces and taught at heritage sites across the United Kingdom.

Anne Koval is Associate Professor in Art History at Mount Allison University, New Brunswick. She co-authored *James McNeill Whistler: Beyond the Myth* (with Ronald Anderson, 1994, reissued 2002) and has written several essays on the artist. She has contributed to exhibition catalogs at Tate Britain (*Whistler and His Time*, 1994), the Edward Day Gallery (Toronto), and the Art Gallery of Hamilton. She has also curated exhibitions including *Framing Nature: The Picturesque in Landscape*, *The Art of the Copy*, *Louis Weldon Hawkins: Shades of Grey*, and more recently the contemporary art exhibition *Paper Doll* held at the Owens Art Gallery (2011) and the Mendel Art Gallery (2012).

Deborah Epstein Nord is Professor of English at Princeton University. Her fields of interest include Victorian literature and culture, gender studies, and literature of the city. Her books include *The Apprenticeship of Beatrice Webb* (1985), *Walking the Victorian Streets: Women, Representation, and the City* (1995), and *Gypsies and the British Imagination, 1807–1930* (2006).

Naomi Stubbs is an Assistant Professor of English at LaGuardia Community College, CUNY. She specializes in the theater and popular entertainments of nineteenth-century America, and recently completed her Ph.D. at CUNY's Graduate Center on the pleasure gardens of America. Her publications include an article on David Garrick in *The Papers of the Bibliographical Society of America*, and a chapter examining the role of technology in pleasure gardens in the forthcoming volume, *Performance and Analogue Technology: Interfaces and Intermedialities*.

Index

Page numerals in italics refer to illustrations.

Abbey Gardens (Shrewsbury), 54
Addison, Joseph, 30–31, 41–42, 68, 82, 87–88, 178
Admiralty, 82, 87–88, 93
Aesthetic Movement, 211–13
African Grove (New York), 15, 142, 280 n.16
African Theatre (New York), 277 n.50
Agus, Joseph, 112
Ahmed III, 105
Albert Hall, 126
Alexander the Great, 105, 108
Alexandra Palace, 126
Alexandra, Queen, 235
Algiers (New Orleans pleasure garden), *155*
Amelie, Princess, 39
Amherst, Alicia, 18, 22
amusement parks, 9, 151–53, 160, 169–76, 217–45
Apollo Gardens (Birmingham), 53
Apollo Gardens (London), 32, *34*
Arban, Jean-Baptiste, 124
Armstrong, Louis "Satchmo," 171
Arne, Thomas, 80, 103
Arnold, Samuel, 103
Arrowsmith, Mr. (singer at London's Vauxhall), 97
Arsenal (Paris), 44
Ashburnham House, 198
assemblies, 63, 76
Audubon Park (New Orleans), 169, 174
Ayton, Fanny, 119

Bach, Johann Christian, 102, 115, *116–17*
Bagatelle (Bath), 53
Bagnigge Wells, 6, 32
Baker, Benjamin, 28, 147
Bakhtin, Mikhail, 240–41
ballet, 119, 146, 198–99, 202
balloons, 124, 145, 168, 177, 190–91
Baltimore, 137, *138*, 144
Bank of England, 88–89
Barber Surgeons Hall (Newcastle), 54
Barcelona, 218
Bartram, C. C., 230
Bartram, John, 20
Bath, 36, 53–54, *56, 57, 59, 60, 61, 63, 72, 74,* 106, 179. *See also* Bathwick Villa Gardens, Gravel Walks, Grosvenor Gardens, King's James's Palace, Orange Grove, Spring Gardens, Sydney Gardens
Bathurst, Lord, 37
Bathwick Villa Gardens (Bath), 54
Baudelaire, Charles, 8, 178, 185–88, 195, 208–9, 212, 243
Baum, John, 202, 204–6, 213
Bean, William, 223, 234
Beethoven, Ludwig von, 124
Bell, Anthony, 69
Belle Vue (Manchester), 230
Belleville, 221
Benjamin, Walter, 178–79, 182, 184–86, 188
Berenger, Charles de, Baron, 198
Berlin, 10. *See also* In den Zelten
Beulah Spa, 5
Billington, Elizabeth, 112
Birmingham, 24, 53, 222, 229, 239. *See also* Apollo Gardens; Casino Theatre of Varieties and Pleasure Grounds; Vauxhall
Bish, Thomas, 119
Bishop, Henry, 102, 119
Blackpool Pleasure Beach, 221–22, *222, 223–24, 224, 225,* 229, 233–35, 239, 241–44, 293 n.48, 295 n.80

Blackpool, 227, 229, 233–34, 241–45, 293 n.48. *See also* Raikes Hall; White City
Blewitt, Jonathan, 119
Bolden, Buddy, 171
Bonaparte, Napoleon, 281 n.32
Boston, 132–33. *See also* Washington Gardens
Boswell, James, 60, 62, 111
botanical gardens, 126, 139, 217–19
Botany Bay, 92
Boyle, Richard, third earl of Burlington, 35, 44–47
Brandon, Alfred, 204–5, 213
Brewer, John, 11–12, 50, 65
Bridgeman, Charles, 19, 44
Brighton, 22. *See also* Promenade Grove
Bristol, 56, 239. *See also* Vauxhall
Brown, John Calvin, 217–19, 225, 230, 238, 291 n.26
Brown, Lancelot, 22, 40–42
Brown, William, 141, 277 n.50
Brussels, 10
Buffalo Bill, 225, 235
Bunbury, Sarah, 14
Bunn, Alfred, 10
Burchell, Isabella, 112
Burlington, Lord. *See* Richard Boyle, third earl of Burlington
Burney, Charles, 100–101
Burney, Fanny, 76, 177, 182–89

Canal Street, City Park and Lake Railroad Company, 172
Canaletto, *37, 63*
Cardiff, 239
Carlyle, Thomas, 198
Carrollton Gardens, 150–51, *155*, 160–63, *163*
cascades, 20, 33, 36, 42–43, 59, 102, 112, 121, 188, 255 n. 20
Casino Theatre of Varieties and Pleasure Grounds (Birmingham), 229
Castle Garden (New York), 17, *128*, 138–39
Castle Hill (Shaftesbury), 58
Castle, Terry, 70, 178–79, 182, 184
Central Park, 23
Chambers, William, 40
Chandler, Mary, 56
Charles II, 93
Charleston, 144, 156, 159. *See also* Vauxhall
Chelsea Hospital, 71
Chester, 55, 243

Chicago Exposition, 226
Chichester, 55
Children, 8, 144, 156–57, 161, 168, 238
chinoiserie, 35, 43, *109*
Chiswick, 35, *36*, 44–45, *45*, 46, *47*
City Park (New Orleans), 169, 174
Cleethorpes, 222
Cobham, Lord. *See* Richard Temple, first Viscount Cobham
Cochran, Charles Blake, 222, 226
Cocking, George, 124
Colley, Linda, 41, 94–96
Collins, Pat, 229, 293 n.48
Columbian Gardens (Baltimore), 137, *138*, 144–46
Coney Island, 9, 130, 170, 220–21, 229, 244
Cook's Circus (New York), *131*
Cooke, Tom, 119
corsairs, 93–95
Courbet, Gustave, 208
Cours La Reine (Paris), 24, 26, 44
Coventry, 53
Cremorne Gardens, 15, 21, 195–216
Cremorne Stadium, 198
Cruikshank, George, 180, *190*
Cruisers and Convoys Act (1708), 87–88
Crystal Palace (London), 126. *See also* Great Exhibition
Crystal Palace (New York), 275 n.22
Cuper's Garden, *33*, 51, 53, 61

dancing, 74, 120, 143–44, 146–47, 157–58, 168, 198, 200, *201*, 202, 224, 227
D'Argenville, Dézallier, 20–21, 24
Davis, Lucy, 205
Debord, Guy, 216
Degas, Edgar, 208
Delacroix, Joseph, 131–32, 135, 137, 139
Denbies (Jonathan Tyers's estate), 19, 36
Derby, 239
Devil's Dyke (Sussex), 221
Dickens, Charles, 8, 102, 119–20, 124, 177–78, 184, 189–90, *190*, 191
Digby, John, 3
Dignum, Charles, 275 n.16
dioramas, 121, 198
Disney, Walt, 223, 244–45
Dodsley, Robert, 80
Dogger Bank, 96–97
Dorchester, 55

Douglas (Isle of Man), 222
Doyle, Arthur Conan, 242
Dreamland (Coney Island), 220–21
Dreamland (Margate), 230, 243
druids, 42
Drury Lane (theater), 111–12
du Deffand, Mme. *See* Vichy-Chamrond, Marie Anne de, marquise du Deffand
Durand-Ruel Gallery, 212
Durham, 54

Earl's Court, 218, 222, 225–26, 234–35, 243
Easton's Garden (Baltimore). *See* Columbian Gardens (Baltimore)
Edinburgh, 222. *See also* Marine Gardens
Edward, Prince of Wales, 105
Egan, Pierce, 178–79, *180*, 184
Eglinton, tenth earl of, 60
Ehrlich, Cyril, 11
Eliza Gardens (New Orleans), 155, 156–57
Elvey, Maurice, 295 n.80
Empire Exhibition (Wembley), 245
Esher Place, 30
Ethiopian Serenaders, 124
Evelyn, John, 7, 18, 20, 22, 31, 36
Exeter, 55–58. *See also* Rougemont Castle

fairs, 17, 202, 225–26, 235, 241, 288 n.23
Fasnacht's Garden (New Orleans), 155
Faubourg La Course (New Orleans), 15
Fielding, Henry, 42, 80
Fiennes, Celia, 54
film, 172–73, 193, 224, 242, 292 n.40, 295 n.80
fireworks, 12, 15–16, 42, 75, 118–19, 121, 132, 134–35, 139, 146, 177, *197*, 198–200, 214, 227, 235
flâneur, 26, 177–78, 184–85, 187–88, 202, 208–9
Flint, James, 142
Florence, 39
Folkestone, 221
Foudrinier, Pierre, 80
Fox, Henry, 14
Franklin, Benjamin, 135
Frederick II, 10
Frederick, Prince of Wales, 79–80, 104–7, 112, 178
French Revolution, 9
Frith, William Powell, 211

Garnerin, André-Jacques, 124
Garrick, David, 112
Gay, John, 75–76, 80, 89, 92–93
George II, 12, 81, 105
George IV, 111
George, Prince of Wales (future George III), 108
Gibbons, Grinling, 40
Gilbert, Arthur, 119
Girod, Nicholas, 281 n.32
glees, 115, 118
Goldsmith, Oliver, 40
Gravel Walks (Bath), 54
Gravelot, Hubert, 78
Gray, George, 136
Gray, Robert, 136
Gray's Ferry (Philadelphia), 136–37, 142, 145, 276 n.33
Gray's Garden (Baltimore), 137, *138*, 144
Great Exhibition, 226. *See also* Crystal Palace
Great Yarmouth, 222, 229
Greaves, Walter, 198–208
Green, Charles, 190–91
Green, Valentine, 124
Green Park, 12
Grima, Barthelomy, 281 n.19
Grima, Felix, 281 n.19
Grosley, Pierre-Jean, 49
Grosvenor Gallery, 200, 213
Grosvenor Gardens (Bath), 54
Gye, Frederick, Jr., 119, 124
Gye, Frederick, Sr., 119

Habermas, Jürgen, 11
Hackenschmidt, George, 226
Haddock, Nicholas, Admiral, 88
Hafod, 41
Hall by the Sea (Margate), 228, *228*, 243
Hamoaze, 92
Handel, George Frederick, 12–13, 42, 67, 108, 111
Harris, Gertrude, 74
Harrison, Joshua K., 137
Harrison, Thomas, 56
Harrowgate (Philadelphia), 136–37
Harvey, William, 64
Haughton, Stanley, 295 n.80
Haydn, Joseph, 118
Haye, Charles, 205

Hayman, Francis, 7, 32, 42, 78–79, 79, 91, 96, 109–10
Haytian Retreat (New York), 15, 141, 280 n.16
Hereford, 55
Hereford, viscounts, 54
Hertford, earl of. *See* Seymour, Algernon, earl of Hertford
Hervey, John, first earl of Bristol, 40
Hill, Aaron, 105
Hindle Wakes (film), 295 n.80
Hogarth, William, 66, 75, 78, 83
Holker, John, 214
Holles, Thomas Pelham-, duke of Newcastle, 88
Hook, James, 103, 113, *114*
Horn, Charles Edward, 115
Hosier, Francis, Admiral, 81
Houdini, Harry, 226
Hucknell, 239
Hughes, William, 119
Hyde Park, 24, 32, 53, 63

Ibrahim Pasha, 105
Iles, John Henry, 230
imperialism, 98, 181
Impressionism, 191, 195–96, 206, 208, 212, 215
In den Zelten (Berlin), 10
Incledon, Charles, 111
Infirmary (Manchester), 54
Ipswich, 54
Isleworth, 53
Istanbul, 107
Italian Opera (Covent Garden), 115, 119

Jalland's Gardens (Baltimore), 137
James I, 24, 40
James, John, 20
Jardin Beaujon (Paris), 221, *221*
Jardin du Rocher de Ste. Hélène (New Orleans), *155*, 164–66
jazz, 170–71
Jefferson, Thomas, 135
Jenkins, Robert, 81
jeu de mail, 44
Jones, Inigo, 24
Jones, Owen, 126
Joseph II, 10
Juba. *See* William Henry Lane
Jullien, Louis-Antoine, 124

Keats, John, 8, 178, 185–88
Kensington Olympia. *See* Olympia (London)
Kent, William, 22, 37, 41–42, 104
Kew, 108
King James's Palace (Bath), 53
King's Theatre (Haymarket), 112
Kiralfy, Imre, 222, 226, 234–35
Kossuth Gardens (New Orleans), *155*
Kursaal (Southend), *231*

Lafon, Barthelemy, 282 n.37
La Rabassada Park (Barcelona), 218
Laignel, Simon, 15
Lambeth Springs, 61
Lane, William Henry, 124
Langley, Batty, 36
Large Oaks (New Orleans), *155*
Lazowski, Maximilien de, 62, 74
Le Nôtre, André, 41
Leaver, Mrs. (singer at London's Vauxhall), 115
Leeds, 54–56, 218. *See also* Pasture Spring; Spring Gardens
Levant Company, 105
Levin, Phoebus, 210, *211*, 211–12
Leyland, Frederick, 288 n.37
Lincoln, 239
Lincoln Beach (New Orleans), 153
Lindsay, Sir Coutts, 213
Lion, Jules, 167
Liverpool, 24, 56–57, 222, 239. *See also* Ranelagh
Lockman, John, 13
London, 18–19, 24, 32, 39, 50–54, 60–73. *See also names of individual resorts*
London Spa, 32
Loudon, John Claudius, 18
Louisiana Tivoli (New Orleans), *155*
Louisiana Vauxhall Gardens (New Orleans), 154, 164
Lower Ferry (Philadelphia). *See* Gray's Ferry (Philadelphia)
Luna (Coney Island), 220
Luna (Southend) 238–39. *See also* Kursaal
Lunn, Henry, 242
Lyttleton, George, 80

Macaronies, 6
MacColl, D. S., 195
Magic City (Paris), 218

Index

Magnolia Garden (New Orleans), 155
Magny, Xavier, 168
Maidstone, 56
Mall (Washington), 23
Manchester, 54, 217–18, 230. *See also* Belle Vue; Infirmary; Royal Botanical Gardens; White City
Manet, Edouard, 208, 212
Mann, Horace, 39
Margate, 228, 230, 233, 243, 293 n.48. *See also* Dreamland; Hall by the Sea; Winter Gardens
Marine Gardens (Edinburgh), 239
Marsh, John, 118, 120
Marylebone Gardens, 42, 51, 58, 61, 65–66, 68–69, 72, 74, 103, 111, 120,
masculinity, 98
masquerade, 70–71, 74, 76, 104, 106, 178–79, 182–83, 187–88, 193
Matlock Baths, 221
Matthews, Cornelius, 146
Mavisbank, 41
McArann, John, 139–40
McArann's Gardens (Philadelphia), 136–40, 140, 146
Mead Garden (Brooklyn, New York), 141
Mead Garden (Manhattan, New York), 141
Medici, Marie de, 44
Mercer, James, 205
middle class, 12–14, 142–44, 200, 206
Milneburg (New Orleans pleasure garden), 155, 170
Milton, John, 22, 33, 42
Misson, Francis Maximilian, 24
Monamy, Peter, 84–85, 85, 87, 90, 94, 94
Monconys, Balthasar, 19, 31
Moncrieff, William Thomas, 119
Mondran, Louis de, 44
montagnes russes, 221, 221
Montagu, Lady Mary Wortley, 39–41, 43, 105
Morecambe, 222
Moritz, Carl Philip, 61–62, 64
Mossy, M. T., 281 n.19
Mozart, Wolfgang Amadeus, 124
Mumford, Lewis, 50, 70
Munn, John, 205
Musard, Philippe, 124
Musgrave, Sir Charles, 54
Music for the Royal Fireworks (Handel) 12, 108. *See also* Handel, George Frederick

music hall, 202, 225–26, 228, 242
Myers, Margaret, 137

Nashville, 131
nationalism, 98–99, 129–35, 147–48
Neville, Sylas, 61, 74
New Brighton, 218. *See also* New Brighton Tower
New Brighton Tower, 225, 241
New Orleans, 15, 131, 150–76. *See also* Algiers; Audubon Park; City Park; Eliza Gardens; Fasnacht's Garden; Faubourg La Course; Jardin du Rocher de Ste. Hélène; Kossuth Gardens; Large Oaks; Lincoln Beach; Louisiana Tivoli; Louisiana Vauxhall Gardens; Magnolia Garden; Milneburg; New Vauxhall Gardens; St. Charles Theater
New Orleans and Carrollton Railroad, 160, 278 n.5
New Orleans Pleasure Garden (New Orleans), 155
New Orleans Railway and Light Company, 174
New Ranelagh (Newcastle), 53
New Spring Gardens (Lambeth). *See* Vauxhall Gardens
New Spring Gardens (Norwich), 53
New Vauxhall Garden (New Orleans), 154, 155
New Walk (York), 72
New York, 5, 15, 28, 137, 139, 156. *See also* African Grove; Castle Garden; Cook's Circus; Haytian Retreat; Mead Garden; Niblo's Garden; Sans Souci; Vauxhall
New York Horticultural Society, 138
Newcastle, 53–54, 239. *See also* Barber Surgeons Hall; New Ranelagh
Newcastle, duke of. *See* Holles, Thomas Pelham-, duke of Newcastle
Newport, 222
Niblo, William, 137, 276 n.42
Niblo's Garden (New York), 134, 137, 144, 276 n.42
Nixon, John, 92
Norwich, 53

Oliver, Joe "King," 171
Olympia (London), 222, 229
opera, 119–20
Orange Grove (Bath), 54, 56, 57

Ottoman Empire, 94–95, 106–8
Outhwaite, John, 223

Paganini, Niccolò, 124
Pancras Wells, 32
Pantheon (Spa Fields, London), 74
Pantiles (Tunbridge Wells), 14, 54, *55*
parachuting, 124
Paris, 9–10, 26, 36, 44–46, 100–101, 179, 182–84, 188, 193, 196, 200, 208, 212, 218, 221, 235. *See also* Arsenal; Cours La Reine; Jardin Beaujon; Magic City; "Wauxhalls"
Park Hill (Shaftesbury), 58
Parker, Hyde, Admiral, 96–97
parks, 5, 9, 23, 26, 53, 64, 152–53, 156, 174–75
Parr, Remi, 80
Pasture Spring (Leeds), 54
Pater, Walter, 212
patriotism, 26, 30, 84, 88, 92–93, 107–9, 133–35, 213, 243
Paxton, Joseph, 126
Pelham, Henry, 38
Pellet, Jane, 111
Pellow, Thomas, 95
Pepys, Samuel, 11, 31, 103–4, 183
Percy Lodge, 38
Petersham, Lady Caroline, 30
Petre, Robert James, eighth Baron Petre, 20
Philadelphia, 131–32, 136–40, 142, 145. *See also* Gray's Ferry; Harrowgate; McArann's Gardens; Vauxhall
Pigott, Edward, 61–62, 74
pigs, learned, in song, 146
Pilié, Joseph, 281 n.19
plaçage, 15, 159, 176, 281 n.20
Placide, Alexander, 132, 144, 274 n.13
pleasure gardens: admission fees, 4, 13, 65–67, 73, 100, 102, 111, 143–46, 156–57, 228, 199–200, 228, 274 n.9, 291 n.26, 291 n.26; relationship to city, 17–18, 23–24, 26, 32, 51–60, 135–41, 148, 184; dancing in, 22, 73, 100–2, 170, 272 n.62; definitions of, 3, 5, 20, 37–38, 50, 227, 229; design and layout of, 18, 31, 33, 35, 58, 162, 230–32; food and drink in, 13, 67, 72, 202, *204*; and illusion, 8, 19, 32, 35, 177–94, 216–17; as inclusive space, 12–14, 23, 28, 64–68, 74, 137, 141–48, 156–60, 178–82, 193; lighting, 8, 15, 19, 21, 39, 41, 70, 75, 177–94; music-making in, 52, 67, 74, 100–126, 137–39, 157, 164, 170–71, 277 n.62; as promenade, 19, 24, 26, 33, 43, 61–64, 73, 110, 118; statuary in, 65, 133, 227–28; and social elites; 14–15, 65–66, 77; and violence, 4, 69–70, 76, 144–46, 169, 278 n.73; and voyeurism, 14, 62, 64.
pleasure grounds, 12, 20, 30, 37–39, 41, 43–46
Pleyel, Ignace Joseph, 118
Plymouth, 82, 92
Pococke, Richard, 56–57
politeness, 70–71, 76–77, 98–99
Pollock, Griselda, 196, 208–9, 214
Pontchartrain Beach (New Orleans), 153, *155*
Pope, Alexander, 22, 40, 43
Porter, Roy, 11
Porto Bello (Panama), 80–82, *85*, 85–86, 95–96
Portsmouth Hard, 88–89
Powys, Lybbe, 57
Priestley, J. B., 245
Promenade Concerts ("Proms"), 124, 126
Promenade Grove (Brighton), 22
prostitution, 15, 31, 68–69, 71, 110, 182–83, 192–93, 196, 200, 202, *203*–4, 204–5, 208, 214
Puritans, 5

Queen's Grove (Tunbridge Wells), 54
Queen's Hall, 126

Radnor, Earl of. *See* Robartes, Charles, second earl of Radnor
Raikes Hall (Blackpool), 227
Ranelagh (Liverpool), 24
Ranelagh (London), 14, 24, 30, 38–39, 40, 42–43, 51, 60–65, 69, 71–74, 103, 105, 111, 120, 124, 241
Ranelagh (Norwich), 53
Rasch's Garden (New Orleans), *155*, 164
Repton, Humphry, 22
Retford, 239
Reynolds, Joshua, 40
Rhyl, 222
Richmond (Virginia), 131
ridotto, 40, 42–43, 74, 104, 106
Rigaud, Jacques, 44–45, *45, 46*
Robartes, Charles, second earl of Radnor, 53
Rocque, John, *47*, 51, *52*, 104, 110
roller coaster, 172, 217, 220–21, 225–27, 232–33, 238–40
Rossetti, Dante Gabriel, 198

Index

Rossini, Gioachino, 119
Roubiliac, Louis François, 33, 108
Rougemont Castle (Exeter), 57
Rowlandson, Thomas, *101*, 112–13, 118
Royal Academy of Arts, 78, 92
Royal Botanical Gardens (Manchester), 217–19
Royal Horticultural Society, 126
Royal Navy, 87–89, 111
Ruskin, John, 196, 200, 212–14, 216
Rutter, Frank, 215
Rysbrack, John Michael, 35, *36*

sabbatarianism, 118
Sa'dabad (Ottoman palace), 105
Sadlers Wells, 5, 120
Sala, George Augustus, 215
Sale (Morocco), 95
Salisbury, 61
Sanger, George, 228, 243
Sans Souci (New York), 137
Scarborough, 222
seaside resorts, 57, 219–21. *See also entries for specific resorts*
Sedley, Charles, 17, 28
Selva, Giannantonio, 42
Seraphina, Princess (transvestite), 70
Serres, Dominic, 92
Servandoni, Jean-Nicholas, 12
Seymour, Algernon, earl of Hertford, 37
Seymour, Charles, sixth duke of Somerset, 53
Shaftesbury, 57–58
Shakespeare, William, 42, 243
Sheffield, 239
Shipley Glen, 227, 292 n.40
Shrewsbury, 54, 56
Simmel, Georg, 240
Simpson, Thomas Bartlett, 198
Skegness, 221–22
Smart, Christopher, 108
Smollett, Tobias, 36, 62, 102
Solkin, David, 65, 69, 98–99
Somerset, Duke of. *See* Seymour, Charles, sixth duke of Somerset, 53
Southend, 222, 233. *See also* Kursaal; Luna
Spa Fields, 62
spa gardens, 6, 51, 53, 65, 72
Spanish Fort (New Orleans), 153, *155*, 170–72, *173*, 174
Spire's Spring Garden (Coventry), 53

Spring Gardens (Baltimore), 137
Spring Gardens (Bath), 53, 61, 73
Spring Gardens (Charing Cross), 1, *1*, 4–5, *4*, 18–19
Spring Gardens (Leeds), 54
squares, 54, 156, 283 n.58
St. Charles Theater (New Orleans), 280 n.13
St. Helena (island), 281 n.32. *See also* Jardin du Rocher Ste. Hélène
St. James's Park, 1, 18, 26, 53–54, 61, 74
Stamitz, Carl Philipp, 118
Stansbury, G., Mr. (musical director at London's Vauxhall), 124
Steeplechase (Coney Island), 220
Stevens, R. J. S., 115
Storace, Stephen, 120
Stowe, 39–40, *46*, 47
Strawberry Hill, 39, 42, 48
Sullivan, Mr. (singer at London's Vauxhall), 111
Sullivan, William, 119
Surrey Zoological Gardens, 21, 25
Swartz, Moses, 172
Swift, Jonathan, 189
Swinburne, A. L., 198
Switzer, Stephen, 22–23, 35
Sydenham, 126
Sydney Gardens (Bath), 36, *37*, 54, 59, *60*, 72, 75
Symons, Arthur, 186

tea gardens, 5, 6, 13, 32, 51, 65, 74
Temple, Richard, first viscount Cobham, 44–45
Tenby, 55
Thackeray, William Makepeace, 177–82
theaters, 143, 202, 222, 224
Thompson, La Marcus, 221
Thomson, James, 72
Thorndon Hall, 20
Timotheus, 108
Tivoli (Copenhagen), 227
Tivoli (New Orleans), 154, *155*, 164–65, 167–69
Toeschi, Carl Joseph, 118
Toon's Gardens (Baltimore), 137
Topkapı Palace, 105
Torré, Jean-Baptiste, 75, 100, 102
Treaty of Aix-la-Chapelle, 12
Treaty of Utrecht, 81

Tunbridge Wells, 14, 54, *54*, 106. *See also* Pantiles; Queen's Grove
turquerie, 105, 107–8, 119, 121
Tyers, Jonathan, 7, 12–13, 19–20, 32, 36, 42, 44, 65, 69, 78, *79*, 98–99, 104–5, 112

Udall, John, 69
Uffenbach, Zacharias Conrad von, 53, 61, 74

Vauxhall (Birmingham), 24, 53
Vauxhall (Bristol), 53
Vauxhall (Charleston), 131–32, 140, 144, 280 n.16
Vauxhall (London), 1, 7–8, 14, 24, 30, 31, 33, 35, 37–39, 41–42, 44, 47–48, 51, 53, 58–62, 68–71, 199, 225, 241; admission fees, 65–67, 111, 267 n.3; tin cascade in, 20, 33, 36, 43, 59; dancing in, 120–21, 124, 272 n.62; and illusion, 120–21, 177–94; lighting in, 15, 21, 23, 70, 75, 89, *101*, 101, *114*, 177–94; music-making in, 62, 67, 96, 100–126; and painting, 32, 42, 78–99, 109–10; and patriotism, 107–9, 113, 115; and politics, 79–80, 105–6; "rural downs," 58–59; statuary in, 33, 42; songbooks, 96, 113, *114*; songs, 25–26, 59–60, 96, *97*, 98, 70, 107–12; violence in, 70, 89, 112
Vauxhall (Nashville), 131, 274 n.9
Vauxhall (New Orleans), 131, *155*, 156, 164
Vauxhall (New York), 28, 137, 131–33, *131*, 135, *139*, 143–47
Vauxhall (Norwich), 53
Vauxhall (Philadelphia), 131, 136–37, *136*, 139, 145
Vauxhall (Richmond, Virginia), 131
Velde, Willem van de, the Elder, 93
Velde, Willem van de, the Younger, 93–94, *95*
Venice, 42–43
Vernon, Edward, Admiral, 80–83, 95–96
Vernon, Joseph, 275 n.16
Vertue, George, 44, 93–94
Vichy-Chamrond, Marie Anne de, marquise du Deffand, 31
Victoria, Princess, 235
Victoria, Queen, 124

Vienna, 10
Vincent, S. (New Orleans pleasure garden impresario), *155*

wakes, 17
Walpole, Horace, 18, 22–23, 30–31, 38, 40–41
Walpole, Robert, 81
War of Austrian Succession, 81
War of Jenkins Ear, 81
Warton, Joseph, 48
Washington Gardens (Boston), 133, 144
Waterloo, Battle of, 119
Watteau, Antoine, 78
"Wauxhalls" (Paris pleasure gardens), 9, 100, 102
Wedgwood, 12
Weichsel, Carl Friedrich, 111
Weichsel, Elizabeth. *See* Elizabeth Billington
Weichsel, Fredericka, 111–12, *113*, 115
West End (New Orleans), 153, 170–73
West End Park (New Orleans), 174–75
Wetenhall, Edward, 115
Wharton, Thomas Kelah, 150–51
Whistler, James McNeill, 8, 191, 195–216
White City (Blackpool), 217, *218*
White City (London), 222, *223*, 226, 233–35, *236*, *237*, 239–40
White City (Manchester), 222, 230, 233, 239, 291 n.26
Whitley Bay, 222
Wilde, Oscar, 178, 191–93, 198
Wilkes, John, 31
Winter Gardens (Margate), 230
Wood, John, 72, *79*
Wootton, Henry, 29–30
Wordsworth, William, 192
Worgan, James, 69, 108
Worgan, John, 108
Wroth, Warwick, 10, 51, 65, 198–99, 202, 214–15

Yates, Edmund, 199
York, 55–56, 63, 67, 72–73. *See also* New Walk
Young, Frederick, 205

zoos, 126, 151, 224, 228, 230

Acknowledgments

The impetus for this volume was "Vauxhall Revisited," a conference held at Tate Britain and the Garden Museum which brought scholars from a number of disciplines together with works of art and music associated with pleasure gardens. Thanks are due first and foremost, therefore, to the institutions whose support made this event possible, to our host museums and to the Paul Mellon Centre for Studies in British Art, the Royal Musical Association, the Music and Letters Trust, and the University of Southampton. In particular I would like to thank Brian Allen, Rachel Beckles-Wilson, Anne Curry, Peter Holman, Kasha Jenkinson, Madeleine Keep, David Owen Norris, Martin Postle, Sir Curtis Price, Victoria Walsh, and Christopher Woodward. Several chapters in this book began as papers delivered at this conference; others were especially commissioned for the book. Some papers not included here have been published separately, and readers interested in pleasure garden music in particular should note articles by David Hunter and Berta Joncus in *London Journal* listed in the Bibliography.

This book would not have appeared without the ongoing encouragement of the contributors, all of whom remained patient and supportive, as well as many others who attended "Grounds for Pleasure" and felt something permanent should come of it. For this I thank Peter Borsay, John Brewer, Penelope Corfield, Lake Douglas, Lawrence Klein, David Owen Norris, Bill Weber, and above all John Dixon Hunt, series editor of the Penn Studies in Landscape Architecture.

A Visiting Fellowship at Dumbarton Oaks Research Library and Collection in the summer of 2010 provided much-needed space to edit contributions and write the introduction. I thank John Beardsley, Michael G. Lee, Jane Padelford, and my fellow Fellows in Garden and Landscape Studies for making my time in Georgetown so pleasant and productive. The illustrations to this volume were made possible by a publication grant from the Paul Mellon Centre. Vicky Burrett set the reduction of the musical example on pages 116–17. Ahren Lester did a sterling job of handling the resulting paperwork and liaising with contributors. The final result owes much to them as well as to Noreen O'Connor-Abel, Jo Joslyn, Jerry Singerman, and Caroline Winschel at Penn Press, who pulled it all together.

Milton Keynes UK
Ingram Content Group UK Ltd.
UKHW010642280723
425910UK00002B/35/J